D1596127

From FORM to MEANING

Pittsburgh Series in Composition, Literacy, and Culture

David Bartholomae and Jean Ferguson Carr, Editors

From FORM to MEANING

Freshman

Composition

and the

Long Sixties,

1957–1974

David Fleming

UNIVERSITY OF PITTSBURGH PRESS

Published by the University of Pittsburgh Press, Pittsburgh, Pa., 15260
Copyright © 2011, University of Pittsburgh Press
All rights reserved
Manufactured in the United States of America
Printed on acid-free paper
10 9 8 7 6 5 4 3 2 1

Library of Congress Cataloging-in-Publication Data

Fleming, David.
From form to meaning : freshman composition and the long sixties, 1957-1974 / David
Fleming.
    p. cm. -- (Pittsburgh series in composition, literacy, and culture)
Includes bibliographical references and index.
ISBN 978-0-8229-6153-6 (pbk. : alk. paper)
1. English language--Rhetoric--Study and teaching--United States. 2. Education--Political
aspects. I. Title.
PE1405.U6F6 2011
808'.042071173--dc22

                            2011003387

Contents

Acknowledgments

Substantial research projects are rarely solitary affairs, however much time the researcher spends alone. They are more often the result of collaborations, both shallow and deep, direct and indirect. The research reported here is no exception: many individuals and groups helped me conceive and conduct this research. If there is anything worthwhile in the final product, it is a tribute to them. If there are mistakes, failures, or wrongheadedness, I alone am to blame.

First and foremost, I want to thank Rasha Diab and Mira Shimabukuro, graduate research assistants at the University of Wisconsin-Madison during most of 2005 and part of 2006, who helped me locate and analyze primary documents, conduct interviews with study participants, and conceptualize the arguments that eventually comprised this book. They were also copresenters with me at an English Department colloquium in Madison in spring 2006, the first public airing of the research contained here. Their care for the sources used here—documents and interviews alike—was extraordinary, their good sense and good humor a bonus.

I am also grateful to the former UW-Madison English Department teaching assistants from the 1960s who agreed to talk with us about the events narrated here; they gave us their time and shared with us their memories and insights. Thank you, Burr Angle, Ginny Davidson, Sue McLeod, Bob Muehlenkamp, Ira Shor, and Jean Turner. We also spoke with Frank Battaglia, a former assistant professor at UW-Madison.

UW-Madison professors David Cronon, Nicholas Doane, Standish Henning, and Charles Scott shared memories and insights with us as well. Professor Eric Rothstein showed particular interest in the way former English Department faculty are represented here. Although he objected to some of those representations, I hope he will see that I have weighed his comments carefully and incorporated several of his suggestions for revision. I appreciate the attention he gave to the spring 2006 presentation of this research in Madison and the thoughtfulness with which he read an early draft of this manuscript. I also want to thank former English Department secretary Gini Martens, who helped me access English Department files in the years when I was consumed with them.

The research of other UW-Madison faculty members and graduate students, current and former, helped inform and inspire this project. I want to recognize

Matthew Capdevielle, Mary Anne Fitzpatrick, Bradley Hughes, Susan McLeod, Rebecca Nowacek, Martin Nystrand, David Stock, and Nancy Westphal-Johnson, all of whom have done or are doing their own original historical research about the teaching of writing at the University of Wisconsin-Madison.

The following graduate students from my spring 2005 research methods course summarized and in some cases transcribed audiotaped interviews from the UW-Madison Oral History Program: Cydney Alexis, Heidi Hallman, Rik Hunter, Adam Koehler, Corey Mead, Eric Pritchard, Terry Rodriguez, Mira Shimabukuro, Christine Stephenson, Annette Vee, and Kate Vieira. Two years earlier, in spring 2003, graduate students from Martin Nystrand's research methods course, including Sookyung Cho, Rasha Diab, David Grant, Melanie Hoftyzer, Matthew Pearson, and Katy Southern, did preliminary work on the history of writing instruction at UW. In spring 2004, all of those students, with the exception of Sookyung Cho and the addition of Corey Mead, collaborated with me on a panel presentation of original historical research about writing instruction at UW-Madison for the Conference on College Composition and Communication (CCCC); we learned much from the audience at that session. I also learned from audiences at the UW-Madison English Department in 2006, the University of Massachusetts Amherst English Department in 2006, CCCC again in 2007, and the Center for the Study of Writing at the University of Illinois at Urbana-Champaign in 2007, an especially memorable trip. (Thank you, Debra Hawhee, Gail Hawisher, and Catherine Prendergast, among others, for arranging that visit.)

The Graduate School at UW-Madison provided funding for research assistance at a crucial moment in this project; I am grateful for that help. More recently, both the English Department and the College of Humanities and Fine Arts at the University of Massachusetts Amherst supported me as I tried to finish this book. I want to also recognize the role of the UMass Amherst Writing Program, which I direct, in providing an especially conducive environment in which to reflect on postsecondary writing instruction in this country. The main first-year writing course at UMass Amherst—thoroughly process-based, resolutely student-centered, inordinately flexible—is taken by more than four thousand undergraduate students a year and taught by nearly a hundred graduate teaching associates, most of them MFA and MA/PhD students in English. In directing that course, I am immensely grateful, every day, for the extraordinary institutional and curricular structures built by my predecessors (Charles Moran, Anne Herrington, Peter Elbow, Marcia Curtis, and Donna LeCourt), the talent and dedication of the many teachers and staff members who work for the program, and the vibrant national academic discipline ("comp-rhet") that

Acknowledgments

supports our work but that was largely unavailable to the teachers discussed in this book.

Despite that and other obvious differences, the first-year writing course I teach and direct today is not all that dissimilar from the 1960s course I describe in this book; and both of those courses share core features with typical composition courses from earlier in the twentieth century and even from the late nineteenth century. The fact is, whenever and wherever it has been taught, first-year writing in this country has been a project both uniquely potent and uncommonly vulnerable. As my colleague Charles Moran, the first director of the UMass Amherst Writing Program, once put it, "Freshman English is a soft structure, living as it does outside the protection of disciplines and departments. It is subject to definition from without: cultural literacy, literary criticism, the research paper. Given its ancestry, the freshman course is pressured to teach 'grammar'; given its location in English departments, it is pressured to teach literature. Freshman English draws eagerly, therefore, on anything that may seem to permit it to define itself."[1] Having spent many years now teaching, directing, and researching first-year writing, I think I finally know what Charlie meant.

In addition to the individuals and institutions mentioned above, I also want to thank the publisher of this book. At a time when university presses nationwide are cutting back, even folding, the University of Pittsburgh Press and its Composition, Literacy, and Culture series continue to thrive. The press has been a joy to work with: efficient, resourceful, and intelligent. Thank you to David Bartholomae and Jean Ferguson Carr for beginning and perpetuating the series at such a high level. Thank you to Joshua Shanholtzer for taking me through the publication process from beginning to end. Thank you to the anonymous reviewers who helped me clarify the overall shape and argument of the book. And thank you to Carol Sickman-Garner for working so attentively and patiently on the text itself.

I remain grateful to my friends and family, especially my daughters, Carmen and Isabel, for their continued love and support.

Finally, I want to note here a group of friends and colleagues without whom this book could never have been written—the faculty and graduate students of the Rhetoric Program at Carnegie Mellon University (CMU), where I first found an intellectual home nearly twenty years ago and that first showed me how important a supportive social community is in academic life. They also introduced me to both the centrality of first-year writing in the wider field of composition-rhetoric and that course's anomalous, sometimes fraught, place in a discipline struggling to raise its research profile. There are too many faculty and students associated with CMU to name here. But I want to single out two graduate students who started with me in 1991—Loel Kim and Patricia Wojahn—and two who were already there—Maureen Goggin and Elenore Long. Among many others, these friends and mentors made graduate study in that program at that time bearable, rewarding, even fun; seeing them every year at CCCC is a highlight of my professional year. They represent for me the best of composition-rhetoric: its unusual humility in a world not always known for such, its abiding commitment to social justice in an environment where such devotion ebbs and flows, its deep humanity in a profession that can be cold and aloof.

U.S. academics use a timeworn, three-part formulation to talk about their professional obligations, dividing their work into the categories of research, teaching, and service. Different fields, different institutions, different appointments define, weigh, and interrelate those three components differently. In some places, in some disciplines, from the point of view of some personnel committees, one term lords it over the other two; in other contexts, two terms dominate, and the third is given lip service or even aggressively neglected. I know no field that weighs the three obligations of faculty work more equally, and integrates them more seamlessly, than composition-rhetoric. I know I lack objectivity in saying that, but I am convinced it is true.

And for me, no individuals embody better that thoughtful, equal weighing of research, teaching, and service, that integration of all three into a comprehensive, effective, and *ethical* conception of the academic life, than Loel, Patti, Maureen, and Ellie.

A Note on Sources

Much of the research reported here comes from unpublished, archived documents and original participant interviews. Full reference to those materials occurs in the notes. Interviews are initially cited by names of interviewer and interviewee and by date. My use of interviews from the Oral History Program at the University of Wisconsin-Madison is also cited in the notes. The bulk of the documentary evidence, meanwhile, comes from the files of the English Department office in Helen C. White Hall on the campus of the University of Wisconsin-Madison. This includes official minutes from Departmental Committee meetings, internal reports, memos among department administrators, correspondence between those administrators and university officials, and other miscellaneous documents. I also used materials from the archives of the University of Wisconsin-Madison and the UW Teaching Assistants Association. Photocopies of all documents used are in my possession.

From FORM to MEANING

1 INTRODUCTION

Freshman Composition in the United States, 1885–Present

For more than a century now, the most required, most taught, and thus most taken course in U.S. higher education has been freshman composition. Although its title has varied over both time and space (here First Year Writing, there College English), its basic purpose and configuration have not, remaining remarkably stable over a span of 125 years and across the diverse terrain of North American postsecondary education. The course was more or less invented at Harvard in the 1870s and '80s, when required, year-long instruction in English composition for first-year students, centered on the writing of weekly themes, replaced the primarily oral, traditionally multilingual education in rhetoric that had been distributed across all four years of the older, classical curriculum. The idea of a required course in writing, focused on the "mother tongue" and located at the threshold of higher education, spread rapidly in the fast-growing, newly industrialized and urbanized United States of the last quarter of the nineteenth century. By 1900, according to Robert Connors, freshman composition was "standard at almost every college in America."[1]

The course has maintained its prevalence ever since. If there was experimentation with the requirement in the 1920s and '30s, the surge in postsecondary student numbers immediately after World War II returned it to prominence just in time for the real enrollment boom of the late 1950s and early 1960s. And although the course's standing declined somewhat in the late 1960s and early 1970s with the reduction in educational requirements of all kinds, it rebounded quickly in the aftermath of the national literacy crisis of the mid-1970s. In the 1980s, it was as pervasive as ever, and by the turn of the twenty-first century, "English composition" accounted for more credit hours than any other course in the U.S. postsecondary curriculum.[2] As former Harvard president Derek Bok put it in 2006, "No other single course claims as large a share of the time and attention of undergraduates."[3]

The continued prominence of freshman composition in higher education today is striking for many reasons, not least of which are the dramatic changes in society, schooling, and writing that have taken place since its founding. The last quarter century alone has seen the rise of the personal computer, the explosion of the Internet, and the rapid spread of digital communication devices, together constituting what may be the biggest transformation in literacy since the invention of the printing press. The academy has changed, too, not only in terms of technology but also in the continuing loss of a common intellectual culture, the ongoing decline in public funding, and the growing consumerist attitude among students. In such a world, a required course in expository writing, taken by all students in their first year, might seem outdated. And yet freshman composition persists and even thrives. At schools like my own, it remains the only course required of every undergraduate on campus. What's more, it is arguably both source and beneficiary of the many new projects in literacy development that have sprung up on college campuses recently, like writing centers and writing across the curriculum programs, fostered in part by the size and success of first-year writing even as *their* energy has helped reinvigorate *it*.[4]

The ubiquity of freshman composition in U.S. postsecondary education is remarkable for another reason: because it is so anomalous when viewed from an international point of view. If universities all over the world have courses like history of China, introduction to biology, and macroeconomic theory, freshman composition remains peculiarly American—in fact, it is one of the distinguishing features of the entire U.S. higher education system. True, the course has made some inroads in other Anglophone countries, like Canada and New Zealand, and its links to the European rhetorical tradition make it at least a plausible, if not actual, presence on that continent. But in general, the course remains largely unique to the United States.

Of course, higher education in America is extremely diverse, and freshman composition is no exception. Not all colleges and universities require it; not all students take it even at institutions where it is required; and the course differs, often radically, from institution to institution. There are different assumptions behind it, different attitudes toward it, different ways to staff and teach it, and different relations between it and other projects on campus—including literary studies, technical and professional communication, creative writing, public speaking, and the so-called content areas. Recent figures on course-taking in U.S. colleges and universities exemplify this variation: freshman composition is clearly less commonly taught, for example, in selective institutions than in nonselective ones.[5]

It also varies by region. If the course began at Harvard in the last quarter of the nineteenth century, it soon developed a strained relationship with the nation's elite colleges and universities, especially those on the east and west coasts. Freshman composition flourished, however, in the U.S. heartland: in community colleges, land-grant public universities, branch campuses of state higher education systems, and other more or less "open" institutions of higher learning, especially in the nation's broad middle. This geographic bias is evident in the ubiquity of the first-year writing requirement in the U.S. Midwest; in the Illinois home of both the National Council of Teachers of English and the Conference on College Composition and Communication; in the presence of the biggest and best "comp-rhet" graduate programs in places like Ohio State and Purdue; and in the midwestern provenance, historically speaking, of the discipline's most influential teachers and scholars.[6]

And yet, recent developments in postsecondary education suggest that attention to writing is increasing, deepening, and diversifying everywhere, showing up in contexts that had disdained or ignored it before. There has been growth, for example, in postsecondary writing centers, writing across the curriculum programs, and writing studies curricula in Europe. And writing programs themselves have revived at elite U.S. universities like Stanford and Duke. The fact is, despite the dramatic changes in literacy that have taken place over the last century, the course's anomalous situation internationally, and its awkward fit even in the U.S. academy, first-year writing continues to be very widely taught in the United States and, increasingly, beyond.[7]

Its basic configuration is relatively easy to describe. For more than a century, and nearly everywhere it has existed, freshman composition has been a stand-alone course in expository writing at the college level; required of all or nearly all students on campus; and taken early in their undergraduate careers as both measure of their entering literacy skills and preparation for the demands of their future academic, professional, civic, and personal lives. It's an educational project characterized, in other words, by features that are all rather remarkable in the context: first, *generality* (that is, independence from any particular academic discipline, specialization, or body of knowledge); second, *universality* (that is, applicability to all or nearly all students on campus, regardless of background or aspiration); and third, *liminality* (that is, location at the threshold of higher education—between high school and the major, the everyday and the expert).

For an improbably long time and across an extraordinarily broad range of contexts, these and other features have given the course both its surprising sociocognitive potency and its seemingly inherent vulnerability.

But how could a course so anomalous in its own context spread so rapidly across the varied landscape of U.S. postsecondary education and survive, even flourish, over such a long period of time? To answer that question, we need to leave the academy—in particular, the specialized disciplines where knowledge accumulates and courses are conceived—and make our way toward *society*, toward the everyday culture surrounding higher education. That's because, for most of its history, freshman composition has been driven not by the knowledge-making and -testing activities of a community of experts, but by "social fiat," by the "perceived social and cultural needs" of the world outside the academy.[8] In this, the course was and remains relatively unique in U.S. higher education. Unlike virtually every other postsecondary course—introduction to chemistry, history of China—freshman composition is not part of a generally recognized "content area," and until recently, it lacked every accoutrement of academic professionalism: graduate programs, undergraduate majors, peer-reviewed journals, faculty chairs, and so on. The course was shaped instead by anxiety among the general public about the ability of young people to write correctly and well in the national language. That anxiety was the wellspring of freshman composition's nineteenth-century birth, and it is the main reason for the course's continuing presence in U.S. higher education today.

The form in which that anxiety has most often expressed itself is the literacy crisis, a recurring phenomenon in U.S. history, manifest every generation or so in a flurry of articles and papers about the appalling condition of adolescent writing skills. From "The Illiteracy of American Boys" (1897) to "Why Johnny Can't Write" (1975), from "A Nation at Risk" (1983) to "The Neglected 'R'" (2003), American leaders since the Civil War have regularly looked out over the adolescent population and seen, in terms of writing, a mess: poor spelling, bad grammar, careless punctuation, awkward style. In response, they have routinely declared a literacy crisis: detailing decline, predicting disaster, and casting aspersions. According to Robin Varnum, five separate literacy crises "have disturbed the course of our educational progress" since the Civil War, occurring respectively at the end of the nineteenth century, during both world wars, following the launch of *Sputnik 1,* and from the mid-1960s to the early 1980s.[9] This periodization is debatable, of course; some scholars even argue that the United States has been in a "perpetual" literacy crisis for much of its history.[10]

Evidence for this latter claim comes, in part, from the similarity of the discourses surrounding these events. Take the first literacy crisis, usually dated around 1870–1900 and fomented in part by the four reports published by the Committee on Composition and Rhetoric of Harvard's Board of Overseers. When English composition was first included in Harvard's admissions exam in 1874, the college faculty was stunned by the poor quality of applicants' written English. Asked to "write a short English composition, correct in spelling, punctuation, grammar, and expression," on a subject like "the character of Sir Richard Steele" or "the Duke of Marlborough as portrayed by Thackeray," half the applicants failed.[11] Commenting on the exams in 1879, Professor Adams Sherman Hill complained of "bad spelling, confusing punctuation, ungrammatical, obscure, ambiguous, or inelegant expressions."[12] A decade later, the situation had not improved: in 1892, half the candidates for admission again "could not write their mother-tongue with ease or correctness."[13] And even those who were admitted to the college had problems; in 1897, the oversight committee argued that the most noticeable feature of papers written in English A was their "extreme crudeness both of thought and execution."[14]

The discourse surrounding the literacy crisis of the late twentieth century was not much different. In 1975, after a decade of declining scores on national scholastic aptitude tests, *Newsweek* published its famous cover story "Why Johnny Can't Write." It included a sentence that would be quoted ad nauseum in the coming years: "Willy-nilly, the United States educational system is spawning a generation of semiliterates."[15] Eight years later, the situation had deteriorated further—at least if you believed the 1983 *Nation at Risk* report, which estimated that as many as 40 percent of America's minority youth were "functionally illiterate."[16] A more recent national commission argues that most students today "cannot write well enough to meet the demands they face in higher education and the emerging work environment."[17] They are unable "to create prose that is precise, engaging, and coherent"—the very writing required in a "complex, modern economy."

Now, declarations of such literacy "breakdowns" have almost always turned out to be exaggerated—or worse. Of the mid-1970s crisis, Richard Ohmann wrote that, when one looked carefully at the evidence, the "decline in literacy" was actually "a fiction, if not a hoax"; Robin Varnum said the problem was not so much falling standards as rising expectations; and James Gee argued that the real crisis was one of social justice, "rooted in the fact that we supply less good schools to poorer and more disadvantaged people, and better ones to more mainstream and advantaged people."[18] I'll have more to say about this skepticism below. For now, I will simply note that evidence for broad-based changes in literacy levels is notoriously hard to gauge; there is as much reason to believe that, over time, *more* people have come to writing, in *more* genres and media, with *greater* fluency, as the reverse.[19] Still, the belief that young people in the United States "can't write" and that the situation is deteriorating is persistent and widespread. And for most of the last 125 years, it has helped fuel demand for first-year writing courses.

A typical literacy crisis includes several elements. First, there are the individuals and groups who raise the alarm: who detect, decry, explain, and sometimes even try to solve the crisis they perceive. Above, I named them "American leaders," but they might more accurately be described as spokespersons for, or members of, the educated elite: that is, the upper middle class or, more precisely, the "professional-managerial class" (PMC), a group that arose in the United States between, roughly, 1890 and 1920 and today plays a crucial role in this and all other advanced capitalist societies. According to Barbara Ehrenreich and John Ehrenreich, the class consists of "salaried mental workers," such as teachers, lawyers, doctors, engineers, graduate students, accountants, managers, scientists, advertisers, and other "culture producers," and makes up about 20 to 25 percent of the U.S. population.[20] Although the boundaries between it and other groups are fuzzy, the PMC cannot simply be lumped in with the working class, say Ehrenreich and Ehrenreich, because it exists in an "antagonistic relationship" to that class, having emerged through the "expropriation of the skills and culture once indigenous to the working class."[21] At the same time, it is not part of the ruling class because its members do not own the means of production, and their commitment to the "technocratic transformation of society" often puts them at odds with capital—even as they play an important role in reproducing "capitalist culture and capitalist class relations."[22] For our purposes here, the key markers of the PMC are its devotion to higher education —Barbara Ehrenreich later defined the "professional middle class" as "all those people whose economic and social status is based on education, rather than on ownership of capital or property"—and its affiliation with professional life, "the characteristic form of self-organization of the PMC."[23]

The PMC's sensitivity to issues of literacy is perhaps unsurprising given the role that reading and writing play in contemporary higher education and professional life. But its tendency to look out at the literacy skills of its fellow subjects, especially the young, and see only decline is striking and requires explanation. According to Bronwyn Williams, the tendency is a function of middle-class anxieties about status and privilege. When the middle class reads, says Williams, it does so highly attuned to signs of cultural capital, evidence that the writer has acquired the "refined virtues" of the upper classes.[24] The rich, of course, can afford not to actually display those virtues, since they have economic capital to fall back on; but the middle class has nothing but cultural capital to distinguish itself from the masses—in language as in all else. That is why the "illiteracy" it sees in the general population so often turns out to be little more than breaches of linguistic etiquette.[25] The PMC often claims that what it is looking for is *critical* skill: sophisticated analysis and synthesis of data, compelling logic, precision in the presentation of ideas, and so on. But what seem to most energize it are improprieties of form and deviations from conventional behavior—that is, errors in spelling, punctuation, grammar, and mechanics.[26] The errors themselves may change, but their superficial nature and the anxiety they produce have remained constant for 125 years.

The bearers of "illiteracy" in these crises are usually adolescents and young adults—that is, inexperienced writers. Unfortunately, they are often seen by the PMC less as inexperienced than as deficient.[27] They are also frequently raced, classed, and gendered.[28] In fact, what seems to most reliably provoke a literacy crisis in this country is widened access to higher education for previously excluded groups.[29] "Each time the American educational system has rapidly expanded," wrote Richard Ohmann in the midst of the 1970s crisis, "there has been a similar chorus of voices lamenting the decline in standards and foreseeing the end of Western civilization."[30] And yet what those voices are really lamenting is the greater inclusivity of U.S. society itself. When Ohmann looked at the dip in ACT scores between 1965 and 1975, for example, he noticed that the decline took place almost entirely among women, who went from 45 to 55 percent of test takers. He inferred that "this means young women are less excluded from education now: many who would not have had a go at college then are doing so now. Presumably this new group is less well prepared than the women who used to choose higher education. If so, the "decline in literacy" translates partly into an *increase* in equality and social justice."[31]

Literacy crises like those described here are associated with more than just expansions of higher education, of course. The last quarter of the nineteenth century witnessed a broad shift in the economic and cultural makeup of this country, as the United States moved from an agrarian to an industrial economy, from majority rural to majority urban residence, and from market to monopoly capitalism. The last half of the twentieth century likewise saw dramatic changes: the shift from an industrial to a service economy, from majority urban to majority suburban residence, and from monopoly to late or global capitalism.[32] Both periods also witnessed high rates of immigration, as well as uneasy extensions of the middle class. And these were periods when literacy was changing, too: the late nineteenth century saw the rise of industrialized print, and the late twentieth century widespread digital communication.[33]

So if anxiety about adolescent writing, especially among the professional middle class, is perpetual, changes in the economy, society, and culture do appear to exacerbate that anxiety. But regardless of whether we see literacy crises in U.S. history as perennial or punctuated, the discourses surrounding them probably tell us less about our students and their failings, or our language and its deterioration, than about ourselves and what it means to live in a complex, fast-growing, multicultural society. In such a world, literacy is diverse and dynamic, even if many adults resent and resist that flux, pretending against all evidence that the "rules" of writing are constant and univocal. Those same adults tend to forget how they themselves learned to write, misattributing their own fluency to things like sentence diagramming or "natural" talent. Unsurprisingly, they often evaluate texts, and writers, more on matters of form than meaning, and they do so more for some texts, and some writers, than others. And, finally, they tend to believe that the literacy skills of their own and others' children are deficient and in decline.

———

One response to such "decline" is to argue that the historical expansion of postsecondary education in this country is a mistake and that whole groups of young adults should probably not be going to college, at least not on an academic track. For most members of the PMC, however, curtailing access to education is unacceptable given their devotion to the very idea of meritocracy. The most common response to the literacy crisis, then, is to call for improvements in the quality of primary and secondary schools, which are seen as currently failing to equip young people with the basic skills needed for higher education and work. Thus, the perpetual literacy crisis is also a perpetual blame game. In fact, during the first literacy crisis, in the late nineteenth century, freshman composition was explicitly seen as a *temporary* solution to writing deficiencies, one that would wither away once the high schools started doing a better job preparing students for the demands of the academy and society. Mike Rose has called this the "myth of transience," the belief that "if we can just do x or y, the prob-

8

lem will be solved—in five years, ten years, or a generation—and higher education will be able to return to its real work."[34]

For many college English professors, however, *any* responsibility for writing instruction, even temporary, was a bitter pill to swallow. As Professor Hill put it in 1879, "For [Harvard] to teach bearded men the rudiments of their native tongue would be almost as absurd as to teach them the alphabet or the multiplication table."[35] Similarly, the Harvard Committee on Composition and Rhetoric complained in 1892 about "a large corps of teachers engaged and paid from the College treasury to do that which should have been done before the student presented himself for admission."[36] A few years later, committee member E. L. Godkin ended a speech with this peroration: "College is the place in which to become acquainted with literature. It is not the place to acquire dexterity in the mere daily use of the mother tongue."[37]

Unfortunately, according to Rose, no one ever seemed to notice that this scenario, of colleges teaching composition only until the high schools improved, "has gone on for so long that it might not be temporary."[38] He continues:

> In fact, there will probably always be a significant percentage of students who do not meet some standard. . . . The American higher educational system is constantly under pressure to expand, to redefine its boundaries, admitting, in turn, the sons of the middle class, and later the daughters, and then the American poor, the immigrant poor, veterans, the racially segregated, the disenfranchised. Because of the social and educational conditions these groups experienced, their preparation for college will, of course, be varied. Add to this the fact that disciplines change and society's needs change, and the ways society determines what it means to be educated change.[39]

Thus, the course designed to solve a short-term problem in adolescent literacy skills gradually insinuated itself in the academy, finding a permanent home in the curriculum and adapting itself to needs other than those first imagined for it, in some places even coming to function as a kind of introduction to college itself.

Even more surprising than the survival of freshman composition after a century on the margins of U.S. higher education has been the rise of a bona fide intellectual discipline to support it. At the beginning of the twentieth century, "writing was the most often taught of college subjects and by a great measure the least examined," but by the end of that century, it was the subject of professional conferences, peer-reviewed journals, scholarly book series, and funded research projects.[40] Most striking of all was the rise of the PhD in "composition-rhetoric." If there were no advanced degrees in "comp-rhet" granted during the entire period from 1865 to 1945, the postwar period changed that dramatically.[41] By the early 1990s, there were more than twelve hundred comp-rhet doctoral students in the United States, studying in seventy-two different graduate programs, together granting more than one hundred PhD's a year.[42] And even that number was apparently insufficient to meet the demands of the job market. According to the Modern Language Association, a third of the fifteen hundred or so English language and literature faculty positions advertised annually in the United States use "composition and rhetoric" as a search term, more than for any other term, including both "British" and "American literature."[43] Given these numbers, the field may actually be underproducing PhD's, an astounding claim given the state of the academic job market in general.[44]

The teaching, study, and administration of first-year writing have been dramatically improved during this process. And the field of "comp-rhet" has come to define itself in ways that go well beyond that single course, becoming an active and capacious site for research and teaching throughout U.S. higher education.

———————

And yet, freshman composition and its attendant field remain curiously unknown, invisible to both the general public and other academics. What's worse, when they are noticed, they are often disparaged and dismissed. Why? Because accompanying the belief that young people in the United States are ill-prepared for the writing required of them in college and on the job is the notion that the acquisition of such skills is a rather basic proposition. According to this view, writing is simply the transcription of speech, itself merely the outward sign of interior ideas and impulses. Learning to write is thus little more than learning the rules of graphic correspondence: how to produce and arrange the visible marks needed to represent one's meaning to nonpresent others. Such skill should be acquired early in one's schooling since it is mainly a mechanical, rather than an intellectual, accomplishment.

Now, everyone admits that there is nothing mechanical about the written expression of literary artists; but ironically, that skill is also seen as unassimilable to traditional academic curricula. The reason in this case is not that the skill is basic, but that it is inaccessible, dependent on such factors as the "spontaneous overflow of powerful emotions" or the creative musings of genius.[45] Learning to write, in other words, is either basic or wonderful, accessible to all or only a few, a matter of memorizing rules or of tapping into rare talents of expression. There appears to be no middle ground: no course of study stretched over time and

Introduction

leading to the gradual acquisition of a fluency that is schooled but within the reach of all. The set of assumptions that makes such a project unthinkable has served the interests of fluent adult writers because it mystifies their skill, enhancing its value even as it obscures its source. But it has distorted writing for everyone else, treating it as perfunctory, rule driven, and uninteresting.

The modern anxiety about literacy and young adults, the motivating impulse of freshman composition, is therefore often accompanied by the belief that literacy instruction for that group is, properly speaking, a remedial subject. Despite half a century of research and practice calling this belief into question, it retains its hold on public opinion and continues to both motivate and destabilize freshman composition itself. Unfortunately, disparagement from outside the field is often matched by an odd kind of self-loathing within. Once introduced to high theory and advanced research, newly minted PhD's in "comprhet" sometimes chafe at the seemingly narrow confines of the first-year course. Years of advanced study have led them to want what other fields have: full, autonomous departments awarding degrees at every level, with multicourse curricula, independent research programs, and scholarly profiles that are irreducible to the expertise needed to teach a single, "basic" course. Decades of research have also produced in them profound skepticism about the very idea of "General Writing Skills Instruction," the notion that eighteen-year-olds can be taught to write in one or two semesters.[46] In other words, while the general public continues to endorse the idea of "learning to write" even as it reduces that process to the acquisition of a basic skill, the field of composition-rhetoric itself, charged with superintending that education, no longer fully believes in its flagship project. We are thus faced with the curious situation of the most widely required and taught undergraduate course in U.S. higher education backed by a professional community that no longer fully endorses it.

In fact, throughout its 125-year history, freshman composition has probably been more vulnerable to complaint, disparagement, and even elimination than any other project in U.S. higher education. The attacks have been strikingly similar regardless of when and where they occurred. We've already encountered the earliest and perhaps most persistent criticism of the course—that it simply doesn't belong in college. But other charges have been equally damning: according to the 1892 Harvard report, reading and "correcting" freshman themes is "stupefying" work, "drudgery of the most exhausting nature"; the teachers who end up with the job, wrote Yale professor Thomas Lounsbury in a much-cited 1911 article, are thus unlikely to be well qualified for it.[47] Students, meanwhile, "loathe" the course and, as Michigan professor Warner Rice put it in 1960, are ill motivated to do well in it.[48] Finally, the course simply doesn't work: to teach writing apart from content, wrote Columbia professor Oscar Campbell in 1939, is "intellectually dishonest as well as futile."[49] And even if it could be shown to have positive effects, one or two semesters is not enough to accrue them.[50]

All these arguments were marshaled in a scathing broadside against the course published in the November 1969 issue of *College English* by Leonard Greenbaum, an English professor at the University of Michigan. In the article, Greenbaum claimed that the single most distinctive feature of freshman composition was the "tradition of complaint" that had accompanied it since its founding, a tradition that revealed, he argued, anxiety both within and without the profession regarding the course. In tracing the history of that anxiety, Greenbaum also summarized the main arguments against composition itself: it was a tedious and disagreeable course to teach; the only instructors who could be compelled to teach it were the least qualified to do so; it positioned writing in an intellectual vacuum; and there was little evidence that it actually improved student skills—in fact, it probably contributed to increased dislike and fear of writing. For these and other reasons, the course has been perennially subjected to calls for its elimination. Greenbaum made his own take on all this abundantly clear: "I'm for abolition, too," he wrote.[51]

———

Given the complex narrative told so far—of the perpetual literacy crisis that has characterized public perceptions of adolescent writing in this country since the late nineteenth century; of the stand-alone course in composition that emerged out of that crisis and is today the most widely taught course in U.S. higher education; and of the "tradition of complaint" that has accompanied that course from the beginning, both within and without its own field—one would think that histories of higher education in the United States would have devoted some time and space to freshman composition. In fact, the course has been almost completely ignored.

Take histories of "general education"—the suite of required courses usually taken in the first two years of college and meant to provide all students on campus with a shared cultural heritage, or at least common exposure to a range of fields and skills, before they concentrate on their major course of study. Studies of "gen ed" have been focused for more than half a century now on the long-standing tension in U.S. postsecondary education between the ends of breadth and depth, between distribution or core requirements for all, on the one hand, and major requirements for each, on the other.[52] Freshman composition, unfortunately, doesn't really fit either category; it's more about activity, application,

Introduction

and skill than content, whether broad or deep. Historians of general education have tended therefore to ignore it.

Similarly, histories of English studies often completely ignore writing instruction.[53] From the point of view of most scholars of British and American literature, in fact, the study of English in the United States *is* the study of reading, though historical evidence clearly shows that college-level "English" in this country began as much with, and has been as much about, writing and rhetoric as literature and philology. Histories of modern rhetorical theory, meanwhile, often act as if written composition doesn't exist, and compositionists who write about the history of rhetoric sometimes seem embarrassed by their own field.[54] Linguists, creative writers, critical thinking advocates, and other scholar-practitioners who would seem to have a stake in first-year writing sometimes seem surprised that it even exists.

As for histories written by compositionists themselves, enormous progress has been made in understanding the long, complex story summarized here—in fact, according to Brereton, "historians of composition have created the single most impressive body of knowledge about any discipline in higher education."[55] And yet the field as a whole, I would argue, has tended to marginalize the very part of the story that I've dwelled on here—the social anxiety that has historically motivated (and disparaged) first-year writing—treating it as important only in the early years of the discipline. From this point of view, composition began developing into a bona fide academic field in the 1950s and '60s and then gradually built a sophisticated body of knowledge through the 1970s and '80s, by which time it had more or less achieved full disciplinarity. The message of such histories is that we've now made it.

The discipline has good reason, of course, for wanting to present itself as a fully autonomous academic field. After all, scholars in the field suffer when it is not so seen. Many grant agencies still don't list "composition" as a field of study. Tenure, hiring, and other decisions are still often based on disparagement and misunderstanding. And people still sometimes ask compositionists, "But what's your area of *research?*" So it's understandable that the field would have a chip on its shoulder. But is it possible that comp-rhet is under the spell of its own "myth of transience"? That, just as freshman writing will eventually wither away once the high schools finally do their job, the field's lack of disciplinary status will also turn out to be temporary, a situation that improves once writing studies is granted the academic respect it deserves?

But what if comp-rhet will *never* be a true discipline? What if, like the freshman course, it's a project that will never fit comfortably in the academy? And what if there is some benefit in that? What if there is virtue in the very aspects of the field that impede full disciplinarity? "Composition is a good field to work in," David Bartholomae once wrote, "but you have to be willing to pay attention to common things."[56] What if the field has not yet learned to take those "common things" seriously? And what would happen if it did?

Earlier, I introduced features of freshman composition that make it anomalous in the academic context: its generality, universality, and liminality. Is it possible that these and other features are also the source of the course's potency? After all, composition is the only course in U.S. higher education that comes more or less untethered to a traditional academic discipline, that doesn't therefore have to introduce students to a particular body of knowledge, that is relatively unburdened by the "content fetish" that characterizes the rest of the academy.[57] It's also, arguably, the only truly activity-based course in higher education and the only one genuinely focused on students themselves: their opinions, their backgrounds, their hopes and aspirations, their language. And, located as it is on the threshold of students' adult lives, composition is also uniquely positioned not only to help them write their way into the academy but also to help them become full members of their own society without being tyrannized by it.[58] It's also, on many campuses, the only course required of all students and thus can work against the fragmentation the rest of the academy actually promotes.

But it's still, after all, a *course.* If the field of composition has had some influence on the teaching of English K–12, it remains a thoroughly postsecondary phenomenon. It may be linked to "common things," in other words, but it's still a project of higher education—a site of study, practice, and learning *for adults* (albeit mostly young ones). As we'll see in this book, first-year writing is a space not only for acculturation but also for growth, change, even critique. If it's an educational project uniquely beholden to social convention, it's also a site where young people can begin to develop their own voices. If it's a space unusually susceptible to social influence, it's also by design free of predetermined content.[59] And if it's a course thoroughly saturated by history, it's a project that has also been unusually stable over time.

Perhaps this is the key to freshman comp's power as an educational project: its remarkable *commonness* within the uncommon environment of the academy. It may also be what makes the course so vulnerable to critique and even abolition. After all, the course imposed by social and cultural forces can always be deposed by them as well.

Introduction

One of the most dramatic events in the history of freshman composition in this country—indeed, one of the most dramatic events in the history of U.S. higher education—occurred in November 1969 in Madison, Wisconsin, on the main campus of that state's public university system.[60] At the time, the University of Wisconsin (UW) was 121 years old, and, like other midwestern land-grant universities, it had grown rapidly, if unevenly, in the hundred years spanning the last half of the nineteenth century and first half of the twentieth. But the boom of the late 1950s and early 1960s was exceptional. In those years, UW experienced unprecedented growth in its student enrollment, its faculty hiring, and its physical plant. For professors and graduate students, it was a time of rampant specialization, unrelenting focus on research, and seemingly unending federal largesse. It was also a period of rapid growth in the size and diversity of the undergraduate population and the resources dedicated to their education. Every part of the university seemed to be expanding, diversifying, and flourishing. As UW's official historians would later put it, it was the campus's "golden age."[61]

The late 1960s changed all that. The U.S. economy began to contract as the costs of the war in Vietnam and new social programs at home continued to mount. Opposition to the war itself grew louder, and domestic unrest on a variety of issues became more violent. The baby boom started to slow. And students and faculty began to turn on one another. On campuses, the years 1966 to 1971 were tense and divisive. Antiwar protests, civil rights demonstrations, union battles—they rocked colleges and universities across the country.

One hotbed for tension at UW was the huge English Department, and many of its deepest conflicts swirled around the two-semester Freshman English course, English 101 and 102.[62] The course was required of every undergraduate on campus, a group clamoring (if inchoately) for relevance and freedom in their studies; it was taught by a cadre of politically active, newly unionized graduate teaching assistants (TAs), anxious about their future in a society they now saw as morally bankrupt and an academy whose decade-long spending (and hiring) spree was clearly coming to an end; and it was directed by an English faculty who affiliated not with first-year writing but with the advanced study of British and American literature and who, given the disaffection of the two groups mentioned above, felt themselves under siege by the late 1960s.

In November 1969, shortly after Leonard Greenbaum published his article about freshman composition's "tradition of complaint," the English Department at UW voted 27 to 8, with 4 abstentions, to cease offering the second semester of Freshman English, English 102, beginning in fall 1970, essentially abolishing a campus-wide composition requirement that had been in place for nearly a century.[63] In justifying its move, the faculty argued that improved high school preparation made the requirement unnecessary and that any remaining responsibility for writing instruction should be borne by students' major departments.

The abolition of Freshman English at UW actually occurred in two stages: in the spring of 1968, the department rescinded the requirement for the first-semester course, English 101, keeping it on the books for the small number of students who were thereafter said to need it but allowing the majority of freshmen to proceed straight to English 102. Then, a year and a half later, in November 1969, the department eliminated outright the second course, thus effectively, and unilaterally, abolishing the university's writing requirement altogether.

These decisions were not minor: in the decade prior to 1968–69, three to four thousand students a year took six credit hours each of freshman composition at UW, a huge undertaking that employed scores of graduate TAs from English, occupied countless hours of faculty training and supervision, and constituted a major part of the undergraduate experience at the university and one of the largest and most important undertakings in the school as a whole. In fall 1970, by contrast, the number of undergraduate students taking any first-year writing course at all was in the low hundreds, and the number of English graduate students was reduced dramatically.

Nor was the abolition a momentary blip: the remedialization of the first course and the elimination of the second held, despite fervent and broad protest, and for the next quarter of a century there was no real writing requirement at UW, putting the university out of step with its peer institutions and preventing the English Department there from fully joining the "composition revolution" of the 1970s. In fact, it was not until the early 1980s that the department hired a tenure-track faculty member trained in composition studies, not until the early 1990s that it began to offer a graduate degree in composition studies, and not until 1996 that something like a universal writing requirement was revived at UW.[64]

Nor did this case of abolition take place in an out-of-the-way institution with no tradition in or commitment to the teaching of writing. From 1898 to 1968, for nearly three-quarters of a century, UW's freshman composition course had been a vital, professionally run program, in a university with a prominent public mission and an English Department with a long record of thoughtful attention to writing and rhetoric, including a role in national debates about first-year composition itself. The reduction and then elimination of the Freshman English requirement at UW were thus high-profile events, playing out on a very public stage, in one of the largest departments on campus, at a leading institution of higher learning, during one of the most turbulent times in the country's history.

And yet, for all the significance of these events, and the drama of their unfolding, the story of the abolition of Freshman English at UW has never really been told. It has been recounted in print only once, in a couple of paragraphs in the fourth volume of *The University of Wisconsin: A History*, published in 1999.[65] This silence is all the more surprising given the amount written about 1960s-era Madison and the later prominence of some of the "freshman comp" teachers of the time, from Lynne Cheney to Ira Shor.[66]

That's not to say that the events in question were forgotten. In fact, a particular narrative about the elimination of the second-semester course survived and continues to be recounted orally in the hallways of the university. According to that narrative, English 102 was abolished in the fall of 1969 because the graduate TAs who taught it were not doing their job; they had become more interested in politically indoctrinating their students and disrupting the university than in actually teaching writing. Given the number of TAs and the general tumult of the time, the faculty decided that the best course of action was to drop the course altogether, justifying their decision with the two-part argument mentioned above, which claimed improved skills among entering students and a campus-wide responsibility for writing instruction.

There are taped interviews in the university's Oral History Program, dating back to the early 1970s, that seem to bear out this unofficial story, which blames radical TAs for the abolition of the course. And there is an extensive collection of primary documents in the English Department, including minutes of committee meetings, official correspondence, and memos to and from the dean of the College of Letters and Science, which seems to confirm it. These materials are rich and useful, but they provide only a partial view of the events in question. The English Department's official records, for example, reflect almost exclusively the senior faculty's point of view about Freshman English. The Oral History Program is similarly biased toward tenured faculty, including not a single interview with an English Department teaching assistant from the late 1960s.[67] There are almost no records anywhere, meanwhile, concerning how undergraduate students experienced these courses or the changes to them.[68]

This book began as an attempt to recover those voices. When I arrived at the University of Wisconsin-Madison in fall 1998 to take a position as an assistant professor of English, I was surprised by the relatively small size and generally muted profile of freshman composition (English 100) there. After all, my new professional home was a storied English Department on the flagship campus of a world-famous, midwestern, land-grant, state university. It should have had a more substantial writing program, I thought, with a more robust administrative structure, a larger teaching staff, more tenure-stream faculty, a higher profile in the English Department and on campus, and more sustained traditions behind it.

Now, the situation could be explained in part, I surmised, by the program's youth. After all, English 100 was only a year or two old in 1998—itself something of a shock. But youth didn't explain everything. After I had been there a few years, it became clear that "comp" was probably never going to be as prominent or as well supported at UW as at comparable programs in other Big Ten universities. The composition faculty at Madison was the smallest in its peer group. And only a third of students at the university ever took a first-year writing course, certainly one of the lowest proportions among comparable institutions. I was puzzled: how could *this* be freshman comp at one of the premier midwestern land-grant universities in the country, the very heart of my field?

So I started to ask around. And when I did, I began to hear stories about the 1960s, about radical TAs using Freshman English to politically indoctrinate their students. Because of such misconduct, I was told, the course had been abolished and the university's writing requirement rescinded for nearly a quarter of a century. What I heard about all this, however, came entirely from senior faculty members who had survived the trauma of that era. Other than their stories, there didn't seem to be much institutional memory concerning the old freshman course; I heard nothing from the TAs' point of view, and I never saw anything about the episode in print. So the question began to nag at me: what really happened to freshman composition at UW during the late 1960s?

At first, I envisioned a small study designed to answer that question, conducted with a few graduate students and culminating in a journal article or book chapter of some kind. But even that modest idea was a long time bearing fruit. Finally, in the spring of 2003, when I was invited to guest-teach a graduate research methods course for three weeks, I designed a unit on local history that used UW's own Freshman English course as ground for the students and me to excavate together. The idea was to focus on primary documents and be open to whatever we might discover about composition at UW, at any point in its history. In fact, some of the first documents we found concerned the English Department's surprising national prominence in composition instruction in the early decades of the twentieth century, when the celebrated handbook author Edwin Woolley directed Freshman English.

Introduction

That group of students uncovered something else in the spring of 2003, which had a dramatic impact on how this project unfolded. Deep in the files of the English Department, they found a faded, two-page memo, dated October 13, 1969, recording the minutes of a meeting about UW's Freshman English program. Written by stewards of UW's Teaching Assistants Association (TAA) and distributed to that group's English Department members, the memo recounted a heated exchange between nearly one hundred graduate TAs and two faculty members—the chair of the English Department and the director of Freshman English—about English 102, the second semester of the required freshman course. The minutes began by airing a disagreement between one of the TAs and the chair over the use of a nonsanctioned text in class. As the document proceeded, however, that disagreement broadened to include other disputes, and it escalated quickly into personal denunciation and ideological recrimination. At the end of the meeting, according to the minutes, the assembled TAs voted to take over the Freshman English Policy Committee, then under faculty control. At that point, the chair left in frustration, and the memo drew to a rapid close.

The document remains to this day an unnerving artifact for me, and much of this book can be seen as an attempt to explain it—how that meeting came to be, what happened in its aftermath, and what those events reveal about the history and nature of my own field.

Unfortunately, the three-week research unit quickly came to a close, and we all moved on to other things. And yet I found myself hooked on the 1960s. I began reading everything I could about Madison during that era. David Maraniss's haunting book about October 1967, *They Marched into Sunlight,* with chapters set alternately in Vietnam and Madison, came out about this time. It led me to Barry Brown and Glenn Silber's documentary *The War at Home,* also set in Madison, which in turn led me to Tom Bates's *Rads,* a stunning account of the 1970 bombing of Sterling Hall on the UW campus. It was also about this time that I discovered the oral history archive at UW, which included interviews with key faculty members from the 1960s. And I came across the fourth volume of the official history of UW, by David Cronon and John Jenkins, published in 1999, which included chapters on the Vietnam War era. As I learned more about the place and time, I began to realize that part of the story of 1960s Madison was missing from these accounts: the huge Freshman English course, which—because it was taught in small sections to nearly every undergraduate on campus; because it was staffed by graduate TAs, themselves both students and teachers; because it centered on reading and writing in general rather than on disciplinary "content"; and because it was thus unusually open to influence from its own time and place—was an especially rich source for studying higher education in that moment of radical change.

So I began to imagine a research project about late 1960s Freshman English at UW, centered on the TAs who taught the course and based on archived documents and oral history interviews. In September 2004, I applied for a grant from the UW-Madison Graduate School to pay two students to help me do the primary research. The application was accepted, and after putting out a call, I hired Rasha Diab and Mira Shimabukuro, two talented doctoral students in rhetoric and composition at UW-Madison. We set to work. Through the spring and summer of 2005, Rasha, Mira, and I unearthed documents and talked to former UW TAs from the 1960s. We located the TAA archive and read intently the two issues of its short-lived journal *Critical Teaching;* we pored over the English Department's own records, including committee minutes stretching back through most of the twentieth century, documents that were astonishingly detailed precisely for the period—the late 1960s—we were most interested in. We listened to the audiotapes stored in the university's Oral History Program and conducted our own original interviews with former TAs and junior faculty members. As the summer wore on, we began to realize that we were accumulating a wealth of untapped data about a fascinating chapter of U.S. history. It was a thrilling experience.

When we later shared our research in a presentation to English Department faculty and graduate students in the spring of 2006, two things became clear: First, there was still intense interest in and continuing controversy about the 1960s, at least among academics in Madison, Wisconsin. Forty years after the events in question, the topic elicited raw emotions. Second, the material we had accumulated, and the depth with which we were beginning to talk about it, had quickly exceeded the article-length parameters I had imagined for this research.

So, in the summer of 2006, my funding now exhausted and working largely on my own, I made a unilateral decision: rather than keep cutting an ever-expanding story to fit the confines of the essay genre, I would expand the narrative into a book. The summer looked blissfully free in terms of practical responsibilities: my oldest child was out of the country; my younger one had joined a pool and was swimming all day long; I had finally finished a draft of an earlier, unrelated book project; and I was now between jobs, having resigned my faculty position at Wisconsin and accepted one at the University of Massachusetts-Amherst, where I would move in August. So for three months, I worked full-time on the UW story. By the end of the summer of 2006, when

I left Madison for a new life on the East Coast, a first draft of the manuscript was complete. Without quite setting out to do so, I had recounted not just the events of the late 1960s, but the whole story of composition at UW, from the mid-nineteenth to the late twentieth century: 150 years of stability and upheaval, innovation and stagnation—perhaps the fullest account available of a writing course in a North American university.

It was also clearly now about more than just that one course. Having read widely in the history of my own field, I knew that what had happened at UW was not entirely out of sync with the broader story of freshman composition in this country. Add to that my own complicated relationship with composition, my sensitivity to its role in contemporary English departments and university general education programs, and my scholarly background in the history and theory of rhetoric, and I was primed to see in the story of this specific course broader lessons about freshman composition and higher education in general.

I thus follow here a long tradition in historical research of trying to tell a general story by focusing on a particular one. This is, in other words, a case study, which involves gathering and analyzing data about an individual example as a way of studying a broader phenomenon. It is done on the assumption that the example (the "case") is in some way typical of the broader phenomenon. The case may be an individual, a city, an event, a society, or any other possible object of analysis. The advantage of the case-study method is that it allows more intensive analyses of specific empirical details. The disadvantage is that it is sometimes hard to use the results to generalize to other cases.[69]

I hope the advantages of such a method will be evident in the book itself: the narrow focus afforded by concentrating on such a well-bounded topic, the rich detail provided by access to such large amounts of data concerning that circumscribed world, and the continuous narrative arc made possible by holding nearly everything else constant. It is this specificity, I believe, that makes history come alive here (to the extent that it does). The details concerning these real people, living in this real place, working in a real program in a real institution, and interacting with others through the complexities of their lives together, give the story authenticity and, I hope, value. As John Brereton once wrote, in our attempts to understand the past, *theory* is relatively easy to get at; what often gets left out is *detail,* "the everyday fabric of history."[70]

That detail enabled me to tell what I believe is a surprisingly gripping story, but also to avoid reducing my research subjects (whether people, places, projects, events, or even whole eras) to stereotype. My main methodological goal, in fact, was (as much as possible) to let the documents collected and the interviews conducted speak for themselves, without heavy theoretical or ideological overlay. In fact, except for the introduction and conclusion, there isn't much overt theoretical reflection here. And I don't spend a lot of time situating the history of UW's Freshman English program in a grand narrative of national scope. Overviews and surveys have their uses; what I wanted to do, rather, was stay close to the ground, privilege the local and particular, and build the project up from primary sources.[71] Now, admittedly, I exert agency here; the focus on the TAs, for example, clearly affected the conclusions reached. But I try to be explicit about why I made the choices I did, and I refer to alternative interpretations of these events and the data on which they rely.

But of course none of this rebuts the traditional criticism of the case study, which is that researchers using such an approach often fail to make the individual case relevant for others, to make their conclusions, based on their research, more broadly applicable to other cases. The study might reveal in rich, detailed, and comprehensive ways a particular person, place, time, program, or event, but it's not clear what the research community as a whole, or the public at large, learns from such work about the world beyond that case. To put this in the form of a question and bring us back to the project at hand: what will readers learn from this study, focused on a single course at a single institution, about freshman composition in general, about the 1960s at large, or about U.S. higher education more broadly?

First, I believe this study tells us new things about the history of freshman composition. In particular, it helps compositionists across the country make better sense of a period that, oddly, has not been well accounted for in our disciplinary histories, narratives that have tended, in my opinion, to privilege the decades from 1946 to 1966, when "comp-rhet" emerged as an academic discipline, and 1971 to 1991, when the process paradigm established itself as the dominant approach to teaching writing in this country, but have largely skipped over the handful of tumultuous years in between, from 1967 to 1970.[72] Consequently, much has been written about composition's professionalization, from the 1949 founding of the Conference on College Composition and Communication (CCCC) to the 1963 publication of Braddock, Lloyd-Jones, and Schoer's *Research in Written Composition*;[73] the rise of the so-called new rhetorics of the late 1950s and early 1960s, including the 1963 CCCC panel on the "New Rhetoric" and the 1965 publication of Edward P. J. Corbett's *Classical Rhetoric for the Modern Student;* and the gradual emergence in the late 1960s and early 1970s of the process paradigm in the teaching of writing, including Gordon Rohmann's pioneering 1965 work on prewriting, the 1966 meeting of British and American English teachers at Dartmouth, and the groundbreaking work of Janet Emig, Donald Murray, Peter Elbow, and others in the early 1970s.[74]

But as important as all these trends were in the field's development during the last half of the twentieth century, *none* shows up in the sources we uncovered about Freshman English at the University of Wisconsin during the Vietnam War era.[75] The few references we found to "rhetoric" were almost all pejorative; there is little indication that writing research or composition pedagogy might be an intellectual or academic field in its own right; and there is almost no mention at all of "process."[76] Is it possible that the field has overstated the role of certain intellectual and pedagogical movements during the last half of the twentieth century and overlooked others that, at least at UW in the late 1960s, were more significant? Have we missed something historically crucial, in other words, between 1966 and 1971, between the Dartmouth seminar on the teaching of English and the publication of Janet Emig's *The Composing Processes of Twelfth Graders?*

In the mid-1960s, after all, Freshman English at UW, as elsewhere, was still under the sway of a "current-traditional" paradigm that had been developed nearly a century before, amid a rapidly expanding postsecondary educational system in North America that was designed to prepare students for an urban, industrial, print-based economy dependent on widespread skills in "standard" English written prose.[77] It was a paradigm that proved remarkably durable and can still in fact be detected in writing instruction today.

But by the late 1960s, with massive changes under way in the global economy, in the social, political, and cultural conditions of the United States, and in the modern North American research university, that paradigm was proving to be both limited and limiting. Unfortunately, no new approach had emerged to replace it. In 1968 and '69, therefore, the freshman course at UW was essentially set adrift: the faculty in the English Department were no longer interested in it; those directing it were treated, in general, as low-level administrators and not provided the resources needed to accomplish the huge task before them; many of the graduate student TAs who shouldered its burdens were deeply ambivalent about it; and the students taking it were often resentful of the requirement and the mechanical way the course was often taught. What's worse, no new theoretical paradigm had appeared that could change any of this: the so-called new rhetoric had not made the slightest inroad at UW; the alleged professionalization of writing studies was nowhere in evidence; the "process" movement was years away.

Still, the teaching of general education reading and writing at UW in the late 1960s was, for many of its instructors, a serious—and relatively autonomous— intellectual and social project that demanded and rewarded reflection, experimentation, and self-evaluation. In the UW Freshman English program, the most important development during these years was the rise of a short-lived but potent pedagogy, simultaneously critical and humanist, developed almost entirely by English graduate student teaching assistants working by and among themselves, and reflective of (but not reducible to) the new world created by the war in Vietnam, the civil rights movement, the struggle for ethnic studies programs, and the other political, cultural, and ideological transformations of the time—as well as by the changing socioeconomic conditions of the 1960s and the new university that had materialized in response to them.[78]

It was a pedagogy that promoted relevance as the key criterion for selecting and evaluating educational materials and tasks, that advocated a radical decentering of classroom authority away from the teacher, that used "emergent" curricula responsive to the day-by-day life of the course and the growing human beings involved in it, and that rejected conventional grading as the ultimate assessment of student work.

It was a pedagogy that was also profoundly unacceptable to the tenured faculty in the English Department at the time, who were unwilling either to relinquish control over the freshman course or to take an active interest in it. They responded to the new world of postsecondary literacy education, therefore, by retreating into advanced, specialized literary study and abandoning, almost overnight, the department's long-standing commitment to general education writing instruction.

The second main contribution of this project, I hope, is the illumination it provides on the 1960s in general, especially the momentous changes in higher education that took place during that decade. In fact, as I argue here, the most important influence on writing instruction at UW during this time was not any new theory or pedagogy of composition, but the massive cultural, demographic, political, economic, and institutional changes that were taking place in the country at large, changes felt especially acutely on college and university campuses and affecting general education courses, like first-year composition, more than any others. The story of English 101 and 102 at UW in the late 1960s, in other words, needs to be told in the context of the changing material conditions of U.S. higher education and North American society during those years, when a rapidly expanding and increasingly diverse student population, mounting federal support for education and research, and a relative liberation of both politics and culture came up against massive civil unrest, foreign war, and the growing anxiety, disillusionment, and alienation of young people.

I show here, for example, how, during the 1960s, growing pressure on English Department faculty to specialize, expand their graduate programs, and develop stronger research profiles coincided with increasing needs in undergraduate general education at the time, a contradiction that was resolved, temporarily and uneasily, by expanded reliance on graduate student teaching assistants, whose rising numbers signaled a perilous overextension of the profession. In all this, the year 1969 turns out to have been a key year, a "hinge," or moment of rupture, and the freshman composition course a more important cultural, institutional, and pedagogical battleground than we have previously thought.[79]

But to understand what happened in the English Department at UW in 1969, we need to put that year in the wider context of "the long sixties," a period stretching from around 1957 to around 1974—from the launch of *Sputnik* to the end of the Vietnam War, "from the heyday of the Beat movement and the rise of popular youth culture to Watergate."[80] It is a period that historians are increasingly using to mark a kind of watershed era in the history of the West.[81] The period is bookended, economically, by two recessions (1957–58 before and 1973–75 after), at least in the United States; but it cannot be characterized therefore as simply an era of growth between two contractions. That's because "the long sixties" itself needs to be divided into at least two subperiods: an early time of expansion, prosperity, and liberalization (say, 1957–64) and a later time of decline, unrest, and reaction (1965–74), the latter years effectively setting up "the long downturn" that began in the mid-1970s and continues, arguably, today.[82]

Looked at from this wide-angle view, "the long sixties" functioned as an extended, complex, dramatic transition in the West—a kind of borderland between modernism and postmodernism, monopoly and late capitalism, print and digital literacy, and the industrial and the service economy. It was also a consequential period for the North American university, with the clash between "research" and "teaching," mentioned above, constituting one battle in a broader war for the heart and soul of higher education in this country. As I argue here, freshman composition was an important, if overlooked, front in that war, and studying it can tell us much about the story of modern U.S. postsecondary education, not only because first-year writing has often been, in general, a site where the contradictions in our academic institutions play themselves out, but also because we can see in it, at least in terms of general education, how the old conservative order (at its peak in the mid-1950s) collapsed, a radical alternative emerged (in the 1960s) but then also collapsed (around 1969), and then a new paradigm—more liberal than the old order but more congenial to the new service economy than the radical alternative—began to take shape (in the early 1970s). In the terms of first-year writing, this is the story of the demise of current-traditional rhetoric and the birth of the process movement.

And that brings us to the third, and I believe the most important, lesson of this book, which concerns freshman composition itself. Let's briefly return, then, to Leonard Greenbaum's 1969 article on the "tradition of complaint" that has accompanied freshman composition in this country since its birth. If Greenbaum's goal was to inaugurate a new period of anticomposition ferment, to add to the prior periods recounted in the essay, he was not entirely successful.[83] There is some evidence for a nationwide reduction in the freshman English requirement in the late 1960s and early 1970s, mostly likely as part of a general turn away from course requirements at the time; but the changes were modest and largely reversed by the late 1970s and early 1980s.[84] But what Greenbaum could not know was that prominent proposals to abolish the course would reappear a quarter century *after* his article appeared, in, for example, Sharon Crowley's 1991 call to eliminate the universal requirement, and continue right up to the present (see, for example, David Smit's 2004 *The End of Composition Studies*).[85]

One might disagree with these pronouncements, but it's hard to ignore the fact that they exist; that they recur with remarkable regularity; and that they have been based for more than a century now on a surprisingly stable set of arguments, some of which even defenders of the course concede. In other words, we are dealing here with an educational project that has probably produced more criticism than any other curricular effort in the postsecondary academy. In fact, it's hard to imagine another course so firmly ensconced in our colleges and universities that is under such constant threat of elimination, or at least disparagement, even at the hands of its own professors.

And yet, oddly, given how threatening the phenomenon of abolitionism is, and how historically self-conscious composition studies has become during the last generation, the field has produced very few case studies of actual abolition. Most of the writing on this topic, in fact, has taken the form of either polemics for or against the course in general or surveys of others' arguments for or against it, a là Greenbaum.[86] What the field lacks, however, are rich, careful empirical studies of actual first-year composition courses, requirements, and programs under stress, told in a way that situates the courses and the opinions and decisions regarding them in their particular spatiotemporal contexts but also allows for reflection on the long-term effects and broader implications of those opinions and decisions.

I offer the following narrative, then, not only to help correct local misrepresentations of the history of Freshman English at the University of Wisconsin but also to help compositionists at large better appreciate the role of "the long sixties" in the story of their discipline and to help everyone involved in higher education make better sense, even today, of "freshman comp," a course that is, at once, inherently unstable and enormously resilient, constantly at risk of marginalization and yet surprisingly central, even inescapable, at key moments in our nation's cultural, intellectual, and material history.

2 A PREHISTORY, 1848-1948

There has been rhetorical instruction at the University of Wisconsin since its founding in 1848. One of the first six professorships at the university, in fact, was a chair in "mental philosophy, logic, rhetoric, and English literature."[1] The charge given to the holder of that chair reflected the amalgamation of literary study, oral and written composition, and moral philosophy typical of those predisciplinary times, and the training its professor provided was, in turn, integrated within a much more unified course of undergraduate studies than we have today.

John Brereton's description of the antebellum college curriculum in the United States fits 1850s UW well: there were "no majors, hardly any electives, no sections, and precious little coursework outside of classics, mathematics, and some science."[2] In many ways, the education offered at UW before the Civil War mirrored the training provided at the time to wealthy young men in private colleges back East, despite the young state legislature's attempts to make sure the new university at Madison was a thoroughly utilitarian institution: open, public, and practical.[3] Those more democratic goals did sometimes peek through, however: Daniel Read, the first professor of mental philosophy, logic, rhetoric, and English literature at UW, was also given the "Normal Professorship," responsible for imparting "the art of teaching" to future "educators of the popular mind."[4] When that department finally opened in 1863, 112 students enrolled, nearly half the university's total; 76 of them were women.[5]

What was rhetorical education like in these early years? First, it was closely interwoven with instruction in literature, logic, and moral philosophy. Second, it was spread across multiple languages, ancient and modern, a linguistic abundance that was one of the central features of the premodern college curriculum.[6] Third, it emphasized oral recitation, declamation, and debate without neglecting written composition.[7] Fourth, it was distributed throughout the student's academic career and was an integral part of nearly every class hour, though it was given special attention in the junior and senior years.[8] Fifth, it was oriented to *public* communication, preparing young men and women for the verbal performances of their future scholarly, professional, and civic careers, and was thus more the culmination of the undergraduate curriculum than its gateway. In fact, up until the 1870s, every senior at UW had to deliver an oration at commencement, often in Latin, Greek, or German.[9]

When Stephen Carpenter took over from Professor Read in 1868, however, the center of gravity in UW's logic, rhetoric, and English literature chair began to shift toward the last term in that trilogy.[10] A belletristic approach to rhetoric had been common in Anglo-American academic circles since the late eighteenth century; and when Carpenter replaced Blair's *Lectures on Rhetoric and Belles Lettres* with future UW president John Bascom's *Principles of Rhetoric,* there was no real change in the course's fundamentally literary approach to composition. But Carpenter, unlike Read, had been schooled in the new German philology; he was a specialist in *Beowulf* and Chaucer, and in 1872 he published the groundbreaking textbook *English of the Fourteenth Century.*[11] With that, the intimate connection between literary studies and public life, inherent in the institution of the original chair in mental philosophy, logic, rhetoric, and English literature and fostered by both Daniel Read and Bascom himself, began to weaken.

Perhaps that's why, when Carpenter retired in 1878, the chair split into two, and, for the next twenty years, one professor (John Charles Freeman) handled English literature, and another (David Frankenburger) rhetoric and oratory. At first, literary studies seemed to stagnate: Freeman was well liked but not especially scholarly, although this may have appealed to the humanities students of the time—mostly "young women preparing to teach in the secondary schools or young men with journalistic careers in view." But by the early 1890s, a number of Johns Hopkins graduates had joined the faculty, and the specialized, advanced study of English literature finally began to deepen and grow.[12]

The study and practice of public oratory, on the other hand, flourished throughout these years. Frankenburger, a graduate of the UW law school, was a popular lecturer, revered and loved by the students, and the campus as a whole enjoyed an extraordinarily vigorous "oratorical culture" during the second half of the nineteenth century.[13] The phenomenon was most visible in the popular literary societies of the time, the Athenaean and the Hesperian societies for men and the Castalian and Laurean societies for women, which sponsored weekly declamations, debates, and essay readings about pressing matters of the day, such as U.S. territorial expansion, women's suffrage, and socialism. When newly elected UW president John Bascom visited Madison in 1874, he attended a debate of the Athenaean Society on "whether workingmen's unions are combinations for the best interest of the laborer."[14] The societies were not always scenes of such idealism, however: "When the Athenaeans debated 'whether four years spent in the University of Wisconsin be of more benefit to a young man than two thousand dollars at twelve percent,' the society voted decisively for the two thousand dollars."[15]

The highlight of the oratorical year at UW was the annual "joint debate" between the two leading literary societies—so popular that in 1895 more than a thousand people paid fifteen cents each to hear the debate in the Assembly Hall of the state capitol building.[16] These societies, and the orations, essays, and debates they sponsored (together with a thriving student journalism movement), were the most vital part of campus life in the decades right after the Civil War.[17] And they were apparently effective in preparing students for their future civic and professional careers: Merle Curti and Vernon Carstensen, in their history of the University of Wisconsin, claim that of 336 known participants in the fifty-six joint debates between 1867 and 1926, two became governors of the state, two presidents of large state universities, and several university and college professors, state and federal judges, prominent business executives, and successful lawyers.[18]

But the joint debates continued long after oratory had lost its centrality in undergraduate intellectual and social life at UW. In fact, the heyday of oratory at the university appears to have been the two decades after the Civil War. By the 1890s, write Curti and Carstensen, the competition from intercollegiate athletics, fraternities, and school dances was too much for the literary societies, and the common culture that they represented became fragmented by the many majors, schools, and interests of the turn-of-the-century years.[19] The university between presidents Bascom and Van Hise—from 1887 to 1903—was changing dramatically, and the old rhetorical theories, pedagogies, and practices changed with it.

For one thing, UW experienced phenomenal growth during these years, expanding from 539 undergraduates in 1887 to more than 3,000 in 1903, a nearly sixfold increase in just fifteen years.[20] The period also witnessed the demise of

A Prehistory, 1848–1948

the old classical course of study and the emergence of new curricula centered on scientific, technical, and business studies, programs that had evolved in the last quarter of the nineteenth century to meet the needs of the country's growing professional-managerial class.[21] In fact, the most rapid growth at UW between 1887 and 1903 occurred in the College of Engineering, though the Colleges of Agriculture and Letters and Science also grew rapidly.[22] Underlying these new fields of study was an increasingly influential model of higher education, imported from Germany, which privileged research over teaching; graduate over undergraduate training; specialization, departmentalization, and electives over a single, unified curriculum; and freedom of inquiry over a common culture.[23]

Meanwhile, the multilingualism of the old curriculum gave way to what Bruce Horner and John Trimbur have called "unidirectional English monolingualism."[24] Inheritors of an academic system based almost wholly on the vernacular, we have forgotten that the linguistic environment of higher education in this country was not always so: as late as 1874, the UW Board of Visitors was publicly complaining about the university's "indifference" toward English, and the twenty-year period after that complaint was made can be seen as the time when English emerged as, essentially, the sole medium of scholarly life at UW.[25] Related to this development was the rising importance of written over spoken discourse in the university; in 1893, for example, written theses replaced oral declamations as the main way graduates demonstrated their knowledge at UW.[26] Since that time, formal speech-making and debate have played relatively minor roles in academic life on the campus.

In the 1880s and '90s, in other words, the University of Wisconsin embraced what we would call today a thoroughly modern undergraduate curriculum: the ancient languages and literatures receded, the technical disciplines advanced, and rhetoric itself was transformed from a capstone, integrative, and vital social practice to a basic skill, studied (if at all) only in the early years of students' academic careers and subordinate in nearly every way to the specialized subjects that constituted the "major" work of their last two years.[27] It wasn't that reading, writing, and speaking were no longer important or not acknowledged as such, but their configuration changed radically: language study was now increasingly monolingual, increasingly focused on written discourse, increasingly compartmentalized into one or two stand-alone courses, and increasingly seen as preparatory to the real academic work of the "content areas."

As part of all this, in 1898, rhetoric and English literature were reunited at UW after a twenty-year split; and Frankenburger and Freeman (with their assistants) were given joint charge of a new universally required, yearlong, freshman writing course, English 1, modeled on Harvard's famous "A" course.[28] The Harvard course, as we saw in chapter 1, comprised two semesters of English composition; originally placed in 1874 in the sophomore year, it moved in 1885 to the first year.[29] It was a stand-alone, yearlong course in written exposition, meant to train Harvard students and certify their abilities in the writing of their mother tongue.[30] It was also, from the beginning, tied to an admissions exam requiring students to write, in legible, correct, clear, and forceful English, impromptu essays on literary topics, the demands of which exerted extraordinary influence on high school English classes nationwide.[31] As for the course itself, English A involved the writing of both short (daily) and long (weekly and "fortnightly") themes, most done without benefit of outside reading, on topics chosen by the students themselves, and corrected sometimes mercilessly by a cadre of overworked instructors and assistant professors.[32]

As we saw earlier, the course was motivated by a "crisis" concerning the literacy skills of incoming Harvard students. Despite the well-publicized defects of those students' compositions and the "drudgery" involved in reading and correcting them, the faculty associated with English A argued that the course succeeded, both in improving students' writing skills early in their academic careers and in encouraging secondary schools to pay more attention to students' written English.[33] By 1900, a version of the course was in place in nearly every university in the country, including UW.[34]

At the turn of the new century, in other words, written English had emerged as the central feature of the modern North American university: the main problem of entering students, the key medium of academic inquiry, the primary mechanism for testing students' performance, and the dominant intellectual tool of the professional-managerial class that students hoped to join when they finished. Yet, for all that, the one course dedicated to *writing* in the new university was given scant intellectual respect. Writing was central and crucial, but it was, after all, merely the transcription of speech, a mechanical activity, uniform across situations, and governed by rules the violation of which was the result, usually, of inadequate primary and secondary schooling before the student even came to college.[35] As we saw earlier, the late nineteenth-century birth of freshman composition in the United States is thus intimately tied up with the idea that postsecondary general education writing instruction is a temporary, stopgap measure until the high schools do a better job of preparing student writers.[36]

English 1 at UW was therefore a devil's bargain. Written composition was made a universally required course, but in the process, it was severed from its rich rhetorical roots and turned into an elementary skill, one that, in a better world, first-year students would have acquired before they even started college. To make matters worse, in the years immediately following the birth of the course, composition at UW lost the intellectual connections to practical life and public discourse that Frankenburger and the literary societies had done so much to foster in the 1870s and '80s. What would soon become stand-alone (and groundbreaking) departments of journalism and public speaking emerged during these years, breaking off from English forever. In 1903, Professor Willard Bleyer offered the nation's first university course in journalism, and before a decade was over, it would be a separate department at UW (in 1927, it became its own school). Similarly, in 1906, the Department of Public Speaking was carved out of English; it would soon become the leading speech program in the country (in 1920, it would drop the word "public" from its title and in the late 1960s would become "Communication Arts").[37] If composition at UW had, in the 1860s and '70s, lost its titular ties to ethics and logic, it now said goodbye to public speaking and journalism. The loss was immeasurable.

What it retained in the new English Department, however, was significant: a social problem that generated wide public and academic anxiety (the "illiteracy" of American boys and girls); apparently attainable pedagogical goals (correctness and clarity in written English); and, perhaps most significant of all, *every student on campus.*[38] At the turn of the nineteenth century, freshman composition was one of the few universally required courses, not just at UW but in American higher education more generally. After 1898, it had something else as well: renewed ties to English literature.

At the time, English literary studies at UW was trying to establish its own research and disciplinary credentials; it would hardly seem to help its case to be saddled with a large, low-status, introductory skills course.[39] No doubt some of the new professors in the department expressed their distaste for the work: in a history he wrote in the 1940s, chair Merritt Hughes said of this period, "The concern of the Department with Freshman Composition was the perennial matter of low standards," its burden the "doubtful literacy of entering freshmen."[40] Why, then, did English literature at UW forge this fateful bond with composition-rhetoric at the turn of the twentieth century, especially when the two had lived apart quite happily for two decades? Was it a decision made on high, with both sides at the mercy of campus leaders? Or did the literature scholars have their eyes on the students, jobs, and funding that would come with English 1? Or was it something else—a sense that composition and litera-ture were bound through literacy itself—opposite sides of the same coin, one focused on writing, the other on reading—and shared responsibility for im-proving students' fluency in their mother tongue? Was it a moral and develop-mental impulse that literary studies simply could not shake, a refusal, in the end, to become a "real" science like chemistry, sociology, or linguistics or an empirical field like history? Or a reminder of its old ties to the Normal Depart-ment, of its historical involvement in the liberal arts and the common educa-tion they have traditionally sponsored?

As for composition, why did it not go the way of journalism and public speaking, developing its own academic identity apart from literature? Connors writes of the lack of a rhetoric PhD in nineteenth-century German universities: perhaps it never occurred to anyone that composition could be a stand-alone intellectual discipline.[41] Or perhaps composition needed and wanted the pres-tige of literature, to have access to its major, its graduate programs, its research profile, its works of art? Or perhaps those associated with composition just couldn't abandon their commitment to belles letters, especially the nonfiction essay, which kept Freshman English within the orbit of literary studies rather than public speaking or journalism.

However it transpired, in 1898, rhetoric and literature together created the new UW English Department, and the mark of their (re)union was the birth of English 1, Freshman English. It was a marriage that would last for nearly three-quarters of a century, and the required first-year composition course was on center stage the whole time. If the two parts of the department never really achieved parity, they were always connected, mutually informed, and incon-ceivable without one another. The key to this situation was undoubtedly the role played by writing instruction in the department. In fact, Brereton describes UW's English Department in the opening decades of the twentieth century as one of only five departments in the country that could rival Harvard's national reputation in composition (the other four were Columbia, Michigan, Vassar, and Cornell); he writes that UW was one of only *two* schools (the other was Michigan) that maintained serious faculty attention to composition all the way through the 1920s. Everywhere else, including Harvard, composition was by 1910 "apprentice work," responsibility for its oversight "the province not of a scholar . . . but an administrator."[42]

Those same years, the opening decades of the twentieth century, were also when graduate students first came to UW in significant numbers for specialized study in British and American literature, according to Hughes's unpublished history from the 1940s.[43] In other words, the English Department at UW dur-

A Prehistory, 1848–1948

ing this time was sponsoring flourishing composition *and* literature programs: senior faculty taught in both, published articles and books about both, and apparently saw both as legitimate parts of English studies.

This image of an English Department firmly embedded in the civil society surrounding it, taking seriously its educational service mission but enjoying as well a national reputation for scholarship, enthusiastically committed to both introductory-level reading and writing courses and advanced literary studies, can be seen in a 1907 statement of the department's aims, quoted by Hughes. The statement is remarkable for its synthesis not only of composition and literature but also of teaching and research, introductory and advanced work, and utilitarian and scholarly goals. The purpose of the UW English Department, it says, is:

> (1) to train students in the use of English as a means of expression or communication for the ordinary demands of social, commercial, and professional life; (2) to continue that training to suit the special needs of those who take up journalistic or professional work; (3) to develop literary appreciation and extend the knowledge of those who find in English and American literature the readiest means of obtaining the advantages of a liberal education; (4) to prepare teachers of English for school or college work; (5) to fit students for and assist them in scholarly investigation.[44]

A hundred years later, the statement remains a remarkably capacious vision of English studies at the service of the people.

The union of "comp" and "lit" in the early twentieth-century UW English Department can also be seen in English 1 itself, which, in 1905–6, just a few years after its birth, is described in the University of Wisconsin *Bulletin* this way:

> Freshman English. English prose style. Composition. The elements of effective writing in prose, based upon direct study of selected authors, with training in composition. Three hours a week throughout the year. Twenty-three sections. For hours and rooms see time table of required studies. Required of all freshmen in the colleges of Letters and Science, Agriculture, and Engineering.[45]

Teaching the course at this time was the department's entire instructional staff, from graduate students to full professors, many of the latter becoming nationally known figures for their work in it. Between 1907 and 1915, according to Brereton, seven different UW faculty members produced *eight* separate composition textbooks, some of them groundbreaking: Frances Campbell Berkeley's

1910 *A College Course in Writing from Models,* for example, was the first reader to use student papers, and Edwin Woolley's 1907 *Handbook of Composition* was the first comprehensive, rule-governed writing handbook and one of the most influential of its kind ever—Brereton calls it "the handbook that made the genre famous."[46]

Woolley in fact directed English 1 from 1909 to 1916, inaugurating what Hughes would call its "modern phase," when Freshman English at UW had "devoted and intelligent leadership"; deep and sustained support from the department, college, and wider community; and the "mass proportions" of a rapidly expanding student body and growing university.[47] Woolley's English 1 was clearly beholden to the handbook he had written, and it was notable for its lack of a reader—something true of Harvard's original "A" course as well: students mostly wrote on "familiar" topics of their own choosing rather than more traditional literary ones.[48] But they were not simply set adrift. Curti and Carstensen write that freshmen in the course "were trained, by systematic conferences and by carefully controlled classroom exercises, to express their ideas and to describe their interests and experiences in clear, grammatical English and to recognize the qualities of good writing."[49]

Toward the end of Woolley's reign, fellow UW English professor Karl Young provided details about English 1 for NCTE's *English Journal.* The course enrolled about eleven hundred freshmen annually, he wrote, all subject to an entrance exam, the students meeting three times a week for a year, in sections of twenty-five, and taught by faculty of all grades, from instructor to full professor.[50] The course was divided into two semesters. The first, English 1a, attempted to secure in students "grammatical correctness and the orderly arrangement of simple expositions." Students wrote one theme of five hundred words per week (more or less)—a pattern that would reappear at intervals over the next fifty years in UW's Freshman English. The second course, meanwhile, English 1b, was meant to encourage "analysis of thought in substantial essays . . . nine long expository themes dealing with ideas."[51]

After Woolley's death in 1916, Freshman English at UW came under the direction of Frederick A. Manchester, who like his predecessor published several composition textbooks and was a national figure in the field. The course continued to evolve in response to both the growing number and sophistication of UW students and the development of the Freshman English program itself. Perhaps the biggest change from Woolley's course was the much greater use of

A Prehistory, 1848–1948

essay "readers," intended to provide models for student writing, content for themes, and preparation for sophomore and advanced literature courses as well.[52]

The department's 1917–18 "Instructions to Students in Freshman English" now listed, in fact, six required textbooks for English 1: a "rhetoric," *Composition: Oral and Written,* by the well-known Columbia University rhetorician Charles Sears Baldwin; Woolley's *Handbook of Composition* (which would go through multiple editions even after Woolley's death, eventually becoming the *Heath Handbook*); three readers: Makower and Blackwell's *Book of English Essays,* Walker and Milford's *Selected English Short Stories,* and *Freshman Themes,* by UW's own Warner Taylor and Frederick Manchester; and, finally, a dictionary.[53]

Brereton characterized the Manchester version of English 1 as an "idea course" to distinguish it from both the readerless version that Wooley had adopted at UW and more literature-based Freshman English courses offered elsewhere. The new approach involved students in close analysis of "literary nonfiction" with an emphasis on "the structure of ideas."[54] The principal aims of the course, according to the "Instructions" distributed to students, were:

1. Clear thinking.
2. Correct and clear expression in writing and speaking.
3. Intelligent reading.[55]

This precedence of thinking over expression, a shift from the prototypical late nineteenth-century freshman composition course, would continue at UW for the next twenty years, not to be abandoned until the immediate post–World War II years, when the influx of a suddenly large and diverse class, including many war veterans, led the course back to its late nineteenth-century mechanical roots and an overarching concern for correctness and order.

The 1917–18 "Instructions" provide additional information to students on how clear thinking, correct and clear expression, and intelligent reading are to be secured. To attain the first, "constant attention is given to accurate definition, natural classification, orderly arrangement of parts, and logical conclusions." As for the second,

> *Correct* expression involves chiefly accuracy in matters of grammar, spelling, pronunciation, idiom, and the meaning of words. *Clear* expression involves chiefly the accurate use of terms; the natural, orderly, logical arrangement of material; the indication of the relation of ideas by such means as word order, connectives, pronouns, and other reference-words. The principal subjects of study for the attainment of clear expression are (a) arrangement of material

in the sentence, the paragraph, and the whole composition; (b) sentence structure; (c) vocabulary.

Intelligent reading, meanwhile,

> involves chiefly (a) an accurate knowledge of the words and idioms used; (b) a perception of the relation of ideas, whether in sentence, paragraph, or whole composition; (c) a knowledge of matters necessary for an understanding of the figures of speech, references, and allusions met with.[56]

Ten years later, these aims, and the language detailing them, were still being used, verbatim, to describe UW's Freshman English course.[57]

The 1917–18 "Instructions" also provided students with information about the form their themes should take, from the ink used to the folding of their papers; it decoded the abbreviations employed by instructors in annotating student themes; and it alerted students to the distinction between "rewriting" (which was substantial) and "revising" (which was not). The "Instructions" also contained warnings about plagiarism and informed students that they were to meet in conference with their instructors three times in the first semester and two times in the second. As for the actual calendar of the course, the first semester prescribed twenty-four themes spread across sixteen weeks, most of them quite short, around 150 to 200 words long, though a few were 300 to 450 words each, and two were what we would call moderate-length: an autobiography of 1,000 words and a "long narrative" of 1,000 to 1,200 words. Many of the themes were impromptu essays written in class in testlike situations (a practice that would continue all the way up to the late 1960s); there were also tests and summaries of course readings.[58]

Importantly, the stratification of the freshman class by skill level, already evident in the early years of English 1, became more pronounced as the years unfolded: the 1917–18 "Instructions," for example, indicated that while most of the sections of the course were "regular," some were reserved for "advanced work," and a few were for students who had failed the placement test and were thus required to take the noncredit course "Sub-Freshman English" until their "deficiencies" were removed and they could enroll in the regular course.[59]

Manchester died in 1921, and Professor Warner Taylor began that year his two-decade directorship of the program. By 1922–23, the number of themes in English 1a was back to sixteen (about one per week, a pace that would remain

A Prehistory, 1848–1948

constant up to the late 1960s), the essays becoming longer as the semester wore on.[60] The overall improvement of students also appeared to continue, enrollment at UW leaping at the end of World War I and rising gradually through the 1920s, increasing especially rapidly between 1925 and 1927 to about 7,500 total undergraduates, double the prewar number.[61] This growth, and the economic expansion that accompanied it, allowed the Freshman English program to stratify students even more rigidly. By 1925–26, there was an exemption from the second semester, English 1b, if a grade of "excellent" was received in the first, English 1a, so that while most students continued to take two semesters of composition, some were now taking only one semester, and, as we've seen, some were taking three or more, including required work in "Sub-Freshman English."[62]

The textbooks for the 1925 Freshman English course were similar to the Manchester version of a decade before: a rhetoric, a handbook, an anthology of model essays, an anthology of freshman themes, and a dictionary. Significantly, English 1b now also included a novel, Hardy's *The Return of the Native*, in addition to a collection of short stories.[63] Within a decade, the second semester of Freshman English at UW, and soon even the first semester, would be almost indistinguishable from an introductory course in literature.[64] But in the mid-1920s, Taylor's course still resembled the version from 1917–18 that we saw above: in 1a, for example, students were writing seventeen themes per semester, beginning with 150–200-word "sketches," including some impromptu ones, and moving up to 450–600-word "essays" with a few longer "themes," 1,000 words or so, thrown in.[65]

Another development during this period, probably related to the overall expansion in student numbers at the time, was the gradual withdrawal by senior faculty from the course and the increasing reliance on graduate student teaching assistants (TAs) to teach it. In his *National Survey of Conditions in Freshman English,* published in 1929 by the University of Wisconsin Bureau of Educational Research, Taylor wrote that when he started at UW in 1911, "every member of the department save one . . . had at least one section of Freshman English. It was a policy of the department. Today I am the only [tenure-line faculty member] instructing in the regular course."[66] In fact, Taylor discerned a nationwide trend in this regard, noting that TAs accounted for 47 percent of all Freshman English sections at the large institutions in his survey. And, in a comment of almost premonitory significance for the research reported here, he wrote of late 1920s freshman composition, "The graduate-student teacher has apparently come to stay."[67]

That was written, however, before the stock-market crash of late 1929. In the early 1930s, the University of Wisconsin found itself, almost overnight, with substantially fewer students and significantly diminished resources. Enrollments dropped dramatically: between 1929 and 1934, the number of students fell from 9,400 to 7,400, the decline especially sharp in the nonresident student population, which had always been strong at UW.[68] There was also a serious budget shortfall, so class size was ratcheted up, "quiz" sections were eliminated, and the faculty took across-the-board pay cuts.[69] They had no choice in the matter, since there were so few academic jobs available in the 1930s. When future UW English professor Mark Eccles finished his PhD at Harvard in 1932 under the direction of George Lyman Kittredge, he sent out over one hundred letters of application but didn't receive a single job offer in reply. A year later, he was offered a lectureship at UW and was glad to have it.[70]

The Depression also brought intense social turmoil and ideological tension. English professor Madeleine Doran, who, like Eccles, was a young faculty member at the time, remembered the tumult of the 1930s as comparable to the campus strife of the late 1960s, which she also witnessed.[71] We often forget how politically charged the 1930s were in this country. David Cronon and John Jenkins, in their history of the university, tell the story, for example, of how, one spring evening in 1935, a group of fraternity students from a house on Langdon Street barged into a meeting of the socialist Student League for Industrial Democracy in the Law School auditorium and dragged its leaders outside, where they were taken down the street and dumped into Lake Mendota.[72]

But what did all this mean for English 1? Well, declining enrollments and tight budgets meant that, for the first time in twenty years, the senior faculty in the UW English Department became active in Freshman English again, perhaps against their wishes, sometimes to the detriment of the course and its students, often with benefits for all concerned. Let's begin with the numbers: if, in 1929, Taylor was the only senior faculty member still teaching the course, the situation was very different just a few years later. The sudden enrollment declines of the early 1930s, combined with serious budget shortfalls, made it no longer feasible for Freshman English to be taught in stand-alone, TA-taught sections of twenty-five students each. So the program was reorganized into *divisions*—each one a collection of five to fifteen sections of students grouped by skill level and led by a senior faculty member who lectured once weekly to the whole division. Students then met twice more each week in small groups for recitation and discussion with an assistant professor, instructor, or graduate TA, who presumably would have responsibility for several such sections.[73] At the end of the 1930s, eight members of the senior English faculty were, in the words of frus-

A Prehistory, 1848–1948

trated chair Merritt Hughes, "drawn away from advanced courses" for this purpose.[74] For good or ill, it was the last time in the department's history when there would be such broad and deep involvement by literature faculty in the course.

The change would have at least three effects: first, the Freshman English program increased the stratification of entering students by skill level, continuing the decades-long move away from the idea of a single, unifying freshman composition course for every student on campus. Second, the course became increasingly literary in its content, approach, and aims. And third, it became the site of a rather remarkable burst of pedagogical experimentation as faculty members used the course to respond, in dramatically different ways, to the rich stimulus offered the academy by the 1930s. Let's take each of these effects in turn.

First: stratification. In 1930, according to a report of the English Department's Committee on High-School Relations, Freshman English had four divisions indexed to students' performance on the English composition part of the UW admissions examination: the "A" division of the course enrolled about 5 percent of entering students, those considered the best qualified for the class; the "B" and "C" divisions, respectively, comprised about 50 and 40 percent of the freshman class, the former containing the better-prepared "regular" students and the latter the poorer ones; the "D" division enrolled the final 5 percent of the entering class, students who had failed the entrance exam and were thus assigned to the "sub-freshman" course.[75]

At some point after the report was written, the so-called A students were allowed to exempt Freshman English altogether.[76] This meant that there was now a substantial gap separating the number of semesters of Freshman English that different students at the university had to take, from zero (for those fully exempt) to one (for those who received a grade of A in the first-semester course) to two (for all "regular" students taking both 1a and 1b) to three or more (for those who first had to pass Sub-Freshman English before they could even register for 1a). The implication for students must have been inescapable: "freshman comp" was punishment, and the more you had to take, the more trouble you were in academically, at least in terms of writing.

This must have raised eyebrows within the department, however, because in mid-1935, a Committee on the Undergraduate Curriculum recommended abolishing the exemption and imposing "more severe standards for admission" to the course. (The committee proposed compensating for the change by creating an honors version of the course, English 3a, which would satisfy the Freshman English requirement if the student received a grade of A; the committee also recommended abolishing the exemption from English 1b for students who received an A in English 1a but allowing them to take a special English 3b if they

41

chose.)[77] But the recommendations were rejected by the department as a whole, which decided to continue both the complete and the one-semester exemptions from Freshman English.

So stratification increased, now with a new "thematic" twist. By 1938–39, the program was dividing freshmen into (1) fully exempt students (about 5 percent of the total); (2) regular "Upper Group" students (presumably about 50 percent of freshmen), who were allowed to choose from three new strands of the course: "Masterpieces of Literature," "Contemporary Affairs" (later called "Language in Action"), and the "Traditional Course," which stressed "the study of fundamentals" more than the other two "Upper" versions; (3) regular "Middle Group" students (about 40 percent of freshmen), whose curriculum was like the "Traditional Course," but for the less well-prepared; and finally, (4) "sub-freshman" students (the final 5 percent of freshmen), who needed remedial work before they could join the regular course. This amounted to five large divisions of the course if one ignores the exempt students and assumes that the second semester, 1b, followed the descriptions above. Each division was put under the direction of one or more senior faculty members, who must have treated their classes as personal fiefdoms, lecturing once a week to as many as three hundred to four hundred students and supervising anywhere from five to fifteen "quiz" sections, each led by an assistant professor, lecturer, or TA.[78]

If, according to the 1938–39 "Instructions," all five versions of Freshman English shared "an insistence upon the development of 'clear thinking and correct writing'" (echoing the old 1920s-era aims for the course) and all had students writing fifteen themes each semester, roughly one per week, from about 150 to 1,500 words each, the description above shows clearly that the course was changing radically during the 1930s and in more than just placement and staffing. The biggest change was the increased role of literature in the course. This is most evident in the Upper Group courses "Masterpieces of Literature" and "Contemporary Affairs/Language in Action," which became, in a way, the marquee versions of Freshman English during this time. In 1938–39, the former, directed by Mark Eccles, prescribed Shakespeare and modern drama in the first semester and the Bible, Homer, the novel, and the contemporary short story in the second.[79] In 1941–42, the "Masterpieces" version of Freshman English was divided into six lecture groups of five discussion sections each (two led by Eccles, two by Henry Pochmann, and one each by Helen C. White and Paul Fulcher); all followed a heavily literary syllabus. Professor White's English 1b, for example, included lectures on *Agamemnon, Oedipus the King, Job, Othello, Romeo and Juliet, Cyrano de Bergerac,* Galsworthy's *Justice,* Rice's *Street Scene,* O'Neill's *The Hairy Ape,* and Sherwood's *Abe Lincoln in Illinois,* students writing weekly themes, most 350 to 500 words long, about their reading, presumably in their discussion sections.[80]

But even the Traditional and Middle Group students received substantial doses of literature, especially compared to the Woolley course of a quarter century back. In the first semester, the Traditional group, for example, under the direction of Warner Taylor, read essays from *Modern English Readings* and *Writing and Thinking*, by former UW professor Norman Foerster and his coeditor John Steadman, as well as *Thought in English Prose* and *The Autobiography of Lincoln Steffens;* they also read the poem *John Brown's Body,* by Stephen Vincent Benét. For the Middle Group, textbooks included the first three above, plus a modern novel and a play by Shakespeare.[81] By this time, English 1b was thoroughly literary in all versions of the course.[82]

But Freshman English at UW from 1930 to 1945 differed from earlier versions of the course in more ways than just the role of literature. The aims were also quite different, and they appear to have been constant across the divisions of the program. According to the "Instructions to Students in Freshman English, 1938–1939," the goals of the course were as follows:

1. a) At the beginning of the course, to offer a student the stimulus of new information and ideas which will be pertinent to his present needs and which will help him to organize what he already knows and feels. This implies that Freshman English should be administered so that it may start with the point at which a student finds himself and give him ideas about the world in which he lives. b) To continue by giving the student sufficient knowledge of the past and present to see his world and himself in some perspective.

2. To give the student intellectual and imaginative discipline, as a basis for sound thinking and for the coherent evaluation of experience.

3. To help the student, on the foundation laid by such thinking and the whole imaginative experience arising from it, to exercise and develop his power of expressing himself effectively through language. This implies, naturally, that language should be a useful tool to the student, and further that learning to write presupposes learning to use the mind.

4. To approach style in writing as organic form, arising from and appropriate to content and the character and purpose of the writer.[83]

These "ideals" may be the most interesting ever articulated for a Freshman English course at UW and about as far from the old Woolley course as imaginable. In fact, most of the 1930–45 versions of Freshman English omit a handbook altogether (though the *Heath Handbook,* a direct descendant of Woolley, was required for the Middle Group in 1941).[84] Why is that? Because the students were better writers? Because literature faculty were unwilling to teach a dull, mechanical course? Because of the stimulus provided by the 1930s themselves, which seem to have prompted a high level of pedagogical innovation among the faculty, as the 1960s would among teaching assistants? It's hard to say. What is clear is that Freshman English had become in the 1930s, at its best, a place where students could think through their ideas; write about their experiences; and argue with one another about politics, books, and language. If the course was not especially sensitive to struggling students, if it was stratified in a way that must have increased alienation and division among the undergraduate population at UW, if at times it seems excessively literary for a first-year writing course, it was nonetheless lively and imaginative, at least on paper, and it seems to have engaged senior literature faculty in general education reading and writing instruction in a way not seen before or since.

Still, the English faculty must have missed their advanced undergraduate literature courses and graduate seminars. In 1940, chair Merritt Hughes was publicly bemoaning the responsibilities his faculty had taken on at the freshman and sophomore levels during the 1930s and wished that they could be redeployed to more advanced courses.[85] In the postwar years, he would get his wish.

Between 1945 and 1946, with most of the soldiers home from World War II, the GI Bill paying their tuition to college if they wished to go, and the energies of the nation—pent up during fifteen years of depression and war—finally released, the University of Wisconsin experienced the greatest single burst of growth in its history. In one year, the number of undergraduate students literally doubled, from 7,643 to 15,475, many of them students who would not, before the war, have been able to attend the university.[86] The need to educate these students and to prepare a whole new professional-managerial class for a teeming postwar nation made English 1 more important to the department and university than it had been since its inception at the end of the nineteenth century.[87] And what these students apparently needed from the course was not what the department had been offering them in the 1930s.

So in 1946, Freshman English at UW returned to its original incarnation, a universally required general education writing course for freshmen, focused on clarity and correctness and organized into instructor- and TA-taught small sections using a uniform syllabus. Gone was the "ideas" course and Masterpieces of Literature. And gone was the intense involvement of literature faculty. But ironically, the department returned to the rough parity between composi-

A Prehistory, 1848–1948

tion and literature that had obtained in 1898, as its efforts—at least in terms of numbers and money—became more or less evenly divided between a massive program in general education reading and writing instruction for every freshman and sophomore at the university, on the one hand, and advanced literary study for majors and graduate students, on the other.

That general education program amounted, not just at UW but across the country, to four semesters (twelve credits) of elementary composition and introductory literature across the first two years of college study: As Edward P. J. Corbett put it, "In those days, virtually every college and university required all beginning students to take at least two years of English: a freshman English course and a sophomore survey course in either English or American literature. A veteran just beginning a college education became one of the twenty-five to thirty students who were packed into one of the dozens of newly created sections of freshman English."[88]

Fortunately, there was on hand in Madison a new generation of faculty members interested in and committed to running a large general education writing program. Warner Taylor had resigned in the spring 1945, after more than twenty years directing the course, and the dean of the College of Letters and Science convinced Professor Robert Pooley to take over Freshman English, seeing his background in English education and his experience in teacher training to be just what the suddenly huge program needed.[89] In the fall of 1945, 130 sections of English 1a were offered, and Pooley—assisted by long-time secretary Charlotte Wood and professors Robert Doremus and George Rodman, who had directed divisions of the course in the 1930s—recruited and trained the staff needed to do that job. He also eliminated the exemption from the course (there were too many candidates to make the determination responsibly, he said), though he continued to allow students who did well in the first semester to skip the second.

But Pooley did not stay long. In 1948, he was asked to take on the directorship of UW's new Integrated Liberal Studies program (an attempt to retain something like a small liberal arts college in the context of this rapidly expanding, quickly fragmenting, and increasingly scientific-technical university).

Coming into Freshman English at this time were two individuals who, together, would craft a curriculum and training program for English 1a and b that would prove remarkably durable in the postwar years. They would stay closely associated with Freshman English at UW for the next twenty years, exerting an enormous influence on its shape and operation and having a hand even in its demise in the late 1960s: it is their course that we'll be focusing on in the next four chapters. They were Edgar Lacy and Ednah Thomas.

3 THE POSTWAR REGIME, 1948-1968

Born in Kentucky in 1914, Edgar W. Lacy received his BA (1936) and MA (1937) in English from Vanderbilt University and his PhD (1939) from the University of Illinois, writing his thesis on the fifteenth-century English jurist and author Sir John Fortescue. After serving in the U.S. Army from 1942 to 1945, he landed an assistant professorship in 1946 at the University of Wisconsin, where he was, within two years, put in charge of the Freshman English program.[1] His scholarly career never really blossomed, and for the next thirty-five years Edgar Lacy was mainly a teacher and administrator at UW, serving as director of Freshman English for twenty years and then associate chair of the English Department for another twenty years, in the mid-1960s holding both positions simultaneously for a time.

Ednah S. Thomas, meanwhile, received her BA in 1923 from Mount Holyoke College, with a major in composition, and her MA in English from Bryn Mawr the following year.[2] A teaching assistant (TA) in the English Department at UW in the mid-1920s, she never finished the PhD but did accumulate some high school teaching experience in Madison. In 1942 she began teaching in the U.S. Armed Forces Institute program at UW and was hired in 1945 to help Robert Pooley manage the suddenly massive Freshman English program in the immediate postwar years. When Lacy took over the program in 1948, Thomas became his indispensable partner.

The freshman comp course these two ran, beginning that year, was a two-semester expository writing course, required of all first-year students at UW;

taught predominantly by English graduate teaching assistants in stand-alone sections; and organized pedagogically by the writing of weekly themes, defined by the traditional modes of discourse and methods of development and evaluated by reference to literary models and rules of correctness.

It was an exceptionally large program, typical of the land-grant, midwestern research universities of the time. After the huge increase in student numbers between 1945 and 1946, enrollment growth at the undergraduate level was flat or even in decline in the years immediately after.[3] But by the early 1950s, the UW Freshman English program was processing over 3,000 freshmen a year. In the fall of 1952, for example, 2,200 freshmen out of a total class of 3,074, or 72 percent, were enrolled in English 1a, meeting in ninety sections of twenty-five students each, taught by a staff of fifty-eight instructors, almost all of them graduate TAs. These large numbers were managed in part by a return to the department's earlier tradition of fairly rigid stratification by skill level. Under Lacy and Thomas, freshmen were divided into four groups by their performance on the university's entrance exam and in the course itself, the groups distinguished by how many semesters of Freshman English the students had to take: (1) the very few "exceptionally well-trained" students who needed no further composition training at all; (2) those who needed one semester and were placed in English 11, an Honors version of Freshman English; (3) the "great bulk" of the class, who needed two semesters of composition training and were placed in English 1a, to proceed afterward to 1b; and (4) "those exceptionally poorly trained or poorly equipped by nature, who are not in a position to profit at all by composition training at the college level" and who were therefore placed in English 0, a noncredit course, before being able to apply again for English 1a.[4]

As for the course itself, the early 1950s Freshman English course at UW returned to a Woolley-era "current-traditionalism," with some literature thrown in for the better students in 1a and for everyone in 1b.[5] Lacy described the 1952–53 syllabus this way:

> Freshman English is a basic training course which aims to develop the highest possible writing skill. From the fact that Freshman English is required of virtually all students, it follows that this writing skill is not that of the "literary" writer, but simply clear and effective command of language, a practical necessity for every student, whether he is studying engineering or agriculture, humanities or science, law or physical education, medicine or music. It endeavors to develop his power of collecting, selecting, and organizing material, and presenting the result in acceptable written form.[6]

He then went on to describe the first half of the course:

English 1a: The aim of English 1a is the achievement of conventional correctness, clear and direct expression, and simple organization. The units are grammar and usage (grammar is presented as a basic tool essential for competent and intelligent writing); spelling; punctuation; the sentence as a composition unit; outlining and the principle of selecting details; use of a college-level dictionary; use of the University Library. The student learns to write clearly about what he knows and sees.

The second semester was described this way:

English 1b: The aim of English 1b (building on the foundation acquired in English 1a) is the achievement of effective and interesting expression, and complex organization, applied to the handling of ideas. The units are the paragraph; complex organization, exemplified by a research project; words and phrases as stylistic units; variations in individual style. The student learns to analyze and organize ideas and write interestingly and convincingly about what he thinks.[7]

Both classes used Lacy and Thomas's own *Guide for Good Writing: A Composition Text for College Students,* published in 1951, in addition to readers of various kinds; both involved the writing of weekly themes, most pegged to the old modes of discourse or methods of development (narration, description, comparison and contrast, and so on), as well as several in-class, impromptu essays; both were organized by three types of "class hours": first, composition discussions, based on the students' own themes; second, analyses of published essays in the interest of modeling various writing techniques; and third, content lessons (for example, about sentence structure) based on assignments from a rhetoric text.[8]

We can see all this at work in an actual syllabus from spring 1953, this one for English 1b. Students in the course used Lacy and Thomas's *Guide for Good Writing;* the anthology *Patterns in Writing,* edited by UW's own Robert Doremus, Edgar Lacy, and George Rodman; the novel *Henry Esmond,* by Thackeray; and a dictionary. They wrote twelve themes over the sixteen-week semester, half of them impromptu, the others defined largely by genre or mode (for example, evaluation, persuasion, literary analysis, and so on). The writing was almost all reading driven, with composition discussion hours, lectures and exercises on composition principles and rules, and a great deal of in-class writing, also usually driven by course reading. It all culminated in a research (or "source") paper based on a topic from *Henry Esmond.*[9]

Let's take a typical week from this syllabus and see how it unfolded, at least on paper. During the fourth week that semester, Monday's class was devoted to

48

a "composition discussion" of the impromptu "Theme 3" written the previous Wednesday (about an essay students had read titled "Are Families Passé?" from the course anthology); Wednesday's class then involved work on "methods of paragraph development" from pages 278 to 288 of the course textbook *Guide for Good Writing;* and on Friday, students turned in "Theme 4" (an evaluation essay). The following week, the fifth of the semester, these activities were largely repeated: there was a "composition discussion" hour on Monday, presumably about the "Theme 4" turned in on Friday, students worked with the *Guide* again on Wednesday, and on Friday they reviewed for an hour-long test the following Monday.[10]

In many ways, the heart of the course, however, was the instructor's comments (or "annotations") on and evaluation of the students' themes, along with the students' reading of and response to those comments, an activity that took place largely outside of the class. Methods of instructor response in UW's English 1 during the 1950s reflected a predictable current-traditional obsession with correctness, but Lacy and, especially, Thomas were more enlightened than our stereotypes of 1950s composition, or of current-traditional rhetoric in general, allow.[11] In fact, they dictated that no grades be given on student themes, only comments, and genuine effort seems to have been put into helping each student become aware of his or her strengths (and weaknesses) as a writer.[12] None of this lessened, however, the ultimate control that Freshman English instructors at UW in the postwar years exerted over the meaning, quality, use, and even ownership of the student texts turned in to them.[13]

Commenting on papers in English 1 was greatly facilitated, after 1955, by the publication of Ednah Thomas's *Evaluating Student Themes*—a "pamphlet" of forty pages that served for the next decade and a half as the centerpiece of UW's composition program and probably its most influential and distinctive feature—at least from the point of view of the TAs who worked in the program. The book, which went through four printings (1955, 1957, 1962, and 1966) and was for some time the biggest-selling publication of the University of Wisconsin Press (at seventy-five cents a copy), contained fourteen student themes, in their entirety, written in impromptu conditions by actual UW freshmen and "representing the range from superior to inferior work," each theme annotated with an extensive terminal comment reflecting on its strengths and weaknesses by a kind of ideal writing teacher.[14] The book also served as the basis for TA training at UW, with new instructors learning to teach Freshman English essentially by learning to comment on student papers the Ednah Thomas way.

From our point of view half a century later, it's hard not to read the book as a tool in the institutional ordering—that is, "disciplining"—of student writing and thus of students themselves, but it should also be admitted that the book shies away from formal and mechanical issues, and in some ways its conceptual underpinnings are quite forward looking. There is an early version of the writing process at work here, an invitation to new teachers to read their students' writing with care and sympathy, and a palpable tone of respect throughout:[15]

> No student should be left without hope and no student should be left without challenge; and each should receive a specific comment which will put him in the frame of mind to write a better theme—next time. . . . If we show the student that we respect his work, are interested in it as a whole, and expect him to take the main responsibility for improving it, he is most likely to take the same attitude.[16]

The overall approach of the "pamphlet," however, combined with the dominant role it played in the UW program in the 1950s and '60s, reveals clearly the extent to which student writing in English 1 during these years was prototypically school "composition": "a private interchange . . . written for the teacher's eyes . . . [whose] role was to point out the errors."[17]

Just who were the teachers buying Ednah Thomas's pamphlet and, presumably, following its example? In the 1950s, as in the 1920s, UW's Freshman English course was taught almost entirely by graduate student teaching assistants in stand-alone sections. The days of serious faculty involvement in the course, a striking feature of English 1 in the 1930s and early '40s, were gone forever. Fortunately for the program, the university was expanding at the graduate level during these years even more dramatically than it was at the undergraduate level. There was, consequently, from the late 1940s on, a whole new army of English graduate students at UW ready and willing to teach first-year composition. If enrollment of freshmen at the university was either flat or in decline from 1946 to 1957, usually hovering around three thousand new students per year, the number of graduate students in fact went up every year in the two decades after World War II except four, most of those in the early 1950s.[18] The increases were especially dramatic from 1957 to 1967, when graduate student enrollment at UW rose by five hundred to one thousand new graduate students *every year,* almost tripling by the end of that ten-year period.[19]

In English, graduate students could teach freshman composition as long as they had completed the master's degree and were working toward the PhD.[20] To anyone who questioned whether such inexperienced teachers, admitted to

The Postwar Regime, 1948–1968

the university solely on the basis of their *scholarly* credentials, could handle such an important and trying *pedagogical* assignment, the faculty replied that these students were in fact quite capable of teaching the course since "the top and bottom layers of the freshmen—those who are exceptionally well prepared and those who are poorly prepared—are skimmed off," apparently to be taught by more experienced graduate student TAs, instructors, or tenure-track faculty members.[21]

By the early 1950s, Lacy and Thomas had developed a well-run and multifaceted training program for TAs, which included a four-day orientation before the fall semester started, when the basic nature of Freshman English—"a service course, designed to supply students in humanities, agriculture and engineering alike with the command of clear straightforward written English"—was established and concrete illustrations of the three types of "class hours" provided. Regular staff meetings were held weekly throughout the year, "timed to anticipate units of work and student questions on those units," and TAs had individual conferences with a program administrator, especially concerning theme grading (or "annotation"). There were two classroom visits per year, also accompanied by conferences, and, finally, committee work, "assigned sparingly to teachers who have had at least a full year of experience."[22]

From our later point of view, the Lacy/Thomas Freshman English program of the 1950s doesn't look especially enlightened, not when compared to the broad faculty involvement of the Woolley years, the sophistication of the early 1920s "ideas" course, or the curricular experimentation of the 1930s. At least on paper, the 1950s program pales. Worse, it seems at times to have been based on a dismissive attitude toward beginning college students and their facility with English. The old "myth of transience," so typical of the last years of the nineteenth century, seems to have come back with a vengeance. As chair Merritt Hughes wrote in a letter to a high school English teacher in May 1953, "We are teaching students to write simple, direct, *complete* sentences because they have not learned to do so in high school."[23]

Still, the program during this time was well organized, professionally managed, and fully supported by the department. It was also almost frighteningly stable. From 1948 to 1968, for twenty years, freshman composition at UW was overseen by a faculty committee chaired by the same person, Edgar Lacy, assisted throughout by Ednah Thomas, and staffed by the same trio of senior faculty members—Robert Doremus, Robert Pooley, and George Rodman.[24]

Together, these five, but especially Lacy and Thomas, managed a curriculum that in its broad strokes, and even in most of its details, literally did not change for more than two decades.

This stability can be seen by taking a snapshot of the second semester of Freshman English in fall 1969, just before the crisis erupted that is the main topic of this book. More than twenty years after beginning her career at UW, Ednah Thomas was still as active in the program as ever. And though he had given up nominal directorship of it a year before in order to concentrate on his associate chair's duties, Edgar Lacy was still pulling the program's levers from behind the scenes. The new director, starting in the fall of 1968, was William Lenehan, a native Texan born in 1930 who had received all his academic degrees at the University of Oklahoma, specializing in American literature, and who had begun as an instructor at UW in 1962, rising to assistant professor in 1964.

Assisting Lenehan and Thomas in the program was another new face: Joyce Steward, a high school English teacher from Madison who had joined the department in 1966, first as a lecturer, then as a faculty member, to help out with Freshman English. Though, like Ednah Thomas, she lacked the PhD, Steward would play a vital role in writing instruction at UW, founding the Writing Lab in 1969 and directing it through the 1970s. She also taught generations of future English teachers in English 309, Composition for English Teachers, and offered the first course in women's literature in the department.[25]

Teaching Freshman English at the time were more than 150 graduate student TAs, all with master's degrees, most pursuing the PhD in English and American literary studies.[26] According to an English Department document titled "1969–1970 TAships in English," most TAs taught two sections of Freshman English per semester. Their pay, at least in fall 1969, was $1,095 per section for inexperienced TAs, $1,135 per section for experienced ones. As for their own studies, TAs teaching two sections usually enrolled in two graduate courses; those teaching one section typically took three or even four courses. Graduate student tuition for TAs at the time was around $200–250 per semester, the in-state rate even if they were not Wisconsinites, since the state legislature granted an out-of-state tuition waiver for teaching assistants at UW.[27]

Meanwhile, by the mid-1960s, the two courses supporting most of these TAs, English 1a and 1b, had been renumbered English 101 and 102. But perhaps the biggest change in the program in the years leading up to 1968–69 was the introduction of a new level of administration between the course director (who was supported by the faculty-led Freshman English Policy Committee) and the instructional staff. "Master teaching assistants" were experienced Freshman English graduate student teachers who devoted one of their section assignments

The Postwar Regime, 1948–1968

each semester to mentoring a small group of new Freshman English TAs during their first year in the program. The system began in the 1965–66 academic year and was described in a short article that Lacy, Lenehan, and Thomas wrote for *College English* in 1966.[28] With these master teaching assistants, the three wrote, "we have succeeded this year in placing every new English TA, on a campus of 30,000 students and in a staff of 165 teachers, in a small group, where he will be known and attended to from the first day."[29] The main argument for the project, in fact, was demographic, a desire "to maintain the quality of instruction and show concern for the individual against the wave of increasing students and increasing staff."[30] When the group of new TAs had numbered twenty to twenty-five per year, the authors argued, the program's training procedures (as we saw above—a preservice orientation, weekly staff meetings, a theme annotation conference, and classroom visits) had been adequate. But when, in 1965–66, the number of new TAs in the program shot up to seventy-five, a result of the nearly 20 percent jump in freshman enrollment that year, something more was needed: "Not only had teaching assistants been losing contact with administrators; they had been losing contact with each other."[31]

Each master TA worked with about seven or eight inexperienced TAs, sharing an office with them, visiting their classes, allowing them to visit his or her class, and conducting about half of the weekly Freshman English staff meetings with his or her group, which was small enough that questions and discussion could be "completely free."[32] The program seems to have been a success: former TAs Susan McLeod and Virginia (Joyce) Davidson said in interviews that they appreciated the master TAs. "They helped us get through the hour," remembered McLeod. "They would say, 'Here's an activity that'll take the full fifty minutes.'"[33] Davidson especially appreciated help with crafting assignments.[34] Another former TA, Burr Angle, however, saw the master TAs as one more way that the faculty shirked their duty in training and supervising the department's graduate student teachers.[35]

<hr/>

Other than the two new administrators (Lenehan and Steward), the new course numbers, and the new master teaching assistants program, Freshman English at UW does not appear to have changed much between the late 1940s and the late 1960s. Let's look, for example, at English 102—the old English 1b —on the eve of the crisis to be narrated below. Despite a major change to English 101 (the old 1a) the previous year and the addition of four TA members to the Freshman English Policy Committee at the same time (developments treated in some detail in the next chapter), the curriculum of English 102 in the fall of

1969 was virtually indistinguishable from the 1b course of the early 1950s, itself not significantly different from the Freshman English of 1925, 1917, or even 1909. In a May 14, 1969, memo from the Freshman English Policy Committee to prospective 1969–70 TAs, committee chair William Lenehan admitted that the revised syllabus for the coming year was essentially the same as that of the previous year, except for "the introduction of literary materials in the form of a short story collection and a casebook related to literature," which had originated with the TAs themselves.[36]

As for the purpose and structure of the course, it too was reminiscent of past versions. In its presentation of the 1969–70 syllabus, the Freshman English Policy Committee noted:

> English 102 is designed to improve the student's ability to write expository prose. The course is designed to challenge the student with increasingly difficult problems of presentation while offering the rhetorical techniques to solve these problems. The essays will provide the basis for the explanation of rhetorical techniques. The short stories will present concrete, self-contained examples furnishing a specific ordering of experience; they are not to be used as literary examples.[37]

The texts used included a combined rhetoric/handbook (Crosby and Estey's *College Writing: The Rhetorical Imperative* [Harper and Row, 1968], apparently replacing Porter Perrin's *Writer's Guide and Index to English*); two readers: an essay anthology (Travis Merritt's *Style and Substance: Reading and Writing Prose* [Harcourt, Brace and World, 1969], apparently replacing the *Norton Reader*) and a short story collection (Leo Hamalian and Frederick Karl's *The Shape of Fiction: British and American Short Stories* [McGraw-Hill, 1967]); and the *Random House College Dictionary*. Added to these was a yet-to-be-determined fiction "casebook" to be used in the writing of the research or "source" paper.[38]

According to the syllabus, students in English 102 in 1969–70 wrote twelve essays in the course, down from the sixteen themes of the prewar years but still suggesting frequent writing of short- or moderate-length essays, all composed, read, and revised at a fairly fast pace. Of the twelve essays, three to four were to be done in class as "impromptu" tests of student writing, and two were to be related to the research (or "source") paper, which, at UW as elsewhere, was the centerpiece of the second-semester Freshman English course: one of those two consisted of note cards and outline, the other of the research paper itself.[39] As for the other essays in the course, they were to be "substantive" rather than "general," that is, based on course reading rather than on personal observations

3.1 *English 102 Curriculum, University of Wisconsin, 1969–1970*			
Time	Purpose	Method	Material
Three weeks	The nature of rhetoric	Exemplification	Essays
—	Finding something to say	—	—
—	Observation	—	—
—	Overall organization	—	—
—	Introduction to methods of development	—	—
Three weeks	Explanation and writing concretely	Description	Short stories
—	—	Narration	—
—	—	Comparison and contrast	—
—	—	Classification	—
—	—	Definition	—
Five weeks	Persuasion	Logic	Essays
—	—	Causal analysis	—
Two weeks	The rhetoric of the long paper	Methods in combination	Casebook (short story or other)
Three weeks	Style	Diction, sentences, and paragraph style	Short stories and essays

Source: Freshman English Policy Committee (chair, William Lenehan) to prospective 1969–70 TAs, memo, May 14, 1969.

or ideas. And they were in most cases to be followed by a "composition discussion hour" and, occasionally, by a student-teacher conference.[40]

The assignments were grouped into five units, each about three weeks long and distinguished from one another partly by mode of discourse (exposition, description, narration, or argument), partly by method of rhetorical development (exemplification, comparison and contrast, classification, definition, or causal analysis), partly by rhetorical canon (invention or style), and partly by method of literary analysis.[41] On top of that conceptual mélange, a dose of academic research was thrown in. The key organizing principle, though, seems to have been to divide up themes by mode and method, to have students read published examples of different types of themes, and then to ask them to try out what they had learned in their own writing (see table 3.1).[42]

Former TAs interviewed for this project remember above all else the mode-driven quality of English 102. According to Virginia (Joyce) Davidson, the instructor would read an essay with his or her students, treating it as an example of a particular mode of discourse (for example, comparison and contrast), then help them generate topics that they could write about in that mode. "We had to stick to that," she remembered.[43] Susan McLeod and Jean Turner pointed out the main problem with this pedagogy: the approach drained the meaning out of discourse. McLeod remembers the syllabus as fundamentally "belletristic" and recalled the problems that both students and TAs had in 1968–69 with an essay in the *Norton Reader* titled "The Joys of Sport at Oxford."[44] "What were you supposed to do with that text that year?" she asked.[45]

Jean Turner also found that the approach fit uneasily into the times: students would read a "classification" essay and then try it themselves, an experience that was inescapably "sterile" and "superficial."[46] She first taught the course a year earlier than McLeod did, in the fall of 1967, during the semester of the now-famous Dow riot, when UW and city police officers beat and tear-gassed students participating in a peaceful "sit-in" against the corporation that manufactured napalm, an event that Turner described vividly nearly forty years later as one of the intellectual and moral turning points of her life.[47] The contrast between the riot and the reading and writing her students were doing in Freshman English was nearly unbearable for her.[48]

How exactly were these TAs of the late 1960s taught to teach Freshman English at UW? They were trained the same way TAs had been trained there in the early 1950s, with the one difference being the addition of the master TAs. In 1966–67, for example, when most new English TAs taught English 101 in the fall and English 102 in the spring, the main components of Freshman English training were (1) study of textbooks and syllabus during the summer before teaching the course for the first time; (2) attendance at three orientation meetings during registration week, organized according to the three types of class hours in English 101 and 102 (composition discussions, analyses of published essays, and content lessons) (new TAs received at this time a copy of Thomas's *Evaluating Student Themes*, which explained and modeled that part of the TA's responsibility); (3) attendance at weekly staff meetings during the semester; (4) participation in master TA groups; and (5) participation in two conferences with course administrators or their faculty designees, one devoted to theme annotation, the other to the conduct of the TA's class hour (the first-semester visit was by Freshman English administrative staff, the second by a senior member of the department).[49]

As we'll see later, many Freshman English TAs in the late 1960s objected to the course's mode-driven syllabus, its belletristic readings, its focus on mechanics,

56

the apparent apathy toward the course shown by other faculty in the department, and the general expectation that TAs would teach without complaint a standard syllabus to which they had had so little input. But former TAs interviewed for this project were unwilling, even forty years later, to blame Bill Lenehan, Ednah Thomas, or Joyce Steward too sharply for these problems (about Edgar Lacy, there was less restraint). If their faculty directors were often conservative and occasionally authoritarian, they were also, according to Susan McLeod, "enlightened" and helpful.[50] She and Davidson in particular seem to have appreciated the help of Ednah Thomas and Joyce Steward. According to Davidson, "they contributed so much and were valued so little."[51] McLeod, fully aware of the limitations of the course and its instructor training from a point of view nearly forty years later, nevertheless described the atmosphere established for new writing TAs by Thomas and Steward as "facilitative."[52]

The help was not appreciated by all, however, especially toward the latter part of the 1960s. There was disrespect, even rudeness, shown to Ednah Thomas and Joyce Steward by some of the TAs; Jean Turner and Ira Shor, who were among the more radical instructors at the time, admit as much.[53] Some of the antipathy, according to Davidson, was related to the "canned" nature of the syllabus and the resentment felt by some TAs about the restrictions on their freedom.[54] As we'll see below, others objected to the current-traditionalism of the curriculum itself—for example, its use of out-of-date model essays and its seeming emphasis on formal features of genre, style, and grammar over student meaning-making through writing. But there may have been other things going on: Ednah Thomas and Joyce Steward were not only administrators of freshman composition at UW; they were also women, from an older generation than the TAs they were supervising, and, importantly, without PhD's.[55] It is perhaps not surprising, then, that Davidson remembered them as silent at meetings and undervalued by their faculty colleagues.[56] They were the "comp women," Jean Turner said, and disregarded for that reason.[57]

Despite these tensions, most of our interviewees remembered both Thomas and Steward fondly. Joyce Steward was hailed as a good mentor and class visitor: "I admired her. . . . She was an excellent supervisor," Susan McLeod remarked.[58] But it was Ednah Thomas and, especially, her book *Evaluating Student Themes* that were remembered most vividly by the former TAs interviewed here. According to Davidson, "That book, and the staff meetings organized around it, was the most important training I got in composition"; she found it all enormously helpful.[59] Turner referred to the discussions about annotating student papers as "norming sessions," but she admitted that they were helpful to her: "we were good paper markers," she said.[60] Shor complained about Thomas's deflection of his questions about politics during English 102 orientation sessions, but he acknowledged that the training program was well organized.[61] That's not to say that Ednah Thomas didn't intimidate many of the TAs: Joseph Williams, who was an English graduate student at UW from 1960 to '65, remembers having to show her a sample student paper from one of his classes and having to explain every mark he made on it.[62] Susan McLeod recalled having the same session with Thomas; in fact, she still has her copy of *Evaluating Student Themes,* which she described as extraordinarily well thumbed. The pamphlet showed genuine respect for student writing, McLeod told us, and still reveals today Thomas's "essential humanity" and her enormous concern for the way teachers responded to student papers.[63]

Despite the regard felt for their former course directors, these interviewees showed little affection for Freshman English itself.[64] Susan McLeod found it "boring"; Jean Turner described it as "grunt work," and Burr Angle as "labor-intensive." According to McLeod, "The students didn't talk; they were from small towns, and everything was overwhelming." Turner said she was bad at teaching the course and found the students "disaffected." Several of the interviewees described the syllabus as "canned," offering little room for experimentation or innovation by the instructors. Fortunately, if the TA made it through English 101 and 102 that first year, at least after 1968, he or she was rewarded with a teaching assignment in the new universally required English 200 course, Introduction to Literature. In that course, remembered McLeod, the TAs knew what they were doing: "I had been taught close reading; I had models for that and tacit knowledge." Davidson also found English 200 "freeing"—she remembers teaching Machiavelli's *The Prince* and Mario Puzo's *The Godfather* together in the same unit. Similarly, Jean Turner found English 200 "liberating": she had her students read *Tess of the D'Urbervilles* and develop a feminist and class-based analysis of society. And she remembers teaching in the post-1968 remedial English 101 program, which will be described in some detail in the next chapter, as "thrilling" and "invigorating." But English 102 was pure "torture."

We'll return to all of this in a moment; for now, the point to be emphasized is that the Lacy/Thomas Freshman English program at UW, essentially conceived in 1948, was still fully intact, in both its broad strokes and most of its details, two decades later. This curricular and administrative constancy is all the more remarkable given the dramatic changes that had taken place in the department, university, and society at large during the intervening years. Let's back up for a moment, then, and take a look at this era using a somewhat wider-angle lens.

To do so, we need to divide "the long sixties," as we did earlier, into two periods: one from about 1957 to 1964, and the other from about 1965 to 1974. The former was a period of momentous cultural and material changes, at least in North America and Europe. First among these changes was dramatic economic expansion, which brought about extraordinary affluence, consumerism, and international trade. The economic boom of the 1960s was real, at least in the United States and Western Europe. According to Samuel Rosenberg, "The longest cyclical upswing on record to that time, running for eight years, began in 1961."[65] As for the stock market, according to Robert Shiller, the highest price-earnings ratio between 1929 and 2000 occurred in January 1966, the end of a 52 percent surge that began in May 1960.[66]

But there were other notable features of this period. For example, it was a time of rapid demographic change, including the rise of an "unprecedentedly large, and unprecedentedly well-off teenage presence."[67] It was also a period of astounding technological development, including the relatively sudden mass prominence of televisions, record players, telephones, appliances, jet travel, and even birth control. The period also witnessed a remarkable opening up, or liberation, of personal, cultural, and ideological expression.[68] In place by the mid-1960s, in other words, at least in large segments of Western society, was an increasingly knowledge-based, technologically oriented, multinational, post-industrial service economy, in which young people—increasingly affluent, mobile, and sophisticated—played an increasingly important role. All of this would have major implications for the literacy skills needed in society and for the kinds of enculturation young people demanded in order to secure those skills.

How did these forces impact U.S. higher education? For one thing, this was a period of astounding growth. According to the U.S. Census, in 1946, there were two million Americans enrolled in institutions of higher education; by 1961, that number had doubled to four million; by 1966, it had tripled to six million, and by 1971, it was close to nine million, a more than fourfold increase in the number of college students in just a quarter of a century.[69] Meanwhile, the proportion of the college-age population attending college also rose dramatically during this period, from 16 percent in 1940 to 48 percent in 1961, by far the highest in the world.[70]

At UW, the number of students and faculty skyrocketed. In 1945, there were 7,643 undergraduates, 911 graduate students, and 809 faculty members (28

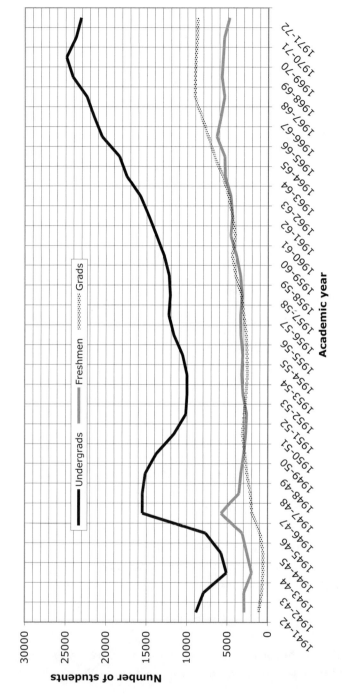

Figure 3.1. Enrollment at University of Wisconsin, 1941–1971. *Source:* UW-Madison, Office of the Registrar, "Enrollments 1888 to Present," available at http://registrar.wisc.edu/enrollments_1888_to_present.htm.

in English) on the Madison campus. In 1970, just twenty-five years later, there were 23,725 undergraduate students (a 310 percent increase), 8,777 graduate students (a 963 percent increase), and 2,324 faculty (70 in English) (a 287 percent increase).[71] The growth of the university in these years was nothing short of stunning.

That growth was not, however, steady, and the spurts are important for this story (see figure 3.1). After the huge leap in enrollment at UW between 1945 and 1946, there was actually negative growth in undergraduate student numbers from 1947 to 1953. Thereafter, between 1954 and 1960, enrollment grew modestly (3–7 percent increases annually). But then, starting in 1961, the increases were staggering: 7–12 percent each year for the next four years (from 14,727 undergraduates in 1961 to 20,496 in 1965).[72] Just between fall 1964 and fall 1965, as we've seen, the number of freshmen alone increased by nearly 1,000 —forty new sections of Freshman English virtually overnight.[73] Along with these increased numbers came increased resources.[74]

Then, between 1966 and 1969, undergraduate growth at UW was again fairly modest; and in 1970 and 1971, the numbers actually went down. After that, there was low or negative growth for the next thirty years, a situation that obtains even today.[75] In fact, it is not an exaggeration to say that today's University of Wisconsin-Madison—in Cronon and Jenkins's words, a heavily bureaucratic, multifaceted, multifunction "megaversity," whose size, complexity, and ambition far outstrip the state that sponsors it—essentially came into being during the years 1957 to 1965.[76]

Coinciding with the enormous nationwide expansion in both the number of students and the resources devoted to their schooling during the first half of "the long sixties" was growth in research on campuses across the country, especially in the sciences, and especially at large research universities like UW, much of it funded by the federal government. In fact, prior to World War II, only $31 million was spent on scientific research at U.S. universities: "A quarter of a century later, that figure had multiplied twenty-five times in constant dollars. Virtually all of the increase was the consequence of a federal government that stressed the importance of research as a central university function, a sharp departure from earlier years."[77] At UW, according to Cronon and Jenkins, the research budget grew from less than $1 million in 1940 ($151,290 from the feds) to $65 million in 1970 (over half from the feds).[78] Nationally, most of this growth came after October 1957, when the Soviet Union launched *Sputnik 1,* the world's first artificial satellite; between then and 1968, research and development expenditures in the United States more than tripled.[79] Clark Kerr has argued that the post–World War II federal support of scientific research rivals the 1862 Morrill Act in shaping the modern American university.[80]

Even in the humanities, there was a sharp increase in advanced research during this period; the production of English PhD's nationwide, for example, jumped 310 percent between 1958 and 1972, from 333 to 1,365 new doctors of literature.[81] It was a time of heady expansion. Murray Sperber, professor of English and American studies at Indiana University, tells the story of arriving as an undergraduate at Purdue University in the fall of 1957, where and when English didn't even have an undergraduate major. Ten years later, he writes, the Purdue English Department offered the BA, MA, and PhD degrees. The growth created unprecedented employment opportunities across the country. Indiana's English Department, for example, ended the 1963–64 academic year with sixty-three faculty members: it added ten the next year, nine the following year, and eight more the year after that. Departments in other universities, including UW's, were expanding at a similar 10–15 percent annual rate. The profession was changing along with these numbers: at Purdue in 1957, faculty taught four courses a semester; when Sperber began his own teaching career at Indiana in 1971, he was assigned half that number, a sweeping change in job description that can be recast as a doubling of the research responsibility of English faculty members in the United States in the span of a decade.[82]

The effects of all this reached beyond research universities and their faculty, however. There is some evidence that post-*Sputnik* federal spending on education from 1958 to 1964 may have contributed to rising verbal and mathematics skills across the school-age population.[83] What also took place from the late 1950s on—after McCarthy, after Eisenhower—was a relative freeing up of political debate and cultural expression in this country. In fact, Madison, Wisconsin, was a center of the New Left during this period. In Madison, and on the UW campus in particular, the late 1950s and early 1960s are remembered as an especially exciting time for liberalism (in 1959, for example, students of UW history professor William Appleman Williams founded the journal *Studies on the Left*). There was growing sophistication among students and faculty both; a rising consciousness about civil rights and social justice; and, by 1964, even a nascent antiwar movement.[84]

All of this—population growth, increasing government support for education, the opening up of the culture in general—helps explain why the years between 1957 and 1965 at UW have been described by Cronon and Jenkins and others as a "golden age": there was money, jobs, construction, new research fields, intellectual excitement, institutional ambition, and growth nearly everywhere you looked, and there was an emerging mass culture of relatively affluent and well-schooled youth to take advantage of it.[85] The University of Wisconsin at the end of this period, in other words, was a very different place from the UW of a decade earlier.

That's why the *lack* of change in the Freshman English program during this time is so striking, if not especially surprising. In the early to mid-1950s, Lacy and Thomas were working in a university with around 10,000 undergraduate students, 2,500 graduate students, and 3,000 freshmen; Dwight Eisenhower was president; and anti-Communist Senator Joe McCarthy from Wisconsin was at the height of his power. Ten years later, there were 20,000 undergraduate students at UW, 7,000 graduate students, and 6,000 freshmen.[86] Lyndon Johnson was in the White House announcing a war on poverty, signing a civil rights bill, and beginning to radically escalate U.S. involvement in Vietnam. The university had doubled and, in some measures, tripled in size; the country was more preoccupied with public education than at any other time in its history; and liberalism was enjoying a heyday never before seen here.

———————

How quickly things change. By the second half of "the long sixties," starting around 1965 or so, a dark cloud began to form over U.S. higher education. That year, for example, SAT scores began their long decline down to the 1980s.[87] This was also when the University of Wisconsin "community," by all accounts, started to fall apart. The reasons for the collapse are complex, but according to Cronon and Jenkins, they include the increasing size and complexity of the institution itself, a condition that exerted enormous pressure on campus resources and personnel; the intellectual fragmentation produced by the explosive growth of the late 1950s and early 1960s, with faculty increasingly loyal to their disciplines rather than to their departments or the university as a whole; the competition among those faculty, prompted in part by their chase for external research funds; and the increasing suspicion felt by students toward the university and its leaders, which they came to see as impediments to the social and intellectual movement they were trying to wage.[88]

We can see all this play out by looking more closely at the English Department during these years. According to Professor Charles Scott, who joined the department in the early 1960s and was chair in the early 1970s, the department from 1962 to 1965, when Helen C. White was chair, was a relatively quiet place: the leadership was authoritarian but benign; assistant professors were deferential; the Departmental Committee met monthly but didn't do much; power was wielded mainly by a small group of senior faculty members working behind the scenes and in the Executive Committee.[89] Madeleine Doran's interview confirms this picture: from the early 1950s to the mid-1960s, the department was a conservative place, and, more important for her, there was goodwill among faculty and between faculty and students. It was a calm between the storms of the 1930s and the 1960s.[90]

But during Walter Rideout's chairmanship, from 1965 to 1968, the department began to unravel, and it did so very quickly. Some of the turmoil can be attributed to simple numerical growth. There were dramatic increases during the mid-1960s in the numbers of faculty and students (undergraduate and graduate) alike.[91] In the fall of 1960, for example, according to chair Ricardo Quintana's tally of full-time equivalent positions, there were 15.5 full professors, 3.5 associate professors, and 6 assistant professors in the department, for a total of 25 tenure-stream faculty.[92] Less than a decade later, in the spring of 1969, chair Simeon K. (Tim) Heninger would count 25 full professors, 15 associate professors, and 25 assistant professors, for a total of 65 tenure-stream faculty.[93] In one year alone (1966), 13 new assistant professors came on board, the same year that the department's fall tea, historically sponsored by the Freshman English program, was dropped due to "the increased size of the department."[94]

Like other parts of the university, the English Department just couldn't keep pace with this growth; it was stretched beyond its capacity. As we've already seen, Lacy, Lenehan, and Thomas admitted in 1966, for example, that their master TA program was an attempt to deal with "the great problem confronting American education today: to maintain consideration for the individual in the face of numbers."[95] But it wasn't just growth that was causing problems here: it was the polarization that accompanied growth during these years. As we saw above, faculty at UW were becoming increasingly competitive with one another during this time, and their increasing research specialization contributed to fragmentation. In the English Department, new assistant professors were coming on board already hostile to Freshman English since, as Charles Scott indicated in his interview, job candidates were promised that they wouldn't have to teach that course. (Walter Rideout's interview confirms this: to attract competent faculty, he said in 1976, you needed to "spare them" Freshman English.)[96] And with the 1968 reorganization of the graduate program into seven areas of specialization (a development covered in the next chapter), the faculty became, in a sense, opposed to one another, their allegiance increasingly tied to their research field rather than to the department or university as a whole.

But the most crucial division during this time was clearly ideological. The figures cited above—high numbers of full professors on one end, high numbers

The Postwar Regime, 1948–1968

of assistant professors on the other, with relatively few associate professors in between, a pattern true for both the beginning and the end of the 1960s—reveal how the department was splitting into two camps—one older, more conservative, tenured, and powerful; the other younger, more radical, untenured, and relatively powerless—with a presumably moderate group in between that wasn't, however, large enough to bridge the gap in any meaningful way.

Departmental polarization reached a kind of head in the spring of 1968 with the election of Rideout's successor as chair: support for the two leading candidates was so evenly divided—twenty-eight votes on secret unsigned ballots for Mark Eccles (the choice of most of the senior faculty), twenty-nine votes for Karl Kroeber (the choice of most of the junior faculty), and one abstention—that Dean Leon Epstein stepped in and found a third, presumably independent, faculty member, Simeon K. (Tim) Heninger, to lead the department starting in the fall of 1968.[97]

The breakdown of community in the English Department at this time was occurring in other campus units and organizations as well, even in groups and among individuals who shared a supposedly "liberal" political viewpoint. In the late 1950s and early 1960s, social protest at UW had been a relatively unified affair, involving faculty and students alike and giving the campus a nationwide reputation for liberal activism. But starting around 1966 or so, student demonstrations on campus were increasingly directed against the university itself, including its administrators and faculty. As other historians have commented, even the tone of campus protests changed from the early to late 1960s.[98] One of our interviewees confirmed this change: when Susan McLeod was in Madison in 1964–65 to get her master's degree in English, the civil rights movement was on everyone's mind, the forces of social injustice were largely outside of the university, and nonviolent protest was the preferred mode of action. When she returned in 1968 to get her PhD after three years away, she didn't recognize the place.[99] After the 1967 Dow riot, it seemed, the student protest movement had become increasingly violent, divisive, and directed against the university itself.

One result of this breakdown of late 1950s and early 1960s campus liberalism was growing tension between graduate students and faculty. By the middle 1960s, according to Cronon and Jenkins, graduate students were forging links with one another across department lines, building coalitions *against* UW faculty and administrators.[100] There are signs of this rift as early as the spring 1966 student sit-in at the Peterson Building, which was as much a protest against the university as it was against the war and which marked the birth of the Teaching Assistants' Association (TAA), the groundbreaking TA union at UW.[101] If, during 1967–68, there were still moments of student-faculty collaboration on the left (note, for example, the involvement of sociology professor Maurice Zeitlin in the Dow protests), by September 1968, the UW chapter of Students for a Democratic Society (SDS) had formally abandoned efforts to bring together radical students and faculty in joint protest and was instructing its members to "push the student-faculty contradiction" during the coming academic year.[102] It apparently worked: 1968–69 was a time of rapidly deteriorating unity among leftists on campus; in February 1969, for example, student activist Jim Rowen complained in the *Daily Cardinal* about the lack of faculty participation in the Black Strike of that year.[103] The Mifflin Street riot in May no doubt alienated students and faculty even further, though the diversity of positions within both groups (in many departments, for example, there was as much division between senior and junior faculty, and between conservatives, liberals, and radicals regardless of rank, as there was between faculty and students) makes any simple dichotomy a distortion of a complex and ever-shifting reality.

Still, rising faculty-student tensions were evident at UW during these years, in the English Department as much as anywhere else on campus. The rise in the number of graduate students there was even sharper than the increases in undergraduates and faculty; by 1969, there were close to 600 graduate students in the department, 240 at the master's level and 357 at the PhD level, only 225 of whom were supported by the department, 186 by TAships, most in Freshman English.[104] In his 1976 interview with the university's Oral History Program, Walter Rideout noted that the English graduate program in the mid- to late 1960s was "the size of a small college."[105] With this growth came conflict: already in the fall of 1967, there were intimations of TA unhappiness in the minutes of the Departmental Committee.[106] And in the spring of 1968, a fairly nasty dispute erupted between the nascent TAA and the department over the faculty's nonrenewal of James Marten's TAship for the following year.[107]

Things grew worse in the fall, when Heninger took over as chair. A forty-six-year-old Louisiana-bred scholar of Renaissance literature, who had served in the U.S. military during World War II, earned his bachelor's and master's degrees from Tulane and his PhD from John Hopkins, and was still relatively new to the University of Wisconsin (having been on the faculty at Duke from 1955 to 1967), Heninger opened the 1968–69 academic year by sending a memo to the entire department—faculty, staff, and graduate students—warning of attempts by campus protestors to disrupt classes that semester in the name of "relevance" and vowing to defend the department against the forces of "chaos and old night," a quotation from Milton's *Paradise Lost* that two former TAs, Susan McLeod and Jean Turner, would vividly remember, and still find ridiculous, nearly forty years later. Here are excerpts from that memo of September 12, 1968:

The Postwar Regime, 1948–1968

There are persistent rumors that classes will be disrupted this fall by vociferous dissidents on the pretence of challenging the professor about the relevance of his course. . . . Apparently the protest groups consider national politics a lost cause, and the Viet Nam war is rapidly waning as a focus for protest. Therefore they have decided to attack the university on the relevancy of its operation. Their tactic will be, if rumor is correct, to challenge the individual professors by disruptive confrontation in the classroom. . . . I . . . urge that you avoid both extremes: neither scowl and storm out without retort, nor go limp and suffer public humiliation without remonstrance. I hope that we can steer a course somewhere between these poles; but of course our antagonists are extremely clever and they will try to push us to one extreme or the other. . . . This is hardly a cheerful message to go out as a new chairman's first memo to all staff members. Let's hope that it is an unnecessary precaution and that it will soon be as obsolete as a bomb shelter (how's that for dispelling fear and gloom?). In any case, if we can face the question of relevancy from serious students, we shall be all the better for it. And we must protect ourselves from the anarchists who will exploit the issue of relevancy to bring in chaos and old night.[108]

Heninger later admitted at the first Departmental Committee meeting that year that "a small group of teaching assistants had taken umbrage" at the memo and had asked for a meeting with him to discuss the department's relations with its TAs.[109] That September 17 meeting, attended by over one hundred English TAs and apparently quite stormy, led to two others, on September 24 and 30, at which the TAs called for a radically increased role in the departmental committees that affected the courses they taught.[110] More will be said about those meetings in the next chapter; for now, they show that in the fall of 1968—in the words of the secretary of the September 23 Departmental Committee meeting, quoting Heninger—"the Department of English had on its hands an incipient case of teaching assistant disaffection."[111]

Meanwhile, in October of that year, an incident allegedly involving undercover police presence in an English 102 class resulted in a unified protest from undergraduate students and their TAs against the department and university.[112] Later that same semester, two thousand undergraduate students petitioned the department for pass/fail grades in English 102, a move that was actively supported by the TAs as well.[113] Then, in the spring of 1969, during an especially tumultuous semester, negotiations about recognizing the TAA as bargaining agent for the department's teaching assistants furthered the breach between faculty and graduate students in the department.[114]

In his interview with us, Ira Shor suggested that by the spring of 1969, the authority of senior faculty in the English Department, from the point of view of their graduate students, had been completely undermined. These were people, Shor said, whom the students no longer emulated, whose careers they no longer desired for themselves: "They were not inspiring scholars," he remarked.[115] Increasingly, for graduate students in the late 1960s, the university and those in charge of it were part of society's problem rather than its solution. This explains why demands for a greater role in educational planning became so important for both undergraduate and graduate protestors at UW in the late 1960s. The movement was no longer just about civil rights or war in Vietnam. It was about the university itself. Students and TAs wanted to be more involved in education, and they saw themselves allied against senior faculty in this desire.[116]

It's easy to blame the students, of course, for the breakdown of community at UW in the late 1960s, even for the collapse of liberalism on the campus—to see them becoming during this period increasingly radicalized, irrational, and violent.[117] But the story is more complicated than that. The students were not consciously betraying the Old Left, and they hadn't simply lost their moral and intellectual bearings, descending headfirst into Heninger's "chaos and old night." The times had changed, and their response to those changes was in many ways a predictable and rational one. As Cronon and Jenkins indicated, and as Ira Shor's interview confirmed, students felt that the institutions of modern society had let them down, and they became, as a consequence, inordinately suspicious of all authority figures and groups.

The Vietnam War gave them good reason to feel that way. The expansion of U.S. involvement in the war during the middle and later 1960s mirrors almost exactly the growing tension between faculty and students at UW charted here. At the end of 1963, there were still only 16,500 troops in Vietnam; two years later, there were 185,300, a huge increase, but a number still not much higher than the troop levels in Iraq in 2006. The next year, 1966, though, was the fateful one: by the end of that year—also the year of the Peterson sit-in and the beginnings of the TAA—there were 485,600 U.S. troops in Vietnam, and the numbers would stay at that level for the next two years, through all of 1967 and 1968, reaching their peak of 542,400 in January 1969.[118] Between 1964 and 1973, twenty-seven million men reached draft age in the United States, and eleven million of them served in the military in one way or another, almost sixty thousand of them killed in Vietnam.[119] But none of those numbers express what so many young people in the 1960s saw in that war: the participation of their own country in unimaginable violence, destruction, and immorality.

At UW, the change in student opinion regarding the war was dramatic. According to Cronon and Jenkins, in 1965, 72 percent of students *supported* the war; in 1970, five years later, 79 percent *opposed* the war.[120] UW faculty and administrators also changed their minds about the war, but neither in such vast proportions nor with such profound disappointment about their own country.[121] The students also came to believe something about the war that their professors never fully accepted: that the university itself was implicated in the war's worst features through the very knowledge that it produced (or failed to produce).[122]

In other words, students and faculty during these years came to occupy significantly different positions in a cultural debate about higher education itself, about whether the university could, at one and the same time, ambitiously pursue specialized, often government-funded, research and still participate actively in the democratic project of general (liberal) education.[123] Some of this conflict was ideological: the war taught students to be dubious of any neutral representation of "science" or "research," whether in the natural sciences, the social sciences, or the humanities.[124] But some of it was demographic and economic. The 1960s saw increasing numbers of students, from increasingly diverse backgrounds, faced with increasing demands from their society for high-level analysis, synthesis, and criticism, entering research universities like UW (themselves increasingly important to the economy and the culture as a whole), where increasingly well-resourced faculty members appeared to be withdrawing from general education in order to devote themselves to advanced research—research that often seemed, from the point of view of the students and the graduate assistants teaching them, to be part of an unjust, inhuman, and oppressive political and social order.[125] It is this fundamental tension between competing visions of the university itself that is key to understanding what happened on U.S. campuses during the 1960s.

Roger Geiger has traced that tension back to the "shock" that *Sputnik I* produced in the U.S. military, political, and educational establishment and the "golden age of academic science" that followed.[126] The most important effects of that event on U.S. colleges and universities, he argues, were, first, the rise of university scientists to positions of influence in the federal government (for example, the creation of the President's Science Advisory Committee [PSAC] in November 1957); second, the "ascendancy of an ideology of basic research" (epitomized by the PSAC-sponsored Seaborg report in 1960, which called for greater federal support of basic, "disinterested" research and the graduate education on which that depended); and third, the "surge" in federally supported university research, much of it from civilian rather than defense agencies (that is, the National Aeronautics and Space Administration, the National Science Foundation, and the National Institutes of Health, rather than the Department of Defense).[127] That surge was substantial: "From fiscal year 1959 to fiscal year 1964 this figure jumped by annual increments of 33, 23, 23, 24, and 21 per cent. In this half-decade federal funds for university research rose by 200 per cent. In comparison, they had increased by 91 per cent in the preceding five years and grew by 74 per cent in the following five years. A large portion of the extraordinary gains of the 1959–64 increases can thus be regarded as the post-sputnik surge—the direct fiscal response to the shock of Sputnik 1."[128] One outcome of all this is that from 1953 to 1968, the proportion of basic research in the country conducted by universities rose from 25 to 50 percent.[129] Similarly, the weight of university research in the gross national product went from 0.07 percent in 1953 to 0.24 percent in 1968, a threefold increase. Further, university research became more dispersed in this period; in 1958, 37 percent of federal research funds went to the ten largest university recipients; in 1968, the proportion had declined to 28 percent as more institutions, like UW, became "significant performers of research."[130]

Geiger has written elsewhere about how the 1960s' "revolution in federal support for university research" interacted with three other revolutions during that "most revolutionary" of decades.[131] There was a "student rebellion," the most vividly remembered of the four, as well as a boom in access to colleges and universities, which made the sixties "the most expansive decade in the enumerated history of our system."[132] But it's the interaction of the "Sputnik surge" with an "academic revolution" that Geiger is most interested in here. Borrowing the phrase from a 1968 book by Christopher Jencks and David Riesman, Geiger defines the "academic revolution" as the 1960s' "emancipation of faculty in the academic disciplines from meaningful control by lay society. Academics at those colleges and universities that mattered were now able to devote themselves wholly to the theoretical concerns of their discipline with scant regard for the wishes of those whom they taught or those who ultimately supported them."[133] This development was spurred on, of course, by the post-1957 surge in federal fiscal support and the ideological preference for basic or disinterested research that accompanied it: "Faculty needed only to delve deeply into their own disciplinary paradigms to be assured of rapid career advancement. Graduate departments mushroomed in size and number, and their graduates staffed the burgeoning academic departments in colleges and universities across the country."[134] The federally fueled "academic revolution," therefore, helped exacerbate the "ivory tower" mentality of U.S. faculty, an attitude ironically supported by the student rebellion since protesting students disliked any university-society partnerships (whether of a military or a corporate nature) that they thought turned them into "cogs in a machine."[135]

The Postwar Regime, 1948–1968

For Geiger, "the legacy of Sputnik, the academic revolution, and the student rebellion, was that the university in the 1960s lost its bearings in a number of respects. The ivory tower mentality made it lose sight of the numerous ways in which the university needs to be and ought to be connected with its society; and the exaggerated moral sensibilities that prevailed by decade's end obscured any realistic appreciation of the university's many functions."[136] For my purposes here, the analysis is most useful in helping us understand how "the long sixties" presented university units like UW's English Department with fundamentally incompatible conditions: just as huge numbers of students were coming to college needing increased support in acquiring the ever more sophisticated "basic skills" on which the new economic, social, and cultural order was based, enormous pressure was being put on faculty, including in the humanities, to spend more and more of their time and energy in the production of research. In the analysis of David Laurence and John Guillory, American higher education was being riven by competing impulses: on the one hand, to radically expand the college-going segment of the population and, on the other, to significantly increase academic and scientific research.[137] How could these two impulses, exemplified by the student-loan program and the National Science Foundation, respectively, be reconciled? How could the university meet its growing student body's escalating needs for general education while satisfying society's (and the government's) increasing hunger for advanced research?

The answer was disarmingly simple: to increase the number of *graduate* students available to teach lower-division courses, sit in on faculty-taught graduate seminars, and become themselves the next generation of researchers. In a prescient 1967 article on the growing exploitation of graduate student teaching assistants in U.S. universities during this time, Robert Dubin and Fredric Beisse pointed to the dramatic increases in both undergraduate and graduate enrollment in U.S. colleges and universities between 1953 and 1964, noting how the undergraduate student-faculty ratio during this time could be statistically stabilized only by considering graduate student teaching assistants as faculty.[138]

As these numbers show, the phenomenal increase in graduate enrollment during this decade—from 74,630 to 182,706—outpaced the rise in undergraduate enrollment, which also grew spectacularly, from 493,817 to 1,005,173 (see table 3.2).[139] This growth in both populations meant increasing pressure on faculty during this decade because of their educational commitments at both undergraduate and graduate levels. The pressure was relieved only by letting the faculty "retreat from its undergraduate teaching responsibilities" and turn those responsibilities over to graduate student TAs, a situation that was possible only because of their increased numbers.[140] In fact, from 1953–54 to 1963–64, the

71

3.2 Enrollment and Student-Faculty Ratio, U.S. Public Universities, 1953–1964				
Year	Undergraduate Students	Graduate Students	Undergraduate-Faculty Ratio	
			Faculty Only	Faculty and TAs
1953–54	493,817	74,630	10.61	8.53
1955–56	628,580	84,141	11.34	9.12
1957–58	691,527	97,392	10.78	8.54
1959–60	722,281	120,144	11.03	8.46
1961–62	839,754	146,438	11.84	8.70
1963–64	1,005,173	182,706	11.71	8.61

Source: Modified from Robert Dubin and Fredric Beisse, "The Assistant: Academic Subaltern," table 1, "Enrollments, Teaching Staff, and Student-Faculty Ratios," p. 524.

number of graduate teaching assistants in public U.S. universities tripled, from 11,352 to 31,083.[141]

At UW-Madison, these same patterns of growth were playing out. As the numbers in table 3.3 show, undergraduate enrollment at UW almost doubled during this period, from 11,457 to 19,567, but graduate enrollment nearly *tripled,* from 2,764 to 7,238. These graduate students were increasingly being called on to serve as teaching assistants, thereby taking some of the burden for undergraduate general education off the faculty's shoulders and giving the latter more time and energy to pursue their research agendas and the graduate teaching with which those agendas were so closely connected.

As we've seen, the English Department at UW therefore allowed its master's and doctoral programs to expand exponentially, with most of the new graduate students funded by TAships in freshman and sophomore English.[142] But this expansion led to growing tension between the graduate student TAs and the faculty members who were now both their professors and their supervisors. After all, as the 1960s wore on, TAs at schools like UW were shouldering increased responsibility for teaching at the undergraduate level, teaching that was increasingly challenging due to both the number and the diversity of new undergraduate students and the growing demands from society for high-level intellectual skills from them. In that work, unfortunately, the TAs were receiving less and less mentoring and supervision from the faculty, who seemed increasingly *un*interested in general education. What mentoring and supervision they did receive often seemed removed from the reality of the undergraduate general education classroom of the 1960s and hostile toward the new pedagogical approaches that were attractive to so many graduate student TAs.

The Postwar Regime, 1948–1968

3.3 Enrollment at UW, 1956–1966			
Year	Undergraduate	Graduate	Total
1956–57	11,457	2,764	15,017
1957–58	11,343	3,013	15,130
1958–59	11,424	3,425	15,672
1959–60	12,001	3,789	16,556
1960–61	13,110	4,050	17,932
1961–62	13,986	4,270	18,997
1962–63	15,283	4,790	20,822
1963–64	16,638	5,590	23,048
1964–65	17,612	6,510	25,055
1965–66	19,567	7,328	27,880

Source: "Enrollment Facts at a Glance: The University of Wisconsin, Madison Campus, Second Semester 1966–1967."

On top of all that, large numbers of new PhD's, from across the academy, were beginning to flood the job market looking for faculty positions, the numbers of which simply couldn't keep pace. And the year in which professional saturation occurred in British and American literature, the year in which there were literally more candidates for faculty positions than there were jobs, was that hinge year, 1969.[143] As we'll see, that was the fateful year for freshman composition at UW as well.

4 FACULTY WITHDRAWAL, 1966-1969

The first sign that any of the changes described above had affected first-year composition at the University of Wisconsin came in the spring of 1968. On March 6 of that year, associate chair Edgar Lacy, at the end of his two-decade tenure directing the Freshman English program and speaking now on behalf of the 1967–68 Ad Hoc Committee to Study Undergraduate Course Offerings, presented to the English Department a proposal that had already been approved by the department's Curriculum Committee and even applauded by the dean: that the two-semester English composition requirement at the university be reduced to one semester. Under the new policy, the majority of freshmen would proceed straight to English 102 (the old English 1b) when they enrolled at the university and would satisfy the composition requirement with a passing grade in that single course, while a small number of students, because of their low scores on the university's entrance exams, would be placed in English 101, the old English 1a, and allowed to register for English 102 only after passing the former.[1]

In making this proposal, which envisioned the most significant change in the Freshman English program at UW in seventy-five years, Lacy passed out an "Interim Report" from the Ad Hoc Committee that outlined the group's rationale. Here's the section of that report addressing the "Composition Requirement":

During the last five years or so, the quality of freshmen coming to the Madison campus has improved. One indication of this improvement is revealed by the high school rank of entering students and by scores on tests taken by entering students at the time of initial registration at Madison. One explanation for this improvement is the change in high school preparation, change both in emphasis and in quality. Probably equally important are recent changes in the University's admission policy (virtually limiting admission of in-state students to those ranking in the upper half of their high school class) and changes in college curricula (esp. in the L & S curriculum, with its emphasis on high school preparation in mathematics and foreign languages): these two changes seemingly not only have excluded some students but also have discouraged other students from applying for admission because they think they are unlikely to succeed.

Because of the improved quality of freshmen, English 101 and 102 have been stepped up during the last five years. (For example, formal review of fundamentals has been dropped, and the individual student still having difficulties with mechanics has been told that he himself is responsible for reviewing fundamentals.) For many years the Department has placed the best students in a one-semester course (English 181) on the theory that those students did not need more than one semester of training in composition. For the same reason those students earning an A in English 101 have been given exemption from English 102. With continued improvement in the quality of entering students, the next logical step is to increase the number of students exempted from one of the two semesters.

On the basis of the writing of individual students in sophomore-level or upper-division courses, any member of the faculty might feel that those particular students need not less but more training in composition. Members of the committee, however, have reached the conclusion that although some—comparatively few—students will continue to need two semesters of composition, the great bulk of entering freshmen have profited from stepped-up high school training and are not receptive to more than one semester of college composition.

RECOMMENDATION: *Hence, the committee recommends that the bulk of students currently required to take two semesters of composition be required to take only one. The method for achieving this reduction would be the use of current placement tests to assign to English 102 the bulk of students currently assigned to English 101 (followed by English 102).*[2]

The proposal, along with another complicated one concerning sophomore literature, was approved at the March 6, 1968, meeting of the Departmental Committee ("by a large majority"), and on May 15 of that year, the minutes of the UW College of Letters and Science Faculty Meeting record that "Professor Lacy presented a *report from the Department of English on Change in Placement Procedures* to result in one semester rather than two semesters of required composition for most new freshmen."[3]

Beginning in fall 1968, then, Freshman English at UW was essentially cut in half, and English 101, the old "1a" course, required of more than 90 percent of freshmen one year before, was turned overnight into a tiny remedial program for students who had failed the university's verbal placement test. Why did the department at this time reduce so dramatically and so suddenly its long-standing two-semester English composition course, remedializing the first semester and leaving the second without its former prerequisite? Because, Lacy's committee argued, entering first-year students at UW were benefiting from stepped-up writing instruction in the state's high schools and thus no longer needed two semesters of Freshman English. Was this true?

During the March 6 meeting, when the "Interim Report" on undergraduate course offerings was presented, Lacy provided, or at least alluded to, evidence supporting his claim about the improved writing skills of entering UW freshmen. He indicated, for example, that "recent CQE scores have shown a steady and even dramatic improvement," though he gave no further details orally (at least according to the official minutes of the meeting). In an appendix to the "Interim Report," however, statistics on the high school rank of UW freshmen showed, for example, that the proportion of incoming freshmen in the top 10 percent of their high school class had risen from 29 percent in 1962–63 to 35 percent in 1967–68.[4] Another appendix showed that a raw score on some unspecified test (perhaps the College Qualification Examination) placing a male student in the 91st percentile of freshmen in 1963 would have put the same student in the 90th percentile in 1967; a raw score on the same test placing a female student in the 80th percentile in 1963 would have put her in the 75th percentile in 1967. These changes suggest a somewhat higher-performing entering class in the latter as compared to the former year.[5]

Of course, none of these scores came from an actual *writing* test, and the gains reported on multiple choice vocabulary tests and in high school rank are rather modest (the change in male scores mentioned above, for example, is virtually imperceptible). But an even more compelling reason for skepticism about Lacy's argument is the general silence that surrounded it. There's nothing in the minutes or in any other document from before spring 1968 to suggest that entering UW students in the 1960s were suddenly becoming better writers and that their Freshman English requirement could therefore be cut in half.

Faculty Withdrawal, 1966–1969

There was no discussion of the issue in prior Departmental Committee meetings, no shared anecdotes about increasingly skilled freshmen writers, no department-wide celebration of improved high school English—nothing. Admittedly, there are no recorded *rebuttals* to Lacy's claims either, no voices raised in support of or opposition to it. Did faculty silence on this question betray unease about Lacy's argument? Or did the secretary of the Departmental Committee fail to register the full reaction? According to Frank Battaglia, who was an assistant professor at the time, when Lacy repeated the claims about improved freshman writing skills during the fall 1969 discussions regarding English 102, there was audible laughter in the room.[6]

In fact, among former teaching assistants (TAs) interviewed for this project, the argument about improved writing skills among UW freshmen in the 1960s was seen, both then and now, as laughable, a smokescreen for other, unstated reasons for getting the department out of the freshman comp business. Virginia (Joyce) Davidson, for one, called the argument about rising skills "bullshit." The students in her classes, she reported, were "farm kids"; they needed *more* practice writing, not less.[7] Susan McLeod agreed: she never saw any persuasive evidence that students' writing skills were improving during the 1960s, and her own experience teaching English 102 in 1968–69 convinced her that first-year students at UW needed *more* work on their reading, writing, and critical think-ing. Her students were from little towns, she said, and they were struggling at college.[8] Similarly, Bob Muehlenkamp stated that there was "no reality" to the argument about rising skills: the students in his classes were "ill-prepared" for college-level reading and writing.[9]

Meanwhile, mean national SAT verbal scores were actually falling when Lacy was praising the improved "quality" of UW freshmen and their "stepped-up high school training." In fact, the so-called great decline in SAT scores, which would last for nearly two decades and be especially acute in the verbal test, began at least four years *before* Lacy's 1968 presentation to the UW English Departmental Committee.[10] The possibility that better-positioned universities and colleges like UW were able to exempt themselves from these national trends, attracting increasingly well-prepared freshmen up until the end of the 1960s, will be addressed below, but the SAT data do cast doubt on one of Lacy's hy-potheses for the *cause* of the alleged improved quality of entering UW freshmen in the late 1960s: "stepped-up" high school instruction.

The most persuasive counterargument to that hypothesis remains Janet Emig's *The Composing Processes of Twelfth Graders,* a case study of the writing of eight Chicago-area public high school students, all identified by their teachers as either skilled or interested writers, during the 1967–68 school year, the very year when Lacy made his case for the improved quality of entering UW freshmen.[11] Published by the National Council of Teachers of English (NCTE) in 1971 and thought by many to have single-handedly inaugurated the "process" paradigm in writing theory, research, and pedagogy in the 1970s, the study was Emig's 1969 doctoral dissertation for the EdD at Harvard and the main evidence for her failed tenure case at the University of Chicago.[12]

Where Lacy paints a portrait of improved high school preparation of student writers, Emig—who actually interviewed such students, collected their writing histories, and watched them compose aloud—found only a stultifying and "neurotic" activity.[13] Her pessimism shows through most clearly in her case study of a student writer named Lynn, who could be described as a classic prospective UW freshman from the time. The oldest child of a lawyer and in the top 5 percent of her high school class, Lynn, in the spring of 1968, was a college-bound senior from an academically rigorous public high school in South Chicago. In many ways, she fit the bill for Lacy's "improved" high school students, and Emig presents her as clearly skilled in the literacy of school. But what Emig means by that, it turns out, is that Lynn had been trained to find in her academic writing assignments "programmable" topics that could be processed quickly and efficiently without her having to actually discover anything meaningful or explore in any genuine way herself or her society.[14] The resulting composing process was fluent but shallow: it involved little planning, no written prefiguring, and almost no reformulation or revision. Instead of a concern for invention, Lynn was obsessed with superficial "amenities" like the length of her essays and the avoidance of clichés. Writing was for her a thoroughly "limited, and limiting, experience."[15]

The reason? According to Emig, Lynn had been conditioned by years of contact with teachers who were "interested chiefly in a product [they] can criticize rather than in a process [they] can help initiate through imagination and sustain through empathy and support." Lynn herself provided support for this criticism when she said at one point of her teachers, "They seem to have this thing about spelling."[16] But Emig is even more brutal: she complains of "teacher illiteracy" in U.S. high schools, describing educators who do not themselves write and who thus "underconceptualize and oversimplify" the process of composing so that "planning degenerates into outlining, reformulating becomes the correction of minor infelicities."[17]

Emig's subjects were clearly capable of self-sponsored writing in a more "reflexive" mode, one focused on "the writer's thoughts and feelings concerning his experiences" in a "tentative, personal, and exploratory" style.[18] In that mode, they demonstrated longer prewriting periods, more contemplation about their writing, and more reformulation of their ideas and language. Unfortunately, says Emig, school writing is almost always "extensive," a mode focused on "the writer's conveying a message or a communication to another" in an "assured, impersonal, and often reportial" style—the hallmark of which is the five-paragraph essay, "so indigenously American," Emig writes, "that it might be called the Fifty-Star Theme."[19] In that mode, teachers set rigid parameters for writing that "students find difficult to make more supple."[20] The result? "Outward conformity but inward cynicism and hostility" and a universe of discourse in which "the good student writer is the polite student writer."[21]

The upshot of Emig's detailed case study, in hindsight, is to cast doubt on Lacy's claim of "stepped-up" high school writing instruction in the 1960s. Now, it's possible that the rising affluence of the population and the general freeing of expression and debate that took place in this country from the late 1950s on, combined with the post-*Sputnik* surge in federal support for education, may well have improved some aspects of U.S. student literacy during this period. But the modest nature of the gains Lacy points to, the lack of any other support for his argument, the anecdotal counterevidence of our informants, and the empirical rebuttal provided by Emig suggest that high school training in English during these years, even at the best high schools, was not keeping up with the increasing diversity of students and the ever-growing demands for critical literacy from both the academy and the culture at large. If anything, the academic preparation of student writers in the 1960s was falling further behind social needs and would, by the middle of the next decade, precipitate a national literacy crisis.[22]

And even if incoming UW freshmen in the late 1960s really were more skilled writers than earlier cohorts, that may have been less a function of improved secondary education than of the increasing stratification of U.S. higher education during this period, stratification that allowed universities like UW to admit increasingly well-prepared students and push off the rest onto the nation's fast-growing branch campuses and community colleges. Lacy admits as much in the report quoted above. As Clark Kerr put it in a 1982 addition to *The Uses of the University,* "The growth in the 1960s of universal access to higher education was absorbed mainly by the community colleges and comprehensive colleges and universities, not by the research universities and particularly not by the Research I universities. . . . Elite institutions remained elite; and some became even more elite."[23]

The fact is that UW at this time was benefiting from the increased competition among high school students for college admission brought about, quite simply, by their skyrocketing numbers. If this doesn't disprove Lacy's claim about Freshman English, it certainly shines a different light on it, and it points to a potentially troubling contradiction between the alleged fact of more "competitive" students enrolling at UW in the late 1960s and the university's and department's stated interest at the time in opening up the campus to groups historically underrepresented there.[24] All this would suggest that the writing skills of U.S. students were not so much getting "better" during this period as becoming more diverse.

But let's put aside for a moment these rebuttals and qualifications about "stepped-up" high school training and "improved" freshman writers in the 1960s and, for the sake of argument, accept Lacy's claims at face value—after all, those of us in public education should *want* to see a positive effect from the increased support for education that took place in this country between the launch of *Sputnik* in 1957 and the budget-draining escalation of U.S. military involvement in Vietnam in the mid-1960s.[25] If the nation's primary and secondary schools were really improving during this time, and if, as a consequence, the average writing skills of entering UW freshmen were also increasing, isn't there another response the English faculty could have had besides getting rid of the first-year writing course altogether? Couldn't they have reimagined the course itself so that it better reflected and responded to the actual literacy experiences of the students taking it and the actual discourse needs of the society in which they lived? Couldn't they have made it more challenging, more interesting, and more *effective*? Aren't there other options for freshman composition besides stagnation and irrelevance, on the one hand, and outright elimination, on the other?[26]

Is it possible, in other words, that the problem at UW in 1968 was less an unneeded than an outmoded English 101? And that the solution was not to eliminate the course but to improve it? After all, when English Department chair Walter Rideout announced the new Ad Hoc Committee to Study Undergraduate Course Offerings in fall 1967, he indicated that it had been motivated, in part, by TA complaints "about the courses they teach."[27] Perhaps the TAs, like their students, found Freshman English boring and were complaining about it? Interviews with former TAs seem to support this interpretation, as does a 1970 study of freshman composition at UW by the College of Letters and Science's Curriculum Review Committee; Lacy's March 6, 1968, presentation to the Departmental Committee hints at it as well.[28] An anonymous article in the *TAA Newsletter* of March–April 1968, meanwhile, claimed that English 101–102

Faculty Withdrawal, 1966–1969

was "one of the most disliked courses in the university, by both students and TAs alike," and suggested that this was due to the faculty's rigid control over the course, preventing TA experimentation, especially in terms of literary content.[29] But if the curriculum of the course was outdated, no longer able to respond to the discourse needs of its society and the literacy goals of its students and TAs, why didn't the faculty try to *revise* English 101, rather than unilaterally eliminate the requirement for it?[30]

────────────

That question brings us to what may have been the real reason for the spring 1968 reduction of Freshman English at UW from two semesters to one. In his September 1967 charge to the Ad Hoc Committee to Study Undergraduate Course Offerings, English Department chair Walter Rideout had said that, among other things, the department needed to "correlate and extend" the previous year's revision of the *graduate* curriculum to the *undergraduate* years. Taking that as a cue, I went back one year and looked at the work of the department's 1966–67 Ad Hoc Committee to Study Graduate Course Offerings.

That committee had recommended in the spring of 1967 the creation of seven new "Area Committees" meant to make graduate study in the department more efficient and specialized—that is, more *disciplined*.[31] The proposal was based on two principles: first, that the department's MA degree needed to be structured more in relation to the PhD than to the BA, thus helping the department draw a sharper line between undergraduate and graduate study; and second, that the PhD itself needed to more rigorously emphasize specialization through such changes as a revamped "prelim" structure, earlier declaration of the student's "area of concentration," and the requirement of more seminars in that area. In his 1980 interview with the university's Oral History Program, former department head Charles Scott confirmed that the impetus behind the department's 1967 revision of the graduate program was the perceived need for specialists in all fields, scholars and researchers grounded in very specific areas of intellectual and scientific inquiry.[32]

So, on May 9, 1967, Rideout presented the recommendations of the Ad Hoc Committee to the department. First, the group identified several problems with the English PhD program: prelims were an endurance contest; too many students waited until after prelims to specialize; students were inadequately prepared for advanced graduate seminars; they were typically hired because of their specialties but did not have a chance to actually specialize, and so on.[33] In response to these problems, the committee recommended shortening the time required to complete the PhD at UW, while maintaining the quality of the program; putting greater emphasis on specialization, though maintaining the program's traditional breadth of coverage; and, perhaps most important of all, creating the aforementioned area committees, "which would include all faculty of any rank in a given area and which would set and read prelims, admit students to candidacy for the PhD, and direct, read, and approve dissertations."[34] There would be seven such committees: English Literature to 1500, the Renaissance, the Eighteenth Century, Nineteenth Century British Literature, American Literature from the Beginnings to 1914, Twentieth Century British and American Literature, and Linguistics.[35] Composition-rhetoric was not included. On May 16, 1967, after extensive discussion, the motion to revise the graduate program passed.[36]

If, then, the changes in the undergraduate curriculum approved a year later, in March 1968—changes that included the reduction of Freshman English to one semester—were meant to "correlate and extend" this earlier May 1967 revision of the graduate program, the implication for the story being told here is inescapable: the changes in Freshman English were part of a concerted effort to move the department in the direction of advanced, specialized, literary (and linguistic) research and away from undergraduate general education. The UW English faculty in 1968 cut Freshman English in half, in other words, because they no longer saw it as an important part of the department's mission.

The silence that attended Lacy's proposal about Freshman English on March 6 and April 30, 1968, when the Departmental Committee dealt with the Ad Hoc Committee's recommendations, provides some evidence for this interpretation. Most of the discussion in the first meeting and all of the discussion in the second were devoted to the committee's recommendations about *sophomore* literature. By contrast, the English 101 proposal was met with almost total silence.[37] Faculty apathy is confirmed by a short statement from English TA David Middleton in the spring of 1968, printed as "The Ad Hoc Committee Meetings: An Interpretation" by the TAA or an English subdivision of it.[38] Middleton remarks that the meetings of the Ad Hoc Committee, which he attended as an observer, concerned two things: Freshman English ("which got a hatchet job") and the Mulvihill Report (discussed below). As for the first, "most of the faculty members were frighteningly silent, from which I infer a sizeable group of English Department faculty who think there is nothing wrong with freshman English as is."[39] I believe Middleton was being charitable here. The silence came not because the faculty thought there was nothing wrong with Freshman English, but because they simply didn't care about it anymore.[40]

82

Now, admittedly, there were other things going on in the department, at the university, and in the society at large at this time that might explain the faculty's decision about English 101. For example, it could be attributed to a growing distaste, among students and faculty alike, and not just at UW but nationwide, for all requirements.[41] There was, after all, *some* reduction in Freshman English requirements during this time, though as indicated earlier, any claim of a late 1960s trend toward "abolition," like that suggested by Lacy in the March 6, 1968, meeting and repeated by Heninger during a crucial November 18, 1969, meeting is clearly an exaggeration.[42] It is true, however, that Freshman English at UW had, by the late 1960s, become unmanageable for the small staff that ran it and the moderate-sized department that sponsored it: there were too many students to teach (as we've seen, an increase of nearly one thousand first-year students just between 1964 and 1965) and too many TAs to supervise (the master TA program was an acknowledgement of that). But if so, why did Heninger appeal to the dean in the spring of 1969 to let the department continue to expand?[43]

Among the possible reasons for remedializing English 101 and essentially cutting the Freshman English program in half, it's hard not to think that the main one was that the faculty by the spring of 1968 just no longer cared very much about it, that their attention was concentrated elsewhere, that the course didn't fit their new post-*Sputnik* image of themselves and the department. They were focused now on research, their own national profiles, and the prestige and productivity of their department; and they wanted to move English studies at UW in the direction of advanced literary study, to help it become a more focused department, one oriented to the needs and goals of its majors and, especially, its graduate students, not freshmen and sophomores. To do so, they needed to shed, or at least deemphasize, the department's general education responsibilities. The faculty looked for a good reason to do that, and they found it in allegedly rising freshman verbal test scores.

Ironically, in the spring of 1968, at the same time that the English faculty were trying to withdraw from general education reading and writing instruction at UW, the department's graduate student teaching assistants were showing increased interest in freshman and sophomore English and taking on greater responsibility for these subjects, something that their professors seemed in fact to be encouraging, if sometimes grudgingly. We can see this in the department's response that semester to the work of the University's Committee on the Teaching Assistant System, established as a kind of high-level study group by the chancellor in the summer of 1966, just weeks after a large number of UW students, graduate and undergraduate, had congregated in a key administration building on campus to protest the university's provision of student grades to the Selective Service agency for military draft purposes, an event that also led to the formation of what would eventually become the UW Teaching Assistants Association, or TAA. The twelve members of the chancellor's Committee on the TA System included faculty representatives, undergraduate students, and two TAs; its chair was Edward R. Mulvihill, a professor in the Spanish Department; and one of its members was the ubiquitous Edgar W. Lacy.[44]

The committee's twenty-page report, published in February 1968, and known ever since as the "Mulvihill Report," was (and remains) a rather remarkable document. It included findings and recommendations about four main issues: the selection and funding of TAs at the university; their orientation, training, and supervision; the teaching situation itself as it pertained to TAs; and channels of communication between faculty and TAs at UW. The goals of the report were to raise the quality of TA instruction across campus, to provide opportunities for TAs to develop as teachers, to improve their pay and working conditions, to provide for more TA input in course planning and content, and to encourage better faculty-TA communication about TA policies and procedures. But behind all of the committee's work was a simple double fact, admitted early on in the report: that TAs had been granted increased responsibility for teaching undergraduates at UW (in 1965, 76 percent of instructional time received by freshmen and sophomores on the Madison campus was provided by TAs), but that their professional status and role remained highly problematic.[45] As the TAA itself put it in another document of that time, "Faculty control of TA classes is, throughout this University, a myth. In many cases this is due to the necessities of mass education . . . ; in other cases, it is due to faculty lack of interest and/or inability."[46] But despite the *teaching* responsibilities being thrust on them, TAs were still seen primarily, by their own professors and the university itself, as *students,* dependent, in theory at least, on the supervisory power and intellectual tutelage of the faculty.

This conflict was causing problems at universities across the country. In their 1967 article on "the Academic Subaltern," cited in the Mulvihill Report, Robert Dubin and Fredric Beisse wrote that TAs everywhere in the 1950s and '60s had been granted increased "teaching responsibilities without corresponding legitimation of their authority and prerequisites to carry them out."[47] That is why so many of them were so intent at the time "to claim professional recog-

Faculty Withdrawal, 1966–1969

nition as college teachers by securing a voice about, and even control over, professional activities necessary to perform teaching functions."[48] Unfortunately, TAs faced the difficult situation of literally being teachers in the same departments where they were students, "incompatible if not irreconcilable positions."[49] They were thus in a bind: to work as an educator, especially in the low-enrollment, stand-alone sections of courses like English 101 and 102, each TA needed "treatment comparable to the regular teaching faculty, including consulting him regarding the courses he is assigned to teach, when classes meet, the outline and content of instruction, the text and supplementary material used, and tests and other evaluation methods employed."[50] But professors continued to treat TAs as apprentices whose lack of full credentials disqualified them from a right to these very prerogatives.[51] The situation was exacerbated by the fact that those professors seemed to be increasingly uninterested in, unqualified for, and even hostile to the classroom work that the TAs were engaged in.[52] Yet the TAs needed the faculty both to keep their jobs and to make progress toward their degrees.

To resolve some of these problems at UW, the Mulvihill committee recommended guaranteeing long-term financial support to PhD students in good standing, support that would include, across a recommended four years, a combination of TAships, RAships, and fellowships—hopefully encouraging departments with substantial research funds to give their best students more opportunities to teach and helping departments that relied heavily on TAships to give their best students more opportunities to do funded research.[53] According to the report, 67 percent of graduate students and 79 percent of faculty surveyed by the committee concurred that teaching was a necessary facet of professional training and should be *required* of all doctoral candidates at the university, a suggestion that the committee formally proposed.[54] Such a move, the report noted, would benefit both undergraduate students, who would therefore have exposure to the best graduate students across campus, and graduate students themselves, for whom teaching experience would become a more significant part of their training. In addition, the committee recommended pay raises for TAs and other improvements in "bread and butter" issues.

Importantly, the committee also endorsed the desire of the majority of TAs at UW for *both* more and better teacher training and supervision from their faculty *and* more "independence, creativity, and responsibility" as teachers.[55] The committee therefore recommended extension of departmental orientation programs for new TAs, extensive in-service programs led by faculty recognized for teaching excellence, and personal conferences between faculty and TAs regarding teaching.[56] But TAs also clearly wanted freedom to experiment and innovate, and the committee specifically recommended "the *encouragement of initiative and creativity on the part of TAs*" in course planning and execution, a line that would be quoted frequently by English Department TAs over the next couple of years.[57]

Finally, because TAs had expressed dissatisfaction with faculty-student communication in their departments, the Mulvihill committee recommended more formalized and equitable means for incorporating TA input in policy and other decisions that affected TAs, especially appointment procedures. TAs needed to be informed of policies affecting them, the report urged, to be consulted on those policies, and to have available to them mechanisms whereby their problems might be brought to the attention of appropriate faculty members or supervisors.[58] Thus, the committee recommended the promulgation of better procedures regarding TAs, but it also recommended setting up in each department a graduate student–faculty committee "with equal numbers of faculty and elected students, including proportional TA representation," to determine and publicize procedures affecting TAs and also to serve as a kind of grievance appeal board.

The English Department voted in favor of the Mulvihill recommendations on May 21, 1968, just a week after the reduction of Freshman English and the remedialization of English 101 were reported to the Faculty Senate.[59] Earlier that semester, the department had allowed for an expanded TA role in the policy committee of the new TA-taught sophomore literature course, English 200 (permitting faculty members of that committee to "appoint several teaching assistants to work and consult with it in matters of course content").[60] But the real implementation of the Mulvihill recommendations in the English Department, at least as regards more equitable participation by TAs in course planning, didn't occur until the following September. As mentioned above, new chair Tim Heninger's first memo to the department that semester, which seemed to blame student protestors for bringing "chaos and old night" into the department, had touched a raw nerve with the TAs, and they asked to meet with him. That meeting, which took place on September 17, 1968, and was attended by over one hundred TAs, was contentious, and it ended with a call for yet another meeting on September 24.[61] At that meeting, Heninger later told the Departmental Committee, the teaching assistants seemed to be "chiefly interested in obtaining voting-power in the policy-making committees of the English Department"; he discussed how they "demanded responsibilities and representation equal to their duties in the English Department, how they regarded themselves as 'experienced' teachers, and how they thought of themselves

Faculty Withdrawal, 1966–1969

almost as firmly established in the life of the Department as many 'full-time' faculty members."[62] The students called for another meeting on September 30 to examine specific proposals for constituting the policy committee of the new English 200 course, on which Heninger believed they were "working toward full voting representation."[63]

At that September 30 meeting, the TAs in fact presented Heninger with recommendations about the participation of TAs in policy committees of the department, including a motion (approved by a TA vote of sixty yeas, fourteen nays, and one abstention) that they be "represented on the 200 committee with voting rights equal to those of the four faculty members."[64] As significant a change as this would be in procedures, and even in the overall balance of power in the department between faculty and TAs concerning general education teaching, Heninger interpreted the motion favorably, not as an ultimatum from the TAs, but as an attempt to show their "legitimate desire to know where they belong in the department." They were, he said, asking for a "line of responsibility to be drawn," and he believed they would abide by the line the Departmental Committee drew.[65]

Heninger reminded the committee that, even configured as the TAs proposed, with equal voting members from the faculty and the TAs, the English 200 Policy Committee, and others similarly configured, would still have one more faculty member than TAs, since the chair was not a "regularly voting" faculty member but could vote in the case of a tie. He also mentioned that the department's Curriculum Committee (on October 3) and the dean himself had approved the TAs' proposal, which was also in line with the recommendations of the Mulvihill Report. And he noted that, in his opinion, the TAs' claim that "they should in reality be at least partially responsible for the courses which they teach and their concurring argument that this responsibility should be openly acknowledged by the English Department through the granting of voting-powers . . . in the policy committees for the courses in which [they] were most used" were not unreasonable demands. After considerable discussion, the motion to accept the TAs' proposed reconfiguration of the English 200 Policy Committee was accepted by the faculty with only a single negative vote.[66]

More important for the focus of this book, in October 1968, the Curriculum Committee recommended extending the English 200 model of shared faculty-TA governance to the Freshman English Policy Committee, which was soon reconfigured to have four "regularly voting" faculty members (professors Elmer Feltskog, George Rodman, Joyce Steward, and Ednah Thomas, all appointed by the chair); four voting teaching assistant members (Michael Krasny,

Faculty Withdrawal, 1966–1969

Albert Logan, Jeffrey Sadler, and Michael Stroud, all elected by their peers); and one faculty chair (Lenehan) able to break ties.[67] For the 1968–69 school year, this was the main policy-making body for English 102.

In August 1969, at the end of that academic year, and less than two months before the crisis that will be detailed in chapter 6, Freshman English Policy Committee chair William Lenehan wrote a long memo to Heninger evaluating the experiment.[68] The nine members of the committee, he wrote, had met weekly during the year.[69] He complained a bit about the TA members—mainly because their presence lengthened the time necessary to reach decisions—but he also admitted that the committee's discussions were "consistently relevant and civilized."[70] There was, he said, general agreement on the purpose of Freshman English: to improve the writing ability of students. And despite a campus climate of extreme polarization that year, committee members dealt openly with all issues. The faculty sometimes felt that the TAs wasted time with old or unworkable ideas, but this was perhaps to be expected:

> The teaching assistant, lacking professional experience, has to be educated on two common sources of error: first, his tendency to form generalizations out of his unique experience as a teacher, not realizing that his particular strengths and weaknesses as an instructor will not adequately reflect those of a staff of 120; second, his tendency to present enthusiastically, as his new idea, approaches to comp which have been tried again and again in the past without success (that is, communications approach, lecture method, and so on). On the other hand, I suspect the TAs often left the meeting feeling that the faculty members were not facing the real problems of the instructor in a comp class.[71]

Each group learned from the other, wrote Lenehan, although in his opinion, the TAs learned more: after all, few new ideas in teaching freshman composition ever crop up. Still, there was something to be gained by having student members: "What the teaching assistant can contribute to the Committee is his concrete awareness of what is happening in the classroom." Also, "Since the teaching assistants teach the courses, it seems to me we have an obligation to let them be represented in planning the *means* of teaching these courses." Lenehan ended the letter on a positive note: "If the existence of TAs on this Committee has offered no panacea for our problems, *their presence [has] made a sufficiently significant contribution that I strongly recommend its continuance.*"[72]

Faculty Withdrawal, 1966–1969

But it was in English 101, the old first half of UW's Freshman English program and the course that the department had remedialized in spring 1968, that TA participation in undergraduate reading and writing instruction at UW was most felt in 1968–69. By February 1969, as an extraordinary report from the English 101 staff reveals, the course had changed dramatically to meet this new set of conditions. Unmoored from the large English 102 program, disattached from a university-wide requirement, set free from prior constraints, English 101 was reinvented in ways both intriguing and disturbing.[73]

The spring 1969 report on English 101, written by Ednah Thomas and the five TAs who were teaching the new version of the course in the 1968–69 academic year, describes an educational experiment based on the pedagogical principle that instruction should always be adapted to students' experiences, abilities, needs, and goals. In some ways, the remarkable reorganization of English 101 that occurred at UW in the late 1960s shows more vividly than anything else the road not taken for English 102, especially in the development of an emergent, self-directed, and meaning-driven curriculum run by a genuinely empowered and collaborative staff. But what may be most noteworthy here is that these TAs produced, essentially on their own, and years before the rise of anything like a "basic writing" movement in this country, a sensitive, flexible, and truly student-centered writing course for an "at-risk" population.

Although each of the TAs wrote a page or two of their own concerning the new English 101, the opening pages of the report are a joint statement about what the group learned about the new course and how they believed it should develop in the future. The main point they make is that the course should be about more than just preparing students for English 102; its true aim rather should be "to inspire confidence in the student and help him, as far as possible, to overcome any psychological barriers which may interfere with his success in his college career." In this, the group argued, the instructor of English 101 has a "special obligation," one that should be felt by any writing teacher, but "with particular sensitivity" by the instructor in 101.

The group began their report proper with placement issues, arguing for provisions that would allow students, early each semester, to move between 101 and 102, but also between different sections of 101: not only to make sure each student was placed in the right course but also to equalize the size of sections and accommodate student and instructor wishes for either heterogeneity (to have a diversity of backgrounds, interests, motives, abilities, and even ages in the class) or skill-grouping. The group also recommended scheduling all sections of English 101 at the same time, preferably 12:05 P.M. daily. And it recommended a class size between eleven and eighteen: not too large for individualized attention but big enough to keep classroom discussion lively.

As for the course calendar, the group asked for maximum flexibility: classrooms should be made available five days a week at the appointed time so that TAs could meet with their students daily at the beginning of the semester and less often later; the rooms should also be available for individualized instruction and small group meetings. Regarding a syllabus, "no common calendar is possible since instruction must depend completely upon the needs of the students, which will vary widely." Similarly, no specific texts should be prescribed, and TAs should be free to experiment in this area.

Meanwhile, the report recommended that the instructional staff be in close touch with one another; because of the problems the course presented for teachers, they needed one another's aid and comfort. The department was encouraged therefore to assign all English 101 TAs to a common office where they would be in close, regular contact with one another and where they could help one another's students when they came for individualized help.[74] In this, as in the other aspects, the revised English 101 suggests a dramatically different kind of writing course: inordinately flexible, insistently student centered, run by a teaching collaborative. (Importantly, the report was signed not only by the five TAs teaching it but also by Ednah Thomas herself; it was later roundly praised by Lenehan, Lacy, Heninger, and even the dean of the college.)[75]

There are also, of course, problems attendant on remedializing composition in these ways; in this case, the most serious problem was an incipient racialization of the curriculum and pedagogy. "A distinction must be made here," the staff writes, "between the black students in the course and the others"; the report goes on to include advice on how to deal with black students, particularly black men, in the course. It is said that they "use fluently a special dialect of their own" that interferes with their acquisition of Standard English pronunciation, vocabulary, and grammar. The desire of these students not to lose touch "with their own people," however, presented opportunities since they often were "deeply and genuinely concerned with having something they want to say." Still, they often exhibited lack of confidence about their writing, exacerbated by knowing that they had been placed in English 101 because "they have a deficiency in writing skill which does not handicap the bulk of the students in the entering class."

Several of the TAs, therefore, proposed using more "relevant" texts for these students; three of the five TAs, for example, used books by James Baldwin

Faculty Withdrawal, 1966–1969

in the course. And they recommended creating a classroom environment in which the instructor tried harder to get to know his students, was more intimately concerned with their writing ("always a personal matter"), and attempted more energetically to help all of them improve their writing: encouraging, giving advice, and providing useful information. "Most of all, first, last, and all the time," the report continues, the instructor should be "a sympathetic listener."

The individual statements show a group of TAs demonstrating enormous flexibility and a willingness to work through difficult teaching problems; they also include moments that would make writing teachers today wince: one TA lists as the first problem of "special importance" in his students' writing that many of them, especially the black students, were not aware that the past tense of "use" requires a final "d." But the document in general reveals a committed staff experimenting, largely unaided, with what would later be called "basic writing." The last paragraph of their report summarizes the approach that the TAs were working with:

> By and large, the students in English 101 have more problems and more diffi-
> culties than the average student entering the University. The instructor in
> English 101 should be aware of this, and of its corollary, that he himself will
> have more problems and difficulties than if he were teaching the average
> course. He should feel a commitment to the course and be prepared to call
> upon his inner reserves of patience and understanding. If he does this, he
> may well find the experience one of great value.[76]

The report also clearly reveals the excitement and pride the TAs must have felt in this particular teaching assignment.[77]

By the spring of 1969, then, graduate student teaching assistants in the English Department at UW were clearly taking an active role in the planning, design, and execution of the courses they most frequently taught: namely, undergraduate general education reading and writing courses. And as we'll see in even greater detail in the next chapter, they were doing more than just serving on policy committees. They were reading and writing about pedagogy; they were experimenting on their own and with other TAs; and they were increasingly organized, working through the Teaching Assistants Association and other outlets not just to secure better working conditions for themselves but also to enhance their professional development as teachers and improve the learning of their students. In March 1968, two-thirds of English TAs signed a petition calling for recognition of the TAA, an organization increasingly concerned at the time with pedagogical and curricular matters.[78] In other words, the English TAs were seeing themselves not just as budding scholars and future professors, and not just as employees concerned about pay, health care, and work conditions, but also as committed and responsible teachers, striving to do a better job in the classroom for their students.

5 TA EXPERIMENTATION, 1966-1969

with Rasha Diab and Mira Shimabukuro

In the fall of 1969, 4,360 students, or about 78 percent of the 5,569 freshmen at the University of Wisconsin that semester, enrolled in Freshman English. One hundred and forty-nine registered for English 101 (11 sections), the newly remedialized writing course examined in some depth previously. Another 329 were in 18 sections of English 181, the Honors version of Freshman English. But the vast majority, 3,882 students, enrolled in English 102, the only composition course most UW students took that year. They were divided into 164 sections of around twenty-four students each, and like their peers in English 101 and 181, they were entirely in the hands of English Department graduate teaching assistants (TAs).[1] The department employed 158 such assistants in fall 1969, two-thirds of them (or 101) assigned to English 102. Many of them taught two sections of the course that semester.[2] The other 57 TAs were assigned to English 101, 181, or 200 (sophomore literature), or they assisted faculty in upper-level courses.

What were those TAs doing in fall 1969? In particular, what were the 120 or so TAs assigned to Freshman English doing that semester? We saw in the previous chapter what a small number of them were doing with the newly liberated English 101 course. But what about the still-required English 102? What were TAs doing with *it* in the late 1960s? Now, we know from chapter 3 what TAs were supposed to be doing at this time: we saw there the course's focus on genre and mode, the heavy use of model essays, the prevailing concern with correctness. We've seen the training TAs were provided in orientation and weekly staff meetings: the modeling of different kinds of "class hours," the emphasis on theme annotation, and so on. And we've seen evidence that this training was highly insufficient in a variety of ways.

There were, after all, no faculty at UW in the late 1960s doing research in composition-rhetoric, no graduate courses in "comp-rhet" theory or pedagogy, no departmental colloquia treating writing studies or instruction as bona fide intellectual projects. In fact, the most sustained instance of faculty reflection on composition during this entire period was the statement about clarity and effectiveness that Professor William Lenehan issued in February 1970—three months after the dismantling of Freshman English![3] Before that, the faculty were largely dismissive of innovations in composition studies or pedagogy. In his August 21, 1969, memo to Heninger, for example, course director Lenehan (a specialist in American literature) wrote, "The idea that the fresh point of view and youthful enthusiasm will enable the teaching assistant to create new means of teaching composition is fallacious. After 150 years (if we begin with Harvard's appointment of a Professor of Rhetoric) of rather hectic experimentation in composition, few new ideas crop up."[4]

The TAs certainly couldn't rely on their own backgrounds, prior training, or professional interests to help them teach writing better or differently. As Virginia (Joyce) Davidson recalled, "None of us had experience in teaching writing; we were steeped in the criticism of literature."[5] Jean Turner likewise admitted that, at UW in the late 1960s, she had no real theory for teaching Freshman English and was never very good at it.[6] Though she learned about critical pedagogy from more advanced TAs like Margaret Blanchard and Bob Muehlenkamp, she had difficulty translating those insights pedagogically. Similarly, Susan McLeod told us that, although (like Jean Turner) she had experience teaching high school and college English before she came to UW, she had never taken any coursework in comp theory and lacked confidence as a writing teacher. She was forced to rely, therefore, on the "enlightened current-traditionalism" of Edgar Lacy and Ednah Thomas, which is why, she told us, her copy of *Evaluating Student Themes* was so well thumbed—it was how she learned to teach English 102. As for the new rhetorical theories then emerging, McLeod said, they simply weren't available at UW in the late 1960s.[7]

Ira Shor confirmed all this: "We were lit students," he said in his interview; "we weren't plugged into the composition crowd."[8] The TAs had no idea, said Shor, that the groundbreaking Anglo-American Conference on the Teaching of English had been held at Dartmouth in 1966; they hadn't read Albert Kitzhaber's

TA Experimentation, 1966–1969

Themes, Theories, and Therapy: The Teaching of Writing in College, published in 1963, or Donald Murray's *A Writer Teaches Writing: A Practical Method of Teaching Composition*, from 1968. "We were urged to read *PMLA* and maybe *College English*," said Shor, "but not the other journals, so we didn't know about 4Cs and the 3Cs journal and the comp books that started appearing. . . . The discourses that began didn't reach us. We were on our own searching for something else educationally that we didn't even know about."[9]

As that last comment makes clear, the TAs' lack of training in composition did not mean that they weren't interested in learning. And it certainly didn't mean that they were arrogantly or randomly making stuff up as they went. They recognized at a profound level that they didn't know how to teach writing the way they wished, and they tried to correct their ignorance. On at least three occasions, in fact, English TAs at UW in the late 1960s publicly asked the faculty for graduate coursework in composition theory and pedagogy. Lenehan himself reported in his August 1969 memo to Heninger that "the teaching assistant members were unanimous in their support of a more rigorous training program with heavy emphasis on rhetorical theory applicable to composition. Some would like to see the development of graduate courses on the teaching of college composition. One TA would like to have the opportunity to do graduate specialization in composition problems."[10] Similarly, in their 1969 "Contract Proposal for English 102 and 200," English Department TAA members proposed the hiring of two quarter-time TAs, paid by the department to administer and encourage TA pedagogical seminars, which shall "reflect the interest in course form and content of the TAs involved and shall serve as a continuing evaluation of 102 and 200, as well as a means of exchanging info and ideas between TAs."[11] And though he was speaking primarily about the teaching of literature, English TA David Foster argued in the Fall 1968 issue of the TAA's journal *Critical Teaching* that

> save for the indoctrination of freshman composition TAs there is nothing done at UW to help new teachers of literature learn about teaching. The TA who is assigned quiz sections in a lecture course may get directions and advice from the lecturer, but usually he is merely given the syllabus and told to go to it. Now the freedom to teach sections the way one likes is important and valuable, of course, and no lecturer would try to tell his quiz instructor how to run his sections. But the crucial problems involved in the direct relationship between TA, student, and literary work are deep and complex, and I suspect very many TAs in literature would enjoy the opportunity to discuss the teaching of literature not only among themselves but with more experienced teachers on a regular basis.[12]

The author then proposes a series of seminarlike discussions on teaching among TAs and faculty, a proposal that, like those mentioned above, was summarily ignored by the department.

If the English TAs at UW in the late 1960s had limited access to theoretical developments in composition-rhetoric, they were not, however, intellectually adrift when it came to the classroom. Their pedagogical reflections and experiments were clearly informed by wider discussions taking place at the time, especially on the left, about human development, critical pedagogy, and participatory democracy. We can assume, for example, that they were reading what other students at the time were reading—Marcuse, Laing, Fanon, and Barthes, for example. And we can assume that some were also reading Marx, Guevara, and Cleaver. The popularity of the anthology *Sense of the Sixties* (ordered, as we'll see in the next chapter, by one English TA for his English 102 sections in fall 1969 but also used by some English 101 TAs in 1968–69 and at least one English 102 TA in the summer of 1969) gives us additional clues about what TAs were reading at this time: Paul Goodman's *Growing Up Absurd*, Claude Brown's *Manchild in the Promised Land*, and Staughton Lynd's "The New Radicals." Former TA Jean Turner mentioned to us the outsized role of Jerry Farber's essay "The Student as Nigger" in her own political and pedagogical awakening, and she cited Andre Gorz's *Strategy for Labor* as well (a book included in the 1969 TAA seminars on "The University and the Economic System" and mentioned in the TAA *Newsletter* of September 1969, where it was said to be "seminal to a full discussion" of the role of unions in counterimperialist work).[13] Another important intellectual source for the TAs was A. S. Neill's *Summerhill*, a 1960 account of an experimental British school, which is mentioned three times in the two issues of the TAA journal *Critical Teaching* and also plays a role in Martin Duberman's 1968 *Daedalus* article about his pedagogical experiments, which will be discussed below.[14]

As is clear from the above references, the new TAA provided important intellectual support for UW graduate instructors in the late 1960s. English TAs active in the TAA (72 percent of the department's TAs were dues-paying members in 1969–70) were able to deepen their understanding of higher education both theoretically and practically by attending TAA-sponsored conferences, reading groups, and seminars. Through the organization, they were introduced to publications like *New Directions in Teaching*, the journal *Radical Teacher*, and the treatise *Degrading Education*, written by leftist faculty and students associated with the Ann Arbor–based New University Conference. And during the summer and fall of 1969, the TAA organized a seminar entitled the "The University

TA Experimentation, 1966–1969

and the Economic System" for TAs who wanted to engage in more sustained and penetrating analyses of higher education. The summer seminar was described in the September 1969 TAA *Newsletter* as "a concerted internal education effort aimed at understanding the imperialist nature of the U.S. economic system and its manifestations in the University." In sessions titled "Background in Political Economy," "The Transition from Capitalism to Socialism," "The University's Place in the Structure," and "Strategy for the Future," TAs worked "to delineate the role of the University in fostering imperialism and to explore possible functions of unions in representing the needs of their constituent groups within an imperialist structure." According to the *Newsletter*, the seminar was "a solid beginning" that gave the organizers "the experience and bibliography necessary for organizing a better course for this semester. It is abundantly clear that a disciplined, on-going process of self-education is necessary if we are to thoroughly understand the university's motives and actions."[15]

At the fall reprise of the seminar, advertised in the same September 1969 TAA *Newsletter*, TAs read many of the same texts summer participants read, including Clark Kerr's *The Uses of the University;* the Winter 1968 issue of *Daedalus*, focused on "The Student Left in Higher Education" (which included Martin Duberman's article on classroom experimentation); Che Guevara's *Man and Socialism;* and Staughton Lynd's *Restructuring the University.* But fall students also benefited from a new session entitled "Educational Philosophy," which included readings from the first issue of TAA's own journal *Critical Teaching*, Michael Faia's *Dunce Cages, Hickory Sticks, and Public Evaluation: The Structure of Academic Authoritarianism,* and Ronald Sampson's "What Is a University?" which will be quoted below.

In the meantime, TAs in the English Department tried to educate themselves about new ways of teaching writing. At some point during the 1968–69 academic year, a handful of English 102 TAs, dissatisfied with both the formal training provided by the composition faculty and the piecemeal efforts in self-education that individual TAs were undertaking, formed a "study group" to learn more about the teaching of writing and, eventually, craft an alternative curriculum for the course. The group had grudging support from the department, though it seems to have always occupied a peripheral position there. According to Ira Shor,

> A group of TAs and I got together and formed our own study group. And we started to develop our own syllabus, and we got a faculty advisor—I'm trying to remember who it was— . . . I can't remember . . . Anyhow, they sponsored it, and we sort of met on our own. What we did was form what

would later be called in the field "staff development seminars." That's what we formed. I took this experience with me to Staten Island Community College when I became an assistant professor there in '71 because this was so *useful* and helpful, *inspiring*. We spoke very concretely about what we were teaching, what was going on, and we were trying to develop a mutual syllabus. It was a TA-organized group. I can't remember exactly which semester and for exactly how long, but I do know we did it, for at least one semester, and I found it wonderful. So we were already trying to develop from the bottom up a curriculum design process, and it wasn't just anarchic. We were asking very serious questions. And you know, it was far more useful than the fall session they [Lenehan and Thomas] offered us.[16]

Unfortunately, no record of the group survives, and neither participants nor outsiders could remember much about what it actually did. There were apparently only about five TAs involved, and they met for only one or two semesters. And yet, without any prompting from us, Susan McLeod (who was not a member) remembered well both the study group and its plan to produce an alternative syllabus for English 102—suggesting that the group's existence was widely known, if controversial, and its work highly anticipated, at least among the TAs.[17]

Yet another group of English TAs conducted original research on other writing programs. In 1968, the English Students Association wrote to twenty different English departments at UW's peer institutions to inquire about the structure of their first-year composition programs. Afterward, the TAA reported the details of what they had learned, especially in relation to the "balance of personal choice and community needs" evidenced by the other universities' composition programs. "So many other large state universities," the TAA noted, "are able to give their TAs a fair amount of autonomy combined with a flexible syllabus and a training program which assumes that both sides can learn together. Perhaps the secret of TA-administration rapport . . . is an attitude encouraging TA planning and experimentation in their courses."[18] The research also seemed to support the TAs' contention that other programs were allowing more literary content in freshman composition.

But perhaps the most powerful example of how these TAs were teaching themselves to reform English 101 and 102 is the writing they did about pedagogy, especially through a TAA project mentioned several times now, the remarkable and, in many ways, unique scholar-practitioner journal *Critical Teaching*, which was written, edited, and published entirely by UW TAs in the late 1960s. Appearing in two separate issues, once in fall 1968 and again in fall 1969, *Critical*

Teaching served as a forum where TAs from across the university could share and reflect on their teaching experiments and present arguments for retheorizing their instructional roles. In the first issue, the editors announced that the journal would publish essays about "the role and methods of teaching assistants . . . from conceptual discussions of the role of the TA in higher education to discussions of specific classroom methods and strategies."[19] The idea was that TAs would benefit from a written exchange of experiences, whether "sweet or bitter," as the editors put it.[20] Both issues contained a dozen articles or so, most three to five pages long, and were produced with especially vigorous participation by English Department TAs (see figure 5.1). The Fall 1968 issue, for example, included "The Degrading System" by English TA Inez Martinez, "Reviving Freshman English" by Anonymous, "Workshop on Communication" by English TA Anne Mulkeen, "Improving Hoop-Jumping" by English TA Timothy Drescher, "Growing Free" by English TA and future TAA president Bob Muehlenkamp, and "Reflections in a Jaundiced Eye" by English TA David Foster. At least six of the fifteen essays in the first issue were written by English TAs. The second issue of the journal, published a year later, included the articles "Rugged Individualism and the Blue Book" by English TA Bernice Mennis, "On Drama Workshops" by English TA Carla Shagass, "Excerpts from 'Kling Peer,' a Drama" by Margaret Blanchard and Bernice Mennis, and "Becoming a Radical Teacher" by Sea Unido (a pseudonym for an English TA). In that issue, at least four of the twelve essays were by English TAs.[21]

By my count, between a third and a half of all the entries in the two issues of *Critical Teaching* were written by English Department TAs, all of them teachers of Freshman English, for whom the problems of *that course* were clearly uppermost in their minds as they wrote about pedagogy. In fact, the centrality of Freshman English in that journal, and the leadership provided by Freshman English TAs, suggests that general education writing instruction may have played a more important role in 1960s student activism, at least at UW and at least in regards to educational reform, than historians have heretofore acknowledged. In Madison at this time, English 101 and 102 were a kind of petri dish for rethinking higher education itself.

We've seen something, then, about what English TAs at UW were reading, writing, and talking about in regards to freshman composition. But what were they actually doing in the classroom? Many of them, it's clear from the evidence,

Volume 1, September 1968

1. "The Teaching Contract," Harold Nelson, 2–3
2. "The Degrading System," **Inez Martinez**, 4-6
3. "The Greed System," 7–9
4. "Catalogue of Creative Methods," 10–16
5. "Surveyors and the Endless Terrain," Bernie Johnson, 17–20
6. "Teaching History 290," Richard Scheidenhelm, 21–25
7. "Questions about Teaching Math," Henry Haslach, 26–31
8. "Reform in Ed Psych," El Ehvhen, 32–34
9. "Reviving Freshman English," **Anonymous**, 35–38
10. "Workshop in Communication," **Anne Mulkeen**, 39–41
11. "Improving Hoop-Jumping," **Timothy W. Drescher**, 42–43
12. "Growing Free," **Bob Muehlenkamp**, 44–50
13. "Reflections in a Jaundiced Eye," **David Foster**, 51–54
14. "Creative Drama," Shirley Parry, 55–56
15. "A Semi-Utopian Vision," **Margaret Blanchard**, 57–58

Volume 2, September 1969

Preface: "There's no success like failure, and failure's no success at all," **Margaret Blanchard**, 1–2

1. "Disconnections," David Siff, 3–7
2. "Rugged Individualism and the Blue Book," **Bernice Mennis**, 8–10
3. "TAA Analysis of the University," 11–14
4. "Bringing It All Back Home," Ed Zeidman and Linda Zeidman, 15–19
5. "On Language Requirements," Anna Marie Taylor and Leslie Dorfman, 20–24
6. "Training for Cages?" Alan Stein, 25–27
7. "Radical Speech," Karl A. Tunberg, 28–33
8. "On Drama Workshops," **Carla Shagass**, 34–36
9. "Music and Self-Development," J. Bauerlein, 37–40
10. "Excerpts from 'Kling Peer,' a Drama," **Margaret Blanchard and Bernice Mennis**, 41–50
11. "Becoming a Radical Teacher," **Sea Unido**, 51–58

bold = English Department TA

underline = English Department faculty

Figure 5.1. Table of contents, *Critical Teaching,* September 1968 and September 1969 were experimenting. If some of their statements during the fall 1969 crisis read like the ultimatums of an assured, even dogmatic group, the evidence concerning their actual teaching practices suggests that, in the classroom at least, the TAs didn't quite know what they were doing and were acutely aware of that fact. That's why "experimentation" is such an apt word to describe these projects: it highlights both the boldly innovative and the surprisingly tentative nature of the TAs' interventions in Freshman English at UW in 1968 and 1969. It's also a word that shows up repeatedly in the documents uncovered and interviews conducted here.[22]

And what were these experiments about? In his interview for this project, Bob Muehlenkamp said that "there was experimentation in both the reading materials used in the course and in grading and also in how to teach," a statement that comports well with the surviving documents.[23] The most common area of experimentation concerned the selection of course texts. Although English 101 and 102 were ostensibly courses in writing, instructors used readings of various kinds to model rhetorical techniques for students, to center class discussions, and to serve as subject matter for student writing. These texts occupied an especially important place in Freshman English at UW, and for TAs interested in transforming the course, the opening salvo was often a proposal to change the readings. The attempted adoption by one TA of an unauthorized textbook for his English 102 students in fall 1969, an event narrated in some detail in the next chapter, is only the most obvious example of how the TAs were searching for new reading materials for their students, texts that could move the course away from the formalistic, rule-bound, and belletristic and toward the relevant, engaging, and critical. Proposals for alternative course texts by the TAs can sometimes look superficial in hindsight, but most were the outcome of extensive trial-and-error by committed classroom teachers, many of whom taught two sections of the course semester after semester for years. Bob Muehlenkamp, who taught English 102 eight times between 1966 and 1970, put it this way in an interview: "Some of the TAs, especially those who had taught the course more than once, would have a feel for what worked and what did not, and then they would try to experiment by substituting their own texts."[24]

Even TAs who weren't actually supplanting approved course texts with alternative ones could be critical of the standard English 102 reading materials. During one fall 1969 meeting between the TAs and department administrators, for example, TA Connie Pohl described the required textbook *College Writing* as "politically biased" and said that she objected to teaching it.[25] Two weeks

TA Experimentation, 1966–1969

later, text-selection issues were a key source of public contention between faculty and TAs.[26] And two TAs, Pauline Lipman in a November 25, 1969, letter to the *Daily Cardinal* and Susan McLeod in a June 2005 interview, independently of each other singled out the same text from the 1968–69 academic year, "The Joys of Sport at Oxford," as an example of the kind of outdated and irrelevant reading that students were being asked to write about in Freshman English at UW.[27] In a later email, McLeod wrote, "It made no sense to us to be teaching such stuff, ignoring what was going on all around us, especially since half of our students were worried about being drafted if they didn't do well in school."[28]

To replace such essays, reformers often proposed literary texts. In the spring of 1969, TAs at UW were pushing for more literature in all three Freshman English courses, the remedial 101, the regular 102, and Honors 181. As we saw in the previous chapter, the February 1969 reports about the reform of English 101 place heavy emphasis on the use of more "relevant" literary texts, like the novels of James Baldwin.[29] Meanwhile, in spring 1969, TA members of the Freshman English Policy Committee proposed (and secured) the adoption of a short story anthology in the English 102 syllabus.[30] And in the English 181 committee that semester,

> there was universal agreement among the instructors [that] at about mid-point in the course, the students should move from sole reliance on the anthology to literature as a subject matter for writing. . . . They would spend the first half of the course on examples of expository writing and the last half on short stories and the novel chosen as the subject matter of the source paper. It was generally agreed that *The Adventures of Augie March* and *Sons and Lovers* had been good choices for the novels, but that *Middlemarch* was too long, even for the superior student.[31]

This may look to us today like a regrettable folding of composition into literature, writing into reading, invention into interpretation—an admission that the project of general education writing instruction lacks disciplinary content and must depend therefore on literary studies for intellectual integrity and pedagogical effectiveness. Even the composition faculty, for all their foot-dragging on the reform of Freshman English, seem to have been ahead of the TAs on this score. Here, for example, is William Lenehan in his August 1969 report to Heninger on the work of the Freshman English Policy Committee:

> The central issue in the discussion of the [English 102] program was how to keep the focus on the central purpose of the course—the improvement of writing—and yet increase both staff and student interest in the course. The

TA Experimentation, 1966–1969

solution suggested was that of giving the course some kind of subject matter —the argument being that good writing is possible only if the student has something in which he is interested to write about. We wandered over the various possibilities, concluding predictably with a strong recommendation on the part of the TA members for literature as subject matter. All of the standard arguments against this were raised: that most experience with literature-based composition courses indicates little attention to the problem of composition; that a staff such as ours with many inexperienced instructors would turn the course completely away from composition; that literature as subject matter teaches only a very specialized kind of writing—that of explication. The responses to these arguments were consistent: the training program should be designed to train the staff to keep the focus on composition; those who would tend to subvert the purposes of the course are doing it anyway; imaginative theme assignments could prevent the writing from becoming over-specialized. The final consensus was that the structure of the course should remain traditionally rhetorical, that a short story anthology be used as a source of illustrative models, and that a short story anthology be used as a background for theme topics.[32]

Working in a discipline now largely autonomous from literary studies, we might wish that the TAs from the late 1960s had not so often proposed using literary texts as their principal way to make the first-year writing course more meaningful and effective for students. But the fact is, for these instructors, advanced graduate students in literary studies, literature was the most accessible way to reform Freshman English during a time when composition had no real intellectual status of its own in North American postsecondary English departments and certainly none at UW; the TAs can hardly be faulted for thinking that *Go Tell It on the Mountain* would engage student writers better than "The Joys of Sport at Oxford."[33]

The search for alternative reading material by some UW English TAs in the late 1960s can be seen as part of a general effort at the time to make coursework more "relevant" for students. These TAs fought consistently and energetically for assignments and materials in English 101, 102, and 181 that were pertinent to the pressing issues of the day, connected to students' worlds outside of class, and alive with import and even urgency. For senior faculty, on the other hand, "relevance" was code for lack of standards and loss of control. This can be seen in Heninger's infamous fall 1968 memo to English Department faculty and students, where the word is used four times in two pages:

There are persistent rumors that classes will be disrupted this fall by vociferous dissidents on the pretence of challenging the professor about the *relevance* of his course. . . . . Apparently the protest groups consider national politics a lost cause, and the Viet Nam war is rapidly waning as a focus for protest. Therefore they have decided to attack the university on the *relevancy* of its operation. . . . In any case, if we can face the question of *relevancy* from serious students, we shall be all the better for it. And we must protect ourselves from the anarchists who will exploit the issue of *relevancy* to bring in chaos and old night.[34]

The word occupies a more honorific place in the preface to *Sense of the Sixties,* the anthology that one TA sought to adopt for his sections of English 102 in fall 1969 and that precipitated the crisis in UW's English Department that semester. The book, its editors claim, was designed to provide students— "those Americans, born after World War II, now flooding the colleges, the generation of rising expectations that has crowded the universities"—with "materials of immediacy and present concern," materials "for here and now." Its selections are thus "all from the Sixties and they are all relevant. Our purpose is to show students their world interpreted in a variety of prose styles which they might emulate . . . to give some perspectives, some angles of vision, on the world the students have inherited." The topics included—God, the Negro, War, Science, and so on—are, according to the preface, central to the students' world, and "we are all in trouble" if they can't respond to them. The editors admit that all good prose is "relevant," but the topics and selections in their book have "an immediacy that should save some time in engaging students in thinking and in determining the quality of their thought."[35]

Clearly, "relevance" was not a superficial concern for radical educators in the 1960s—a matter of simply pandering to students' tastes and past experiences. For TAs active in educational reform at UW, it was a more serious issue, especially given what was happening in the "outside" world at the time. In the words of the pseudonymous English TA Sea Unido, who wrote "Becoming a Radical Teacher" for the second (1969) issue of *Critical Teaching,* "the demand for relevance is a mortal challenge to imagination and understanding to ensure that knowledge be related to human fulfillment rather than human destruction."[36]

Former TA Ira Shor was especially intent at the time on transforming Freshman English into a space where social and political problems in the real world could bear directly on students' thinking and writing in school, where their lives outside and inside the classroom could connect and interpenetrate, and where they might relate on a deeper level both with one another and with their teacher. "Oh yeah, we were tossing [the syllabus] aside," Shor recalled in an interview, as he related how the TAs searched for new ways to motivate intellectual progress in their students:

TA Experimentation, 1966–1969

For example, we would bring in problems. . . . I was trying to figure out a way to raise the issue of social inequality and to pose it as a thinking problem. So I remember bringing in the Gross National Product of America at that time. And then I asked students to divide it by the number of American's living in the country and come out with a per capita figure. So I think at that time we came out with about $17,000 per American per capita—you know how many years ago this is? Thirty seven years ago—so then I said, okay, now here's the median family income in America, which I got from some census source, and I put it on the board. It was very low, like $18,000, right, and so I asked them to write, or something like that, to give a context to inequality and base it in data and so on and so on. I probably wasn't the only one doing that.[37]

Shor claims that the students appreciated the approach: "It was very militant times, activist times. I never ran into objections or protests or resistances that became common in the '80s. The atmosphere among young people and on campus was so *activist* that the idea of relevance was a common theme. And also I think the students were tired of being lectured with the same old *same old*, that this was not just another course in grammar, usage, and punctuation."[38]

The senior faculty were a different story. They were not necessarily opposed to political analysis—after all, most were nominal liberals, and some were even old leftists from the 1930s. But in the late 1960s, they were, in general, opposed to what they saw as the reduction of intellectual and cultural problems to ideological position, the collapsing of historical perspectives into a pervasive "presentism," and the surrendering of classroom expectations to the "chaos" of the outside world. The difference between TA and faculty attitudes about the "outside" world was drawn especially sharply during a well-publicized panel discussion entitled "Relevance and the Teaching of Literature" convened at Hillel, the campus Jewish center, before an audience of about two hundred on March 19, 1969.[39] The panel, sponsored by the English Colloquium at UW, was comprised of two English graduate students, Ira Shor and Richard Miko, and two faculty members, assistant professor of comparative literature Cyrena Pondrom and associate professor of English Eric Rothstein. During the discussion, all the panelists agreed that literature was "relevant," but each articulated that relevance differently. For Eric Rothstein, literature was serious and worthwhile, "more than just a source of excitement"; it was a means of organizing one's emotions and attitudes by analogy to fictional experiences. Student Richard Miko stressed, however, that "reality" shouldn't be ignored in literary study, that art was always a reaction to reality and thus "a means of letting people know how our society runs." For Cyrena Pondrom, meanwhile, a work of literature might have contemporary relevance, but it must be placed "within the horizon of when it was written." In contrast, Ira Shor defined literature as a "vast treasury of absorbing crises, an art that emphasizes powerful moral realities," one with an important role to play in education: "The teacher's duty in class is to clarify the relevance of social problems outside of that class . . . [but] at a certain point the teacher must leave the classroom and take action on those social problems." Pondrom disagreed: "It is not morally better to carry a placard than to ask your class to reflect on what it is to be living. If he is concerned with the relevancy of teaching he has put me on the picket line for too many hours to prepare a proper lecture." But Shor was given the last word: he emphasized the personal relations that need to be established between professors and their students: "If teaching literature really means attacking problems at their roots then it is important to get close to people. 'I would like to know that a professor of a large lecture could walk into a room, talk to only eight people, and not be afraid of it.'"[40]

Shor remembers bringing up such issues in the Freshman English program as well. During orientation for English 102, for example, he asked Ednah Thomas about raising social problems, like civil rights, in class. According to Shor, she replied, "Well, those are interesting questions, Mr. Shor, but they're not really appropriate for this teaching session."[41] Other former TAs also remembered senior faculty members at this time resisting the intrusions of the "outside world." According to Virginia (Joyce) Davidson, the faculty believed intensely that literature was one thing, and politics another.[42] Susan McLeod also remembered her professors working energetically to separate the ivory tower from everyday life: Heninger in particular, she said, was "exemplary in this kind of elitism."[43] And though he was critical of the tactics and pedagogies of his more radical colleagues, former TA Burr Angle shared with them a distaste for what he saw as the "monasticism" of the English faculty. Concerning their treatment of Freshman English, for example, he said that they had clearly decided they'd rather be "a small group of effete scholars than actually deal with the needs of the commonwealth." But did they really think, Angle asked, that the legislature would pay them to teach Melville for thirty years? "You can't have an English Department without freshman composition!"[44]

If the faculty had blinders on regarding the "outside" world, the TAs did not. They were acutely aware of "the needs of the commonwealth" during this period, and at no time more so than during that "hinge" year, 1969. Our national narratives of the Vietnam War era have tended to portray 1968 as the year of greatest cultural and political upheaval, but in many ways, 1969 was more tumultuous and more consequential. In terms of U.S. war casualties, it was less

TA Experimentation, 1966–1969

devastating than 1968, but spring 1969 actually marked the highest U.S. troop level of the entire war (543,000 in March), and it was also when Nixon inaugurated both his ill-fated Vietnamization policy and his disastrous expansion of the war into neighboring countries. At UW, meanwhile, spring 1969 was an especially turbulent semester. In February 1969, seven to ten thousand UW students and their supporters struck to demand the creation of a black studies department at UW; campus administrators responded by calling in the National Guard. For nearly a month, the campus was shut down, with protesting students faced off against armed soldiers in a confrontation the stark antipathies of which even that turbulent campus had not seen before. The strike further eroded the strained relations between radical graduate students and liberal faculty, the old intergenerational coalition of campus leftists now a thing of the past. It was well known among English TAs, for example, that senior members of their faculty had petitioned the chancellor to bring in the National Guard during the strike, suggesting to them that their own department was hostile toward social justice.[45]

The following month, the *Daily Cardinal* began running a series of investigative articles by former English graduate student Jim Rowen, son-in-law of U.S. senator George McGovern, about the university's "Profit Motive," and by fall, the close relationship between UW's Army Math Research Center and the U.S. military had been fully exposed, in part by Rowen but also by English Department assistant professor David Siff, whose nontenure decision from the department would be announced in the same issue of the *Daily Cardinal* that carried news of English 102's abolition. In May, meanwhile, the Mifflin Street riot broke out near campus, turning a student "ghetto" into a veritable war zone for nearly a week.

Things seemed to be coming apart nearly everywhere in the United States that spring and summer. In April 1969, a branch of the leftist organization Students for a Democratic Society (SDS) seized control of the main administration building at Harvard, and in June SDS itself splintered, with the Weatherman faction emerging as the most potent group; it later organized the Days of Rage in Chicago and other violent protests. The summer of 1969 also saw the Manson murders in California and the Woodstock music festival in New York. In terms of antiwar demonstrations, meanwhile, the fall of 1969 saw some of the largest protests of the whole period, most notably the October 15 National Moratorium in Washington, D.C. A month later, on November 12, the story of the civilian massacre at My Lai broke, putting American war atrocities in Vietnam front and center in an especially graphic and horrifying way.

Given such headlines, English TAs at UW saw faculty moves regarding Freshman English as just another example of the conservative establishment using its authoritarian prerogatives to quash the spirit of the young—as TA Richard Damashek put it in the *Daily Cardinal* in November 1969: "The [English] Department faces the same crisis that American society today faces: because it fears the loss of power to the young and the vital, it chooses not to accommodate but to stifle its impulses."[46] From the TAs' point of view, Freshman English was one of the few spaces on campus where all students, of all backgrounds and interests, undergraduate and graduate alike, could explore, converse, critique, create, and grow, as readers, writers, thinkers, and human beings, free of disciplinary imperatives and authoritarian strictures. It was a place where the cruelty and injustice of contemporary society could be exposed and opposed, where new forms of language could be developed and freedom and truth pursued. The TAs wanted to know that their teaching, their classrooms, their labor, their department, their university, and their society were involved in human progress, not death and destruction. In this sense, they saw English 101 and 102 as fully embedded in their students' lives and part of a wider movement for personal and social change.

But if the TAs cared deeply about the *content* of Freshman English—about what their students were reading, writing, talking, and thinking about—they also paid close attention to pedagogical *structure:* where authority resided in the classroom, how goals were established and students evaluated, and so on. In fact, the TAs' experiments in educational process and procedure at UW in the late 1960s may be even more interesting, and far-reaching, than their search for "relevant" content. I examine three such innovations below.

First, the evidence indicates that many of the more radical English TAs at UW in 1968 and 1969 were trying to develop what one might call a teacherless writing class, in which authority is dramatically decentered and the student's responsibility for his or her reading, writing, and thinking—his or her own education and life—radically heightened. The idea is simple but, in the context of the old Lacy-Thomas course, revolutionary: in learning to write, students need to be personally engaged in what and how they are writing, to care enough as writers (as human beings, the TAs might have said) to truly reflect on and improve the ideas and language they are creating. The course could not be taught, therefore, in top-down fashion, by simply applying rules from a handbook, holding up model essays from an anthology, imposing the authoritative

TA Experimentation, 1966–1969

comments of an ideal reader (that is, the teacher), while the student passively absorbed the principles of good writing and tried to manifest them in his or her own work.

Learning to write, in other words, could not be motivated from outside and above; it had to be a self-initiated and self-controlled process in which students themselves were empowered to take responsibility for their own education and allowed to discover meaning through their own language. This required transforming the classroom into a genuinely collaborative space, what the TAs at the time referred to as a "democratic" classroom, in which the teacher abdicated his or her prerogatives, and the student, perhaps for the first time in his or her life, claimed the right to genuine self-education and true self-determination.

We saw all this in chapter 4, when we examined Janet Emig's 1971 claim, based on her observations of high school writers in the mid- to late 1960s, that young adults in U.S. schools needed more opportunities to write in self-centered and self-directed modes, as opposed to the other-centered and other-directed modes usually rewarded in school. "American high schools and colleges," she wrote, "must seriously and immediately consider that the teacher-centered presentation of composition, like the teacher-centered presentation of almost every other segment of a curriculum, is pedagogically, developmentally, and politically an anachronism."[47]

Former TAs interviewed here shared this antipathy to the teacher-centered classroom. Ira Shor put it this way: "The students were being lectured to death, so several of us figured we had to do something else, to interact with the students and find a method." He connected this pedagogical insight to a political one: "Those kinds of feelings were widespread then because, you know, it was a participatory period. Participatory democracy was an idea whose time had come through SDS and was widely in circulation. Participation, bottom-up politics, was discussed a lot."[48] Similarly, in his interview, Bob Muehlenkamp said that the goal of the TAs he worked with was to get students to actively participate in the course itself. As teachers, they didn't see themselves as dispensers of wisdom, so they experimented with having students participate in the design and teaching of the courses. And the students liked it, he said, especially because it was something that made learning less rote.[49]

Concerned more with younger students but serving nonetheless as an inspiration in the 1960s for radicals at the postsecondary level, A. S. Neill had written in *Summerhill* that "the function of a child is to live his own life—not the life that his anxious parents think he should live, not a life according to the purpose of an educator who thinks he knows best."[50] One of the teachers inspired by *Summerhill* was Princeton history professor Martin Duberman, who in fall 1966 tried to empty his "American Radicalism" undergraduate seminar of all authoritarianism: he required no readings, assigned no papers, held no exams, and gave no grades.[51] Instead he provided students with a starting list of topics and various reading lists and then essentially turned the class over to them, letting them determine, singly and together, what they would study, as well as how, when, where, and, most important, why. Published in the journal *Daedalus,* in its important Winter 1968 special issue on "the Student Left in Higher Education," Duberman's account of his experiment was one of the texts read at UW in the 1969 TAA seminars on "The University and the Economic System." In its egalitarianism—"Each man can, must, become his own authority," Duberman argues—and its stress on self-initiated and self-directed learning—"The young have their own interests and timetables"—it's a classic story of 1960s pedagogical experimentation.[52] The piece also evokes well the spirit of these alternative classes: the endless bull sessions, the late-night extraordinary meetings, even the free-flowing beer. The piece is remarkable as well for Duberman's honesty in admitting his flaws, failures, and doubts regarding the experiment.

Neill and Duberman weren't, of course, the only educators experimenting with decentered authority at the time. The TAA journal *Critical Teaching* contains several extended narratives of attempts by TAs at UW to turn their classes over to the students. In the second (1969) issue, for example, history TAs Ed Zeidman and Linda Zeidman complain explicitly about the lack of democracy in the contemporary university—"The student still must learn and memorize what teachers tell him, and no one consults him about his needs"—and detail their own experiment in the codesign of a survey course on Roman history: students in that course were provided, in the first half of the semester, with a broad survey of the topic but then encouraged in the second half to follow their own impulses concerning detailed individual study.[53]

English composition was also a site for such experiments. The anonymous English TA who wrote "Reviving Freshman English" for the first issue of *Critical Teaching* was discouraged by the passivity and grade-chasing of UW students and, recognizing his/her own responsibility for fostering that attitude, decided to experiment with "letting the students run their own classes."[54] Although initially dubious, the students' hesitations were "rapidly dispelled":

> The class amazed me because they became genuinely interested in interpretation; they would argue with each other about wording, characterization of

TA Experimentation, 1966–1969

speaker, and authorial bias (point of view). Several students advocated a completely subjective approach; that is, whatever I think the author meant is right, but someone else is equally right in what he thinks. One of the most interesting discussions was raised by the class over this critical approach. Had *I* asked them to discuss the two views, I am quite certain that they would not have become involved, would not have learned anything. But because the discussion came from *within* the class and was characterized by a diversity of viewpoints vigorously supported, it was a truly educative experience—the students learned because they were involved.[55]

The writer closed with an important caution about his/her proposal: "My approach does not call for the TA to stop teaching, to make no preparation for the classes; it merely calls for an abandonment of the role of TA as authoritarian. My workload was doubled, not cut in half, for the TA should consider how he can participate in, although never dominate, the discussions; how he can take issue with points to generate arguments but not win every time. To stimulate discussion, not play Socratic games, to encourage involvement and interest, not alienate the majority, should be the intention of every member of the class including the TA."[56]

An even fuller account of a student-run writing course at UW during this time is Bob Muehlenkamp's remarkable article "Growing Free" from the first (1968) issue of *Critical Teaching;* in fact, it's the most detailed account available of an actual Freshman English class at UW in the late 1960s.[57] Muehlenkamp was a doctoral student in the English Department at UW from fall 1966 to spring 1970, teaching throughout that time and also serving in the high-profile position of president of the TAA during the spring 1970 campus-wide TA strike. At the beginning of spring 1968, he had already taught English 101 two semesters and English 102 one semester and realized, like Martin Duberman (whose article appeared at this time), that he needed to do something different in the course. Muehlenkamp wrote that he had no problem with the official goal of English 102, "to develop skill in writing logical and convincing essays," but he did have a problem with its methods: the focus on style, the use of propriety as the key criterion of performance, the analysis of models, the neglect of self-realized purpose in meaning-making—in short, the tyranny of writing's formal aspects. The student can never improve his writing, Muehlenkamp wrote, if he isn't genuinely responsible for it. Both effective use of rhetorical tools and development of style depend on purpose, and this depends on the student taking responsibility for his own education.

To accomplish all this, Muehlenkamp tried, like "Anonymous" above, to turn the course over to the students, discarding (more or less) the standard syllabus and letting the students work toward the reading and writing course they themselves wanted. So he asked them on the first day of the 1968 spring semester what *they* wanted in the course, in light of their past experiences in such classes—he pressed them for more fundamental objections to the first-semester course (English 101) they had just taken and sent them home to think more about what they would like the second course to look like. He was prepared to discuss educational matters for as long as they wanted, that is, until they decided on a direction. This was important because, Muehlenkamp told the students, they were responsible for what occurred in the course.[58] After discussing this question for the rest of that week and into the next, the class decided that the teacher should pick out from the first six weeks of the departmental syllabus those elements that he thought most valuable, and they'd begin there. "During the third week," meanwhile, "they decided that the existing syllabus, because its limitations in subject matter and organization prevented their being involved in the course, would result in a course of as little interest and profit as their other (composition) courses. So we began to look for other subject matter and methods."

Because the students had already purchased the anthology of short stories specified in the standard English 102 syllabus, they decided to keep working with that—but doing so meant that there would be a month between finishing the anthology and beginning the novels that Muehlenkamp himself had earlier selected, so they began looking for a suitable bridge between the two. They settled on Joyce's *Dubliners:* short stories connected into a novel-like narrative. And they followed the same technique of "evolving ideas and alternatives" for other course matters, increasingly accepting responsibility for the class. Though this might sound disorganized to some, chaos was not the problem. As Muehlenkamp notes, "High school graduates have been so successfully conditioned to receive and accept that they seriously lack imagination. The problem rather is starting students to see through and beyond what they have known and to formulate other alternatives." But they worked at it, he writes, the discussion usually beginning where it had left off at the previous meeting and going wherever the group's interests dictated. Muehlenkamp describes his own role in all this: "As individuals felt more at ease in an atmosphere of cooperation rather than competition and accepted more responsibility for the group, I tried to withdraw myself from the group as leader. For example, the last two weeks on *Dubliners* were run by individual students responsible for each short story. Where discussion lagged, I would not step in to pick up the ball. The ball and plays and goal were all theirs and it was going to be a damned boring game if they didn't play."[59]

TA Experimentation, 1966–1969

Muehlenkamp continues: "We also developed maximum flexibility with regard to composition work." A major purpose of classroom discussion, after all, was to provide content for students to explore, "ideas to go off on." So when class discussion failed to provide a student with ideas he wanted to explore, he could write on whatever else he wanted; "late" papers, therefore, didn't exist because, as Muehlenkamp argues, "we all assumed there was a reason for handing in a paper after the administratively convenient time; assignments were not enforced: since in order for a student to develop his 'style' he had to put everything he possibly could, experiment 'to the fullest,' in every paper, any other kind of paper was obviously useless."[60]

This idea of adopting "maximum flexibility" toward the syllabus brings us to the second structural feature of the alternative freshman composition course English TAs at UW in the late 1960s seemed to be working toward. They were interested not just in the collaborative planning of the course with their students but in a new kind of planning altogether, not just a *democratic* writing class but an *emergent* one as well, involving a curriculum less prepackaged and more sensitive to the life taking place outside the classroom, the personal and intellectual growth of each student, and the unfolding of the group's joint experience across the semester. If the idea discussed above concerns the teacherless classroom, where authority was radically decentered, this one concerns the syllabusless classroom, where the curriculum is every day an open narrative, changing according to the path that the participants, individually and together, pursue. We're talking, in other words, about taking the idea of contentlessness seriously, imagining a curriculum driven not by some prior and externally imposed syllabus, but by the constantly evolving desires of its actual participants, reflecting day-to-day on the meanings they wished to explore and construct, in dialogue with one another and the surrounding world.

In some sense what the teachers were approximating here was a *studio:* a highly flexible pedagogical structure tied to each class's needs and desires at any given moment in the course, with each new activity and its timing determined by what the students themselves were doing, the progress they were making in those activities, and their changing vision of the future, the class radically customized on a day-to-day basis according to background, circumstance, situation, desire, personality, and uptake. As TA Michael Krasny put it in a fall 1969 Departmental Committee meeting, the syllabus for English 102 had to be "flexible" to give it "content," to make it "meaningful."[61] According to this logic, writing teachers needed to take into account the individuality of each student, with all his or her talents, needs, and desires; the unique confluence of different students, with all their different talents, needs, and desires; and, finally, the constantly changing nature of the external world to which all must ultimately respond but that is also an effect of the very activities of such individuals and groups. What all this requires is inordinate flexibility, patience, even bravery, as the teacher surrenders to the unpredictable but relentless flow of events and people, of life itself.

I'll have more to say in the conclusion of this book about how evacuating syllabi in this way often looks to outsiders like you're turning freshman composition into a course about nothing, but some TAs at UW in the late 1960s seemed to realize that radical flexibility vis-á-vis curriculum does not mean emptiness and that the apparently contentless course can in fact be an unusually full one. A good example of this occurred a few days before the U.S. presidential election of 1968, when the English Students Association (ESA) petitioned chair Tim Heninger for permission to use English classes as a space for discussion and debate on current affairs:

> The English Students Association believes that literature should not be studied in an apolitical context. Moreover, ESA believes that the University has the obligation to consider those issues which directly affect the lives of the students.
>
> The national presidential elections will be held on November 5. In accordance with our beliefs, we demand that all English classes devote their entire class hours on the days of November 4 and 5, 1968, specifically to a student led discussion about the significance of these elections and the meaning of the American political process.
>
> This demand is in keeping with the University's tradition of suspending normal operations during periods of great national importance.[62]

What TAs like Bob Muehlenkamp were proposing, however, was not just treating one class meeting, or even a week of meetings, along these lines, but doing so for an entire semester, connecting the course not just to the news of the day, but to the ongoing narrative of the class and the individual students in it. Such a project requires enormous forbearance from the teacher as he or she waits for the students to decide on what *they* want to do in the course, to essentially make it up as they go. These pedagogical virtues are evident in Duberman's history seminar (described above): self-effacement, a sensitivity toward the changing needs of the group and the individuals in it, an ability to adapt to the seeming chaos that results, a willingness as teacher to sacrifice one's singular and original Plan for the many smaller plans that emerge during the semester itself. But Duberman was a tenured professor at the time of his experiment; in doing the same thing but with far less job security and dramatically fewer resources, TAs like Bob Muehlenkamp showed a level of professional maturity, even courage, combined with a youthful openness to unpredictability, that is, in hindsight, quite impressive.

"Becoming a Radical Teacher," written by the pseudonymous English TA Sea Unido for the second issue of *Critical Teaching*, also tells the story of a syllabusless writing course.[63] The piece opens with a critique of the English 102 curriculum, the kinds of reading and writing that students did in the course, as well as its very reliance on a syllabus, "this giving and receiving of lectures and grades, requiring attendance three times a week at a given hour, etc."

> We decided . . . that a syllabus and the lecture system taught submission to authority, acceptance of an authority figure's decisions about topic, method, questions, and answers; that grades taught competitiveness, placed top value on measurable products, and atomized people from each other; and that the three lectures a week taught machine production mentality and submission to bureaucracy. . . .
>
> Within the area of freshman English, many of us tried to synthesize the two [critiques of content and form] by first articulating how writing could be a meaningful tool in the "growth process," and by experimenting in the teaching of writing with different forms. We tried, for example, being non-authoritarian in the classroom, thus creating structurelessness pressuring students to make decisions. We tried replacing grades with student self-evaluation to emphasize student motivation and development and de-emphasize measureable products. In order to thus synthesize and experiment, we had to struggle against the English Department and the ideology underlying the University system.[64]

But the best examples of "emergent" Freshman English classes at UW in the late 1960s are actually from English 101, the old first-semester course that was remedialized in spring 1968.[65] As we saw in chapter 4, the now smaller but liberated English 101 teaching staff issued a remarkable report in early 1969 about their new version of the course that was all about individualization and flexibility in the teaching of writing, especially for disadvantaged students. The TAs argued, for example, that students should be allowed to move between 101 and 102 at the beginning of the semester, as well as among different sections of 101—not only to make sure they were placed in the right course but also to equalize the size of sections and to accommodate different desires among students and instructors for either heterogeneity—"to have a stimulating diversity of backgrounds, interests, motives, abilities, and even ages in the class"—or skill-grouping. They recommended a class size of eleven to eighteen students: "not too large for individualized attention but not too small to make lively classroom discussion impossible."

They also asked that classrooms be made available five days a week at the appointed time so that TAs could meet with their students daily at the beginning of the semester and less often later; the rooms could also be available for individualized instruction and small group meetings. As for a course syllabus, the group wrote that "no common calendar is possible since instruction must depend completely upon the needs of the students, which will vary widely." Similarly, no specific texts were prescribed, so that TAs could be free to experiment in this area. Finally, they asked that all English 101 TAs be assigned to a common office where they would be in close, regular contact with one another and where they could help one another's students when they came for individualized help. As argued earlier, in less than a year, TAs had turned English 101 into an impressively flexible, insistently student-centered course run by a kind of teaching collaborative.

Hand in hand with the teacherless, syllabusless curriculum was an insistence among English TAs at UW in the late 1960s that Freshman English move away from its obsession with the formal evaluation of student writing by teachers and toward informal evaluation by the students themselves, who would thus—it was hoped—be *internally* motivated to write and improve their writing, rather than be driven to do so by external compulsion and fear. The kind of courses described above, after all, could hardly work under a system of grading that seeks, almost by definition, to either index students' individual intellectual and literate journeys to some general, abstract, hierarchically imposed criteria of "good writing" or rank them against one another in a zero-sum competition, a few coming out on top, most lumped together as "average," and the rest left languishing and stigmatized on the bottom. A reformed writing course had to make evaluation, that is, part of the writing process itself—not a terminal mark on students' finished papers, but an activity of continual reflection, testing, and growth, initiated and conducted by the students themselves, and based on *their* desires, capabilities, and time lines.

TA Experimentation, 1966–1969

This antipathy toward grades was tied in the 1960s, at least among radical and leftist educators, to a deeply felt neoromanticism regarding human growth and personal development, itself part of a wider antiauthoritarian, antibureaucratic movement during the times. Thus, Martin Duberman made his 1966 rejection of grades at Princeton a matter of promoting students' personal and intellectual freedom, a step in the direction of *self*-exploration, *self*-discovery, and *self*-validation.[66] Similarly, a document read by participants in the fall 1969 TAA seminar on "The University and the Economic System" described grades as one of two obstacles in the way of "self-development education" at the postsecondary level (the other was degree requirements). "Both persist because of nostalgia for a dying system of liberal education, a mistaken understanding of bureaucratic efficiency, and the sheer inertia of a huge established system."[67]

But "de-grading" the university was also a highly practical matter at this time: early in the U.S. military buildup for the Vietnam War, male students were put at greater risk to be drafted if they had low grade point averages. In fact, the birth of the TAA at UW was connected to TAs' refusal to participate in an educational system in which the evaluation of classroom performance was used in such a deadly manner. According to a TAA history written in the 1970s, "The Association was formed during the spring and summer of 1966 by TA's concerned about the possibility that the grades they gave would affect the draft status of male students. Many TA's did not believe that the function of selecting soldiers should be part of their role as educators and actively opposed the Vietnam War."[68] Grades in first-year composition, in other words, could literally mean life or death for the young men in the classrooms, and TAs did not want such blood on their hands even if a student's academic writing was not yet up to par.

The link between grades and the draft was eventually weakened, but opposition to traditional academic evaluation only increased during this period. In October 1968, for example, a group of English 102 and 181 TAs threatened to withhold the usual six-week reports on freshmen "as a means of protesting the present grading system," as chair Tim Heninger put it in a memo to the TAs meant to persuade them not to do so.[69] But the TAs were not alone in worrying about grades. According to the "Agenda" of William Lenehan's August 21, 1969, memo to Heninger about the previous year's work of the Freshman English Policy Committee, a freshman student appeared before the committee in fall 1968 with "a stack of petitions for a pass/fail system" signed by approximately two thousand students.[70] The committee agreed to pass the petitions on to the

Buck Committee on Grading, which met from the fall of 1968 until the spring of 1971(!) in order to make recommendations on grading reform at UW.[71] The Freshman English Policy Committee, meanwhile, did more than simply accept the undergraduate students' petition.

> The Committee discussed grading extensively, some attacking the current system on both idealistic and practical grounds, others defending [it] on the same two bases. One point of attack on the current grading system was the inconsistency of grading among our sections, leading to unfairness to the student. If the grading system is retained, we must deal with this problem realistically by means of a staff meeting. In the only close vote of the semester, five voted in favor of submitting a report to the Grading Committee advocating pass/fail for English 102 (Krasny, Lenehan, Logan, Sadler, Stroud). Four voted to submit a minority report advocating traditional grading (Feltskog, Rodman, Steward, Thomas).[72]

Importantly, although the four regular faculty members opposed reform of grading in the program, Lenehan himself sided with the TAs, giving them a majority on the issue. Reports from both majority and minority groups were forwarded to the Buck Committee, though it doesn't appear that changes were ever made to grading policy in Freshman English. In fact, as we'll see in the next chapter, during the fall 1969 crisis in English 102, just a few weeks after acknowledging his support for grading reform in the memo to Heninger, Lenehan inexplicably backtracked on the issue, now criticizing TA experiments in grading and portraying them as irresponsible.[73]

If the faculty dragged their feet on reforming the grading system, the TAs worked tirelessly to subvert it. In fact, "de-grading" the classroom was, along with proposals for alternative course readings, one of the two most frequently discussed and adopted pedagogical innovations among English TAs at UW in the late 1960s. TAs developed, in fact, a remarkably shared language for talking about "The Evils of the Grading System," which they accused of conditioning students to accept externally imposed goals, reducing unmeasureables to numbers, destroying student self-confidence, discouraging cooperation among students, objectifying students by categorizing them, generating fear of punishment, fostering dishonesty, creating tension between faculty and students, discouraging initiative and creativity, and supporting the status quo.[74] As English TA Inez Martinez put it in "The Degrading System," a short essay in the first issue (1968) of *Critical Teaching*, grades stood in the way of creating a society of self-realized persons—they reinforced a value scheme that equated acceptability of self with

118

performing better than others. Martinez therefore recommended that UW "remove from the freshman year as much of the threat and fear of the grade point average as possible."[75]

We heard about all this as well in our interviews, when, unprompted by us, our informants emphasized again and again the role of grading in the pedagogical battles of the time. Jean Turner said the "multiversity" of that era was oppressing students, making them docile, and she saw "demystifying" grades as a key goal in her classroom work.[76] Bob Muehlenkamp likewise charged that "the university was pumping out students without caring what they learned. . . . We thought if the university doesn't care, why should we care. For a couple of semesters I gave everyone an 'A,' and I would say at the beginning of the semester: 'Who would like to get an "A"?' Once that was out of the way, the class could focus on learning."[77] Susan McLeod, otherwise more forgiving in her discussion of the Freshman English program and its leaders, admitted that her grading practices were influenced by the ideological and practical critique of conventional evaluation: "This was 1968; how could you *not* give them all A's?" she said, referring to the draft.[78]

At least two fairly extensive accounts of "de-grading" appeared in the TAA's *Critical Teaching* journal. In "Reviving Freshman English" from the 1968 issue, "Anonymous" writes:

> The experiment of letting students run their own class cannot work unless the authority role is eliminated altogether; for as long as the TA retains the power of the grade, no matter where he sits, no matter who leads the discussion, the rules of the game are changed but the name remains the same. So I eliminated the standard grading system, encouraging each student to evaluate and grade himself on the basis of his own standards. Their goals were extremely varied. One girl felt that if she didn't participate in every class, do more "outside" reading, and perfect her already lucid style, she should consider herself a failure. Another student felt that increased class attendance, papers handed in on time, and occasional participation should raise his grade to a "C"! But they were also skeptical that the teacher would really abide by their self-evaluations and showed thereby their complete passivity to the external grading system.[79]

It took until the end of the course, "Anonymous" writes, to convince the students that to be able to formulate one's own standards was a sign of maturity and that "one should always question externally imposed criteria." In another essay from the same issue, "Growing Free," Bob Muehlenkamp writes similarly about how he proposed to students on the first day of his spring 1968 English

102 course that they rigorously question the existing grading system.[80] The students began, he wrote, with superficial ideas, but as they kept the subject open and discussed it, there seemed to be less worry about their own grades, more concern for what grades meant, and a desire to find a meaningful way to evaluate their performance in the course.

At six weeks, however, "we had decided nothing." By that time, to evaluate even temporarily according to the familiar method would have set the class back where it had started. So the students decided that everyone would get an A for their six-week report. A few weeks later, Muehlenkamp writes,

> We decided that the students might most profitably evaluate their own performance. We tried it on individual papers: I would return them with my comments; they would return them to me, with more of their own comments which took into account their rereading of the paper and my comments, and tried to clarify their criteria and put a tab on their performance. Our first efforts were halting. But finally we decided this was the best way to grade for a course in "style": each student had only to come to tell me what grade he was giving himself.

Muehlenkamp writes that he learned three things from this experiment:

> First, the students were reluctant to put that "tag" on themselves: They will sit and talk for a half-hour about their criteria, what they "got out of the course," and so on, but they deeply fear defining, classifying, rating, and hence taking ultimate control of their performance, of making any ultimate decisions about their existence—a reflection of their alienation from themselves. Second, it was for many students a very wrenching experience. . . . As a means toward breaking them from their "reality," I considered this of value. Third, the reasons for deciding the grades were consistent and revealing. Some students could not break from the conditioning, and simply put one of the old tags on what they thought my comments (on their papers) indicated; others had decided that grades were absurd, and that on that basis they would give themselves an A—it meant nothing more or less than anything else to them, but within the "system," it showed that they were "above" it; the most common criterion was degree of movement: students who on any other "absolute" systems would have been rated a "C" were giving themselves A's because of the change in their perception of their own and others' writing: growth was the most significant criterion.[81]

Did Muehlenkamp succeed in teaching his students to think more critically and clearly? Most of his students came to realize, he wrote, that ideas must

TA Experimentation, 1966–1969

be there first, that language can and inexorably will express only what is already there; they became more aware of the subtleties of language and found specific directions in which their own writing would have to go. But much of this, he writes, was due simply to the individual tutoring not possible in mass education. The small setting of English 102, combined with his reforms of the curriculum, made students look more intensely at their goals, question their assumptions more deeply, and articulate more convincingly what they really wanted from such a course.[82]

Bob Muehlenkamp's attempts to "de-grade" his sections of English 102 in 1968 are a good example of a notable feature of the TAs' pedagogical experiments at this time: for all their fiery rhetoric and wild ideas, they revealed, in *Critical Teaching* and elsewhere, considerable self-awareness, even humility, as teachers, acknowledging again and again the uncertainty of their efforts, the incompleteness of their ideas, and the failures that they experienced in the classroom. It's important to acknowledge this, given the way 1960s student radicals are often stereotyped as ardent protestors, always impassioned, fists in the air, voices raised against injustice wherever and whenever it is found. The English TAs we've been discussing here, however pure their ideological self-presentation, were always unabashedly *in process* as thinkers, teachers, and individuals. That's not to say they weren't often bold: in 1968 and 1969, they were clearly trying to do something significant about a course, Freshman English, that most found to be boring, oppressive, and irrelevant and that they wanted to make more meaningful, for both themselves and their students. Unfortunately, they were doing that without the intellectual and professional resources that successful curriculum reform efforts need. They were thus reaching, sometimes arrogantly, sometimes humbly, often clumsily, for something new, something different from what had been handed down to them—something *else* that spoke better to the times and to their students' lives.

They sometimes stumbled, and they were surprisingly ready to acknowledge that. In her "Preface" to the second issue (1969) of *Critical Teaching,* TA Margaret Blanchard wrote:

> Those of us who have tried both authoritarianism and non-direction know that both are effective and that neither works. We know the conflict between letting students do what they want and getting them to do what we want; and we have found no practical way of bridging the gap between the de-

mand for liberal (personal) education and the demand for radical (political) education. We know more intimately our own failures as teachers, the failures of our students, and the failures of the group dynamic, and we know how hard it is to separate one from the other. We know how little we know about the psychology of young adults and the limitations of applying even the most enlightened principles (Summerhillian or whatever) to higher education. But most importantly, we know that none of these problems can be dealt with creatively within the present university system.[83]

But perhaps the most striking—and touching—instance of a TA from this time exposing his or her own failures and uncertainties as a teacher occurs in Bob Muehlenkamp's essay "Growing Free" in the first issue of *Critical Teaching*.[84] There, after telling the story of his attempt to foster student self-evaluation in his section of English 102, he reminds readers of the tendency of innovative teachers to deceive themselves about the success of their experiments:

> The most tangible evidence [of this self-deception] I had was the final "grade discussions" in which they told me what I so desperately wanted to hear: how much they "enjoyed the course," how much they "got out of it"—even, occasionally, how much they "put into it." And I bought it all for a while, until one of them, very upset, tried for an hour on the last day of the semester, to tell me how many were laughing, behind my back, at my naiveté. That and a little distance sobered my view of my success. Nor can I yet be satisfied with saying it was worth it if "at least three, or two, or even one learned from it." I want more than that: I know that as a teacher my existence is value-burdened, I accept that, and want some significant response to it. I of course learned the most.[85]

In the end, wrote Muehlenkamp, he didn't know whether he had succeeded or not. But he knew he had to continue: "For despite the overwhelming difficulties, what is the alternative?"

In their candor and self-criticism, the TAs' reflections on their pedagogical experiments at UW in the late 1960s are reminiscent of what John Paul Tassoni and William H. Thelin describe as the "blundering" that is inevitable in critical pedagogy:

> To be true to their theory, critical pedagogues—in many ways—must be blunderers, teachers who wind up in the middle of difficult, politically charged teaching situations. Blunderers find themselves wondering what happened on certain days or throughout particular courses, not because they are unskilled, but more often because they are not afraid to try new things in their classrooms, the consequences of which—given the complexity of interests and

TA Experimentation, 1966–1969

1. Employing *relevant* materials and topics
2. *Decentering* classroom authority away from the teacher
3. Opening syllabi to *emergent* needs and desires
4. *De-grading* teacher-student communication

Figure 5.2. Pedagogical innovations of English TAs at UW in the late 1960s

concerns of any group of students in any institution at any given moment—are often impossible to predict. The more decentered the classroom and the more the material challenges the status quo, the less the teacherly safety net of the tried and true can be implemented. Empowering students means losing a certain amount of the order and control that characterize a traditional banking-method classroom . . . as student input is crucial to the direction of the course. To be fresh and relevant, texts and assignments that question the norms of society and the academy must constantly be changed, which prevents instructors from relying on their expertise of canonized material to assert stability during classroom activities.[86]

They continue: "Obviously, there are heroic moments in the critical classroom, just as there are in many life situations, but to represent dialogic methods as accurately as possible, the errors need to be a bigger part of the story. Recounting these errors sheds light on learning and allows us to reconfigure teaching as an activity, not as a presentation or a script."[87] Tassoni and Thelin propose, therefore, reimagining critical teachers in a way "that doesn't allow [them] to ignore self-doubt even as [they] continue to believe in what [they] do."[88]

So what, in the end, were the more radical TAs at UW doing with Freshman English in the late 1960s? They were developing a new kind of postsecondary language arts classroom: insistently relevant, thoroughly student centered and student evaluated, eminently flexible—a collaborative, participatory, and emergent curriculum inextricably embedded in its time and place and yet motivated by the timeless, universal goals of freedom and truth (see figure 5.2). Above all, they were trying to make the course *meaningful* so that their students' growth as readers and writers, as human beings, would be more genuine and effective.

In fact, "meaningful" may be the key term for this whole story. In a fall 1969 joint meeting, TA Michael Krasny told English faculty members that, in seeking more representation on the Freshman English Policy Committee, the TAs only wanted to make the syllabus of English 102 more flexible so that the course

TA Experimentation, 1966–1969

itself would be more "meaningful."[89] This reference to meaning is telling: if the English TAs at UW can be faulted for some ill-considered moves during 1968 and '69, they showed throughout this period, unlike their faculty mentors, a consistent willingness to raise the stakes for reading and writing in the postsecondary classroom; an unabashed acknowledgment and acceptance of the power of language; and a deep-seated desire to inspire students to take responsibility for their own compositions, their own educations, and their own lives. They were working to avoid, that is, the situation Janet Emig found herself in while observing high school writers in the late 1960s. Although those students wrote with ease, and produced (at least superficially) flawless essays, at no point, Emig writes, did any of them *ever* ask the questions: "Is this subject important to me?" "Do I care about writing about it?"[90] Given such thoughtlessness, what does it matter if students spell correctly, write complete sentences, and organize paragraphs logically?

The TAs were not the only ones interested in making the writing course more meaningful. In November 1968, UW undergraduate Anthony Elkan complained in a letter to English Department chair Tim Heninger about the policy requiring that his themes be filed permanently in the Freshman English office, denying him the right to his own writing:

> By implication one may assume that the student cares only for the grade he receives and, beyond that, the future of his written work is of no concern to him. Perhaps you are unaware of this phenomenon but some students have respect for their own creative talents and your attitude towards them is most insulting. Eventually students, knowing that whatever work they do will be consigned to a file and, at some unknown date, destroyed, will not bother to write anything of value. It is in this manner that the University stifles all creative effort and encourages mediocrity.[91]

After consulting with Lenehan, Heninger denied Elkan's request, suggesting that, in the future, he make a carbon copy of any themes he wished to keep for himself.[92]

The "meaning" these students and TAs sought from Freshman English can only fully be understood by acknowledging the importance at the time, at least among many leftists, of an unabashedly utopian belief in the possibilities of individual and social progress in the world. It's easy from the vantage point of the early twenty-first century to read the 1960s as the forerunner of our own postmodernism, with its distrust of metanarratives; its predilection for the fragmentary and chaotic; its detachment, irony, and cynicism. But as Marianne DeKoven

TA Experimentation, 1966–1969

has recently shown, even the most radical political and cultural movements of the 1960s were thoroughly dependent on classically *modern* narratives of freedom, truth, and enlightenment.[93] The SDS's early championing of participatory democracy, for example, was as much about the growth and sustenance of the self, about "personal meaningfulness" through direct action, as about any particular social or economic changes in society.[94] And that self, unlike today, was seen by most radicals as unified, as fully capable of resisting the alienations of modern society and progressing toward genuine freedom, both individual and social. In this sense, the teachers I've been trying to recuperate in this chapter, creatures of the "totalizing, hierarchical master narratives of sixties utopianism," were as much the inheritors of modernism as they were the forerunners of our own postmodernism.[95]

DeKoven reminds us also of the importance at the time of books like R. D. Laing's *The Politics of Experience,* which begins and ends (as does Marcuse's equally influential *One Dimensional Man*) with the individual, unified person and his or her potential to change and grow in positive directions.[96] This explains, at least in part, the rather remarkable faith in self-discovery, self-exploration, and self-generating inquiry that animated 1960s classroom experiments like the one Martin Duberman recounts in the Spring 1968 issue of *Daedalus.* There, each student learned, ideally, to assume responsibility for his or her life and education, in the process resisting the passivity of a society of approval seekers. "The chief function of a university," Duberman writes, "should not be, as is currently assumed, the accumulation and dissemination of knowledge, but rather the encouragement of individual growth."[97]

This positive attitude toward the possibilities of freedom, this utopianism regarding the individual's search for meaning, stood in stark contrast, for radical educators of the 1960s, to the imputed neutrality, scientism, objectivity, and disciplinarity of the universities around them. As Ronald Sampson put it in an article read during the TAA's 1969 seminars on the university and the economic system, "Student unrest reflects a fundamental questioning of and dissatisfaction with the very philosophy of knowledge on which the university as an institution is ultimately based."[98] The TAs, from this point of view, were against the supposedly value-free pursuit of knowledge characteristic of the postwar natural, social, and human sciences, epitomized by the excesses of behavioral psychology and sociology: "Since the spiritual life of man is immaterial, immeasureable, non-empirical, spontaneous and free, it is not susceptible to such treatment and is therefore declared to fall outside the proper scope of the science in question."[99] According to Sampson, "The kingdom of this world is the kingdom of power, whereas the kingdom of God is animated solely by love. It is, accordingly, the duty of each of us to do what he can to transform the former into the latter."[100] What results, however, is not a mystical view of life, "but a rational view of the unity and equality of all men, bound to the universe out of which they emerge and to which they return in a common way. We urgently need a renewal of a common purpose based on an authentic religious vision of the true nature and role of knowledge in the service of the community, where the university is seen as a genuine means of transmitting the best in our cultural heritage to the next generation."[101]

Reading, writing, and talking are always key in such projects because, according to radical teachers, it is only through the personal discovery, criticism, and cultivation of *meaning* that true growth can occur and freedom be attained. And this meaning must be radically substantive, that is, something completely different from the mere form that had previously characterized literacy education and language theory. As Bob Muehlenkamp asked about English 102's formal aspects, "How can one want to write about something which has been assigned, within a context which requires that it be written? One cares only when he is responsible—and no freshman is responsible for anything—criteria, assignments, texts, rate of 'development', evaluation, and so on—in his composition course."[102] He continued: "The development of 'effective' writing involves much more than analysis of logical and rhetorical methods: it means having something which you want to say and seeing the necessity of saying it in certain ways. . . . These new goals call for a creative environment in which the student is responsible for his activities: growth requires caring, and caring requires deciding and controlling."[103] In the article "Becoming a Radical Teacher," from the same journal, Sea Unido, a pseudonymous English TA, agreed with Muehlenkamp: you learn skills not by memorizing rules, but by desiring to use the skill.[104]

In their attempt to create a meaningful Freshman English class, as opposed to a formalistic one, the TAs in Madison were, perhaps without knowing it, participating in a wider intellectual narrative, one recounted by Martin Nystrand, Stuart Greene, and Joseph Wiemelt in their 1993 history of post–World War II composition studies. In that story, the post-1971 development of the discipline, fueled in part by epistemological changes from the late 1950s through the 1960s and on, was predicated on the turn away from behavior and form and toward meaning and meaning-making.[105] The present research concerning graduate TAs at UW in the late 1960s, however, suggests, first, that these individuals were largely innocent of the disciplinary developments that Nystrand and his col-

TA Experimentation, 1966–1969

leagues describe; and second, that their "meaning" harbored a holism that would be elusive in subsequent decades, as composition self-consciously sought a theory for itself. The search for meaning in post-1960s discourse studies split between 1970s expressivism and cognitive rhetoric, both of which located meaning in the writer, and 1980s social constructionism, which located it in the reader, or rather, in society itself. The research reported here suggests that that split did not yet exist in TAs' pedagogical work or self-consciousness—to their and their students' credit.

Ira Shor complained in his interview, for example, that the unified search for meaning, growth, and criticism, involving both the individual person and the whole society, that characterized late 1960s critical pedagogy was lost on later compositionists, who tended to bifurcate the student into an inside and an outside.[106] In the late 1960s, Shor told us, the search for meaning in the course certainly included helping students locate "relevant" topics to write about.

> But it was more than that. . . . At that time, it was a package deal. The students' lives and social issues were all a bundle out of which we drew relevant subject matters. And that synthesis was very characteristic of the age. It's worth going back to because I think it was the model that I later understood as Freirian generative themes. So when I began to theorize problem-posing in a deep, more rigorous way, I understood the importance of not splitting the everyday from the social, or the academic from the experiential, or so on. They had to be integrated. But that wasn't the way our field developed. Our field radically split them in the '70s. My stream of critical pedagogy was marginalized by expressivism and cognitivism, which identified subject matter as socially outside personal experience or socially inside personal experience, but not connected.[107]

Still, even Shor, after nearly forty years of his own intellectual growth, in a discipline that itself has changed, may not fully realize the extent to which the "critical pedagogy" of late 1960s freshman composition was far more humanist, far more "utopian," to use DeKoven's word, than that which would emerge, partly under his leadership, in the 1980s—the earlier version could even be called neoromantic, a label that does not fit well the later redaction of critical pedagogy. On this, the English 101 and 102 TAs at UW in the 1968 and 1969 were after something quite different from the designers of, say, the controversial first-year writing course at the University of Texas-Austin in the late 1980s, which was also vehemently opposed by those in power.[108] The Vietnam War–era TAs certainly were committed to unrelenting social and political criticism; but they also seem somehow more forgiving of students' *individual* quests for meaning and more sensitive to both the demands and the potential benefits of letting students themselves, these eighteen-year-olds away from home for the first time in their lives, chart the meaning-making path they would personally engage in.

In fact, one of the great surprises of this research has been the recovery of pedagogical projects that, contra every stereotype of radical teachers in the late 1960s, can*not* be charged with a doctrinaire spirit. Clearly there was an attempt to influence students at this time, and many TAs no doubt saw their task, at least in part, as contributing foot soldiers to the antiwar movement. But the evidence of their actual teaching reveals a different picture, of teachers trying to create in first-year composition a site for each student's own *self*-education and *self*-discovery (though, admittedly, this personal journey was imagined in far more radical terms than what would later be called "expressivism" in the 1970s).

If all this neoromanticism, utopianism, and holism seem too free, too loose, too extreme, we need to remember how extreme the opposition appeared at the time: how formalistic, stale, sterile, and mechanical seemed the old curriculum. If it sometimes looks like TAs of the late 1960s went too far in one direction, we need to remind ourselves how far current-traditionalism had proceeded in the other direction. The "official" Freshman English of this period, even from the point of view of its defenders, was a pedagogy of unabashed error hunting, teacher responding, and model following; it was handbook, anthology, and teacher tyrannized. What the more radical TAs were trying to do was vitalize a course that had been boring both students and instructors to death. What they devised in its place was inordinately flexible in part because the old syllabus had been so rigid.

All this brings us to the final and perhaps most controversial aspect of the TAs' efforts to reinvent Freshman English at UW in the late 1960s. The most radical among them knew that the only way to achieve the curriculum described above, one focused on meaning rather than form, dedicated to the pursuit of personal and social freedom, and requiring therefore a relevant, decentered, emergent, and nonevaluative pedagogy, was by wresting control of the course away from the faculty and concentrating it in the hands of those instructors actually teaching it, who, with their students, were the individuals most committed to it. This required not just flexibility, in other words, but power: raw political power. We need to leave, then, the pedagogical and curricular matters of grading and textbooks and enter the realm of collective action. By the end of the

1968–69 school year, a confrontation with the faculty not just about grading, texts, and syllabi, but also about power, was beginning to look inevitable. For the TAs, the two (curricular reform and administrative power) were clearly intertwined. In her interview, Jean Turner, for example, complained about the faculty in this regard, charging "how little they understood or could accommodate the degree of power we needed to develop the course. . . . If we didn't control the course, it would be rotten."[109]

Wresting such power from the senior faculty, many of whom had exercised unfettered control over the course for decades, would not, however, be easy. As Ira Shor indicated to us, these individuals were used to their superiority, to giving orders and announcing rules that the TAs would then follow: "There was no consultation, really. There was no participation by TAs in policy making, and these things had been emerging as essential to that age, so without consultation or collaboration having any real foundation in the department, it suddenly emerged at a level of sophistication, an organizational level that completely caught them off guard. They were trying to catch up to events . . . trying to get ahead of history instead of behind it."[110] Bob Muehlenkamp confirmed this impression: there were faculty in the English Department at UW who had been there for a very long time: they felt that they owned the department and the curriculum.[111] And TA Pauline Lipman, in a letter to the editor of the *Daily Cardinal* that will be quoted more extensively in the next chapter, also made the political story here central. By late 1969, she wrote, "many TAs had come to understand that only by controlling the courses they teach will they be able to develop genuine education."[112]

But whatever one thinks of the TAs' political tactics in fall 1969, they should be situated in an overall context that also includes intense study, thoughtful classroom experimentation, and self-reflective theorizing—work that is deserving of careful attention even today. In fact, as indicated above, I was surprised when I actually looked at what the TAs were doing at UW in the late 1960s at how little of it seemed stereotypically leftist. Many of the most radical TAs in fact seemed more concerned with freeing the course from constraints than in using it to turn students against the war in Vietnam. Ironically, English Department chair Tim Heninger admitted this in a May 1969 letter to Dean Leon Epstein. The dean had charged the English Students Association with being a haven for "SDS types"; Heninger defended his students: "Their criticism of the English Department and the University is much more pedagogical than political, though several have expressed the intention of applying their criticism to society as a whole and of reaching out into the community."[113] The present investigation of the classroom experiments of English TAs in the late 1960s has led me to the same conclusion: that the TAs' impulse was student centered and surprisingly nondoctrinaire. That said, the evidence also shows how revolutionary many of these TAs were and how far they were willing to go to achieve their pedagogical goals.

What I hope to have shown in this chapter is that for about two years, from the publication of the Mulvihill Report in early 1968 to the abolition of English 102 in late 1969, English TAs at UW engaged in a burst of classroom innovation, pedagogical reflection, and teacher organizing that may well be unique in the history of postsecondary education in this country. They experimented with new materials and techniques, organized and attended their own symposia, read extensively in educational theory, created study groups meant to develop alternative syllabi, conducted research on other writing programs, and reflected thoughtfully and honestly about their own teaching. And they did it all without full-time jobs, without PhD's, without dedicated funding for curricular and professional development, without any significant background in or disciplinary commitment to the courses they were teaching, and without meaningful support from their own faculty.

And their goal in all of this seems to have been, quite simply, to make Freshman English a better course. Despite what the faculty would later say, the TAs do *not* appear to have sought through their reading, discussing, organizing, and experimenting license to do whatever they wanted in the classroom. Nor do they appear, forty years later, to have been incompetent and irresponsible as classroom teachers. For the most part, based on the materials uncovered and memories elicited here, they seem to have worked in a serious, thoughtful, collaborative, surprisingly humble spirit to reform Freshman English at UW. TA Gary Kline's claim in a fall 1969 meeting of the Departmental Committee that "the TAs were capable of bearing the brunt of English 102" was not, in other words, an idle boast.[114] They wanted the responsibility to teach and run this course, and they were training themselves to do that.

Something else is clear by this point. When the developments analyzed in these last two chapters—the English faculty's attempts to withdraw from Freshman English and the English TAs' growing interest in and commitment to that very program—are combined, one is left with a picture of a department digging

TA Experimentation, 1966–1969

itself into a serious institutional contradiction. The faculty, officially responsible for Freshman English, were abandoning it, while their teaching assistants, subordinate in every way to them, were taking it up.

The two trends are related, of course. Faculty could only move to a more research-oriented model of their work if there were enough willing and able graduate students to fill their advanced seminars and teach their freshman- and sophomore-level courses. In other words, although the faculty were still very much in charge of "English" at UW in the late 1960s, managing the institution so that they could pursue their research largely unbothered by general education duties, they were increasingly dependent on graduate students to help them resolve a glaring contradiction in their professional identities. They saddled those students with year-by-year employment contracts, evaluated them *as teachers* largely on the basis of their performance *as students,* and refused to grant them ultimate control over their own classrooms.[115]

The irony in all this was nowhere better expressed than in a letter English chair Tim Heninger wrote to Dean Leon Epstein in April 1969:

> Over the years the English Department has spun its excellence out of itself by developing the teaching assistant system. It is not inaccurate to say that the Department is built upon the teaching assistant system. . . . The graduate program rests squarely upon it, and the graduate program is the greatest attraction for superior staff. If the teaching assistant system goes, and if there is no alternative way of supporting graduate students, the graduate program will shrivel, and the Department will decline in size, and even more in quality.[116]

And yet just a week later, at a stormy meeting of the Departmental Committee, English graduate student Bob Muehlenkamp, president of the UW TAA, complained to the faculty that, a year after the Mulvihill Report, "Teaching Assistants were being used more and more in undergraduate instruction at this institution, though . . . the University had made no specific plans for this eventuality and thus had made no effort at all to protect either undergraduate students or the TAs themselves from so haphazard a development."[117]

Tensions swirled in an especially confused way around a proposed faculty revision of one part of the university's rules and regulations, which read:

> Teaching assistants are entitled to enjoy and exercise constitutional rights and liberties, including academic freedom; and this shall be considered in deciding whether there is adequate cause for dismissal. All teaching assistants, however, are subject to faculty supervision in the conduct of their duties;

TA Experimentation, 1966–1969

and in such academic matters as course content, procedures, and grades, are subordinate to the faculty members whom they assist and who have the responsibility for the teaching of the students assigned to the assistants.[118]

The very language here trapped all concerned in a maze of contradictions and ambiguities.

So the national trends discussed at the end of chapter 3 were playing themselves out in the UW English Department in the late 1960s in a particularly striking way: the complexity of general education was growing at the same time faculty were withdrawing from it in order to concentrate on their own research. For a while, the conflict between these two trends was resolved by granting to graduate student teaching assistants the de facto responsibility to teach general education courses at the freshman and sophomore levels. But it turns out that that grant did not include the right to actually *change* those courses in any meaningful way, that is, to have genuine control over them. The TAs, occupying an increasingly crucial position at the university as teachers, were increasingly frustrated by their inability to implement educational reform; they were also increasingly well organized in their complaints about this state of affairs.

The situation was ripe for a direct confrontation.

6 1969 BREAKDOWN

On the morning of September 25, 1969, Joseph Carr, a second-year teaching assistant (TA) in University of Wisconsin's English Department who had been assigned two sections of English 102 that semester, walked into the office of Professor William Lenehan, director of the course, to say "that he and his students had decided that they could not profitably conform to the texts and approach to English 102 prescribed by the Freshman English Policy Committee," as Lenehan reported the incident later that day in a letter he wrote to his chair, Tim Heninger.[1] Carr himself would put it this way in an October 13 memo written to his fellow TAs: "Like many others, I was disappointed with the selected texts for English 102 and with the seemingly total lack of any substantial changes in the structuring of the course as had been promised in the spring. I therefore informed my classes that they could sell both *College Writing* and *The Shape of Fiction* back to the bookstores as we wouldn't be using them during the semester."[2]

But when a manager at Brown's Bookstore wouldn't take the books back, claiming that he knew which textbooks had to be used by all sections of the course and that TAs weren't allowed to make changes, Carr decided to meet with Lenehan personally to explain the reasons for his actions and inform him that his classes would be using the anthology *Sense of the Sixties* rather than the prescribed books. Lenehan, however, didn't sympathize with Carr's arguments and told him he would be making his actions known to the chair. The following day, Carr received word from Heninger that he wanted to meet with him; he was also told by the manager of University Book Store that he couldn't accept his order for *Sense of the Sixties,* having received a letter that day from Lenehan "asking him to continue just such a policy."[3]

In his letter of September 25 to Heninger, Lenehan praised Carr for "exhibiting honesty and even bravery" in coming to him, and he summarized the reasons the TA gave for thinking he could make unilateral changes in the English 102 syllabus: "that he was competent to judge the best way for him to teach composition and that it was his right—even his obligation—to teach the way he preferred."[4] Lenehan wrote that he thought Carr was an isolated case of TA disaffection but warned Heninger that if the English Department was to take responsibility for Freshman English, it must have some power to guide it:

> The issue is one that has been more or less obvious for the last two years: are we going to enforce the faculty responsibility clause of Chapter 10D or are we going to accept *de facto* individual direction in classes taught by teaching assistants? In fairness, if we are to allow Mr. Carr to follow his conscience, I must assure 101 teaching assistants in English 102 that each is free to follow his conscience. I doubt that under these predictable conditions the English Department, the Curriculum Committee, the Freshman English Policy Committee, or I will be willing to accept responsibility for this course to the University Committee.[5]

Two weeks later, on October 9, Joseph Carr finally met with Heninger to discuss his "discomfort" (Heninger's word, according to Carr) in following the prescribed course structure and content of English 102.[6]

In the memo he wrote a few days later to his fellow TAs, Carr said that, at the meeting with the chair, "questions were raised concerning the extent to which a T.A. is free to determine the structure and content of a course . . . which he has been delegated with the responsibility of instructing."[7] According to Carr, Heninger said that if he couldn't abide by the prescribed structure and content of the course, he should resign, using Chapter 10D as support for this position. "It is Mr. Heninger's position," Carr wrote, "that Mr. Lenehan is responsible for the instruction of English 102 and that any responsibility I feel either towards myself or my students is unfounded. I told him that insofar as I *had* to teach the course that the greater share of that responsibility was mine and that I felt more of an obligation to my students than I did towards the Freshman English Policy Committee."[8] According to Carr, Heninger replied that this was his (the TA's) error: "to think that he *has* to teach any course."[9]

1969 Breakdown

Carr interpreted that last line as a threat of dismissal, a charge Heninger later refuted.[10] But regardless of interpretation, by mid-October 1969, the Carr episode was presenting faculty and TAs alike with a potential impasse regarding the administration of English 102.

A few days later, on October 13, Carr distributed his memo to the department's TAs, summarizing his meetings with Lenehan and Heninger. That day there was to be a previously scheduled TA staff meeting, with Heninger and Lenehan attending, called to fill vacancies on the Freshman English, English 200, and English 201/203 policy committees.[11] On receiving Carr's memo earlier in the day, however, the English TA Steering Committee decided that the agenda of the meeting needed to be changed in order to focus on the threatened dismissal of Carr and on English 102 policy more generally.[12]

The meeting of October 13 is perhaps the key event in the story told in this book, and I will summarize it, and its aftermath, in some detail here.[13] According to the minutes of the TAA stewards, at the beginning of the meeting, TA Eliot Rich, "ad hoc chair of English TA staff meetings," reported to department chair Tim Heninger that the English TA Steering Committee had received feedback from TAs that they preferred the meeting to be chaired by a TA, "so that Mr. Heninger could speak to questions from the floor." Heninger reluctantly agreed. TA Pauline Lipman then moved that the original agenda of the meeting be amended to include "discussion of the Joe Carr case and an evaluation of English 102 policy."

Jean Turner began the discussion by asking Lenehan to "explain the present 102 policy" regarding the different TAs teaching the course. Lenehan replied, according to the minutes, that the course policy was meant to "lay down guidelines and select materials appropriate to carrying out the goal of the course—teaching effective writing effectively. He said further that it was understood that part of the policy was to use a single set of texts." Turner then asked "if Mr. Carr's refusal to use the selected texts constituted a 'deviation' from the policy. Mr. Lenehan answered yes." Michael Krasny, a member of the English 102 Policy Committee, spoke next, saying that his understanding was that neither syllabus nor textbook was mandatory, and he questioned the purpose of the committee: "Was it to set up the course, administer it, or enforce the guidelines?" At this point, Lenehan refused the role of enforcer; he said that Mr. Carr had voluntarily stated to him that he had rejected the texts for the course and that he had felt obligated to report this to Mr. Heninger.

Heninger himself then entered the discussion, accusing the TAs (at least according to the minutes) of using the Carr case as a "handle" for political purposes. He and Carr proceeded next to dispute the details of their October 9 meeting, specifically whether or not Heninger had tried to dismiss Carr from the English 102 staff. At this point, as the minutes relate, a number of TAs stated that they considered it unjust to take punitive action against Carr for changing course texts and that his academic freedom was probably being violated. As one of them put it, "TAs should be responsible for selecting course materials since the TA is ultimately responsible for the conduct and result of the course."[14]

According to the minutes, TA Jeff Sadler then stated that in his opinion the makeup of the English 102 Policy Committee made it impossible for TAs to obtain their objectives in the course, and other TAs complained that the committee had not responded to their criticisms from the previous spring. Lenehan suggested that the committee was "not as recalcitrant as had been alleged, and that we should give it another try."

Here, Heninger entered the fray again. He stated, according to the minutes, that he felt "that the important thing was to maintain a flexible equilibrium between the freedom of the TA in the classroom and the responsibility of the faculty for the course." Tim Sloan and other TAs claimed, however, that the equilibrium's balance was weighted against the TAs and their students. Connie Pohl, for one, thought that the textbook *College Writing* was politically biased, and she objected to teaching it. Heninger then asked the body "if they felt their academic freedom was being violated. Almost everyone responded 'yes.' Mr. Heninger then concluded that if the TA system as a whole can not ensure academic freedom for TAs, then it is probably archaic and should be done away with." The writer of the minutes added, in parentheses, "Groans were audible here."

The meeting now reached its climax. TA Gary Kline moved "that the faculty be instructed to establish a Committee to administer English 102 composed of 7 TAs and 1 faculty advisor."[15] Heninger pointed out that the faculty, by statute, could not relinquish its responsibility for the 102 course. But TA Steve Groark replied that, since the Curriculum and Departmental committees had veto power over the actions of any 102 policy committee, the faculty could in no sense be said to be relinquishing their responsibility. A vote was taken, and, according to the minutes, Kline's motion passed 41–17.[16]

The final paragraph of the minutes is chilling in its depiction of a rupture within both the Freshman English program and the department as a whole, between faculty administrators, on the one side, and graduate student teaching assistants, on the other: "Someone moved that we recess to a later date to elect members to the English 200 and other committees. Mr. Heninger said that he would be calling no more English TA staff meetings because he had obviously lost control of his staff, because there were not enough TAs present, and because the TAs had acted against his advice. Adjournment was moved and passed."[17]

The meeting was a watershed moment in the history of freshman composition at UW. It clearly distressed both Heninger and Lenehan, the former especially. And it was remembered long into the future: when asked in a 1976 interview about the abolition of Freshman English at UW in the late 1960s, English professor and longtime Freshman English Policy Committee member Robert Doremus said that it came about, in part, because the chair had been turned off "by a TA takeover at a meeting."[18] I have also located a handwritten note, from Heninger himself, written just three days after the October 13 meeting, and right after a previously scheduled meeting with the dean of the College of Letters and Science, in which he wrote, "I broached the TA problem, 'to alert the Dean in case the English Department comes to feel that it can no longer take responsibility for English 102.'"[19]

On October 20, Heninger communicated his frustration about the TA meeting in a long memo to the Departmental Committee.[20] After informing the faculty of the proposal to increase the number of TA members on the Freshman English Policy Committee from four to seven and to decrease the number of faculty from four to one, he wrote, "It is clear that the teaching assistants are demanding complete control of English 102 with no faculty supervision, that the newly constituted English 102 committee proposed in the motion would allow each teaching assistant to do exactly as he wished with his students, and that the teaching assistants consider this motion, at the very least, an impasse."[21] He summarized the Joe Carr case for the other faculty members and said that, in the October 13 meeting, "The charge was made that Mr. Lenehan and I had not given him [Carr] license to do as he pleases with his students; his academic freedom had been violated."[22] Heninger continued, quoting the university's rules and regulations:

> The issue as I see it, and as I expressed it to the teaching assistants on October 13, is simply stated. The faculty in the English Department has responsibility for teaching English 102; the teaching assistant, however, like any teacher, must have opportunity to develop pedagogical methods that he personally finds most effective. There must be an equilibrium between the responsibility of the Department for instruction in the course and the freedom of the teaching assistant in his classroom. In the last few years this point of

equilibrium has moved considerably toward greater freedom for the teaching assistant. But the motion passed in the TA staff meeting on October 13 asks that the faculty relinquish its responsibility for English 102 and holds out the promise that each teaching assistant have complete autonomy. The English Department cannot accede to such a request.[23]

This language about responsibility and autonomy, evident in Heninger's comments here, in the earlier memo Joe Carr wrote to his fellow TAs, and in debates between English faculty and TAs as early as the fall 1968 discussions about TA participation in course committees, had become by this point a key locus of contention between the two groups, but it did not play out exactly as one might expect, with faculty pressing for "responsibility" and the TAs for "autonomy." This became clear in a meeting between TAs and faculty the following week.

On October 28, 1969, the Departmental Committee met to discuss the English 102 crisis for the first time with, in an extraordinary change in procedures, TAs present.[24] Heninger opened that meeting by resolving the TAs' October 13 motion "into what he considered to be its central matter, involving five questions":

1. Can the English Department legally accede to the motion passed by the teaching assistants in the October 13th staff meeting? Do not statutes of the State of Wisconsin and legislation by the Madison campus faculty prevent the reconstitution of the Freshman English Policy Committee to include only teaching assistants?
2. Whether or not the English Department can legally accede to the motion, would the Department *want* to relinquish responsibility to this extent?
3. Can the guidelines for English 102 in the present structure of the Freshman English Policy Committee be loosened sufficiently to solve the problems implied by the motion before us from the teaching assistants?
4. If the guidelines were loosened, would the reality of the situation—that is, the present practice of teaching assistants in the classroom—make it possible for the English Department to assume responsibility for English 102?
5. Given present circumstances, can the needs of students be met by a course such as English 102, or should some other means of meeting these needs be devised?[25]

Concerning the first question, Edgar Lacy read from Wisconsin state statutes that gave the regents ultimate power to regulate instruction at UW, a power that was then delegated by statute to the faculty. "Professor Lacy added that the regents assume that the faculty exercise very tight control over the TAs."[26]

1969 Breakdown

Here, the meeting opened up to include the TAs, and the atmosphere quickly became antagonistic, at least according to the minutes of the meeting. TA Tom McGlinchy asked which departmental committees had oversight of English 102. Heninger provided information about the Freshman English, Curriculum, and Departmental committees, but then asked the TAs what the intention of their motion could be "when it excludes faculty members from the Policy Committee of English 102," adding that "the thrust of the motion was to give TAs complete freedom." Lenehan added that this interpretation of the motion was confirmed by "the spirit of the TA meeting in which it was drafted." But Gary Kline, the TA who had drafted the motion, noted "that he did not feel that the motion was asking for autonomy. The intent, he pointed out, was to show that the TAs were capable of bearing the brunt of English 102. If the motion were passed, he added, it would result in a group of TAs functioning under the Departmental and Curriculum Committees, and not totally running the Freshman English program."[27]

In response to a faculty question about why the TAs wanted seven of their own members on the committee but only one faculty member, Kline claimed:

> The TAs had not wished to secede . . . but only that they would make up a curriculum, with the help of a faculty advisor, who would report the resolutions of the seven TAs to the Curriculum Committee, who would in turn report to the Departmental Committee. . . . Their motion should not be interpreted as a bid for autonomy, but rather as a desire to work within the structure. . . . All the TAs really wanted was that they be allowed experimentation with English 102.[28]

According to the minutes, "Professor Pochmann then noted that further questioning was futile."[29]

At this point Professor Standish Henning proposed that the discussion move to the second question; but the issue of autonomy persisted, with faculty complaining that the TAs' motion amounted to a bid for complete freedom in the course. TA Eliot Rich countered that the motion should be seen rather as about "pedagogy and not autonomy." TA Bob Muehlenkamp reminded members that in the April 26, 1969, TAA agreement with the university, two of the points considered "bargainable" were "(1) work loads and (2) participation in educational planning"; Heninger replied that "course content was not bargainable."[30] According to the minutes, more discussion followed on the legality of the TAs' motion and the extent to which any TA-dominated committee would feel bound by the Departmental Committee or any other faculty committee. Heninger said,

1969 Breakdown

according to the minutes, "that the new committee formed of TA's would not agree to anything contrary to its own ideas, and that if the Departmental Committee disagreed with them, they would secede."[31]

It was TA Steve Groark who this time took up the charge, replying that the TA motion was only about "asking for action and interest on the part of the faculty" and that it was not an ultimatum.[32] TA McGlinchy agreed and suggested that perhaps the phrasing of the motion was "unfortunate." Another TA repeated that secession "was not the issue at all."

There followed a discussion about the Freshman English Policy Committee and its work the previous spring, in particular whether or not the TAs on the committee truly represented their peers. In response to a question about the textbooks chosen for the course, Lenehan said that the decision had been made by the whole committee and that the TAs in fact had chosen two of the three. But one TA member of the committee, Jeff Sadler, complained that the decisions had been reached primarily on the basis of the color, thickness, and cost of the books, a claim that Joyce Steward staunchly refuted. "The texts were chosen on the basis of their adequacy to fit the course concept," she said. Like Lenehan, she argued that in at least once case, that of the fiction text, the faculty members on the committee had been convinced of its value by the TAs: "She had thought the TAs and faculty [were] in good agreement, but now knew she was wrong."[33]

At this point, Michael Krasny, another TA on the Freshman English Policy Committee, summarized what he felt was the TAs' vested interest in participating actively in course planning and execution for English 102, stating "that one of the freshman's worst problems was Freshman English, and that the TAs were faced with the problem of trying to make it meaningful. They had attempted, he noted, to turn it into a writing course dealing mainly with the principles of writing. He said that it was necessary to have a flexible syllabus in order to put content into the course, but thought the syllabus should be only a guideline."[34] Krasny felt that "flexibility should be guaranteed to TAs, since they had full responsibility for teaching the course."[35] But Lenehan countered that no criticisms of the new syllabus had been offered before the present semester started and that it was too late in the second week of September to change course requirements: "The time for criticism was last year when the course was being constructed."

An exchange between TA Ira Shor and chair Heninger ensued, Shor arguing, as Muehlenkamp had previously, that educational planning *was* a proper subject for collective bargaining between the TAs and the university; he also complained that Heninger had already committed the Departmental Committee to a particular position with regard to the matter and that neither bargaining nor discussion was now possible. In reply, Heninger said that he "saw the success of the Freshman English policy-making committee as intentionally being scuttled by a small cadre of TAs"; Shor countered that Heninger was being unfair to the TAs "by raising the spectre of anarchy and conspiracy" and that the word "scuttling" was too strong.[36]

TA Ron Dewoskin then asked how many faculty taught English 102 and how qualified the TAs were who taught it. Professor Walter Rideout answered that "few faculty members teach English 102, and that most TAs do it very well, but he added that it was necessary to distinguish that while TAs teach 102, faculty members are responsible for it."[37] Discussion followed about why TAs in English 200 could choose their own texts, but TAs in English 102 could not. Lenehan replied that, although it would present problems for ordering, such an arrangement was a possibility, but there had been no demand for it from either faculty or TAs and that the idea had not been raised last spring when the policy committee was deliberating about the upcoming year's syllabus. Somewhat confused discussion followed, with at least one TA arguing that he for one did *not* want to surrender his rights to seven TAs and asking that the department continue to give direction for the course.[38]

Professor David Siff, an untenured assistant professor and well-known campus leftist, whose contract nonrenewal would be made public at the same time the department was grappling with English 102, argued next that the problem was neither the Freshman English Policy Committee nor its composition—the success of the English 200 experiment proved that—but the entire system. He claimed that the faculty had "abandoned its teaching [and] fallen back on the prerogative of power."[39] He concluded that "the entire issue should concern only pedagogy and not legalistic principles, and that it should be realized that the present program simply does not work and that a new program should be begun." Heninger replied that this was too harsh, that there had been an effort "to draw in TAs, and get their opinions." According to the minutes, Professor Howard Weinbrot then argued that he had seen little flexibility in similar programs at other universities and that "inflexibility was necessary here in order to give the TAs discipline, and in order that they learn how to teach boring classes. He also added that it might be good for them to be given a genuine role as assistants rather than being given their own classes."[40] But TA Eliot Rich responded "that he thought that there were among the TAs those qualified as much as any faculty member."[41] Professor Reuben, like Siff an untenured assistant professor, noted that "senior people should also be actively involved in the course."

But time was now up. Professor Heninger announced that the committee would reconvene the following week at 4:30 in the same place, but Professor Curran formally questioned the advisability of repeating what had just taken place. When voted on, twenty-eight faculty members supported her challenge, and eighteen did not: "Professor Heninger therefore announced that the next meeting of the Departmental Committee would be at 4:30 pm, Tuesday, November 4, in 360 Bascom, *without TAs being present.*"[42]

According to the minutes of the October 28, 1969, Departmental Committee meeting, two weeks after their apparent coup d'état of the Freshman English program at UW, the English TAs were still seeking to increase their participation in planning and administering Freshman English. They were also now making more clear their willingness to do so *within* the system of faculty-led departmental committees. The meeting seems to belie, in other words, any notion that the TAs were after complete freedom to do whatever they wanted in Freshman English, that they were trying to wrest all power from faculty and assume it themselves without restraint.[43] It's also clear from that meeting, and its aftermath, that not all TAs were equally radical in their interpretation of "course planning" as it related to English 102.

Soon after the October 28 meeting, in fact, a group of eleven English TAs distributed their own memo, titled "A Third View," to departmental members.[44] The memo argues against both Heninger and his fellow faculty members, on the one hand, and the department's TA leaders, on the other, attempting to stake out a middle ground, or "third view," between them: "First of all we would like to state our belief that the issue of 'complete autonomy' is a false one, a red herring formulated by a few T.A.s and a few faculty members in the heat of parliamentary debate." Second, answering complaints from Heninger and TA leaders alike about attendance at TA staff meetings, they argued that the refusal of a majority of TAs to participate in lengthy and chaotic staff meetings was a sign not of apathy but of sanity. "Finally, we feel, at the very least, insulted at the efforts of both Mr. Heninger on the one side and of some T.A.s on the other to place us in an ideological position with which we have no sympathy," complaining that they had been cast as either "company men" or "union agitators" when they themselves felt like neither: "This does not mean that we do not see a need for some change in departmental policies; most serious T.A.s would be delighted to make a contribution to a reasoned process of planning."[45]

If a moderate resolution to the crisis seems to have been within reach, the momentum nonetheless swung toward greater confrontation, conflict, and extremism. That may be because by the end of October 1969, just two weeks after the Carr episode, the faculty members most directly responsible for English 102 —professors Lacy, Lenehan, Thomas, and Steward—had all lined up against it. I have found in the department's files, for example, the following typewritten statement, dated November 1, 1969, most likely written by Lacy:

On April 1, 1968, the Department of English reported to the University Faculty that, because "the great bulk of entering freshmen have profited from stepped-up high school training and are not receptive to more than one semester of college composition," these students should be assigned, on the basis of placement tests, to English 102 rather than to English 101 (followed by English 102).

The Department now feels that the needs of most students would be best served by shifting to each undergraduate department the responsibility for offering whatever training in composition, if any, a department may decide is needed by its undergraduate majors. In order to ensure that those students who need and may profit from additional instruction in composition will be selected to receive this instruction, the Department of English will be glad to make suggestions and to help departments develop procedures. But at the end of the current academic year the Department of English will cease to offer Freshman English as it is now constituted.[46]

The rest of the faculty would not have to wait long to hear the motion and vote on it.

But first, there was the next Departmental Committee meeting, held on November 4, 1969, this time without TAs present. Heninger opened this meeting by recapping the five questions he had introduced the week before, claiming that the first three had been discussed then and that the faculty now needed to consider the fourth, which concerned "the actual practice of teaching assistants in the classroom."[47] Professor William Lenehan spoke to this issue first: he began by considering the possibility of "increasing the flexibility of 102, so that it might more closely resemble English 200." He noted, however, that the majority of TAs, "while gaining competence in matters dealing with literature, had neither the commitment nor knowledge basic to teaching composition and rhetoric without help from faculty advisors." This lack of interest and training was, according to Lenehan, resulting in too much variation in the course, which was "ultimately destroying" its value. As the minutes note, he therefore recommended "that Freshman English no longer be offered in its present form after this year."[48]

Ednah Thomas spoke next (it's hard not to suspect that she, Lenehan, Heninger, and Lacy had rehearsed their parts beforehand). She presented what she saw as two possible alternatives to Lenehan's proposal. "The first alternative," according to the minutes, "was to keep the present system, an idea she found impossible due to T.A. feeling that they were being exploited. The second alternative," she continued, "was to give in to the demands of the T.A.'s, but she [thought this was] infeasible due to the lack of training in the T.A.'s, both with rhetorical theories on the university level, and the latest rhetorical theory found in high school. She concluded that Professor Lenehan's solution was the only way out of the present predicament."[49]

Professor J. J. Lyons spoke next, saying that he was aware of a planned "phased withdrawal" from the freshman composition program, referring apparently to the spring 1968 reduction of the Freshman English requirement from two semesters to one. He asked how many students were currently exempt from 102, and Lenehan answered that 1.0–1.5 percent of students were currently exempt. Lyons then asked if there was "a technical need" for the course. "Professor Lenehan," the minutes note, "asserted that he thought there was a need, but that judging from the high grades given by T.A.'s, it was evident that his staff did not agree." Lyons then asked about the possibility of using the TAs to teach writing to "underprivileged students."[50] Lenehan agreed that English 101 could be improved and perhaps expanded, but that it would never employ the current staff of 150 TAs. At this point, Ednah Thomas mentioned increasing the use of the Writing Clinic.

Professor Lacy continued on this point of a "phased withdrawal" of Freshman English at UW, noting that "College English had advised getting rid of freshman English, and that what now should be considered is the establishing of new approaches to taking care of poor writers. He noted that other major departments should follow the example of the College of Engineering and set up their own programs to take care of their students."[51] Questions were then raised "concerning the psychological impact such a move might have on T.A.'s." Professor Donald Rowe asked whether it was the confrontation of the prior week that had caused the "present situation," implying that the notion of a long-planned and historically inevitable withdrawal of the department from Freshman English was an exaggeration. To this, Lacy replied that "the present ideas had been in the works for the last two years," an assertion that Heninger confirmed.

Madeleine Doran then asked whether the abolition of English 102 would need to be approved by any college or university committees, but Lacy replied that "all the English Department need say is this: the course will no longer be given." Professor Eric Rothstein raised the question "of whether the present ac-

1969 Breakdown

tion might be precipitous, considering the T.A. motion, and wondered if deviation from the course by T.A.'s was so great as Professor Lenehan had implied." To this, Lenehan gave two examples of deviation—"one of which," the minutes report, "involved a T.A.'s shuffling cards for grades, another involving a T.A.'s discussing the 'pigs' for three solid lectures, causing some of the students to become very upset of the conduct of the instructor." Lenehan noted, however, that "usually the deviation was the result of sheer incompetence, the T.A.'s not knowing how to teach composition."[52] At this point, time was called and the meeting adjourned.

Lenehan's two examples of deviation are both significant. TA experimentation with grades—refusing to grade students, distributing grades randomly, giving all students As—is the category of classroom practice from this period for which we have the most evidence; if the example given by Lenehan is extreme (and unverified), it is nonetheless clear from chapter 5 that many English 102 TAs were in fact refusing to grade their students according to the long-established conventions of the Freshman English program. What is interesting about Lenehan's mention of it here, however, is that he was himself on record as supporting pass-fail grades in the program.[53] It is true, though, that grading was a source of contention between faculty and TAs and that the former generally saw the practices of the latter as irresponsible.

As for Lenehan's example of a TA "discussing the 'pigs' for three solid lectures," a central complaint of the senior faculty during this crisis was that the TAs were infusing curricula meant to impart neutral literacy skills with irrelevant and even dangerous ideological content. For example, though it was not recorded in the department's official minutes, the *Daily Cardinal* noted on November 21, 1969, that at an English Departmental Committee meeting that fall (it must have been the one held on November 4 or 11), "one committee member read an essay on critical teaching by TAA President Bob Muehlenkamp and then suggested to the faculty that English 102 was being used to politicize students."[54] In the last chapter, I tried to gauge with some care this question of the TAs' alleged indoctrination of their students.

Meanwhile, at the next Departmental Committee meeting, on November 11, 1969, the faculty discussion regarding English 102 was comparably short.[55] Edgar Lacy now formally moved that the department abolish English 102, reading the report of April 1, 1968, from the Department of English to the university faculty concerning the assigning of students to English 102 rather than 101 and noting that it was now felt "that the student was best served by individual departments, and that the English Department would help set up the program in these individual departments."[56] He then read a formal proposal to abolish English 102, an earlier version of which is quoted in draft form previously.

At this point, Frank Battaglia, an untenured assistant professor in the department, proposed that deliberation be deferred until TAs were consulted, a countermotion that would not be formally taken up until the end of the meeting. In the meantime, discussion ensued about the reappointment of eligible TAs to other courses. Professors Siff and Kimbrough argued, with Battaglia, for giving TAs a chance to consider the proposal first. Heninger replied, however, that "he did not feel that the T.A.'s were really after flexibility so much as they were after control of the Freshman English program." Professor Roache joined Siff and Kimbrough in asking "that the department not act too hastily."[57] To questions about the merits of Freshman English in general, Lenehan "noted that the present program was simply unworkable; that the students were not motivated to write on subjects in which they were not interested, and that most of the TAs were not teaching composition." Professor Evett noted, however, that "the present move" on the part of the Departmental Committee "looked irrational . . . [like] a move to cut off T.A.'s because of their motion [of October 13]." But Professor Pochmann responded, according to the minutes, that "Freshman English was not a university level course and should be abandoned." Discussion then returned to Battaglia's "sense of the meeting" proposal, "that no final determination on the question of substantive alteration of the Freshman English program shall be taken without a meeting of the Departmental Committee with departmental T.A.'s." By a vote of 12 to 34, the proposal was rejected and the meeting adjourned.

The denouement of the crisis occurred at the following week's Departmental Committee meeting, on November 18, 1969.[58] But before the meeting even began, there was drama: difficulties preventing nonmembers from attending (the *Daily Cardinal* reported that five TAs were barred entrance) required not only moving to a new location, from Bascom 360 to 312, but also securing a police presence at the door to forestall further delays.[59] The start of the meeting was thus delayed almost forty-five minutes so that, in Heninger's words (as reported by the secretary of the committee), "the integrity of the meeting" could be maintained.[60] By the time the meeting started, there were forty-four faculty members present, but some key junior members—Battaglia, Siff, Roache, and possibly others—had decided to boycott the meeting in support of the barred TAs.[61]

When the agenda turned to a "discussion of Freshman English," however, Lenehan asked that discussion be postponed "because of the emotional atmo-

1969 Breakdown

sphere of the Departmental Committee."[62] But chair Heninger and former chair Rideout urged that discussion proceed on the formal proposal, introduced the previous week by Lacy, "to abolish English 102 and 181." Professor Heninger then gave "what he considered to be the four main arguments brought up thus far in the debate about whether or not English 102 should be abolished":

> The first concerned pedagogical arguments on whether English 102 was necessary. Professor Heninger noted that two years ago it was decided that Freshman English should eventually be abolished, and that this was a national trend. The second argument concerned the moral commitment of the department to the present Teaching Assistant staff. Professor Heninger noted that every effort was being made, with the Dean's support, to keep TAs next year who merit reappointment and who are eligible for reappointment. The third argument concerned departmental dealings with the TAA. Professor Heninger noted that the time would come when the English Department must bargain with the TAA, but that the Department must go ahead with its operation and not wait until this time. The fourth argument involved the commitment of the English Department to other departments on the campus to help rectify student deficiencies in writing. He noted that the argument for abolishing E102 included the feeling that the English Department should continue to help other departments, but that the English Department has no more commitment to teach English composition than any other department.[63]

Edgar Lacy then distributed his motion again, asking that the department approve it in principle because "students have improved in their writing upon entering college, and that TAs are less willing to teach composition and are also less willing to accept instruction in how to teach it."[64] Lenehan added "that by diminishing the number of students who take composition courses, more intensive training could be given to those who most need the help. As for others, he added, their improvement is not significant enough to justify the expenditure involved in maintaining English 102. He also noted that the Writing Clinic, while small at the moment, would be increased, never to the size of English 102, but larger than present, and it would be staffed by TAs."[65]

At this point, Professor Henning moved that debate be stopped and the proposal tabled until the following week, "at which time thirty minutes would be given to discussion of the proposal, after which the committee will vote on it." But before the committee could vote on that proposal, Professor Kimbrough brought forth a carefully prepared substitute motion, which was read to the committee:

1. The members of the Departmental Committee are unable to accept for present consideration the resolution of 13 October 1969 which has been forwarded by the Chairman from the Teaching Assistant Staff because we believe that the business of the Department of English should be—in fact, can only be—conducted when a spirit of cooperation, trust, and good will prevails among all committees, areas, and echelons of the whole department.

2. Within this spirit, the Departmental Committee invites the Teaching Assistant Staff to reconsider its resolution of 13 October, and to elect teaching assistants to the various existing departmental policy committees in order that members of, and groups within, the whole department may submit through those committees proposals for the reconstitution both of the committees themselves and of the courses for which they are responsible.

3. The Departmental Committee sincerely solicits the opinions, advice, and recommendations of teaching assistants with regard especially to English 102 because some members of the Departmental Committee feel that the course no longer serves a useful purpose as presently constituted.

4. The Departmental Committee further requests the Chairman to call a meeting of the Teaching Assistant Staff in order to present this motion for its consideration and discussion. We hope that the Staff, in turn, will invite the members of the Departmental Committee to be present to answer questions and to make statements when recognized, but not to make motions or to vote.

The vote to substitute Kimbrough's motion for Lacy's, however, failed (6 yeas, 26 nays, and 6 abstentions). Professor Henning's motion to table Lacy's proposal for a week also failed, though by a much closer vote, 17–20. With all alternative measures now exhausted, the faculty finally voted to call the question on Lacy's motion to abolish English 102 and 181, effective at the end of the 1969–70 academic year. It carried, 27–8–4, and "the meeting was adjourned."

The department had now officially voted to do away with English 102. Given its spring 1968 move remedializing English 101, it had therefore effectively—and unilaterally—abolished the university's seventy-year-old Freshman English requirement and the two-semester course that fulfilled it. In a memo to English Department TAs distributed the next day, November 19, 1969, Lenehan confirmed all this: "At the meeting of November 18, the Department proposed that, at the end of the current academic year, the English Department cease to offer E102 and E181."[66] He assured eligible TAs that they would be reappointed for the 1970–71 academic year.[67] He also provided some "historical background" for the decision: in 1968, he wrote, the department had reduced composition training for most students from two semesters to one because the bulk of freshmen had profited from stepped-up high school training:

> We feel that the writing ability of entering freshmen has continued to improve and that the difficulty of motivating freshmen to improve their writing skills has increased. The Department decided that the area in which the student would be willing and able to do his best writing is that subject matter to which he has made a commitment—his major field of study. Therefore, we suggest that individual departments assume the responsibility for the writing proficiency of their students.[68]

Lenehan affirmed the department's continued responsibility for students with serious writing deficiencies. And he mentioned other factors involved in the abolition of 102: "One is that our teaching assistant staff is academically prepared for and committed to the teaching of literature, in such a course as English 200, rather than composition and that its efforts are better expended in teaching literature."[69]

Less than a week later (on November 24, 1969), the minutes of the UW College of Letters and Science Faculty Meeting record the following notice:

> Dean Kleene reported that the *Department of English* voted on November 18 to *cease to offer English 102 and English 181,* effective at the end of the current academic year, although it proposes to continue to test entering freshmen in order to assign English 101 to the small number who need the remedial course.
>
> The Dean stated that he will ask the new Curriculum Committee for an early report on what needs to be done with respect to the freshmen English requirement.[70]

So, after nearly three-quarters of a century of unbroken and often distinguished history, UW's two-semester Freshman English course, a linchpin of the university's general education program, the sponsor of tens of thousands of credit hours of undergraduate instruction every year, and the employer of hundreds of English PhD students, was effectively dismantled by a few faculty members in less than eighteen months, the elimination of the second-semester course alone taking less than six weeks from the beginning of the fall 1969 crisis to its conclusion. I'll return to the events of late 1969 in a moment, but first I want to try to explain why these professors, at this time, in this way, abolished the largest, oldest, and arguably most important educational project in their own department.

As we've seen, the faculty themselves, especially Edgar Lacy, William Lene-han, and Tim Heninger, *officially* explained their move by a two-part argument about students' writing skills and needs that was fully in place by the end of October 1969, as evidenced by Lacy's November 1 draft motion for abolishing English 102. That argument went like this: first, freshmen writing skills at UW no longer warranted a universally required general composition course; and second, what instruction students still needed at UW was better provided by their major departments. Let's briefly recap and reassess the validity of these two arguments.

In chapter 4 I raised several issues with the "improving skills" argument. First, it's not at all clear that the writing skills of incoming freshmen really were improving at UW during the 1960s. Lacy's spring 1968 evidence is not exactly overwhelming, and his claims were largely met with either silence or derision from his faculty colleagues and TA staff. Second, if skills were improving, it's more likely that the change was caused by the university simply taking advantage of the increased competition for college admission among prospective students in the 1960s than by any improvements in the high school teaching of reading and writing. Third, regardless of the cause, if in fact UW freshmen in the late 1960s were "better" writers than freshmen of prior years, the program could have responded with a more challenging first-year course rather than simply eliminating it altogether.

At the same time, there does appear to have been a modest trend in the late 1960s and early 1970s toward reducing the Freshman English requirement in U.S. colleges and universities.[71] But if this trend explains part of the story I've been telling here, it certainly doesn't explain the entirety of what happened. After all, by the early 1970s, following the period of alleged nationwide aboli-tionism regarding freshman composition, three-quarters of universities and colleges in the United States still had at least a one-semester first-year writing requirement, according to Ron Smith's 1974 survey.[72] By contrast, at UW, where thousands of students and hundreds of instructors were affected virtually over-night, the Freshman English requirement went from two semesters to none in less than two years—the speed and totality of this change cannot be explained, I believe, by reference to national trends.[73]

As for the second argument advanced in 1969 to support the abolition of English 102 at UW, the claim about the responsibility of other departments to teach writing to their majors, this one was entirely new. The first signs of it in the historical record, in fact, are Lacy's November 1, 1969, draft motion and the oral comments he made during the November 4 Departmental Committee meet-ing. Lacy and Lenehan seem to have come to this argument, in other words,

1969 Breakdown

quite late, one reason I have for questioning the depth of their commitment to it. If they were well rehearsed by late 1969 regarding the argument about students' rising skills, having had nearly eighteen months to practice it, they did not fully articulate the argument about "writing in the disciplines" until February 1970, three months *after* the November 18, 1969, vote to eliminate English 102.[74]

Nonetheless, in the abstract, the argument deserves our attention—especially in light of the fact that, on this score, Lacy and Lenehan were actually ahead of the curve in terms of educational trends. The critique of a single writing course for all students across the university, taken early in their postsecondary careers, and promising to transmit general skills in writing, applicable across contents and contexts, has become prevalent in composition studies over the last generation, and the idea that students should receive at least part of their education in written communication from within their own major fields of study is now common. My difficulty with that critique here is its tardiness: it simply appears too late to be, in my opinion, a true cause of the faculty's fall 1969 actions. If the argument against the very idea of a first-year general education writing course remains compelling (though by no means dispositive) in discussions today, in the debate over English 102 at UW in the late 1960s, it seems post-hoc, an after-the-fact justification for a decision that was motivated by other, unstated reasons.

Something, in other words, seems to be missing from the department's explanation for remedializing English 101 and eliminating English 102 in the late 1960s. Is it possible that the faculty, especially professors Lacy, Lenehan, and Heninger, were not being sufficiently candid about why, in 1968 and 1969, they suddenly wanted to eliminate one of the department's most important instructional programs? Were they using claims about rising student skills and a campuswide responsibility for writing instruction to mask why they really wanted to get rid of Freshman English?

I argued in chapter 4 that the 1968 decision to reduce the Freshman English requirement from two semesters to one was actually less about students' "improving" skills than about the faculty's lack of interest in undergraduate general education writing instruction. Those professors were now more focused on graduate education, the pursuit of scholarly prestige, and specialization in literary studies than in teaching writing to first-year undergraduates. This was still true in late 1969, when the argument about entering students' verbal skills was suddenly resurrected to support eliminating freshman composition altogether. But by then, something else was motivating faculty antipathy toward Freshman English, something captured by neither Lacy's rising-skills argument nor Lenehan's writing-in-the-disciplines one.

That other unstated reason is something we've been brushing up against throughout the last few chapters of this book: the growing tension in the late 1960s between tenured English Department faculty, on the one hand, and their graduate student teaching assistants, on the other, especially concerning control of the Freshman English program. Did the faculty abolish English 102 in November 1969 because they couldn't abide their own TAs' attempts to take responsibility for a course they no longer cared much about?

An answer to this question can be heard in taped interviews with English professors collected over a thirty-year period by the UW-Madison Oral History Program, where, from 1972 to 2002, at least six former faculty members recounted the story of the 1969 abolition of English 102 in strikingly similar terms, first by appealing to the "official" reason for the course's elimination—better high school preparation of student writers (the argument about writing-in-the-disciplines was not well remembered in later years, another reason to be skeptical about it)—and then by suggesting that an important but unstated reason for the move had to do with alleged TA misconduct in the course.

So, for example, in 1972, long-time Freshman English Committee member Robert Pooley said in an interview that English 102 was eliminated in the late 1960s because "there [had] been improvement in the high school teaching of comp."[75] He continued: "But another cause, frankly, is that the whole attitude of teaching assistants changed. . . . They became belligerent, self-directed, antagonistic to the department." According to Pooley, Ednah Thomas's early relationship with the TAs was almost maternal, but around 1967 or so, the relationship soured. The TAs were, "well, I don't want to use any opprobrious terms, but they were different. I'll just leave it that way."[76] And so, said Pooley, the earlier close rapport between faculty and TAs became strained. Where before the department had been socially, intellectually, and ideologically integrated, now the younger generation was acting in an "antagonistic" manner toward their elders.

Madeleine Doran, in her 1977 interview, agreed with this latter assessment, describing in some detail the deteriorating relations between English Department faculty and TAs in the 1960s. After the rifts of the 1930s, Doran said, the department had enjoyed a long period of goodwill in the 1940s and '50s: it was a place of "easy informality," where one's word was honored and trust among students and faculty was the norm. All that was lost, she claimed, by the "adversarial" posture adopted by TAs in the 1960s.[77]

In 1976, former chair Walter Rideout echoed this sentiment about the English TAs of the late 1960s, confirming Pooley's two-pronged explanation for what really happened to UW's Freshman English program in the late 1960s. He

1969 Breakdown

began by claiming that "the students we got in those days were better trained in the sense that they were closer to the top and had done more writing in high school." But another reason for the elimination of English 102, he added, was that "the TAs were not teaching the course as it was intended to be taught. . . . They felt that it was more important to liberate the students from old-fashioned ideas, to argue against the war than to proceed with literature or writing as such."[78]

Similarly, in 1980, former department chair Charles Scott recalled in an interview that "the public reason" for the abolition of English 102 was that "the student's ability in writing seemed to suggest that a required Freshman Comp course was not necessary." But, he added, "this was not the only reason why the course was dropped. The other had to do with the fact that in the perception of the faculty at the time . . . there was a lack of confidence and trust in what TAs were actually teaching."[79] According to Scott, the faculty didn't know what the TAs were doing in the classroom, and there was simply not enough time to visit them and find out. (Former TA Bob Muehlenkamp, in his interview with us, remembered the situation differently, describing it as one in which the faculty "dumped the freshmen and sophomores on our end, and there was no interest in what happened there—they did not mentor us." Muehlenkamp couldn't recall, for example, ever being visited by a faculty member or having a discussion with one about freshman composition or pedagogy more generally.)[80]

In a 2002 interview, former Writing Lab director Joyce Steward reiterated the department's official position that students in the late 1960s at UW were better prepared than those of earlier generations. Because of this, she said, they were bored and resented the required writing course. But she also indicated that the TAs at the time were "restless" and that that restlessness may have had something to do with the crisis in English 102.[81]

Chancellor Edwin Young went even further in blaming the TAs for the elimination of the course; in a 1977 interview with the Oral History Program, he complained that TAs at that time (that is, the mid-1970s) were trying to reinstate the very freshman writing program they had once scuttled, their refusal to teach the course "as intended" in the late 1960s being the main factor in its abolition.[82]

So we have numerous English Department faculty members, and even the chancellor of the university, stating in formal interviews, most conducted in the decade immediately following the events discussed, that an important reason—perhaps the main reason—for the elimination of English 102 at UW in 1969 had nothing to do with rising student skills or the responsibility of other departments for teaching writing to their majors; it was the English faculty's lack of confidence in their own teaching assistants.[83]

This TA-centered explanation for the abolition of Freshman English received scholarly imprimatur in 1999 when the fourth volume of David Cronon and John Jenkin's *History of the University of Wisconsin,* covering the years 1946 to 1971, was finally published. According to Cronon and Jenkins, the stated reason for the department's "bombshell" decision to eliminate English 102 in November 1969 was that "entering Freshmen were now better prepared in their writing skills."[84] While admitting that there was some evidence for this, the authors argue that "the unstated reason" for the decision was different:

> Senior members of the department believed they had lost control of the Freshman English courses to the largely radicalized junior faculty and TAs staffing the numerous sections of English 101, 102, and 181. Most of the tenured majority of the faculty objected to unauthorized grading experiments and indications that many freshmen were getting more exposure to Karl Marx and Che Guevara than to the writers and poets from the traditional canon specified in the departmentally approved reading lists. Rather than offer courses whose content and standards the department could neither control nor wished to stand behind, the faculty simply voted to stop offering them.[85]

This, in fact, is the story I heard when I first arrived at UW in 1998.

———————

Were the senior faculty of the English Department in the late 1960s right to question their TAs' commitment to, abilities in, and judgments about the teaching of first-year writing? Were those TAs in fact acting irresponsibly, even incompetently, in the classroom? Were first-year writing students at UW really "getting more exposure to Karl Marx and Che Guevara" than to the materials and objectives specified by course administrators? These are hard questions to answer definitively, given the numbers of individuals involved and the time elapsed. I hope to have at least provided here a wider range of voices than could be accessed previously.[86]

One thing that does warrant further inquiry is the *extent* of TA troublemaking in the Freshman English program at UW in the late 1960s. In fact, the only indications found of *mass* insubordination in the program during this entire period are the threatened withholding of grades in fall 1968—something that one could almost say the 1968–69 Freshman English Policy Committee endorsed—and the attempted "takeover" of that committee on October 13, 1969.[87] Most of the other evidence concerning TA performance in the course during this time points to rather extraordinary subordination of TAs to the faculty-led Freshman English program, even at the height of campus radicalism in 1968 and 1969. We've seen, for example, the generally positive assessments of the TAs by faculty right up until the start of the fall 1969 semester.[88] We have Lenehan's August 1969 tribute to TA participation on the 1968–69 policy committee, participation that resulted in significant revision of the syllabus itself.[89] We have the "Third View" memo from eleven moderate TAs, suggesting that there was a sizable number of TAs who rejected the leadership of their more radical colleagues even as they expressed support for reform.[90] And we have interviews with three former TAs—Susan McLeod, Virginia (Joyce) Davidson, and Jean Turner, all self-professed liberals—who described almost painfully conscientious following of the approved English 102 syllabus in the late 1960s.[91] We can even make some informed guesses here about the actual proportion of TAs in the English Department in the fall of 1969 who were departing from the approved English 102 syllabus and speculate from that whether the levels of "deviation" were as high as Lenehan claimed in the Departmental Committee meeting of November 4, 1969.

Let's begin with the raw numbers. As we saw at the beginning of the last chapter, there were 158 graduate student teaching assistants employed by the English Department in fall 1969. Now, not all of those TAs were teaching English 102, but since the October 13 motion about the Freshman English Policy Committee was voted on by the whole TA staff, and since the majority of that staff was involved with Freshman English at some point or another in their graduate careers, 158 is the relevant number for my purposes here. And the question I want to ask about that number is this: how many of these TAs were not teaching their courses "as intended" by the faculty?

One measure of TA insubordination, imperfect but telling, is simple attendance at TA staff meetings, especially meetings involving controversial issues like the ones raised during the 1968–69 and 1969–70 academic years. Here the numbers fluctuate considerably during this period, but within revealing limits (see table 6.1). Tim Heninger complained in his October 20, 1969, memo to the Departmental Committee that the number of TAs present at the fateful October 13, 1969, staff meeting was a minority of the total number of TAs in the department at the time (58 of 158, or 37 percent, with only 41 of those, or 26 percent of the total, voting for the committee "takeover"), and he provides estimates of similarly spotty TA attendance at staff meetings during the previous fall semester (1968), when there were 186 TAs on staff.[92] According to these estimates, the proportion of TAs showing active interest in the *administration* of the courses they were teaching was as high as 59 percent (110 of the 186 total)

6.1 TA Attendance at Fall 1968 Staff Meetings (according to English Department chair Tim Heninger)	
Date	Number
September 17	about 100
September 23	about 100
September 27	110
September 30	75
October 7	60 dwindling to 35
October 14	70
November 4	36 dwindling to 30
December 9	40 dwindling to 25
December 16	16 increasing to 25

Source: Simeon K. Heninger to English Departmental Committee, University of Wisconsin, memo, October 20, 1969.

and as low as 13 percent (25 of 186), but seemed to settle around the 20–40 percent range (36 to 75 or so).

On its surface, then, there appears to be some validity to Heninger's complaint that most TAs were not participating actively in course governance and were allowing a relatively small number of their colleagues to move Freshman English in unacceptably radical directions. But this same logic could also be used, of course, to cast Heninger's own reaction to the fall 1969 attempted coup as precipitous (Jean Turner called it "hysterical"), given the high number of uninvolved TAs as well as the repeated, subsequent attempts by moderate TAs and faculty members to find a compromise solution.[93] In addition, Heninger's own numbers show that, at times, TA interest in the institutional arrangements surrounding their teaching could be considerably higher. The proportion attending the September 30, 1968, meeting about the new English 200 committee, for example, was 41 percent (76 of 186), with 79 percent of those present (60 of 76), or 32 percent of the total English TA population, supporting the "radical" position on the main vote that day. And at the three meetings prior to that, held weekly after Heninger's infamous September 12, 1968, memo, during a relatively stormy period in the department when there was, among other dramatic events, a threatened grade boycott, TA attendance was nearly 60 percent (100 and 110, respectively, out of 186), by Heninger's own count. Meanwhile, during the semester before that, according to the May 1968 *TAA Newsletter,* 65 percent of English TAs (110 of 170) signed a petition calling for recognition of the TA union, a provocative and, indeed, historic act in the face of intense faculty and administrative opposition—in fact, English was one of the three departments on campus with the greatest TAA strength.[94]

Given these numbers, which point to *average* attendance at TA meetings of less than half the staff, it's hard to buy a charge of *mass* insurrection among English TAs during this time. It's clear, though, that a substantial minority of TAs, hovering perhaps between a quarter and a third of the staff, were openly, actively, and regularly resisting faculty control in 1968 and 1969 and that an even higher proportion, sometimes approaching two-thirds of the total, could be counted on to support liberal reform measures during the most critical junctures.

Let's return, then, to the 41 TAs who voted on October 13, 1969, for the reconstitution of the Freshman English Policy Committee.[95] That number, three to four dozen, or about a quarter of the total TA staff, is a fair estimate, I would argue, of the number of *radical* TAs in the department during the late 1960s, those most committed to overturning conventional educational practices and exerting expanded control over the committees responsible for designing and supervising those courses. Three dozen turns out as well to be the number of TAs who signed a petition protesting alleged police presence in an English 102 classroom in fall 1968.[96] It's also the number, roughly speaking, that Heninger mentions in his October 20, 1969, memo to the Departmental Committee, when he claims that 40 TAs arrived en bloc at the beginning of the October 13 meeting.[97] This proportion of the fall 1969 staff (26 percent) is roughly similar as well to the proportion of the fall 1968 staff (32 percent) that voted on September 30 for greater TA control over the general education courses they taught.[98]

Now, probably fewer TAs than this were genuine political and educational activists, boldly innovating in their Freshman English courses and aggressively pushing for curricular and organizational change in the program. The names of only 23 English Department TAs from 1968–70, for example, show up two or more times in the documents uncovered here (excluding simple lists of department TAs and paid members of the TAA), suggesting the number of TAs who were especially active in professional issues during this period: signing petitions, speaking up in departmental meetings, serving on committees, contributing to course reports and memos, writing essays for the TAA journal *Critical Teaching* and letters to the *Daily Cardinal*.[99] The names of 11 of those TAs, in fact, show up three or more times, some of them, like Bob Muehlenkamp, again and again.[100] Interestingly, 11 is also the number of TAs who are recorded in English Departmental Committee minutes as having spoken up for change in what must have been an especially intimidating rhetorical environment: the

October 28, 1969, English Departmental Committee meeting to which TAs had been invited by the faculty.[101] (The actual number of TA speakers at that meeting was 13, but two were clearly not on the side of the radicals during that exchange.)

Of course, there were conservative TAs in the department as well, opposed in various ways and for a variety of reasons to the more radical members of the staff. We have, for example, a letter from an anonymous TA written to Heninger in fall 1968 sharply objecting to his or her fellow TAs.[102] Further, as we've seen, there were at least two dissenting TAs (of the total 13 TA speakers) at the October 28, 1969, Departmental Committee meeting, one of whom stated that he did not want to "surrender his rights" to a TA-dominated policy committee.[103] There were also substantial numbers of "no" votes to the fall 1968 and fall 1969 radical motions, amounting to 20–30 percent of those present in both cases.[104] The number of conservative TAs in the department, in other words, may well have been as high as a third of the staff—roughly equivalent to the size of the radical group. A third of the staff (60 of 170) corresponds as well to the proportion of TAs who did *not* sign a petition in the spring of 1968 calling for recognition of the TAA, though most of those (51) were not even contacted, apparently disengaged from the debate altogether.[105]

The conservative teaching assistant from the late 1960s who is best known now is Lynne Cheney, who has been interviewed at least twice concerning her experiences as an English TA at UW during this period. In an interview with the *New Yorker* in 2002, she remembered "going to class and having to walk through people in whiteface, conducting guerrilla theater, often swinging animal entrails over their heads, as part of a protest against Dow Chemical" (referring apparently to the September 1967 Dow demonstrations). But what surprised her most, she said, "was that you would enter the classroom and here would be all these nice young people who honestly wanted to learn to write an essay. That, in a sense, was the real university, but this other was what was attracting so much attention."[106] My best guess is that TAs like Cheney conscientiously, even aggressively, followed the faculty-sanctioned syllabi for the courses they were teaching, including Freshman English.

Between these three to four dozen largely unorganized TAs on the right, variously conservative or apolitical, and the three to four dozen well-organized TAs on the left, there was a large number of TAs in the middle, perhaps as many as 75, whose political allegiances were more fluid and unpredictable, but who generally opposed the war in Vietnam; who were committed to most of the other liberal causes of the time, such as civil rights; and who genuinely desired

158

reform in Freshman English even as they were occasionally repelled by the ideas, tactics, and style of their more radical colleagues. Many of these TAs could be called upon to sign a petition, attend a well-publicized meeting, and vote for reform measures, though they probably didn't do much more than that. Some were genuine fence-sitters, siding occasionally with the left, occasionally with the right, and sometimes absenting themselves from the debate entirely.

We should also remember that in the late 1960s there were many English graduate students at UW who were *not* TAs. In 1968–69, for example, when there were 186 TAs on staff, 120 of them in Freshman English, there were 357 PhD students in residence and 597 *total* graduate students in the department— the size of a small college, as Walter Rideout put it in his 1976 interview.[107] Among these were more than 200 MA students, most quite young, unburdened by teaching duties, and probably either actively involved in or generally sympathetic to the protest movements of the time. (One of these was future compositionist Lisa Ede, whose name shows up on the November 1969 petition against the faculty's abolition of English 102.)

The non-TA graduate student group also included many PhD students who were beyond coursework, focused on their dissertations, and supported by the relatively rich array of fellowships at the time. Many of these students no doubt kept mostly to themselves, their spouses and children, their circle of faculty and graduate student friends, and their work. Some were liberals whose political awakening had occurred earlier in the 1960s, when the most prominent leftist cause was the civil rights struggle of Southern blacks. But by the late 1960s, "a significant number" of these TAs were more intent on getting their paychecks and finishing their degrees than in staffing a revolution.[108] Take Susan McLeod, who taught English 102 in 1968–69 but was on National Defense Education Act (NDEA) fellowships for the rest of her graduate career at UW. She had been active in liberal causes as a master's student at UW earlier in the 1960s, but as we saw in chapter 3, when she returned to Madison for the PhD in the late 1960s, after a year spent at a historically black college in Texas and two in the Peace Corps in Ethiopia, she was repelled by the changed tone of student protests. She was also by this time married and focused on her career: "My first order of business was to get my degree and get out of there"—though that didn't stop her from signing the petition mentioned above.[109]

Some of the older English TAs in the fall of 1969 no doubt aligned themselves with their more career-oriented fellow graduate students. Like them, they were trying to finish their degrees after years of work and were unwilling to jeopardize hard-won personal relations with the faculty. Many were living in

UW's Eagle Heights family housing and no doubt felt far removed from the goings-on in the streets downtown and around campus. But even those immersed in graduate student life often kept their distance from the more radical TAs. Virginia (Joyce) Davidson, who described her late 1960s' political self as "moderate," remembers being turned off by the behavior of some of her colleagues, who, she thought, often used their undergraduate students to advance their own political agendas.[110] Susan McLeod also described attempted indoctrination of students and intimidation of fellow graduate students by some TAs.[111] And Burr Angle portrayed protest leaders as sometimes more interested in media attention than in thoughtfully responding to the problems of the times.[112]

Still, I believe that most of the TAs in this large middle group, while generally uninterested in making trouble and turned off by the extreme tactics of their radical colleagues, could be counted on in a crisis or during moments of pronounced faculty obtuseness to sign a protest petition or join a fledgling union. After all, the general direction of political sentiment during this period, at least among U.S. college students, undergraduate and graduate, was leftward: against the war and an educational system that seemed too often supportive of it (or at least insufficiently opposed to it). As we saw in chapter 3, 72 percent of UW students supported the war in 1965; five years later, 79 percent opposed it.[113] Clearly, political conditions could also change from week to week, like in the spring of 1969, when the TAA, considered politically quite radical, recorded a surge in mainstream membership after the state legislature threatened to eliminate in-state tuition benefits for graduate student TAs.[114] But despite these fluctuations, the overall trend among undergraduate and graduate students, at least for the period covered in this book, was toward liberal reform. Richard Nixon might claim, in November 1969, that a "silent majority" of Americans supported him and the war, but the evidence collected here suggests that the broad middle group of English TAs at UW in the late 1960s, silent though they often were, favored change rather than the status quo. They wanted Freshman English to be more relevant for students and more pliable for instructors.

This research suggests, then, that the number of radical TAs in the UW English Department during the late 1960s, the ones who genuinely annoyed Heninger, Lenehan, and other faculty, was relatively small even though its members were well organized. A roughly equal number of poorly organized conservative TAs found themselves at the other end of the political spectrum. Between these two was a large number of TAs who followed the faculty-approved syllabi but nonetheless sympathized with critiques of them. That would give us, in a staff of 150 or so, about:

- 24–48 radicals: a dozen activists and two to three dozen followers who could be counted on to cause trouble for the faculty (perhaps a quarter of the whole);

- 60–72 middle-of-the-road, mostly conscientious, professionally anxious, but generally liberal "regulars" (about a half of the total); and

- 24–48 conservatives, sometimes more disengaged than ideological, but nonetheless opposed to the radicals (about a quarter of the staff).

The evidence suggests, in other words, that no more than a quarter of the English TA staff at UW in the late 1960s could be described as truly "radical" and that probably less than 10 percent were *aggressively* departing from the approved syllabi in the direction of genuinely critical or radical pedagogy.[115] This puts in some perspective the blanket condemnation of TAs by faculty that one finds in the Departmental Committee minutes of fall 1969. And it supports Walter Rideout's observation at the October 28 Departmental Committee meeting that "few faculty members teach English 102, and that most TAs do it very well," leaving aside for now the question of whether activist TAs were teaching English 102 "well" or not.[116] The fact is that there was no widespread clamoring among the TAs for "license" to do whatever they wanted in the classroom, no extensive deviation from the standard syllabus of English 102, and no evidence to support Lenehan's rather stunning November 11 claim that "most of the TAs were not teaching composition."[117] The conclusion is thus inescapable: the English faculty at UW in 1969 exaggerated the incompetence and insubordination of their TAs and, faced with concerted resistance from about a quarter of the staff, resorted to repressing the "initiative and creativity" of the entire TA staff, to use the phrase championed by the Mulvihill Report.[118]

This bears repeating. The received wisdom regarding student radicalism in the 1960s holds that the protest movement defeated itself, imploded at the end of the decade, the victim of its own internal strife, strategic excesses, inner contradictions, and ideological hair-splitting. Madison itself often plays a role in this narrative, since the bombing of UW's Army Math Research Center in August 1970, in which a graduate student was killed, is often cited as the moment when student protests in this country crossed over into the violence, destructiveness, and disregard for human life that activists had earlier opposed in others.[119] As we've seen, the TAs in our story were not blameless—they sometimes acted precipitously, made tactical errors, overreached their capabilities, disrespected potential allies, grandstanded in public, and blundered in the classroom. But the demise of Freshman English at UW can hardly be laid at their feet: as we saw in chapter 5, they paid unflagging attention to the course, innovated in it, and worked energetically to inject life into it. No: the abolition of English 102 was the project of others, and the responsibility for the subsequent quarter-century loss of composition at the University of Wisconsin rests on their shoulders.[120]

When campus and city newspapers reported the English Department's November 18 decision to abolish Freshman English, a barrage of complaints from students, TAs, and other faculty at the university began to pour in. On November 19, the day after the vote on English 102, the student-run newspaper the *Daily Cardinal* published a front-page article, complete with a large photograph of campus police chief Ralph Hanson blocking the door to the Departmental Committee meeting and looking for all the world like a Nazi storm trooper.[121] That same day, both of Madison's local newspapers, the *Wisconsin State Journal* and the *Capital Times,* published front-page articles on the English Department's decision.[122]

The next day, November 20, the assault continued: both the *Daily Cardinal* and the *Capital Times* published articles on the event.[123] And on November 21, the *Daily Cardinal* followed up with an article accusing the English Department of basing its move on political reasons.[124] On November 25, meanwhile, two English TAs published letters in the *Daily Cardinal.* Pauline Lipman and Richard Damashek ridiculed the faculty's rationale for its move and suggested that English 102 was really abolished in order to eliminate the TAs' power base, punish them for their classroom experiments, and exact revenge against unruly insubordinates.[125] Here's what Lipman wrote:

> The decision of the English Department to abolish English 102 should be seen as a political decision. . . . The department has tried to obscure this political struggle by representing the concern of the TAs as simply job security. This is objectively false.
>
> The controversy over English 102 arose because TAs refused to participate in planning another version of standard English 102 under the control of the department. While English professors decided, behind police-protected doors, to abolish freshman English, TAs were debating a proposal to place the course under the collective, democratic control of TAs and students. Through long experience, many TAs had come to understand that only by controlling the courses they teach will they be able to develop genuine education.
>
> Freshman English was abolished partially because faculty members responded to what they saw as the impudence of TAs and the threat of the union [the TAA]. But the decision on 102 took place in a larger context in

which the U operates to serve the needs of a corporate structure which holds the economic and political power of the state. . . .

Until teachers, like other workers, control the work they do, their work will serve the interests of an elite who hold power, or be abolished. Meanwhile real education, the legitimate aim of TAs, will have to operate largely underground.[126]

Meanwhile, about this time, a petition of non-TA English graduate students with eighty signatures arrived in the chair's office. The short statement accompanying the petition indicated that those signing it "oppose the Departmental Committee's abolition of English 102 and 181," arguing that the decision was "completely arbitrary and irresponsible," that student voices had been ignored, and that graduate student funding and professional training needs had not been given consideration. The students also indicated that they supported English Department TAs' demands for "educational reform" and recognition of the "student voice" in policy decisions. "The justification offered for the abolition of Freshman English," they wrote, "is unacceptable to intelligent spectators aware of the background to the controversy." The students ended the statement by calling for a "full and immediate reconsideration" of the abolition of Freshman English at UW.[127]

There was also a string of letters addressed to Heninger and Lenehan from other faculty on campus—all saved in the files of the English Department. Professor Millard Susman, from the Department of Genetics, for example, wrote to Heninger on November 19:

I was distressed to read in this morning's *Cardinal* that the English Department is considering the discontinuation of English 101 and 102. The focus of the *Cardinal* story was on a separate issue; so please forgive me if my reaction is premature or misinformed. I want to express my opinion now— misinformed or not—because I do not want to wait until it is too late to influence your decision.

My teaching responsibilities expose me to small biology classes, a total of about 70 undergraduates and 30 graduates each year. The classes are so small that it is possible to give take-home, essay-type exams. It is obvious from their exam papers that many students are so deficient in the techniques of communication that they cannot express complicated ideas even to themselves, much less to others. I use much more red pencil on the correction of language errors than on the correction of scientific errors. My emphasis on writing skills seems to annoy and to surprise science students, as if it had never occurred to them that communication had any relevance to the study of science or that words have any relevance to the function of the brain. I find that attitude frightening.

The deterioration of language skills is evident also in the writings that are published in professional scientific journals. We pack a lot of scientific rubbish into our heads because good experiments are badly reported in the professional literature. Frightening again.

You will say—and I agree—that this appalling, self-nourishing linguistic catastrophe is the concern and responsibility of science teachers and editors. We both know, however, that the problem extends far beyond the scientific community and that it is everybody's problem.

We must continue to offer our students lessons in composition. No impending advance in communications technology is going to relieve us of the problems that we all face when we have to put thoughts on paper. Relaxation of grammatical rules will never make writing a less exacting chore. Criticism of our secondary schools for their failure to teach writing skills will not help our speechless students to find words when they need them.

I think the University *must* continue to offer freshman composition courses and must do everything possible to ensure high standards in the teaching of these courses. These courses deal with the most fundamental and indispensable of all human skills and should be at the top of our list of curricular priorities, not precariously dangling from the bottom.[128]

Heninger's reply, which was sent almost a month after Susman's letter was received, consisted of two rather brief paragraphs. In the first, he agreed that there was a problem on campus with students' written expression but claimed that freshman composition just wasn't solving the problem, asserting that "the course had reached a point of diminishing returns." In the second paragraph, he proposed that working with students' writing on an individual basis, in their major department, might work better than a course designed to remove their deficiencies "en masse" and asserted that the English Department, far from reneging on its responsibilities in this area, was ready to help in any way.[129]

A few weeks after Susman wrote his letter to Heninger, Dean George W. Sledge of UW's College of Agriculture and Life Sciences wrote a similar letter.[130] This time, the reply came from William Lenehan, who dealt in his letter almost entirely with the technical process of referring students to the Writing Clinic.[131] He agreed with Susman that "there will be students in all colleges, however, who were inadequately trained in composition during their secondary school experience. . . . What we visualize for these students is something like the following: we will ask your faculty to select these students for additional training in our writing clinic. We will not ask any faculty member to analyze the

1969 Breakdown

flaws in the students' writing; he simply makes a distinction between what is acceptable college level writing within a discipline and what is not."[132] The letter is largely a defense, therefore, of the to-be-expanded Writing Clinic, an idea that, writes Lenehan, seemed preferable to other solutions on several grounds:

> The first is the extensive experimental literature suggesting that permanent writing proficiency is not best attained in a one or two semester composition course but by continued scrutiny of realistic writing assignments throughout the student's college career. Second, the student sent to the clinic is motivated to work as hard as necessary because a firm judgment has been made that he will not be successful in college unless he improves his writing. Finally, by encouraging all faculty members in the university to share in the responsibility for the writing ability of the students, I think we will place the true value of good writing in a much more realistic perspective than we have in the past with our required composition courses.[133]

Meanwhile, on December 24, 1969, Professor Roy E. Tuttle, professor of business and chair of the Undergraduate Studies Committee of the UW School of Business, complained about the course's abolition to his dean, E. A. Gaumnitz, who copied the letter to the dean of Letters and Science Stephen Kleene and English Department chair Heninger.[134] Tuttle wrote that his committee in the Business School had voted unanimously that he communicate their opposition to the abolition of English 102.

> It is the opinion of the committee that for the most part freshman students admitted to the University of Wisconsin are in great need of an excellent freshman composition course. In fact for each of the two preceding years, by standards established *by the English Department,* there was a relatively small number of students exempt from Freshman English and a relatively small number of students eligible to take English 181 (honors). These indicate that the English Department also recognized the serious limitations of the writing and communication achievement of our freshmen. . . .
>   Whereas . . . freshman composition is not at the present time meeting all of the needs in development of writing skills, it is going a long way towards the development of the basic concepts and principles that should be applied in subsequent writing areas. Our students, as do the students of all other curricula of the university, desperately need these skills as provided under competent direction of the English Department.[135]

On January 15, Professor G. R. Stairs, chair of the Department of Forestry, wrote the following letter to Lenehan:

The recent announcement that English 102 will no longer be offered is viewed with some concern by our faculty. We do not agree that most of our students are writing effectively and we feel that there is still a need for formal education in this area. It may be that English 102 was not the correct course to fill this need and that dropping it is not our real concern. We do hope that your Department will now make specific recommendations concerning a replacement course for these students who do need additional writing experience. In addition, we would hope that such a course would not have prerequisites other than the equivalent of placing above English 101.

The suggestion that responsibility for developing writing effectiveness be passed on to every faculty member is well taken and we will continue to do as much as we are able in this direction.

In summary, we feel that dropping 102 may be a useful change if a truly innovative writing effectiveness course is developed somewhere in the University to replace it. Perhaps this course should be developed in a journalism department?[136]

Lenehan's response to Stairs—two and a half single-spaced pages of closely reasoned argument—was the English faculty's first sustained attempt to theorize its November 1969 decision, which essentially (and unilaterally) shifted responsibility for writing instruction from themselves onto both the high schools (where students should acquire, and, according to Lacy, largely *were* acquiring, the basic skills needed to write college-level expository prose) and other departments at UW (where students would be motivated to do their "best writing," as Lenehan put it in his November 19 memo to the TAs).[137] The letter justifies this shift of responsibility by distinguishing between "simple clarity" in writing, for which "the English Department is willing to take responsibility," and "fully effective writing," to which "the University must address itself," according to Lenehan.

The letter to Stairs, slightly revised and now titled "Means for Attaining Student Writing Effectiveness Without Required Freshman English," was distributed as a "preliminary report" to the campus community in February 1970. It is quoted here in full:

MEANS FOR ATTAINING STUDENT WRITING
EFFECTIVENESS WITHOUT REQUIRED
FRESHMAN ENGLISH

A Preliminary Report

The entire faculty of the University of Wisconsin is rightly concerned with the effect of the English Department's decision not to offer the traditionally required Freshman English courses. Our common concern is to assure that all of our graduates can write effectively. I hope the following statement will indicate a preliminary outline of means which can be expanded creatively to meet the needs of our students.

The English Department based its action on the following assumptions. Our basic belief is that most students coming to the Madison campus possess the necessary skills to write clear expository prose. For those who demonstrate by means of objective examination that they do not possess these basic skills, we will offer English 101 as a three-credit course. We know that some students will enter whose inability to write clearly will not be detected by our tests. We will establish in the English Department a Writing Clinic to which any member of the instructional staff may send a student. The instructors in the Clinic will analyze the writing problems of the student and recommend a solution to the problems. If the student's problems require a formal course, the instructor will recommend that he take English 102 through the Extension Division here. Usually, the problems will be such that the instructor will be able to solve them through tutorial sessions with the student. This procedure has two advantages over the required course: first, the student is motivated by the fact that a teacher in a course in his major field has told him that he will not succeed unless he improves his writing; second, we will be able to use the most efficient method of teaching composition—the tutorial method. If the faculty cooperates in sending us those students who require help, we are sure that the English Department can achieve the goal of making all of our students able to express their ideas clearly.

We all realize that there is a difference between writing clearly and writing with full effectiveness. It is this gap between simple clarity, for which the English Department is willing to take responsibility, and fully effective writing to which the University must address itself. The best way to solve this problem is not by a required writing course centered in any single department. Several major difficulties mitigate against such a solution. A fully effective writer has to have broad knowledge of his subject and he has to want to express his ideas; the most competent control of the grammatical and rhetorical resources of our language is ineffective without this knowledge and commitment. The shortcomings of any required writing course offered to students with diverse interests is that there is no discoverable subject matter which can motivate even a majority, much less all, of a class to express or indeed to formulate ideas. The right subject for a student to work with to become an effective writer is that discipline to which he has committed himself, whether it be agriculture, engineering, or the humanities.

Perhaps this point is best illustrated by our experience in English 102 in the last two years. All our students experienced something called training in composition during high school; some of it was very good training. Our expectation was that in college, with the practice furnished by Freshman English, their writing effectiveness would improve, and most of the students, we believe, would admit if asked that improvement was possible. But we were disappointed when we tried to measure improvement, and staff opinion quite generally ascribed the meager results to the difficulty of finding a subject matter that would motivate 4,000 students, or even 25 in one section. In the conferences on theme annotation which we have as part of our training program, we concluded again and again that the difficulty in assignment arose from the lack of relevance of material for the student. In our field we are familiar with many graduates who return to tell us how much they now regret that they wasted the opportunity they had in Freshman English; in a very wide range of jobs, on the job, they have become completely convinced of the importance of effective writing. But they did not realize it when they were in college because they wrote themes which had no direct connection with their professional interests. We have, we assure you, done our best to combine our composition training with the diverse interests of university students, and we have concluded that it is not good enough.

All the studies that have been published indicate that the really effective writer is the one who has been challenged to improve his writing throughout his college experience. The only place where an individual student can achieve full effectiveness as a writer is in the discipline he has selected because that is the subject he knows best and cares about most. One concrete way to accomplish this is to make sure each student in any department takes one course per semester that requires a paper. This does not mean that departmental faculty have to become teachers of grammar. The only distinction a faculty member needs to stress is that between effective and ineffective writing. If any of the students seem to have difficulty understanding why their prose is ineffective, our Writing Clinic staff would be glad to offer advice. We are convinced that the kind of student we are getting on the Madison campus today can become an effective writer by the time he graduates without taking a formal writing course; he will only do so if he is forced to write within the discipline he has chosen, if he is reminded on each assignment that writing effectiveness is as important as factual content, and if in fact his instructor penalizes the work exhibiting ineffective writing.

Some disciplines seem to face real problems in adopting this means to assure writing effectiveness because the courses are based upon particular non-verbal skills or means of communication, such as laboratory work or numerical systems. It is disturbing that the faculties in some of these departments insist that the success of their graduates depends heavily on writing effectiveness, and yet they offer no practice in this skill within the discipline. The only solution I can see for these departments would seem to be that they develop a technical writing course within the department. Such a course fulfills the ideals for an effective writing course because it contains students who share a common knowledge and a common commitment to express their ideas. This is a solution for any department whose faculty feels strongly that the writing effectiveness of its students depends upon formal training.

The English Department feels that one of the absolute requirements of a college graduate is the skill of writing effectively. I hope that we may all work together to gain this goal more efficiently than we have in the past.[138]

Faced with criticism from faculty across campus that the department had abandoned its responsibility to teach writing to UW students, Lenehan tried to split the difference: English, he admitted, does have responsibility for ensuring that all students possess the ability to write *clearly*, a basic skill that is of broad applicability and capable of being imparted by general and centralized writing instruction in the vernacular language. Happily for the department, though, most entering students at UW already possessed that skill, and those who didn't would have a remedial class and, later, individualized tutoring available to them. What most students still needed work with, however, according to Lenehan, was writing *effectively*, an apparently context-bound practice that requires work within particular communities.[139]

No direct response to Lenehan's February statement has been found; but given the earlier reaction to the department's decision about English 102 from faculty in other departments, it's doubtful that the expanded argument made much of a dent. As late as March 1971, at least one professor from another department, Professor Fred R. Rickson, of Botany, was still complaining to Chancellor Edwin Young about the loss of Freshman English.[140] Rickson wrote that "Freshman English Composition is needed in any university curriculum. To deny that it is needed is either stupid or intellectually dishonest. The very fact that the chairman of the English department simultaneously dropped the course and yet offered, and in fact continues to offer, to establish all sorts of workshops, clinics, special programs, etc. points to an unfailing need and an obvious understanding on his part that students are not as competent as possible in their writing skills. In my view he simply doesn't want to have the burden of teaching English skills within the English department."

Professor Rickson continued: "I firmly believe that the English department dropped 102 because they did not like the way it was being run rather than because it was not needed. I find this fact to be particularly disturbing in this rural state where many of the students' vocabulary and writing skills are at a somewhat elementary level. I also find it disturbing that a Wisconsin student can come to the University and take courses from Algebra to Zoology but he cannot learn to express himself. Ridiculous!"[141] Here, Rickson levels perhaps a more fundamental complaint: "I think that one of the real dangers here is more academic than actual. It is that any department can drop any course it so desires without considering the needs of the University as a whole. This University is great because of the sum total of its departments, not for a minute because of any one particular department. The sum of those individual departments give us the whole that we call an undergraduate education at the University of Wisconsin. If all or indeed many of the departments decided that they did not want to teach introductory courses any longer but rather concentrate in the more glamorous graduate level education (although I certainly disagree with that statement as to which is more glamorous), our educational system would be in a sorry state. This precedent by the English department now simply says that a department is stronger than the University. I don't believe that."[142]

The English TAs also found Lenehan's attempt to shift responsibility for writing instruction to other departments less than convincing. In his November 25, 1969, letter to the editor of the *Daily Cardinal*, TA Richard Damashek calls the argument that other departments should teach writing "an absurd proposition, as absurd as the Math Department telling the English Department that it should be responsible for the instruction in mathematics of English majors taking courses in math."[143] It must have seemed to these protestors that Lenehan had merely found a post hoc rationalization for something that was a fait accompli.

I have even found in the department's files from this time a handwritten letter to Heninger from an undergraduate English major that includes the following comments: "I am quite disgusted with the recent mysterious actions of the English department. I am particularly concerned about the dropping of English 102. To say that high school provides adequate training in composition skills is either ignoring reality or hiding something else that is actually the issue at hand. . . . Finding solutions by dismissing problems will be disastrous to the quality of education at this university if there is any quality at all. Certainly composition training must be expanded rather than discarded."[144]

A storm also began to brew concerning the *way* the department had reached its decision about English 102 and, specifically, whether it had violated any laws when it forcibly barred nonmembers from attending the November 18, 1969, meeting at which the faculty voted to abolish English 102. The storm reached

1969 Breakdown

as far as Chancellor Edwin Young, who asked Heninger to come see him on February 1, 1970. At that meeting, Young apparently expressed concerns about a possible legal challenge to the university because of the department's actions. Two days later, the English Departmental Committee met and, by a vote of 34–5, rescinded its April 15, 1969, decision to close committee meetings to the public. On February 4, Heninger dutifully reported the decision to Young and promised that a week hence, the committee, in open meeting, would "reconsider ceasing to offer English 102 and 181."[145]

Sometime before that meeting took place, Professor Robert Kimbrough, who had tried unsuccessfully in November to forestall Lacy's motion to abolish English 102, attempted again to find middle ground for the department between acceding to the TAs' October 13 motion and eliminating English 102 outright. He delivered a handwritten note to Heninger asking that on February 10 the Departmental Committee declare "null and void" its November 18 action.[146]

At that February 10 meeting, the faculty voted unanimously to rescind its November 18 decision abolishing English 102, tacitly admitting that the vote had been invalid because the meeting had been closed to the public. But Lacy then immediately reintroduced his motion to cease offering the course at the end of the 1969–70 academic year. The vote to call the question on the motion, however, failed to reach the requisite two-thirds majority (the vote was 29–20).[147] The department would have to wait another week to finally decide the issue one way or another.

On February 17, 1970, the committee returned to the question of English 102. After Kimbrough's substitute motion, which asked TAs to fill their places in the department's various course committees and invited them to a kind of summit regarding the future of English 102, failed to pass (16–33), the question on Lacy's renewed motion to abolish English 102 was called. That motion then passed 33–14, the percentage of faculty voting for abolition virtually identical to that of November 18 (around 70 percent).[148]

The decision to abolish the Freshman English program was now *really* official. And on May 18, 1970, the minutes of the UW-Madison College of Letters and Science Faculty Meeting included the following statement: "On motion of Professor David Cronon it was voted to approve the *interim recommendation of the Curriculum Review Committee* as follows: That Section I,A, of the present degree requirements be changed from 'One year of English composition with the possibility of partial exemption' to 'One semester of English composition with the possibility of exemption.'"[149]

By now, attention in the English Department had turned elsewhere. In fact, the spring 1970 semester was an especially traumatic time at UW. In March, there was a dramatic three-week strike by the TAA, essentially shutting down campus, and in May, news of the Cambodian bombings and then the Kent State killings brought about destructive riots on the UW campus, during which National Guard troops were called in for only the second time in the university's history. On May 8, President Fred Harrington himself resigned. And about this time, Professor Tim Heninger, chair of the English Department, also left UW, not even completing the normal three-year stint.

In August 1970, the bombing of UW's Army Math Research Center seemed to bring the 1960s literally and figuratively to a close. All of Jean Turner's group left around this time, as did Burr Angle and Virginia Joyce. Most of the junior faculty members who had supported the graduate students, meanwhile, were denied tenure in 1970 and 1971. In the words of new chair Charles Scott, the old era was gone.[150] The early 1970s were a time of declining enrollments, diminished protest activity on campus, increasing concern among faculty and others about students' basic skills, and poor job prospects for all—especially English PhDs.[151]

1969 Breakdown

7 AFTERMATH, 1970–1996

By the fall of 1970, Freshman English at UW was a small remedial writing program. Despite widespread protests, the English faculty held their ground and eventually put the episode behind them, at least for a while. As we saw above, even though the spring 1970 semester turned out to be especially traumatic on campus, Madison's revolutionary heyday was quickly coming to an end. As new English Department chair Charles Scott put it later, an era was winding down. Nationally, a kind of cultural hangover set in, evidenced on university campuses by declining federal support for basic research; a crisis in the arts and sciences as business became, during the 1970s, the most popular student major; and the collapse of the academic job market for PhD's.

The "problem" of undergraduate writing skills, and the question of whether a universal freshman composition course was needed at UW, however, never completely went away, and for the next quarter of a century, the topic resurfaced repeatedly.

The first revisiting of the department's decision to abolish English 102 came less than a year after the Faculty Senate's May 18, 1970, ratification of the move when, on April 19, 1971, the College of Letters and Science Curriculum Review Committee issued its long-awaited report on the university's undergraduate course of study.[1] That report had a good bit to say about "freshman comp" at UW and the English Department's actions concerning it. It complained openly, for example, about the way the department had handled the English 102 crisis:

During the 1969–70 spring semester the Committee was obliged to give special and immediate attention to the English composition requirement. This need resulted from the decision of the Department of English on November 18, 1969, to cease teaching its two courses, English 102 and English 181, at the end of the 1969–70 academic year. Inasmuch as one or the other of these two courses was then being used by nearly all freshmen students on the Madison campus to satisfy the English composition requirement of the College and the other undergraduate schools and colleges, the English Department's action had serious implications for the ability of most undergraduates to satisfy their existing degree requirements. Irrespective of the merits of this action, the Committee believes that the proper way to seek to change a degree requirement is to recommend a change in the requirement, not to act unilaterally to abolish the courses which satisfy it.[2]

The committee then turned to the substance behind the department's decision, its arguments about whether a universally required freshman composition course was needed at UW:

Despite evidence offered by the Department of English to support its view that most entering freshmen are sufficiently well-prepared on the basis of their secondary school work not to need further training in English composition, the Committee received many contrary views from students and faculty members. The committee's own survey of a random sample of second semester freshmen and seniors revealed both dissatisfaction with the existing English composition course and significant student support for the availability of good formal training in English composition. As an interim measure, the Committee recommended and the College faculty approved on May 18, 1970, that the English composition requirement be changed to "One semester of English composition with the possibility of exemption." This would permit those entering freshmen whose placement tests indicate the need of formal composition training to meet the requirement through English 101, and other students to receive appropriate help from the new Writing Clinic established by the Department of English.[3]

In its report, the committee went on to formulate the "general objectives of a liberal education" at UW, which the college's requirements were meant to support. The very first of these objectives was "competency in communication."[4]

Further on, the committee wrote that "the central importance of [acquiring the tools of learning and communication skills] makes it necessary for students to acquire competency in composition, language, and mathematics either prior to or during their enrollment in the college." And in its first recommen-

Aftermath, 1970–1996

dation for a reformulated bachelor's degrees at UW, the group argued for "demonstrated competence either through examination or one semester course in composition or public speaking at the college level, plus subsequent certification of competence by the major department or major adviser for an Individual Major."[5] In its most specific statement about composition, the committee wrote that "adequate mastery" by students of expository English was essential and that

> the student's command of English will be tested upon admission. If necessary, a semester course in composition or public speaking at the college level may then be assigned. An important innovation is that the student must also demonstrate command of expository English in his field of specialization. This places upon his major department (or major adviser in an Individual Major) the responsibility for certifying that he has achieved this skill. Departments and major advisers have complete flexibility in testing such mastery of English and in taking appropriate steps to insure that their students meet their standards of expository writing.[6]

In 1971, therefore, Professor David Cronon's Curriculum Review Committee grudgingly ratified the English Department's de facto abolition, a year earlier, of the university's freshman writing requirement, offering both veiled and unveiled criticisms of that move but seeking ways to show that the campus could still be meaningfully attentive to students' general writing skills even with a drastically enfeebled freshman writing program. To all concerned, it was a strained performance; but given UW's tradition of highly decentralized faculty governance, especially in terms of curriculum, there didn't seem to be much else the committee could do.

And here the situation stood—at least until the mid-1970s "literacy crisis" put student writing, nationally and at UW, on the front burner again.

When the article "Why Johnny Can't Write" appeared in the December 8, 1975, issue of *Newsweek,* the magazine was participating in a recurring American cultural phenomenon, the literacy crisis. As noted earlier, the story of freshman composition in this country is inextricably entangled with these crises, which typically occur during moments of economic and sociocultural transformation. Complaints about students' writing abilities, therefore, often reveal more about the complainants than about the students themselves.

Still, concern about a perceived deterioration in reading and writing skills among U.S. youth was widespread in the mid-1970s. In fact, the *Newsweek* article can be seen less as a flash point or catalyst for that perception than one of many symptoms of public anxiety at the time regarding student literacy levels and instruction; after all, both *Time* and the *Chronicle of Higher Education* had published articles about a writing "crisis" at least a year before.[7] What was important about the *Newsweek* article, however, was its prominence—appearing as it did on the cover of a national magazine—and its alarming tone, apparent in its opening paragraph:

> If your children are attending college, the chances are that when they graduate they will be unable to write ordinary, expository English with any real degree of structure and lucidity. If they are in high school and planning to attend college, the chances are less than even that they will be able to write English at the minimal college level when they get there. If they are not planning to attend college, their skills in writing English may not even qualify them for secretarial or clerical work. And if they are attending elementary school, they are almost certainly not being given the kind of required reading, much less writing instruction, that might make it possible for them eventually to write comprehensible English. Willy-nilly, the United States educational system is spawning a generation of semiliterates.[8]

The evidence *Newsweek* adduced for its claims was mostly anecdotal, from frustrated business executives and senior English faculty. Rising enrollment in "remedial" English on some campuses was also reported, with, apparently, half of the freshmen at UC Berkeley taking "bonehead" English the year the article appeared and a 50 percent increase since the late 1960s in the number of students at Temple failing the English placement test there. More "scientific" data, meanwhile, came from a March 1975 U.S. Department of Health, Education, and Welfare study, which showed "a steady erosion" of reading skills among American students since 1965, and a National Assessment of Educational Progress (NAEP) study that revealed "deteriorating" writing performance among students since the late 1960s.

But no educational statistic in the mid-1970s generated as much concern as the decline in mean SAT scores. Nationally, the scores had been falling since the mid-1960s, especially on the verbal portion of the test. The decline was particularly sharp in the early to mid-1970s; in fact, as *Newsweek* reported, the biggest drop in SAT scores in twenty years occurred in 1974, the year before "Why Johnny Can't Write" appeared (see figure 7.1). It was for that reason that, in October 1975, the College Entrance Examination Board (CEEB), in conjunction with the Educational Testing Service (ETS), the main sponsors of the

Aftermath, 1970–1996

SAT, appointed an Advisory Panel on the SAT Score Decline, which two years later published its report, *On Further Examination,* about the crisis.[9] By then, there had been fourteen straight years of declining average SAT scores, resulting, from 1963 to 1977, in an unprecedented 49-point drop in the mean verbal score and a 32-point drop in the mean math score.[10] Clearly, there were complex psychometric issues involved, but, according to the panel, the public was less interested in the technical aspects of the decline than in its widely perceived implication, namely, that a "serious deterioration of the learning process in America" was under way, evidenced by "more and more high school graduates show[ing] up in college classrooms, employers' personnel offices, or at other common checkpoints with barely a speaking acquaintance with the English language and no writing facility at all."[11]

What caused the decline? After first discounting the possibility that there were problems with the test itself—that it had become more difficult, for example, or less valid as a predictor of students' academic performance in their first year of college—the panel attempted to explain what had happened to the students taking the test over the preceding decade and a half.[12] The explanation consisted of a division of the decline into two periods. First, said the panel, from 1963 to 1970, the composition of SAT test takers changed, each year including larger proportions of "characteristically lower-scoring groups of students"; this resulted in an average score decline during that period.[13] In the 1960s, that is, fewer American students dropped out of high school, and more went on to college, meaning that the test-taking population at the end of the decade included more students from groups with typically lower-than-average scores, namely: "students from lower socioeconomic status families, members of minority ethnic groups, and (on the Mathematical but not on the Verbal portion of the test) women."[14] In fact, the panel estimated that between two-thirds and three-fourths of the SAT-score decline between 1963 and 1970 was caused by compositional changes in the test-taking population.[15]

But after 1970, according to the panel, these demographic shifts became less important (accounting for only about 25 percent of the decline), "and other factors in the schools and in the society at large became more significant," explaining three-fourths of the decline.[16] Scores began to drop sharply, for example, among students within the *same* socioeconomic, racial, ethnic, and gender groups; there was even a decrease in both the absolute number and proportion of high-scoring students, suggesting that something more "pervasive" than simple demography was involved.[17] The panel posited several possible explanations for

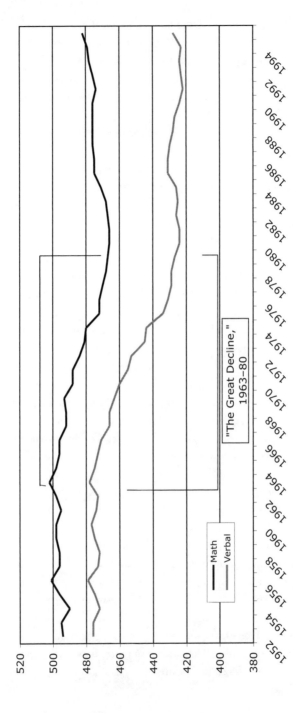

Figure 7.1. SAT Mean Scores, United States, 1952–1995. *Source:* College Board, U.S. Census Bureau.

this later decline. First, there appeared to have been in the nation's schools a "dispersal of learning activities and emphasis,"[18] such that students were now taking fewer basic courses and more electives—science fiction instead of English composition, for example—with critical reading and writing skills suffering the most.[19] Second, academic standards were dropping in U.S. schools, with absenteeism, grade inflation, and automatic promotion all on the rise and students doing less homework and being subjected to less challenging textbooks.[20]

Changes in society at large were also to blame: the country had experienced in the preceding decade a rising divorce rate; an increase in the number of women working outside the home; growth in television watching among the young; and a period of "national disillusionment, especially for young people, virtually unparalleled in American history," which included a divisive war, political assassination, riots, and the resignation of a president.[21] Finally, the panel argued, there had been during this time "an apparent marked diminution in young people's learning motivation."[22]

In 1975, *Newsweek* had rounded up many of these same culprits, especially television; it also blamed overcrowded classrooms and overworked teachers, who were simply no longer able to assign, read, and grade essays from their students because of the sheer size of the task involved. But the most withering criticism in "Why Johnny Can't Write" had been directed at academics, who, under the influence of "structural linguistics," began in the 1960s to privilege speech over writing, seeing the former as prior and primary and the latter as separate and derivative, and to deny any form of English, whether written or spoken, higher objective status over any other. According to *Newsweek,* followers of this approach to language believed that insistence on "standard" English constituted an act of "repression" by the white middle class, and sympathetic teachers began therefore to deemphasize rule following in language education and to favor writing that resulted from natural, speech-based creativity. In fact, for *Newsweek,* a key sign of the influence of the new linguistics on writing instruction was CCCC's own "Students' Right to their Own Language," ratified in 1974.[23]

This conservative explanation for the "great decline" of SAT scores in the 1960s and '70s was still exerting cultural pressure twenty years later. In *The Bell Curve* of 1994, for example, Richard Herrnstein and Charles Murray discounted the demographic explanations for the SAT decline, especially in the 1970s, when skill deterioration seemed to affect even the best-educated students.[24] While others might claim, they wrote, that the drop in mean scores was a function of the "democratization" of U.S. education, the data suggested to them that it was rather a matter of "mediocritization."[25] In the 1960s and '70s, according to this thesis, educational standards in the United States had been "dumbed down."[26] Television played a role as well, but it was teachers who were mostly to blame, especially their championing of multicultural education, self-esteem fostering, and other "politically compromised" agendas that were "antagonistic to traditional criteria of rigor and excellence."[27]

In a review of all the major studies on literacy performance during this period, Lawrence Stedman and Carl Kaestle, from the UW-Madison School of Education, argued in 1987 that the "permissive sixties" interpretation of the "great decline" was flawed.[28] Agreeing with the 1977 College Board study, they found the evidence for a decline in American students' reading and writing skills during the 1960s to be "mixed at best," given the massive demographic changes in the national test-taking group.[29] But even the "dramatic downturn" of 1970–78, for which the data seemed more persuasive, and which was so crucial to the conservative conclusions of both *On Further Examination* and *The Bell Curve,* could be attributed in large part, wrote Stedman and Kaestle, to compositional factors. Considering the lower dropout rate of the period, the increased immigration to the United States that followed federal immigration reform in the 1960s, birth-order effects attendant on the larger families of the baby boom generation, and other phenomena, they put the proportion of the 1970s score decline explained by demographic factors as high as 40 percent.[30] Stedman and Kaestle also pointed to the unrepresentative nature of the SAT itself, still taken by a minority of American youth, and the unreliability of standardized test scores in general. And they raised questions about whether declining scores on such multiple choice tests, concerned mainly with vocabulary (and a particular kind of vocabulary at that), could be connected to deterioration in actual reading and writing performance in schools, the workplace, or civil society.

But even assuming the reliability of the SAT test and the validity of its results, the most rational explanation for the decline in average verbal scores among U.S. high school juniors and seniors in the 1960s and '70s is that students, teachers, schools, and literacy itself had all simply changed during that time. The verbal performance of young American adults in the mid-1970s, in other words, wasn't better or worse than that of earlier cohorts; it was just different —and appropriately so, given the massive social, political, economic, demographic, cultural, educational, and linguistic changes of that period. The one thing that Stedman and Kaestle seemed to concede about SAT scores in the 1970s is that there did appear to be evidence for declining student motivation during the period.[31]

Aftermath, 1970–1996

Put in context, then, the 1970s literacy crisis was probably exaggerated. Between 1940 and 1980, most measures of student reading, writing, and overall academic performance in the United States steadily increased; the median educational level of adults, for example, rose an impressive four grades during this period, from 8.6 to 12.5 years. "The achievement test score decline" of the 1960s and '70s, Stedman and Kaestle concluded, "was not as drastic as many believe and is best explained by a combination of factors, not simply by educators' failure of nerve and drop in standards."[32]

Be that as it may, the faculty at the University of Wisconsin, like their counterparts across the country, were convinced in the mid-1970s that student writing skills were deteriorating. In the fall of 1975, 60 percent of juniors at the university failed the Journalism Department's English Usage Test. At the same time, the College of Letters and Science voted to begin a two-year experiment testing juniors' writing skills to determine if the 1971 Curriculum Review Committee's requirement that all students, before graduating, be certified as competent writers by their major departments was being fulfilled.[33] And in December 1975, after a TA-led symposium in the English Department concluded that "much work" was needed to improve undergraduate writing skills, UW's Teaching Assistants Association (now affiliated with the American Federation of Teachers, AFL-CIO) voted to include a request for an expanded composition program in collective bargaining negotiations that year, a proposal that gained the approval of the Student Association Senate and "Students for Quality Education" but was rejected by university administrators.[34]

Meanwhile, the UW Committee on Undergraduate Education's Task Group on Student Writing and Speaking (chaired by economics professor Lee Hansen, who would remain active in the campus fight for increased attention to student writing skills for the next thirty years) issued a long and detailed report in April 1976, titled "Improving the Writing Skills of Undergraduate Students," sometimes referred to as the Shakhashiri Report, after overall committee chair Professor Bassam Z. Shakhashiri. It represented the fullest account to date of the history of writing-skills instruction at UW and the most powerful argument up to that point for a reinstated freshman writing program. The task force summarized the campus literacy problem thusly:

> By long tradition, basic writing skills have been taught in the nation's elementary and secondary schools. These skills have been sharpened in the

colleges by requiring students to take composition courses during their early college years. They have been further developed and broadened through a variety of writing assignments in students' major fields of concentration during their junior and senior years.

A gradual and substantial improvement in writing and other basic skills of students entering college became evident in the early 1960s, as reflected by test score data and informed opinion. For this and a variety of other reasons, many colleges and universities had by the early 1970s relaxed their composition requirements, by either reducing or, in some cases, eliminating required composition courses.

While these curricular changes were taking place here and elsewhere, however, the basic skills of entering freshmen had already begun to stabilize. And since then, they have declined sharply. Recent and widespread publicity about these declines has strengthened judgments formed earlier by many individual faculty members. As a result, there have been calls for both the colleges and high schools to concentrate greater efforts on the teaching of writing.

The committee's evidence that UW students were having difficulty writing came from a variety of national reports (including aforementioned studies by NAEP, ETS, and the American College Testing Program). But there was local reason for concern as well: most important, a sharp decline in scores by entering freshmen on UW's own seventy-five-item College Qualification Test, scores that, in the mid-1970s, were at their lowest point since 1957, having suffered an especially steep drop since 1968 (from a median score of 57 to 48) (with a score below 35 requiring the student to enroll in and pass the "remedial" English 101 or Comm Arts 102) (see table 7.1).

There were other local data that seemed to support a literacy crisis on campus: a drop in scores on the English Recognition Test, also used to place students into English 101; more students seeking help in the Writing Lab, from four hundred visitors in fall 1973 to one thousand in fall 1975; and anecdotal evidence of increasing complaints from faculty about student writing.[35] Yet despite these signs of trouble, as the task force pointed out, 91 percent of students at UW took no general composition course at all, and those who were taking English 101 were receiving what appeared in historical context to be inflated grades. In 1963–64, when virtually all students on campus took two semesters of composition, over 50 percent of grades in English 101 were Cs (the average GPA for the course being 2.11); by fall 1975, when English 101 was taken only by the lowest-skilled writers among a cohort of apparently increasingly poor writers, the average GPA in the course had risen to 2.55, with the proportion of

7.1 Measures of Student Writing Ability at UW, 1957–1976

Academic Year	SAT—Mean Verbal	ACT—Mean Composite	Mean Freshman GPA	Median Centile High School Class Rank	Median Raw Score College Qualification Test—Verbal	Estimated Percentage of Entering Students Taking Different Number of Composition Courses			
						0	1	2	3[A]
1957–58	N.A.	N.A.	2.23	78	47	0	4	78	18
1963–64	535	24.2	2.24	79	55	0	10	70	20
1968–69	569	24.8	2.59	83	58	0	97	3	0
1972–73	544	21.5	2.62	81	51	93	5	2	0
1975–76	N.A.	N.A.	2.70	81	48	91	8	1	0

[A] The third course here refers not to the old English 0 remedial course but to English 201, Intermediate Composition, required during the 1950s and early '60s for BS and School of Education students.

Source: Task Group on Student Writing and Speaking (Lee Hansen, chair), UW-Madison Committee on Undergraduate Education (Bassam Z. Shakhashiri, chair), "Improving the Writing Skills of Undergraduate Students," April 1976, pp. 5, 6, 20.

students receiving Cs falling to 21 percent and the percentage receiving Ds falling by one-half.[36]

As argued earlier in relation to the SAT and in chapter 4 regarding campus placement tests, there are flaws with any such portrayal of student literacy levels: none of the data comes from actual student writing performance, most of it originating in multiple choice tests of vocabulary or usage; the studies fail to contextualize changes in test performance by considering changing student populations; and they fail to consider that changes in reading and writing skills might be explained by changing sociocultural contexts for and attitudes about literacy itself.

Be that as it may, the task group's report seemed to come from genuine faculty (and student) concern for undergraduate writing performance and instruction at UW. And it ended with a long discussion of possible steps for improving the situation. Some of these steps would *modify* the system of literacy instruction then in place at UW by, for example, instituting a campuswide English competence test at the junior level, combined with mandatory referral to courses like English 101 or the Writing Lab, or by reducing the number of students exempted from the writing requirement and either expanding the number taking English 101 or instituting a dual-level program for those not exempted, with the weakest required to take English 101 and the others required to go to the Writing Lab.

The report also considered policy alternatives that would *supplement* the system then in place by, for example, expanding the Writing Lab, the number of elective writing courses offered, or programs providing remedial help, or by encouraging faculty to place more emphasis on writing and speaking skills or to strengthen their competence requirements. Finally, the report discussed policies that would substantially *replace* the system then in use by, for example, establishing a university-wide English competence requirement for either admission to or graduation from UW; reinstituting a required course similar to English 101 or the old English 102; or developing a set of basic courses, one of which would be required.

The committee didn't make a final determination among these possibilities (in hindsight, probably a tactical error). Instead, at report's end, it merely considered their various advantages and disadvantages. But it did reiterate its argument that effective writing skills were central to the university's instructional program; that the deterioration of those skills among UW students was alarming; and that something needed to be done about them that would involve putting more resources into undergraduate writing on campus. The committee

Aftermath, 1970–1996

also recommended that the university conduct research about the suitability of multiple-choice tests for judging writing competence, that it survey the benefits and costs of implementing the various proposals considered by the committee, that campuswide competence levels in writing be established; and that assistance in developing writing skills be expanded somehow.

Meanwhile, in the spring of 1976, English Department TAs at UW organized the second departmental forum in a year on the composition issue. And a week later, responding to both the Shakhashiri Report and the English TA forum, Chancellor Edwin Young announced the formation of a Special Committee on Improving the Quality of Student Writing Skills to make recommendations about an expanded composition program on campus. That committee's report, issued a year later, in February 1977, argued that UW undergraduate students could be divided into three groups with respect to their writing skills: one-third needed training in both basic (English 101) and intermediate (English 201) writing skills, another third needed only the latter (English 201), and a final third came to college with skills sufficient to be exempt from both courses.[37] Even with that breakdown, which seemed to argue against a one-size-fits-all freshman composition requirement, the momentum seemed to be moving toward some kind of expansion or strengthening of the university's writing requirement and course offerings.

But a few months later, in May 1977, when the College of Letters and Science Faculty Senate considered a proposal to require junior-level competence testing in composition, faculty complained that the policy would penalize students for inadequate skills but provide no new coursework to help them acquire those skills. And with no proposal from the English Department to expand its composition program and no significant effort among departments themselves to increase their writing-in-the-disciplines effort, the motion was voted down.

Once again, it appeared that the English faculty, refusing to reestablish a large, TA-taught freshman writing program, was standing in the way of substantially improved writing instruction on campus. And once again it was the English Department TAs who were trying to push them, less aggressively than in 1969 but pushing nonetheless, into a new posture on the subject. It was clear that once the old Freshman English program had been dismantled, it was going to be difficult to reinstate it, even with pressure from nearly every side to do so. Inertia, the traditional foe of academic reform, had set in. After all, curricula always expand to fill a vacuum, and it was difficult to carve out space for general (or even disciplinary) writing instruction once that space had been taken by other things. Gradually, the mid-1970s literacy crisis waned, and for the next few years, the university's attention was focused elsewhere.

———————

Then, in the spring of 1980, a strike by the UW Teaching Assistants' Association revealed, among other things, continuing frustrations among English Department TAs concerning undergraduate composition and their training in it. It also pointed to growing tensions in overall faculty-TA relations on the campus. After the 1970 strike, the university and union had settled into a kind of tense but stable relationship. But the 1980 strike created a rupture that would never really be healed. The TAA itself tells the story this way:

> The fifth contract between the TAA and the UW expired in August 1979. For some time, the University had grown increasingly impatient with the collective bargaining process, ignoring arbitrators' awards in grievance cases and flouting court decisions ordering it to abide by the terms of the contract. When bargaining began for a new contract in 1979, the UW insisted on across-the-board concessions. It wanted some TAs to work without being paid on the pretext that they were not really working, but fulfilling degree requirements. The UW did not want to post hiring criteria for TAs. Administrators demanded the sole power to decide which grievances could be taken to binding arbitration. Once again, the TAA was faced with the difficult choice—to strike or to work without a contract.
>
> For seven months, the union worked without a contract. Finally, in March 1980, TAs voted to strike. The issue was the union's existence and the right of graduate assistants to have a say in determining their working conditions. Union members and supporters struck for five weeks. Although the TAA accepted a mediator's proposal to end the strike, the UW refused to compromise. In May, just before the end of classes, the TAA returned to work without a contract. Three months later, Chancellor Shain announced that he was terminating the Structure Agreement, which had provided the legal framework for ten years of bargaining. The TAA sued, but the court ruled that the UW had the right to pull out of the agreement. Ten years of bargaining were over.
>
> While in the short term it seemed that the TAA's second strike had failed, in the end, it galvanized TAA members to address the underlying weakness in their position: the lack of legal bargaining rights. A legislation committee was created to coordinate an intensive outreach, lobbying, and research effort designed to secure passage of a bargaining rights bill. With the support of unionists from across Wisconsin, the TAA accomplished what

many had considered impossible: in October 1985, the bill passed despite intense opposition from the university. Once again, TAs had the opportunity to bargain about their conditions of employment—but this time, the university had a legal obligation to sit at the table and bargain in good faith. And, for the first time, PAs had the right to choose union representation. The foundations of a new beginning were laid.[38]

In the English Department, the 1980 strike exposed long-simmering problems in the staffing, training, and supervision of TA-taught undergraduate writing courses, many of which could be traced to the crisis a decade earlier in Freshman English. The semester after the strike ended—fall 1980—department chair Sargent Bush asked the "Committee on Composition Programs," chaired by Charles Scott, to look into possible reforms in how the department managed its writing courses.[39]

That committee issued its report in December 1980. It's not entirely clear what the TAs had complained about during the previous semester, but the report itself suggests that one issue had been whether the department took seriously its responsibility for training and supervision of its TAs, especially in courses like freshman and intermediate composition (English 101 and 201), where the TAs had relative autonomy as teachers. Before delving into specific recommendations, the committee dealt with this complaint in the following statement:

> We believe that the training of teaching assistants for careers in college teaching has traditionally been an objective in this Department, even if at times it has been honored more in the intent than in the practice. Indeed, we hope that one of the effects of this report will be to resuscitate this objective for an area of college-level teaching that has been too much neglected in the vision of this Department during the past decade. We accept as axiomatic that our recommendations should recognize the faculty's statutory obligation for the supervision of teaching assistants, and its moral and professional obligation for the training of teaching assistants.[40]

The report is then divided into two sections: one dealing with the training and the other with the supervision of TAs. In the training section, the committee recommended a series of steps to make teacher-training for the department's writing courses, especially English 101 and 201, more coherent. First, nearly fifteen years after TAs first asked for it, the department would create a graduate-level course in the theory and practice of college composition: a semester-long, three-credit, faculty-taught course required of all TAs in their first semester of residence in the PhD program (the committee didn't consider in depth the content of such a course, but someone on the committee, probably Stan Henning, had done his homework: there is discussion of the writing process, rhetoric, and discourse analysis, and a citation of Gary Tate's *Teaching Composition: Ten Bibliographic Essays*).

The new course was English 700, still offered to this day in the UW-Madison English Department. The purpose of the course, according to the report, was, in a sense, to professionalize the teaching of composition in the department: "Being able to write with clarity and appropriateness of style does not, in itself, guarantee an ability to teach others to do so as well. We suppose, therefore, that an improved—or at least a more enlightened—level of composition instruction ought to be a benefit of this course."[41] Interestingly, the committee paired English 700 with the required Critical Methods course (English 723), the two functioning together in professional development of the department's PhD students.

There are moments in the report, in fact, when the faculty seemed to imagine a balance between composition and literature in the department that had not obtained since the earlier parts of the twentieth century:

> A further motivation [for the new course in composition studies], however, has to do with a broader conception of the link between our program for the PhD and the experience of the teaching assistantship, both of which contribute integratively to the preparation of an individual for a career in college- or university-level English teaching. Just as the required course in Critical Methods might be construed as a kind of professional introduction to the ways in which literary texts can be approached for purposes of elucidation, so also might we consider this proposed course in the theory and practice of composition as a kind of professional introduction to the ways in which written texts can be composed for purposes of communication. The one has a preparatory function for the subsequent study and teaching of literature; the other will fulfill the same function for the teaching of writing skills and composition. The teaching of English at the college or university level encompasses both activities, even more so now and in the foreseeable future than in the recent past.[42]

The committee admitted that its recommendation concerning English 700 also recognized the realities of the academic job market in English.

The committee further recommended the appointment of a program coordinator for English 101 and 201 (a nine-month academic staff assistant to the faculty directors of the two programs), a schedule of regular staff meetings for course instructors, and the continuation of the department's summer workshop

188

for new writing teachers. The committee summed up these four recommendations by describing them as "interlocking constituents of a program for the training of teachers of composition and writing skills," which together would encompass:

> 1) pre-registration week Workshop; 2) course in composition theory and practice in the first semester of residence in the PhD program . . . ; 3) regular staff meetings with faculty director of writing course and Program Coordinator . . . ; 4) consultations with Program Coordinator based on several informal classroom visitations, plus general guidance on such issues as theme annotation and grading patterns; and 5) continuation of staff meetings and consultation with Program Coordinator in second semester.[43]

Under "Supervision," the report recommended:

> 1. Deleting from the Department's statement of policies and procedures governing faculty visitation of TA-taught classes the footnote: "When TAs are working in more than one program the visit should be made to the literature course when possible." . . . 2. Postponing the formal evaluation of TA teaching performance by faculty visitors to approximately the eleventh week of the semester. . . . 3. Requiring each of the faculty directors of English 101, 105, 117, 118, 201, and 203 to check the grading patterns in their respective courses and, in those courses where the practice is not already established, to sign the grade sheets at the end of the semester.[44]

But it's only in the report's "Conclusions" that the committee seems to admit that the department had not been taking its responsibilities in training and supervising TAs in writing courses seriously enough: "A recurrent theme in our discussions concerned the extent to which faculty awareness of what happens in our basic writing courses seems to have diminished in recent years." The committee admits that "only a handful" of faculty members are knowledgeable about the courses, the rest "permitted, by default, to remain largely unfamiliar with such matters." And in a statement that seems an eerie echo of TA complaints from ten years before, the committee remarks that "a consequence of this general condition of inattention and unfamiliarity is to weaken the faculty's claim to authority in issues of educational policy, though no amount of neglect can abrogate the authority. Still, we ought to be in a position to assert more than just a *de jure* claim in such matters."[45] Further down, the committee articulates its plea in an eloquent formulation: "As faith without good works may compromise our fitness for heavenly tenure, so too legislation without participation may exact a toll on our credibility as a departmental faculty."[46]

The recommendations were meant to serve, then, as "a call to a more concerted effort on the part of the faculty to become more actively engaged in issues surrounding the teaching of writing in our Department, including especially the training and supervision of teaching assistants in the basic writing program."[47] And here, the committee returned to its earlier image of parity in the department between literature and composition:

> More bluntly, we do ourselves no service, nor the academic community, if we do not heed the public expectation than an English department is a department of language as well as of literature, and that, among its functions, is the teaching of writing with clarity and appropriate style as well as the teaching of reading with comprehension and critical interpretation. We are long past the time when we could afford to attend to the one and not to the other.[48]

If the 1980 report is a sign that, a decade after the events of 1969, the department was still neglecting not only its composition program but its TAs as well, that it had not really learned its lessons, the tone here is admittedly very different from the tone of the Departmental Committee meetings in the late 1960s: here, the response to "inattention and unfamiliarity" among the faculty concerning general education writing instruction in the department was not to simply abandon responsibilities in that area, but to thoughtfully try to reengage that project.[49]

The 1980 report led not only to the hiring of Joyce Melville as the new assistant to the directors of freshman and intermediate composition and the design of a new graduate Introduction to Composition Studies course (English 700) but also to the hiring of a tenure-track faculty member whose specialty was composition, the first in the department in half a century. In 1982, Martin Nystrand, a former high school English teacher in the Chicago area, who had gone on to do graduate study with James Britton at the University of London in the early 1970s and received his PhD in English Education from Northwestern University in 1974, working with Wallace Douglas, joined the department and quickly raised the intellectual profile of composition there. He spearheaded numerous developments at the graduate level, including new courses, such as English 700, English 900 (Language and Cognition in the Composing Process), and English 901 (The Structure of Written Communication). Then, in 1983, the department hired Deborah Brandt, with a new PhD in hand from Indiana, literally doubling the composition faculty at UW. In 1985, a graduate minor in composition theory was inaugurated, and in 1991, a full-scale PhD program in composition studies began.

190

There were other developments during these years: in 1985 Brad Hughes took over the Writing Center from the retiring Joyce Steward, and in 1987, Dean David Cronon recommended writing-in-the-disciplines coursework for each student in the College of Letters and Science. Still, another decade would elapse before the campus would finally reintroduce a substantial and universal freshman writing requirement. It came about this way: by the early 1990s, faculty concerns about undergraduate general education at UW, in terms of both foundational skills in communication and mathematics and exposure to a range of disciplines, had reached a critical mass, and formal proposals were made to the University Faculty Senate for a new campus-wide general education program, including required first-year general coursework in written communication.[50]

The Committee on Undergraduate Education (chaired by communication arts professor Lloyd Bitzer) recommended on August 20, 1993 (in the "Report of the Committee on Undergraduate Education") extensive new undergraduate requirements in communication, quantitative reasoning, breadth, and ethnic studies.[51] In January 1994, that report was widely disseminated on campus, and on March 15, 1994, a revised draft was published, which was formally approved by the UW-Madison faculty in May 1994. Students matriculating in 1996 were the first subject to the requirements, and on October 7, 1996, an amended set of recommendations and reports governing the university's general education program was published. In 1996, the committee summarized the effort this way:

> Our 1993 report pointed out that UW-Madison has no campus-wide general education requirements, with the single exception of the 3-credit ethnic studies requirement. Moreover, from one school/college to another, considerable variation exists regarding requirements for basic composition and mathematics instruction, as well as for other required subjects, including natural science, humanities, literature, and social studies. Because we lack campus-wide requirements, many students never take college-level work in composition and quantitative reasoning; and some students graduate lacking competence in these basic, important skills. We reported also that numerous peer universities have substantial general education requirements, in comparison to which our requirements are meager. As well, we reported results of a survey of faculty opinion showing considerable support for general education requirements at UW-Madison.
>
> The 1993 report pointed out that the current composition requirement, mandated by several of our schools and colleges, is embarrassingly weak. It calls for taking English 101 or Communication Arts 101 or 105 unless placement scores exempt students from any one of those courses. The exemption

Aftermath, 1970–1996

score is so low that less than five percent of entering students are required to take English 101 (a course in composition) or Communication Arts 101 or 105 (courses in public speaking). Many students who pass the exam cannot write papers free of the most obvious errors of composition. By contrast, the University of Iowa's requirement produces almost opposite results: Iowa's entrance test exempts about 5 percent, while 95 percent take one or two semesters of composition and basic rhetoric. In truth, UW-Madison's composition requirement is the weakest such requirement of all the 20 or so universities whose general education requirements we examined. Even though numerous reports by faculty committees called for serious reform, the requirement has remained in force since the early 1970s.

After much discussion of a literacy requirement and how it might be met, the committee concluded that a new two-course requirement in composition/basic rhetoric should be satisfied by course work in the four modes of literacy (writing, speaking, reading, and listening), with primary emphasis on writing, and in the skills of critical thinking. As well, one of the courses should provide instruction in information literacy, which introduces students to University libraries, information accessing, use of computers to locate materials, and strategies of library research. In the committee's view, students who satisfy the communication requirement should be able to write papers that are largely free of grammatical and stylistic errors, well organized, clear, convincing, and properly documented and referenced; also, students should be able to make oral presentations confidently, coherently, logically. The committee is convinced that students should take courses that focus on: expository and argumentative prose; fundamentals of grammar and style; paragraphing; methods of investigation; kinds of evidence; major types of practical inductive and deductive reasoning, as well as common fallacies; the form and documentation of research reports and papers; organization of effective prose; audience adaptation; principles of critical reading and listening; principles of oral delivery.

After the 1993 report was distributed, the committee received comments from individual faculty members, several of the schools and colleges, the University Committee, academic planning councils, and several students. We received comments in formal reports, letters, conversations, and in three public hearings sponsored by the committee in February. In general, we found strong support for the recommendations. No one disagreed with the committee's finding that our composition requirement must be upgraded markedly. Likewise, there is broad support for general education requirements in quantitative reasoning, natural science, humanities, literature, social studies, and ethnic studies. Finally, we heard strong support from library staff and others for our recommendation that instruction in utilizing the resources of University libraries should be an essential part of the required communication courses.[52]

In the end, the new communication requirement was constituted as follows:

COMMUNICATION: 3 TO 5/6 CREDITS

Part A: 2–3 credits

Each student shall complete, or through examinations be exempted from, a first-year course providing instruction and practice in the modes of literacy. Courses shall be dedicated to literacy proficiency—accurate and critical writing, speaking, reading, and listening, with primary emphasis on writing.

The courses shall contain instruction in "information literacy," including accessing the print and electronic resources of the University's libraries. Students exempted from Part A shall complete comparable instruction in information literacy.

Part B: 2–3 credits

Students who complete or are exempted from the first course shall thereafter earn 2 to 3 credits in course work designed to enhance their literacy proficiency.

Units of instruction within courses not dedicated primarily to instruction in the modes of literacy may count toward satisfaction of the Part B requirement if the school/college determines that the units provide substantial instruction in these modes.

In November 1994, the committee released guidelines for Part A of the new requirement, satisfied for most students by passing either English 100, Freshman Composition, or Communication Arts 100, Public Speaking.[53] The purpose of these new "Comm-A" courses was to promote "communication skills at the college level, developing student abilities in writing and public speaking, for both exposition and argumentation. As such, the course is to serve as a general foundation in the central skills and conventions required for student success in a variety of subsequent course work, as well as in careers after college." The courses were meant to advance basic skills in the four modes of literacy ("writing, speaking, reading and listening, with special emphasis on writing"), along with critical thinking and information seeking, and the teaching method prescribed was "continuous practice in the process of writing and speaking," including planning, drafting, and revising. Students would be allowed to waive the requirement with sufficiently high SAT or ACT verbal scores.

Part B of the new communications requirement, referred to as Comm-B, would be satisfied for most students by an advanced communications course in their major. Beginning in the fall of 1996, all entering freshmen at UW-Madison were required to meet the two-semester communications requirement.

The story of composition at UW after 1970 and especially the battles around the Comm-A and Comm-B requirements in the early 1990s deserve fuller attention than I can devote here. The focus of this book, after all, has been on the late 1960s. But I wanted to show some of what happened after the 1969 crisis and, especially, to make the point that the abolition of first-year composition at UW was, in one sense, astoundingly effective, forever changing the English Department there and leading to twenty-five years without a substantial writing requirement on campus. At the same time, the constant calls to reinstate first-year writing—from TAs, from other faculty, from the public at large—show clearly that freshman comp cannot so easily be done away with. Since the late nineteenth century, both at UW and nationally, the course has clearly met a deeply embedded need in our society, one that the academy (and the discipline of English studies) remains acutely aware of even as it alternately accepts and refuses responsibility for effectively and ethically responding to that need.

Aftermath, 1970–1996

CONCLUSION

Freshman Composition at the Turn of the New Century

Given the repeated attempts, after 1970, to reinstate a universally required first-year writing course at the University of Wisconsin-Madison, attempts that would ultimately succeed (in their way), and reminding ourselves of what we saw in chapters 2 and 3 about the long history of Freshman English at the university before 1968, it would be easy to characterize the period from 1970 to 1996, when the campus essentially had no composition requirement, as an aberration in an otherwise unbroken story of general education writing instruction at UW. We could then explain the faculty's "surprise action" regarding Freshman English in the late 1960s by reference to the tumultuous times in which it occurred, interpreting the abolition of English 102 as a product of history: a function, for example, of the intense generational clashes of the period, exemplified by the conflict between English professors Tim Heninger, Edgar Lacy, and their colleagues, on the one hand, and English graduate teaching assistants Joe Carr, Bob Muehlenkamp, and their colleagues, on the other.[1] Or we could see it as a casualty of the highly charged ideological climate of the time, which often left individuals mired in starkly opposed positions, with little middle ground between them. Or we could see it as part of the collision of incompatible institutional impulses that characterized higher education during the 1960s: the desire to meet the general educational needs of the increasing number and diversity of entering students, on the one hand, and the growing pressure on faculty to produce specialized research, on the other. We could say, in other words, that the story of Freshman English at UW in the 1960s—however interesting, evocative, and telling—is just that: a story of the '60s.

And in fact, it would be a mistake to separate out the events of 1968 and '69 at UW from the larger story of that time, from foreign war, domestic unrest, sociocultural upheaval, and student activism more generally. With that in mind, I have tried here to connect the two, the local and the global, the institutional and the cultural, especially after hearing from readers involved in the events related here that the narrative was factually true but lacked the "feel" of the era. I wished sometimes I could have told this story in the form of a documentary film, with a soundtrack from the Rolling Stones and Jimi Hendrix and archival footage of UW students marching up Bascom Hill as armed troops lined their way.

Even in the admittedly tame form of the scholarly monograph, however, I have tried to situate this story as much as possible within its particular historical context and to embed what happened to English 101 and 102 at UW in 1968 and '69 within a larger narrative about postsecondary education in the land-grant public universities of the United States during "the long sixties," a narrative about how faculty at schools like UW, with full support from their institutions and state and federal governments, tried to reposition themselves in *disciplinary* terms, as producers of original research within highly specialized academic communities, whose key teaching duties, if any, were at the advanced level; and how, at the same time, the number of undergraduate students at public universities like UW was skyrocketing, as young people from increasingly diverse backgrounds, subjected to academic, political, economic, and cultural demands for increasingly sophisticated reading, writing, and thinking skills, needed ever-increasing help at the general education level to meet those demands.

Key to the administration of both developments, at least at large public research universities like UW, was a growing cadre of graduate student teaching assistants (TAs), who were given increased responsibility for teaching at the lower undergraduate level, a situation that left those TAs in the difficult position of being in charge of increasingly important and increasingly complex courses in general education that their faculty supervisors, on whom both their jobs and their academic careers depended, increasingly belittled. As I have argued here, the tensions inherent in this institutional arrangement reached a crisis in this country around 1969.

Part of this project, then, has been about emphasizing the radical specificity of the late 1960s within histories of twentieth-century North American higher education in general and of modern composition-rhetoric in particular. That's because I believe there has been a tendency within my own field to tell stories about writing and writing instruction in which the late 1960s are absorbed into narratives that are really about either the late 1950s–early 1960s and the birth of the "new rhetoric," or the 1970s and the rise of the process paradigm. In such accounts, the years 1967–70 are made continuous with the events of earlier or later periods.[2]

A more accurate account, I believe, would treat the late 1960s, at least in terms of freshman composition, as sui generis, its own cultural moment unassimilable to other periods, a time of radical rupture in the incipient discipline as well as higher education itself, when one era literally and figuratively came to an end and another, haltingly, incoherently, began. The late 1960s, from this point of view, was when current-traditionalism finally came up against a wall it could not surmount. Unfortunately, when that paradigm collapsed, there was nothing waiting in the wings powerful and attractive enough to take its place; at UW, for example, there was no discipline of composition that could supervise a new kind of course, no rhetoric revival in the English Department, no incipient process movement. At other schools, freshman composition might have limped on for a few more years, intellectually orphaned, until the process revolution reinvented it, emerging at the end of the 1970s as the central project of a new, bona fide academic discipline, with full-fledged research programs, graduate degrees, and tenure-track faculty lines. But at UW, when current-traditionalism collapsed in the wake of graduate TA resistance, and the faculty refused to allow those TAs to develop a new curriculum in its place, the course was simply killed, and for the next quarter of a century there was a void in undergraduate general education on that campus, a void that left English studies at UW in the 1970s unable to take full advantage of the writing revolution that was taking place elsewhere.[3]

But what this story also reveals is that, however specific the late 1960s were for composition at UW (and the nation at large), however incommensurate with stories of 1950s professionalization, 1960s rhetoric revival, or 1970s process, however radical the break of those years in any valid disciplinary narrative, the *idea* of freshman composition survived. Even with the very particular personalities and forces involved in that time and place, and the dramatic attempt made by the senior faculty there to chart a new direction for postsecondary "English," one focused exclusively on advanced literary studies, the fact is that for the next twenty-five years a conceptual place for freshman composition at UW was retained, well after the course itself was abolished. It was almost as if the rest of the campus—faculty outside of English, TAs inside, and undergraduate students across campus—were simply waiting for a new institutional arrangement that could sponsor it. In other words, as radically different as freshman composition was at UW across the twentieth century—English 1a and b from 1898 to 1963, English 101 and 102 from 1963 to 1969, English 100 from 1996 on—as inextricably embedded as each version of the course was in its own historical moment, the course itself can be characterized by surprisingly stable features and parameters, benefits and liabilities alike, that seem almost to transcend history.

Which brings me to the final point I want to make in this book. Despite the importance of situating this story fully in its time, of radically contextualizing English 101 and 102 within the late 1960s Madison scene, I have come to believe that the story of Freshman English at UW in the late 1960s is more than just a story of its time and place. It's also a story *about that course,* about an educational project that, over the past century and a quarter, has acquired the status of a kind of transhistorical academic phenomenon, one that, across dramatically different times and places, has occupied roles, sponsored experiences, and satisfied needs of remarkable constancy. It struck me again and again, for example, how often the TAs and faculty I was listening to in this study were arguing, in the end, not about Vietnam, civil rights, or cultural politics, but about the pedagogical parameters of first-year writing itself, this odd entity that, in many ways, has changed very little since its invention in the late nineteenth century. And it struck me as well how the crisis that engulfed freshman composition at UW in the late 1960s was, in many ways, not unlike crises that have engulfed the course in other times and places very different from Vietnam War–era Madison.

To put this another way: although much about the history I have told here is woven tightly into the particular fabric of the UW English Department in the late 1960s, a time and space that needs to be seen in all its particularity and specificity, that story cannot, I believe, be *reduced* to time and place. As much as the events related here were dependent on forces originating outside of the English Department—forces like the war in Vietnam or the large-scale political, cultural, social, and economic transformations taking place in the United States—there were things about freshman composition itself as an educational project, things built into the very structure of that course, that drove the events narrated here as much as those events drove it.

In other words, far from simply absorbing late-1960s freshman comp at UW into the tumult of its times, I want here, at the end of this study, to give that course a measure of independence from its situations and personages. And I want to suggest that "internal," structural features of first-year composition at UW, features that it shared with the course at other institutions and that it shares with the course at other points in time, may have helped it play a more important role in 1960s campus upheaval than historians and others have tended to think. Now, I obviously can't take this argument too far: most of what took place at UW from 1967 to 1970, from the Dow sit-in to the Black Strike to the Mifflin Street riot to the bombing of Sterling Hall, would have happened had there been no English 101 and 102. And yet, I've come to believe that this narrative is not merely a story *of* 1968 and 1969; it's also a story *about* postsecondary composition and composition instruction in the United States.

Here, then, is where I rejoin the "great debate" about freshman comp abolitionism that I mentioned in chapter 1.[4] I believe that the remedialization of English 101 and the elimination of English 102 at UW in the late 1960s were only partly about that particular faculty's rejection of those particular undergraduate students (whom they cast as uninterested in and unaided by the course) and those specific graduate TAs (whom they characterized as insubordinate and irresponsible in their teaching of it). The decisions, I believe, were also about the English faculty's opposition to *the very idea* of freshman composition.

And that opposition transcends the particular time and place of the story I've told here. The fact is that, nearly everywhere it has been taught, and at nearly each juncture in its history, freshman composition has been an unstable institutional phenomenon. Why? Perhaps it's because the course is so beholden to forces outside of the university itself. But perhaps it also has to do with the very structure of the course as it has usually been configured: its position in the curriculum, its "clientele" and staffing, its generally perceived ends and means. Almost by definition, freshman comp lacks "content"; almost by definition it is required of nearly every undergraduate student on campus, regardless of major, background, or skill; almost by definition, it's taken during the first year of college, when those students are literally closer to high school than to their major; almost by definition, it's taught by low-status instructors with (typically) insufficient resources to meet the demands of their job. We're talking about an educational phenomenon, in other words, that is inextricably embedded in the quintessentially American projects of *common* schooling and *general* education, a situation that imbues the course with remarkable potential even as it leaves it radically "undisciplined," undistinguished, and undifferentiated. It's a course that has both thrived and suffered in the face of higher education's modernist pursuit of substantive knowledge, specialized research, disciplinary allegiance, and neutral inquiry. It's a course that is both preternaturally tied to "social fiat" and largely independent of it.[5]

In other words, what most epitomized the freshman composition program at UW in the late 1960s, what most bothered its opponents, is what has always epitomized freshman composition, and generated opposition to it, everywhere. As an educational project, it is both precariously "empty" and dangerously full, relatively untethered to disciplinary content and authority, on the one hand, but replete with all our social concerns and anxieties about language, reason, identity, and community, on the other.[6] To put this another way: what lent the course both cultural resonance and institutional instability in the Madison, Wisconsin, of the Vietnam War era, is what continues to lend the course cultural resonance and institutional instability today. And that is its *generality, universality,* and *liminality.* Let's take each of these in turn.

First, *generality.* By generality, I mean the way freshman composition is almost by design a course without "content" in the academic sense of that word, a course that practices students in skills, habits, and dispositions rather than transmitting substantive knowledge to them. It is a course that is, almost by definition, inordinately flexible and that, from a negative point of view, can thus look empty or thin from the outside. Now, when a skills-based conception of freshman comp served their interests, the English faculty at UW were perfectly willing to define English 101 and 102, and their other general education offerings, in those terms. This is how department chair Tim Heninger put it in an April 1969 memo to Dean Epstein:

> Because of the nature of our discipline, we should have an unusually low student-faculty ratio. . . . We require more than transfer of information; we are teaching students how to write and how to respond to literature. These are highly individualized achievements, and we must interact with the students as individuals in order to be effective. The students' demand for personal attention from us is enormous and insistent; and the more successful we are in our teaching, the more we are badgered by eager students. I maintain that student demands are greater on members of the English Department than on members of other departments where the discipline is largely subject-matter.[7]

A month later, as we saw in chapter 5, Heninger made an even more impassioned defense of the department's role in providing space for student thinking, debating, and arguing. In a letter to Dean Epstein, responding to the charge

Conclusion

that the English Department was a "weak spot" in the university and a haven for "SDS types," Heninger denied that the English Students Association was dominated by SDS: "Their criticism of the English Department and the University is much more pedagogical than political, though several have expressed the intention of applying their criticism to society as a whole and of reaching out into the community."[8]

Heninger went on to claim that the department had a large number of intelligent students, who were asking pointed questions and would not be satisfied with half truths.

> By the nature of our discipline, we are the focal point for such students in the University, and I take it as a genuine responsibility that our department provide a context for these students to explore their ideas while interacting with a mature faculty.
> . . . This is what a liberal education means. . . . I will argue that, rather than being a weak spot, the English Department is a bastion for thinking men, and that we are performing an extremely important function in dealing with these bright young critics in a way that not many other departments are capable of trying.[9]

This view of "English" studies as general, practical, and nonsubstantive was held by students as well. As we saw in chapter 5, a few days before the presidential election of 1968, the ESA had petitioned the chair for permission to use English classes as a space for discussion and debate on current affairs, something perhaps only truly possible in a course with the kind of built-in generality and flexibility of freshman composition.

And yet, ironically, the TAs themselves were not always clear that a "contentless" course is what they wanted. Note, for example, how, in the joint faculty-TA deliberations of the Freshman English Policy Committee during the 1968–69 academic year, the central issue of discussion, according to committee chair William Lenehan, was how to keep the focus of English 102 on its central purpose, the improvement of writing, and yet increase student and staff interest in it. The solution suggested was to give the course subject matter, under the belief that good writing is possible only if the student has something he or she is interested in writing about. TAs recommended literature; faculty argued against. The final consensus was to keep the course traditionally rhetorical, use an essay anthology for models, but allow a short story anthology as background for themes.[10]

But the issue of course content remained a point of contention between faculty and TAs. In spring 1968, in fact, English TA James Naremore complained that the faculty wanted Freshman English to remain rhetoric based, "the pure skills course, the 'service' program which is good public relations" but which, from Naremore's perspective, was anti-intellectual and elementary. He thought that the course should instead be literature based: "I found myself in the awkward position of having to defend the teaching of literature before a panel of literature teachers."[11]

But the *idea* of freshman comp, I believe, is the idea of an education that helps young people engage the real world around them—not from the perspective of a discipline, canon, or textbook, but from that of *activity* itself. The trick has been to imagine such an activity-based course that is not therefore empty, a course without content that is not therefore about nothing, a general experience that is not consequently vacuous.

The move to process in the teaching of writing during the 1970s was, from this point of view, partly right and partly wrong: right because it lessened the earlier pedagogical focus on static, finished, "correct" writing, but wrong because it encouraged the view that "writing" was a neutral method or skill and not a material practice always embedded in time and place even as it was capable of being discussed, criticized, analyzed, and mastered. The contentless nature of the freshman composition course, rightly understood, is thus its genius. As Richard Ohmann has put it, the thinness of the first-year writing class is what makes it "socially useful."[12]

Second, *universality*. By *universality*, I mean the way that freshman composition has been seen traditionally as meeting the needs of *all* students on campus, a course common to all undergraduates that, ideally at least, brings together a multiplicity and diversity of students that would not otherwise come together—given both the social segregation of college students in our society and the academic fragmentation of the modern university. Now, a universal requirement can also be seen, of course, in less generous terms: as a restriction on students' freedom, a flattening out and homogenization of student needs and goals, a reduction of writing to a single thing. I don't deny the potential problems that attend universalization; for now, though, I want to emphasize what is unique, and historically constant, about freshman composition: its application, well after the late nineteenth century rise of elective studies in U.S. higher education, to *all* students on campus, its essential (and rather astounding) commonality even in the fragmented universities of the late twentieth and early twenty-first century.[13]

The faculty at UW in 1969, however, as much in English as in biology, were all about intellectual dispersal, academic specialization, and professional

Conclusion

fragmentation. This attitude can be situated historically within the rise and development of the modern university itself, but it can also be seen in the specific context of the English Department at Madison in the post–World War II decades and especially in the post-*Sputnik* period, when, as Charles Scott admitted in his 1980 interview with the UW-Madison Oral History Program, there was enormous pressure on faculty to specialize and when, as Tim Heninger admitted in his spring 1969 memo to the dean, the department's very identity increasingly depended on the advanced research represented by its graduate program.[14] But nowhere was the English faculty's commitment to a centrifugal model of higher education more evident than in the second reason provided in November 1969 for the elimination of English 102: that students' writing skills should be acquired predominantly within their majors. This commitment to a "writing-in-the-disciplines" model of writing instruction can be seen as an abandonment of the very idea of a common discourse that all students on campus are exposed to and practiced in. As I tried to indicate in chapter 6, this is not a theory of writing or writing instruction to be sneered at. In fact, the general tendency of composition and rhetoric research since the late 1960s has been precisely in the direction of dispersal, particularization, and situatedness: there is no such thing, we now tell ourselves, as a general writing skill or practice and thus no valid universal course in writing in general.[15]

We should not underestimate the break with the historical project of common schooling, public discourse, and universal education that this move marks, but we also shouldn't assume from the success of this model of contemporary social discourse theory and pedagogy that there aren't still good arguments for a common education in practical, ordinary, general discourse for all students, especially in a public institution of higher education like UW —with its supposed openness to all the people of its state and its prominent public mission.

One doesn't need to subscribe to an explicitly ideological set of assumptions in order to advance this critique of language specialization, but many of the TAs in the late 1960s apparently did; for them, the key rationale behind a common course in writing, reading, and speaking at the university, a course like English 102, was precisely that it could help subvert the fragmentation of the Fordist economy, the segregation of America's social and physical landscape, the privatism of modern society, and the vocationalism of the university itself. In a letter to the editor of the *Daily Cardinal,* published a week after the faculty's fateful decision about English 102, English TA Pauline Lipman put that critique this way:

Freshman English was abolished partially because faculty members responded to what they saw as the impudence of TAs and the threat of the union [the TAA]. But the decision on 102 took place in a larger context in which the University operates to serve the needs of a corporate structure which holds the economic and political power of the state. In the context of the University as a training center for the future salesmen, engineers and researchers employed by the corporations and the military, as well as those who will teach their ideology, students must be taught to write clearly and think uncritically. Such vocational training obviously excludes serious questioning of the validity, rationality, or morality of the corporate capitalism students are being trained to serve. The rhetorical approach to writing, discussion of "The Joys of Sport at Oxford," and the subtle anti-communism of "College Writing" do serve the needs of "the system." As a service to all the colleges in the university, Freshman English is responsible for meeting the needs of other departments in training students. . . . When the course no longer functioned to socialize in this way, it had to be abolished. When a few TAs began to redefine education as the development of one's ability to think and act critically in response to one's society and the ideology which perpetrates it, they became a desocializing force. The department acted against all TAs.

But 102 will continue. From now on people will be trained to write and think only in terms of their future jobs.

Lipman then quotes from the November 19, 1969, letter from Freshman English director William Lenehan to the English TAs that shifts responsibility for teaching writing to the several departments of the university, and she concludes:

Now neither the History Department nor the School of Engineering need worry that students are thinking too much, or writing creatively, or reading literature. . . . Until teachers, like other workers, control the work they do, their work will serve the interests of an elite who hold power, or be abolished. Meanwhile real education, the legitimate aim of TAs, will have to operate largely underground.[16]

One of the benefits of freshman comp's universality, in other words, is its ability to counter the fragmenting tendencies not only of the modern university but of modern society itself. The course potentially sees students not as future engineers, nurses, or managers, but as *citizens,* a role that all students—in theory at least—share. And one is left wondering, how could we ever educate young people toward such civic roles in a modern, open democracy without something like a universal course in composition-rhetoric?

In fact, what may be most troubling of all about the department's subscription to a dispersal model of language acquisition (if in fact the faculty really subscribed to it) was the betrayal of the university's own historical commitment to an insistently civic interpretation of higher education. In their discussion of the "state university idea" in volume 1 of *The University of Wisconsin: A History*, Merle Curti and Vernon Carstensen portray the early UW as a thoroughly secular, democratic, and utilitarian institution of higher learning.[17] David Cronon and John Jenkins, in volume 4 of *The University of Wisconsin*, show how UW president Charles Van Hise's early twentieth-century vision of the "combination university" involved not just cutting-edge research and ground-breaking scholarship but also high-quality instruction and genuine social service, a vision that was, in their view, unprecedented among American universities at the time.[18] Similarly, in an interview for this research project, former UW English TA Burr Angle asked of the English faculty who abandoned general education writing instruction in the late 1960s: did they really think the legislature would pay them to write about Melville for the rest of their careers?[19]

In this sense, the defense of freshman comp is the defense of an educational space that belongs to all, is responsive to all, and is meant to bring all together—a space that resists the fragmentation, segregation, and privatism of our society and imagines that we can learn from each other, no matter how different we are, no matter where we come from and where we're going, and we can do this by broad and deep cultural and linguistic contact.

Finally, *liminality*. By *liminality*, I mean the way that freshman comp seems to be always and everywhere on the border of things, the margin or threshold—a course that is, almost by definition, neither here nor there, suspended between other, better-known, and better-understood states, a rite of passage from one condition to another. I take the word *liminality* here from anthropologist Victor Turner, who has used it to refer to that middle place in social life that contains profoundly transformative possibilities.[20] People tied together in a liminal place, according to Turner and others, often share experiences of lowliness, but also of homogeneity and comradeship, a space of hardship where they bond with one another amid rules of suspended normality. As Turner saw it, liminal experiences contain the seeds of enormous creativity and social change: after all, a rite of passage is at once a preparation for the world and a creative response and innovative challenge to that same world.

Though this has not been much discussed in terms of freshman composition, it's hard to imagine a more "liminal" course in higher education: its students positioned between high school and the "real" work of college; its instructors (at least when TAs) between the studenthood of their own graduate curricula and their (pre)professional responsibilities as teachers in the freshman comp classroom; the course itself between complete independence from subject matter (as in, say, writing center tutoring) and full absorption in disciplinary content. But "betweenness" is perhaps misleading here; as we've seen with the "myth of transience," freshman comp might be better characterized as located always on the threshold of "real" college- or university-level work, a course on the margins of the content areas, disciplines, and majors. As such, liminality is perhaps the permanent and eternal condition of the first-year writing course.

But the word also resonates, I believe, with the student and TA protests of the late 1960s, which emanated from individuals who were often exquisitely self-conscious of their liminal status not only in the university but in society at large. Note, for example, how Daniel Cohn-Bendit and Gabriel Cohn-Bendit, leaders of the 1968 French student movement, defined their revolution in the name of radical uncertainty—liminality—rather than militant conviction:

> There are 600,000 of us; sometimes treated as mere children, sometimes as adults. We work, but we produce nothing. Often we have no money, but few of us are really poor. Although most of us come from the bourgeoisie, we do not always behave like them. The girls among us look like boys but are not sure whether they really want to be boys. We look upon our professors as part father, part boss and part teacher, and we can't quite make up our minds about them.[21]

Following on this insight, Bill Readings has argued that, in the late 1960s,

> the narrative of *Bildung*—of simple passage from infancy to adulthood, from dependency to emancipation (the Kantian narrative of enlightenment that characterizes the knowledge process itself in modernity)—[was] rejected by the students in the name of an uncertainty. An uncertainty about maturity, about labor, about wealth, about class, about gender. . . . In this sense, the position of the students has always been that of a troubled relation to the public sphere. The public sphere is proposed as the birthright of citizens, but the students have to go through a period of training in order to accede to their birthright. . . . I would argue that the revolt of 1968 was structured by the way in which students are positioned as capable of enacting the sense in which we are and are not part of society, that we always function in society before we understand what it means to do so, and that we do so until death.[22]

Like their TAs, the freshmen taking English 101 and 102 in the late 1960s at UW were also betwixt and between, neither one thing nor the other. For both students and teachers, the course was neither high school nor college, neither content nor skill—it was something else: an experience, a journey, a passage—one fraught, as all liminal passages are, with both peril and possibility.

The very structure of the first-year composition course, in other words, contributed to its abolition at UW in the late 1960s, and that structure continues to make the course, wherever it exists, vulnerable to abolition today. The fact that it is placed in the first year, as a transition from high school to the "real" work of the university, the fact that it is required universally, even for a heterogeneous body of students, the fact that it often relies on temporary and low-status instructors (something as true today as in 1969 or even 1929), the fact that it has no content of its own—it is a course whose apparent emptiness and low status have always made it easy to disparage.[23]

But the things that most make first-year composition, then and now, susceptible to complaint (to bring back Leonard Greenbaum's word) may also be what makes the course potentially so powerful, even for radical educational agendas.[24] If it's a course that exists at the margins, its very marginality can make it surprisingly central for students and teachers alike. The TAs in the English Department at the University of Wisconsin in the late 1960s, for all their posturing, for all their ignorance about composition and rhetoric theory, and for all their lack of professional commitment to composition studies, realized this more than the faculty did. They realized that the real strength of the course lay precisely in its flexibility, its practicality, its commonness. And when the faculty abolished it, they gave up for twenty-five years one of the only spaces on campus where a common education in social and intellectual action could resist the fragmentation, reification, and even dehumanization of the university itself.

Perhaps that was the biggest loss of all.

Notes

Acknowledgments

1. Moran, "How the Writing Process Came to UMass/Amherst," 142.

I. Introduction: Freshman Composition in the United States, 1885–Present

1. Connors, *Composition-Rhetoric*, 11. See also Brereton, *Origins*, 13. According to Kitzhaber, Harvard's English A course, required of all freshmen starting in 1885, was "the parent of all later courses in freshman composition" (*Rhetoric in American Colleges*, 61). Both Brereton and Connors endorse Kitzhaber's claim; Brereton even titled his long chapter 2 "The First Composition Program: Harvard, 1870–1900." Recent efforts have sought to complicate this "Harvard narrative," which has played such an important role in composition's disciplinary self-consciousness (see, e.g., the studies collected in Donahue and Moon, *Local Histories*). But whether or not freshman composition was "invented" at Harvard in the 1870s and '80s, the influence of English A is indisputable. Also indisputable is the rapid dissemination of the idea behind it, a "curricular endeavor that has no parallel in U.S. college history" (Connors, "New Abolitionism," 5).

2. Adelman, *New College Course Map*, 232. For lists of the college courses most often taken by the high school classes of 1972, 1982, and 1992, see "Contexts of Postsecondary Education," table 30-1, "Top Thirty Postsecondary Courses, 1972, 1982, 1992," in U.S. Department of Education, National Center of Education Statistics (USDE-NCES), *Condition of Education 2004*, available at http://nces.ed.gov/programs/coe/2004/section5/table.asp?tableID=109. According to Louis Menand, "Although the average number of credit hours devoted to courses in English literature has gone down over the last 20 years, the number-one subject, measured by the credit hours that students devote to it, has remained the same. That subject is English composition" ("Ph.D. Problem," 29).

3. Bok, *Our Underachieving Colleges*, 85. This is often literally true; Richard Light has shown how much time and effort college students put into their writing and how much they care about it. In one study, Light asked students about their courses in terms of time commitment, intellectual challenge, and personal engagement. The results, he argues, are "stunning": "The relationship between the amount of writing for a course and students' level of engagement—whether engagement is measured by time spent on the course, or the intellectual challenge it presents, or students' self-reported level of interest in it—is stronger than any relationship we found between student engagement and any other course characteristic" (*Making the Most of College*, 55).

4. "It has been precisely the historical and theoretical construction of the first-year course, with all of its debates about literacy, rhetoric, culture, and technology, that has laid the groundwork for a curriculum devoted to the study of writing. The achievements of the first-year course have made an advanced writing curriculum thinkable precisely to the extent

that our knowledges of writing are too much for a single course to contain. Quantity turns into quality, and in many respects the work of theorizing and enacting the study of writing is to make transparent and teachable the social relations and bodies of knowledge that now silently underwrite the first-year course—to organize the study of writing as an intellectual resource for undergraduates" (Trimbur, "Changing the Question," 23).

5. "Contexts of Postsecondary Education," table 30-2, "Top Thirty Postsecondary Courses by Selectivity of Institution," in USDE-NCES, *Condition of Education 2004*, available at http://nces.ed.gov/programs/coe/2004/section5/table.asp?tableID=82.

6. On this last claim, see Goggin, *Authoring a Discipline*, 157–60 and fig. 5.1. Comprhet's geographical particularity has sometimes been narrativized through the story of the field's turn, early in the twentieth century, away from Harvard, whose approach to freshman composition had by then lost its luster, and toward the "Michigan model," which took more seriously the possibilities of college-level composition-rhetoric (see Stewart, "Two Model Teachers" and "Harvard's Influence"). Why did freshman composition find such a receptive home in the U.S. Midwest? And why is it still so prominent in the public institutions of that region? The reason is probably partly historical accident and partly a function of rhetoric education's traditional strength in the provinces, far away from metropolitan capitals (see, e.g., Miller, *Formation of College English*). But there may be another reason for the particular geographic story of composition in the United States: namely, the progressive traditions of the (especially Upper) Midwest: the long-standing antipathy to elitism one finds there, the historic commitment to economic development among its local and state governments, and the ingrained belief in civic uplift so prominent in the history of midwestern public education. As Merle Curti and Vernon Carstensen claim in the first volume of their 1949 *The University of Wisconsin: A History*, the state universities founded in the old northwest territories in the middle years of the nineteenth century reflected a devotion to secularism, egalitarianism, and utilitarianism that was unprecedented in the educational history of this country—perhaps of the world. Such ideological underpinnings are still evident in midwestern colleges and universities, and they remain, arguably, conditions for the flourishing of postsecondary writing instruction.

7. Take my own experiences in U.S. higher education over the past thirty years. I took English 21, English Composition, as a freshman at tiny Davidson College in North Carolina in 1979; then, as an MA student in English at the University of North Carolina at Chapel Hill in the late 1980s, I observed the doctoral students there teaching English 101/102, English Composition and Rhetoric. After that, I myself taught English 321, Composition and Rhetoric, for two years at Laredo Junior College in South Texas. Later, as a PhD student in rhetoric at Carnegie Mellon University in the mid-1990s, I taught English 100, Strategies for Writing. Then in the late 1990s, I watched my faculty colleagues at New Mexico State University in Las Cruces supervise the graduate teachers of English 111, Rhetoric and Composition. I then directed English 100, Freshman Composition, at the University of Wisconsin-Madison in the early 2000s, and now I teach and direct Englwrit 112, College Writing, at the University of Massachusetts-Amherst. That's three decades studying and teaching first-year writing at seven different institutions of higher education, from the Southeast to the Midwest, the Southwest to the Northeast, from a private liberal arts college to a two-year community college on the U.S.-Mexico border, from a private urban research university to the campuses of four different state universities.

8. Connors, *Composition-Rhetoric*, 7, 112.

9. Varnum, "From Crisis to Crisis," 148.

10. Williams, "Why Johnny Can Never, Ever Read." According to Denis Baron, "our literacy has always been in crisis" ("No Students Left Behind," W424).

11. Hill, "Answer to the Cry," 47, 49.

12. Ibid., 46.

13. Adams, Godkin, and Quincy, "Report of the Committee," 92.

14. Ibid., 103.

15. Sheils, "Why Johnny Can't Write," 58.

16. National Commission on Excellence in Education, *Nation at Risk.*

17. National Commission on Writing in America's Schools and Colleges, *Neglected "R,"* 16.

18. Ohmann, "Strange Case," 231; Varnum, "From Crisis to Crisis," 145; Gee, *Social Linguistics and Literacies,* 33. "As tasks bec[o]me more complex and 'school-like,' less and less of the population [can] do them, with failure being most prominent among those least influenced by, and most poorly served by, the schools" (Gee, *Social Linguistics and Literacies,* 33).

19. What is clear is that, as researchers put it in the mid-1970s, "anyone who says he *knows* that literacy is decreasing . . . is at best unscholarly and at worse dishonest" (quoted in Ohmann, "Strange Case," 232 [emphasis in original]).

20. Ehrenreich and Ehrenreich, "Professional-Managerial Class," 13, 15.

21. Ibid., 11, 17.

22. Ibid., 22, 13.

23. Ehrenreich, *Fear of Falling,* 12; Ehrenreich and Ehrenreich, "Professional-Managerial Class," 26.

24. Williams, "Why Johnny Can Never, Ever Read," 180.

25. Cf. Brodkey, *Writing Permitted in Designated Areas Only.*

26. Perhaps this is why "throughout most of its history as a college subject, English composition has meant one thing to most people: the single-minded enforcement of standards of mechanical and grammatical correctness in writing" (Connors, *Composition-Rhetoric,* 112).

27. "[Basic Writing] students write the way they do, not because they are slow or non-verbal, indifferent to or incapable of academic excellence, but because they are beginners and must, like all beginners, learn by making mistakes" (Shaughnessy, *Errors,* 5).

28. See, e.g., Lamos, "Literacy Crisis and Color-Blindness."

29. Russell, "American Origins," 35.

30. Ohmann, "Strange Case," 234.

31. Ibid., 233 (emphasis in original).

32. See, e.g., Hourigan, *Literacy as Social Exchange;* Varnum, "From Crisis to Crisis."

33. Kaufer and Carley, *Communication at a Distance.* Cf. Socrates's criticism of writing in Plato's *Phaedrus* and the cultural anxiety wrought by the printing press (Kernan, "Literacy Crises").

34. Rose, "Language of Exclusion," 355. "The turmoil [we] are currently in will pass. The source of the problem is elsewhere; thus it can be ignored or temporarily dealt with until the tutors or academies or grammar schools or high schools or families make the changes they must make" (ibid., 356). See also Russell, *Writing in the Academic Disciplines,* chap. 1.

35. Hill, "Answer to the Cry," 51.

36. Adams, Godkin, and Quincy, "Report of the Committee," 96.

37. Godkin, "Illiteracy of American Boys," 9. The belief that freshman composition would wither away once the high schools did their job right—or could simply be pushed back to the high schools whether they were ready for it or not—was still widely held a century later. In his 1966 report on general education at Columbia, Daniel Bell recommended getting rid of freshman composition altogether: "It should not be the function of a college to teach composition as a separate course. . . . One has a right to assume that by the time a student enters college, he can write clearly enough to make a special course in freshman composition unnecessary" (*Reforming of General Education*, 233, 292).

38. Rose, "Language of Exclusion," 355.

39. Ibid., 355–56.

40. Connors, *Composition-Rhetoric*, 15.

41. The exception is twenty-three doctorates produced under Fred Newton Scott at Michigan early in the twentieth century (Connors, "Composition History," 411).

42. Connors, "Composition History," 418. The data come from Brown, Meyer, and Enos, "Doctoral Programs." As for the number of graduate programs, the Consortium of Doctoral Programs in Rhetoric and Composition currently lists seventy-one members (see http://www.rhetoric.msu.edu/rc_consortium/).

43. Laurence, Lusin, and Olsen, "Report on Trends," table 6.

44. Stygall, "At the Century's End," 382.

45. The quoted phrase is from Wordsworth's *Preface to Lyrical Ballads* of 1800.

46. On "General Writing Skills Instruction," see Petraglia, "Introduction"; a similar critique can be found in Smit, *End of Composition Studies*.

47. Adams, Godkin, and Quincy, "Report of the Committee, 75–76; quoted in Connors, "New Abolitionism," 7.

48. Ibid., 7, 16.

49. Ibid., 13.

50. Ibid., 16. For more on abolitionism in the history of freshman composition, see Russell, "Romantics on Writing"; n. 85, this chap.

51. Greenbaum, "Tradition of Complaint," 187.

52. In their study of the U.S. undergraduate curriculum from 1975 to 2000, for example, Brint et al. explicitly define "general education" as "an organizational phenomenon constituted by breadth requirements" ("General Education Models," 608). Likewise, Stevens's recent history of University of Chicago president Robert Hutchins's influence on U.S. higher education is largely a study of "core," "liberal studies," and "breadth" requirements ("Philosophy of General Education"). Both studies at least acknowledge the existence of freshman composition. Daniel Bell's influential 1966 study of Columbia's general education program, by contrast, refers to freshman composition only because its abolition, which he recommends, would open up space for another humanities course in the first year (*Reforming of General Education*). Miller's study *The Meaning of General Education*, meanwhile, completely ignores freshman comp. It should be said that there are hints in these texts of a conception of general education that more readily includes rhetoric and composition: Brint et al. describe an alternative tradition of general education, beholden to Dewey rather than Hutchins and more about practice and application than cultural heritage; Stevens writes of the role of skill development in the general education tradition, though she shows how the

Chicago tradition consistently absorbed skill into content; Bell himself advocates a "third tier" of undergraduate education, beyond both breadth and depth, attuned to application.

53. See, e.g., Graff, *Professing Literature.*

54. See, e.g., Douglas, "Rhetoric for the Meritocracy."

55. Brereton, *Origins,* xiv.

56. Bartholomae, "What Is Composition," 28.

57. Gee, *Situated Language and Learning,* 117–18.

58. Martin Heidegger called Aristotle's *Rhetoric* "the first systematic hermeneutic of the everydayness of Being with one another" (quoted in Aristotle, *On Rhetoric,* 115).

59. As Dilip Gaonkar has put it, rhetoric is at once over- and underburdened with content: on the one hand, it's replete with the beliefs, values, and languages of a particular community in a particular time and place; on the other, it's a portable, content-free process that can be used to respond discursively to any situation, anywhere, any time ("Rhetoric and Its Double," 345). See also Fleming, "Becoming Rhetorical."

60. The University of Wisconsin is a statewide system of higher education with multiple campuses, so that today one cannot say "UW" and mean unambiguously the Madison campus. But in the late 1960s, the system was not fully in place, and the Madison campus *was* the "University of Wisconsin" or simply "UW." I usually refer to it that way in this book and do not mean by that any disrespect to other campuses in the system (see Cronon and Jenkins, *University of Wisconsin,* 4: 174–77, esp. 175 n. 21).

61. Ibid., 4: 210.

62. "Freshman English" (FE) was the name often given in the twentieth century to the standard two-semester, first-year, postsecondary composition course, not just at UW but across the country. That course is more often known today as Freshman Composition, First Year Composition, First Year Writing, Expository Writing, College Writing, or some similar title.

63. The history briefly summarized in this and subsequent paragraphs is fully detailed and referenced in the body chapters of the book.

64. I'll have more to say about all this in chap. 7. It's important to note here, though, that, even with the de facto elimination of the Freshman English requirement in 1969, writing instruction survived at UW and, in some corners, flourished. The postabolition years saw, e.g., the rise of an internationally prominent Writing Lab (now Writing Center) under the direction of first Joyce Steward and then Brad Hughes; the survival (at least until the mid-1990s) of English 101 as a "basic" writing course; the development of a well-regarded English as a Second Language program, including English 117 and 118; the continued requirement of an Intermediate Composition course (English 201) in some degree programs at UW; the success of several elective writing courses at the introductory (English 105) and advanced (English 315) levels; the beginnings in the late 1970s and early 1980s of research at UW on the studio method of writing instruction by, among others, Nick Doane and Stan Henning; the hiring of composition specialists Martin Nystrand and Deborah Brandt in 1982 and '83, respectively; the 1991 inception of what would become a nationally known PhD program in composition studies, etc. For all that, however, the university lacked a substantial campus-wide undergraduate writing requirement from 1970 to 1996—precisely the quarter century when writing studies emerged nationally as a bona fide discipline, and freshman composition itself experienced a kind of golden era (see Fleming, "Rhetoric Revival"). By 2000, even with the developments described above and the institution of a

Notes to Pages 13–16

substantial communication requirement at UW-Madison, the English Department still had the smallest composition faculty in the Big Ten.

65. Cronon and Jenkins, *University of Wisconsin,* 4: 289–94.

66. See, e.g., Bates, *Rads;* Brown and Silber, *War at Home;* Buhle, *History and the New Left;* Maraniss, *They Marched into Sunlight.*

67. See http://archives.library.wisc.edu/oral-history/.

68. Regrettably, little material is presented here from the undergraduate students' point of view, though I do summarize surveys, occasional letters to the chair and campus newspapers, and petitions from undergraduates, as well as statements from the English Students Association and other groups and secondhand reports on student attitudes and activities from the faculty and TAs. I would like to have done more from this angle, though it would have required a vastly different and even more ambitious study.

69. Vogt, *Dictionary,* 30.

70. Brereton, *Origins,* xiii–xiv.

71. In her archive-based study of late nineteenth-century rhetoric and composition instruction at Butler University, Heidemarie Z. Weidner writes that one outcome of working with primary sources "is the web of intertextuality that gradually brings to life an entire period. Infrequently at first, then more often, connections appear almost serendipitously: objectives in a catalogue are borne out by a student diary or supported by recorded observations of a faculty member; the heated discussions in a literary magazine contradict the melancholy assessment of student writing in a contemporary article; evidence of early peer evaluation, student-teacher conferences, and writing across the curriculum tells the researcher that not all pedagogical 'innovations' of the twentieth century are truly new. Finally, such contextualized searches create histories that at times reflect, at times supplement, and at times complicate established historical narrative" ("Chair 'Perpetually Filled,'" 59).

72. The lack of attention by composition historians to these years is somewhat surprising given the political affinity many in the field feel toward the antiestablishment student protestors of the late 1960s and the fact that the period looms so large in our cultural memory of the late twentieth century, especially in higher-education circles.

73. See, e.g., Goggin, *Authoring a Discipline.*

74. See Fleming, "Rhetoric Revival."

75. There's a single reference to "classical rhetoric" in the spring 1968 proposal to reduce the composition requirement at UW from two semesters to one, but it's fleeting and superficial. There are also a handful of references to "rhetoric," but they are almost all pejorative, usually denoting the subdiscipline that would become "basic writing" in the 1970s. The one exception to the almost complete disconnect between the Freshman English program at UW and alleged trends in the field is the experimentation in English 101 from 1968 to 1970, which does seem to reflect cutting-edge developments in language and literacy studies and pedagogy of the late 1960s and early 1970s (see chap. 4).

76. But see chap. 3, n. 15.

77. On current traditionalism, see Connors, *Composition-Rhetoric;* Crowley, *Methodical Memory.*

78. As I'll argue more fully in chap. 5, I use the phrase "critical-humanist" to distinguish late-1960s writing pedagogy at UW from the "critical pedagogy" movement that arose in the early 1980s (and even had links to 1960s Madison through people like Ira Shor) because the former contained, I believe, a neoromantic, utopian element that was largely absent from the latter.

79. A working title for this book was "On the Hinge of History," a phrase borrowed from Clark Kerr, who argued in the early 1960s that the university was "at the hinge of history" (*Uses of the University*). The phrase was later picked up by former UW English TA Ira Shor: the first chapter of his book *Culture Wars* was titled "The Hinge of 1969."

80. Dekoven, *Utopia Limited*, 3.

81. See, e.g., Marwick, *Sixties;* McHale, "1966."

82. Brenner, *Economics of Global Turbulence.*

83. In his 1974 article "The Composition Requirement Today," Ron Smith wrote that, in 1967, freshmen at 93.2 percent of the schools surveyed by Wilcox were required to take at least one term of composition and that at 77.8 percent of the schools, they took two terms. By 1973, according to Smith's own numbers, 24 percent of schools had no composition requirement at all, 76 percent required at least one course, and 45 percent required two or more courses (139). So there was a downward trend during this time, at least if Smith's survey is to be trusted. But note that even by his numbers, three-quarters of universities in 1973 still had a freshman English requirement of at least one semester. It's an exaggeration to say, therefore, as Carol Hartzog did in 1986, that "during the sixties, departments gave up freshman English or at least stopped requiring it" (*Composition and the Academy*, 3). My research suggests that it's more accurate to say that freshman English in the 1960s suffered from benign neglect, neither changing much nor coming under significant threat of elimination. Note also that Smith's survey dates to the *early* 1970s, a few years before what must be seen as the third great expansion of freshman composition in the history of higher education in this country, the first two being the late nineteenth-century birth of the course and its post–World War II, GI Bill–fueled "rebirth" (see also Fleming, "Rhetoric Revival"). Hartzog's research confirms a broad-based resurgence of composition in the late 1970s (4–6). And by 2001, researchers Moghtader, Cotch, and Hague were finding that, of 233 four-year colleges and universities, 97 percent had some kind of writing requirement, and in 85 percent of the cases, it was fulfilled in the English Department ("First-Year Composition Requirement Revisited").

84. Periods of "freshman comp" abolitionism in this country often coincide with times of declining or stagnant enrollment in U.S. colleges and universities and also periods of economic downturn nationwide. Periods largely devoid of abolitionism are usually, by contrast, times of population growth and economic expansion. As Robert Connors once put it, expansionist periods do not generally produce freshman comp abolitionism ("New Abolitionism").

85. See Connors, "New Abolitionism"; Crowley, "Personal Essay on Freshman English"; Smit, *End of Composition Studies.* See also the debate on the first-year writing requirement between John Ramage and Sharon Crowley at the 1999 Western States Composition Conference, available at http://orgs.tamu-commerce.edu/cbw/asu/bwe_fall_1999.htm. See also Goggin and Miller, "What Is New"; Roemer, Schultz, and Durst, "Reframing the Great Debate on First-Year Writing"; Russell, "Romantics on Writing"; Sullivan et al., "Student Needs and Strong Composition."

86. Perhaps the best-known attacks on freshman composition in recent years have involved the writing programs at SUNY Albany and the University of Texas-Austin. On the former, see Brannon, "(Dis)Missing Compulsory First-Year Composition." On the latter, see Brodkey, *Writing Permitted in Designated Areas Only;* Hairston, "Diversity, Ideology, and Teaching Writing." Not only do these stories share the same historical setting, the 1980s culture wars, but they share as well a polemical edge that comes from being told by partici-

pants in the abolition itself—either staunch defenders or avid opponents of threatened first-year writing courses. There are also, of course, numerous stories of freshman composition being *reformed*—i.e., neither abolished nor left standing as is (see, e.g., the story told in Sullivan et al., "Student Needs and Strong Composition"). Such accounts have their value, but the field also needs carefully researched *empirical* studies of composition courses being eliminated or threatened with such.

2. Prehistory, 1848–1948

1. The other five original professorships were in ethics, civil polity, and political economy; ancient languages and literature; modern languages and literature; mathematics, natural philosophy, and astronomy; and chemistry and natural history (Curti and Carstensen, *University of Wisconsin*, 1: 73).

2. Brereton, *Origins of Composition Studies*, 3.

3. See Curti and Carstensen, *University of Wisconsin*, 1: 3–34.

4. Ibid., 1: 74.

5. Ibid., 1: 117.

6. Cf. Abbott's description of Renaissance education in England: "in its entirety a linguistic and literary curriculum" ("Rhetoric and Writing," 103).

7. Brereton, *Origins of Composition Studies*, 4.

8. Sustained, explicit instruction in rhetoric was provided only after the student had established a foundation in the grammar of the ancient and modern languages, read widely, and attained sufficient moral discipline. In the old trivium, rhetoric *followed* grammar but *preceded* dialectic; the quadrivium then followed all that (see, e.g., Murphy, *Short History*).

9. Curti and Carstensen, *University of Wisconsin*, 1: 200. For more on nineteenth-century postsecondary rhetorical education in the United States, see Brereton, *Origins of Composition Studies;* Connors, *Composition-Rhetoric;* Douglas, "Rhetoric for the Meritocracy"; Halloran, "Rhetoric"; Reid, "Boylston Professorship."

10. "Mental philosophy" had now departed from the chair's title, and within a decade, "logic" would be gone as well.

11. Curti and Carstensen, *University of Wisconsin*, 1: 343–44; Merritt Hughes, "The Department of English, 1861–1925," 2, typewritten MS, c. 1946, UW-Madison English Department files. The latter is described as "a sketch prepared for the use of Professor Merle Curti in writing the history of the University of Wisconsin for its centennial year, 1948–1949."

12. Hughes, "Department of English," 5–6.

13. Curti and Carstensen, *University of Wisconsin*, 1: 344. Curti and Carstensen vividly portray this period at UW (1: 422–38). Back East, the "oratorical culture" (see Clark and Halloran, *Oratorical Culture in America*) had its heyday before the Civil War, but it did not fully mature in Western universities like UW until afterward (Curti and Carstensen, *University of Wisconsin*, 1: 423).

14. Curti and Carstensen, *University of Wisconsin*, 1: 428. Bascom offered arguments for the affirmative.

15. Ibid., 1: 427.

16. Ibid., 1: 437.

17. Ibid., 1: 423. Though extracurricular, the intellectual benefits of these societies cannot be underestimated: in 1893, economics professor Richard Ely was so impressed with the

research done on the topic of the joint debate that year (municipal ownership of public utilities) that he proposed publishing the transcript for public edification (ibid., 1: 437).

18. Ibid., 1: 435.

19. Ibid., 1: 659.

20. Ibid., 1: 659–60. Brereton attests to similar growth nationwide: U.S. postsecondary enrollment was largely static between 1850 and 1880, but the three decades between 1890 and 1920 witnessed a veritable boom, student numbers doubling between 1890 and 1910 and again between 1910 and 1920 (*Origins of Composition Studies*, 7).

21. Ehrenreich and Ehrenreich, "Professional-Managerial Class."

22. Curti and Carstensen, *University of Wisconsin*, 1: 660.

23. See, e.g., Bledstein, *Culture of Professionalism*; Brereton, *Origins of Composition Studies*; Connors, *Composition-Rhetoric*; Halloran, "Rhetoric."

24. Horner and Trimbur, "English Only," 594.

25. Curti and Carstensen, *University of Wisconsin*, 1: 343.

26. Ibid., 1: 197–204, 621–22.

27. Curti and Carstensen call this the 2+2 system of higher education, the freshman and sophomore years devoted to "general" education and the junior and senior years to the major, still a hallmark of undergraduate studies in most U.S. universities (ibid., 1: 545–56).

28. Ibid., 1: 649–50.

29. Brereton, *Origins of Composition Studies*, 11.

30. The move from the sophomore-junior level to the freshman year was important because it allowed freshman composition to supplant the classics as the new conceptual and practical underpinning of undergraduate learning but also because it now positioned the course *between* high school and the major, thus, in some sense, taking from one hand what was given by the other: "Putting composition at the beginning of a student's career earned it the right to be a 'foundation' for all that followed. But along with the foundation came its reputation as a transition from high school to college, connected with introductory work, with bringing students up to the required level. In fact, putting composition into the first year was a recognition of its newly-developed remedial overtones: freshman year was to make up for what preparatory schools had failed to teach. That goes a long way to explain composition's lowly status" (ibid., 18, 30–31, 52–53).

31. Ibid., 9. On UW's own placement exam, see Hughes, "Department of English," 10.

32. Brereton, *Origins of Composition Studies*, 11–13.

33. See chap. 1, n. 47.

34. Brereton, *Origins of Composition Studies*, 13.

35. The authors of the 1892 Report of the Committee on Composition and Rhetoric for Harvard wrote that "writing is merely the habit of talking with the pen instead of with the tongue" (Adams, Godkin, and Quincy, "Report of the Committee," 95).

36. On the "myth of transience," see chap. 1, n. 34.

37. For these two departments, see Curti and Carstensen, *University of Wisconsin*, 2: 326–29.

38. See chap. 1 for more on U.S. literacy crises.

39. Curti and Carstensen, *University of Wisconsin*, 2: 329. See also Hughes, "Department of English," 7.

40. Hughes, "Department of English," 10.

41. Connors, *Composition-Rhetoric*, 171–209.

42. Brereton, *Origins of Composition Studies*, 132–33, 21.

43. Hughes, "Department of English," 12.

44. Ibid., 6–7; see also Curti and Carstensen, *University of Wisconsin,* 2: 329ff. Hughes gives no citation for the list, and Curti and Carstensen, following Hughes, quote it without attribution.

45. UW, *Bulletin of the UW: General Announcement of Courses, 1905–06.*

46. Brereton, *Origins of Composition Studies,* 133, 378–86, 359. On Woolley, see also Connors, *Composition-Rhetoric,* 91–94, 146–47; Curti and Carstensen, *University of Wisconsin,* 2: 329. Other composition textbooks written by UW faculty of the time include Frances Berkeley Young and Karl Young's 1914 *Freshman English: A Manual* (Brereton, *Origins of Composition Studies,* 477–91); Norman Foerster, Frederick A. Manchester, and Karl Young's 1913–15 *Essays for College Men, First Series* and *Second Series* (ibid., 391–92); and Warner Taylor and Frederick A. Manchester's 1917 *Freshman Themes.*

47. Hughes, "Department of English," 10–11.

48. Ibid. Hughes bemoans the fact that the original UW admissions/placement exam in English composition, which asked candidates to write "at least two pages" on a work of literature from a list including such texts as Irving's *Alhambra,* Scott's *Kenilworth,* and Goldsmith's *Vicar of Wakefield* (cf. Harvard's similar exam from the same time: Brereton, *Origins of Composition Studies,* 33–37), gave way in 1898 to a "practical examination" on "familiar" rather than literary topics, the stress now on "form, plan, paragraphing, and the 'avoidance of errors in spelling and punctuation'" (Hughes, "Department of English," 10–11).

49. Curti and Carstensen, *University of Wisconsin,* 2: 329.

50. Karl Young, "The Organization of a Course in Freshman English," *English Journal* (1915), as excerpted in Brereton, *Origins of Composition Studies,* 233–34. As Young reports, UW instructors whose work was confined to Freshman English taught three sections per semester.

51. Ibid., 233–34.

52. UW Department of English, "Instructions to Students in Freshman English, 1917–1918," 1.

53. Ibid.

54. Brereton, *Origins of Composition Studies,* 16.

55. UW Department of English, "Instructions to Students in Freshman English, 1917–1918," 1–2.

56. Ibid., 2.

57. See, e.g., UW Department of English, "Instructions to Students in Freshman English, 1927–1928."

58. UW Department of English, "Instructions to Students in Freshman English, 1917–1918."

59. Ibid. In Hughes's description of the early years, "unsuccessful students were to be dropped from English 1 and put into an awkward squad" ("Department of English," 11).

60. UW Department of English, "Instructions to Students in Freshman English, 1922–1923."

61. UW-Madison, Office of the Registrar, "Enrollments 1888 to Present" (see "Fall Enrollment Tabulations from 1888," available at http://registrar.wisc.edu/enrollments_1888_to_present.htm).

62. UW Department of English, "Instructions to Students in Freshman English, 1925–1926." On the stratification of students by skill level in 1920s freshman English na-

tionwide, see Warner Taylor's 1929 *National Survey of Conditions in Freshman English*, reprinted in Brereton, *Origins of Composition Studies*, 545–62.

63. UW Department of English, "Instructions to Students in Freshman English, 1925–1926." In the 1920s, as Brereton confirms, "better students" nationwide were writing mostly about literature in their freshman comp courses (*Origins of Composition Studies*, 16–17).

64. See, e.g., UW Department of English, "Instructions to Students in Freshman English, 1938–1939."

65. UW Department of English, "Instructions to Students in Freshman English, 1925–1926."

66. Taylor, *National Survey*, reprinted in Brereton, *Origins of Composition Studies*, 556.

67. Ibid., 562.

68. Cronon and Jenkins, *University of Wisconsin*, 3; 277.

69. Ibid., 3: 224ff.

70. Mark Eccles, interview with Barry Teicher, Oral History Program, UW-Madison, Archives, #508, 1997 (see http://archives.library.wisc.edu/oral-history/).

71. Madeleine Doran, interview with Laura Smail, Oral History Program, UW-Madison, Archives, #31, 1977.

72. Cronon and Jenkins, *University of Wisconsin*, 3: 290.

73. UW Department of English, "Instructions to Students in Freshman English, 1938–1939."

74. Merritt Y. Hughes, "Report to the Members of the Department of English," Dec. 8, 1940.

75. Committee on High-School Relations of the University of Wisconsin Department of English, "Requirements for Admission to Freshman English at the University of Wisconsin," rev. ed., Madison, 1930.

76. UW Department of English, "Instructions to Students in Freshman English, 1938–1939."

77. UW Department of English, "Report of the Committee on the Undergraduate Curriculum," Apr. 1936. Committee members included Wright Thomas (chair), Ricardo Quintana, Grace Wales, Ruth Wallerstein, Phyllis Barlett, J. J. Lyons, and Hoyt Trowbridge. But why these recommendations? Because of declining enrollments and the need to keep numbers up to employ faculty, instructors, and grad students? Because the quality of entering students (especially with the sharp decline in out-of-state enrollments) had fallen off? Or because the heightened faculty role suddenly involved professors in course administration who had never before paid much attention to Freshman English?

78. UW Department of English, "Instructions to Students in Freshman English, 1937–1938." By 1941, this elaborate subdivision had been simplified somewhat to (1) exempted students (now about 9 percent); (2) regular students, divided into "Masterpieces of Literature," "Language in Action," and "Traditional" groups, the latter further subdivided into "Upper" and "Middle" sections; and finally, (3) students required to take Sub-Freshman English (UW Department of English, "Instructions to Students in Freshman English, 1941–1942").

79. UW Department of English, "Instructions to Students in Freshman English, 1937–1938."

80. UW Department of English, "Instructions to Students in Freshman English, 1941–1942."

81. Ibid.

82. UW Department of English, "Instructions to Students in Freshman English, 1936–1937."

83. UW Department of English, "Instructions to Students in Freshman English, 1938–1939."

84. UW Department of English, "Instructions to Students in Freshman English, 1941–1942."

85. Hughes, "Report to the Members of the Department," Dec. 8, 1940. See Greenbaum, "Tradition of Complaint," and Connors, "New Abolitionism," for connections between abolitionism and a tight economy.

86. UW-Madison, Office of the Registrar, "Enrollments 1888 to Present" (see "Fall Enrollment Tabulations from 1888," available at http://registrar.wisc.edu/enrollments_1888_to_present.htm).

87. "The post–World War II era of rapid economic growth was accompanied by even more rapid increases in the demand for college-educated workers. . . . The percentage of all jobs that were professional or managerial [an index of the demand for college-level manpower] rose from eighteen in 1950 to twenty-four by 1969" (Carroll and Morrison, "Demographic and Economic Influences," 104–5).

88. Corbett, "History of Writing Program Administration," 65.

89. Robert Pooley, interview with Stephen Lowe, Oral History Program, UW-Madison, Archives, #82, transcript only, 1972.

3. Postwar Regime, 1948–1968

1. Why was Lacy selected for this position? Compared to Pooley or Taylor before him, there didn't seem much in his background or training that fitted him for leading Freshman English. Did he volunteer when no one else showed interest? Was he pressured to do it as a new assistant professor?

2. For composition at Mount Holyoke in the early twentieth century, see Mastrangelo, "Learning from the Past."

3. UW-Madison, Office of the Registrar, "Enrollments 1888 to Present" (see "Fall Enrollment Tabulations from 1888," available at http://registrar.wisc.edu/enrollments_1888_to_present.htm).

4. UW News Service, "U.W. News: On Improving Undergraduate Writing," Nov. 3, 1952; University of Wisconsin Department of English, "Freshman English," 1952–53. Note that the attitude toward students in English o became increasingly stingy. In 1960, the department recommended that the university get out of the remedial English business, deferring admission for at least one semester to all students "whose skill in writing is found through testing to be deficient," arguing that of the 123 students in 1959 who were denied admission to English 1a (3.1 percent of the total freshman class), 6.5 percent withdrew from the university immediately, an additional 8 percent withdrew before the end of the first semester, and 48.7 percent were either dropped or had withdrawn by the end of the second semester (UW Department of English, Minutes of the Departmental Committee, Oct. 18, 1960).

5. On current-traditional rhetoric, see chap. 1, n. 77.

6. UW Department of English, "Freshman English," 1952–53.

7. Ibid.

8. Ibid.; Thomas, "Devices for Training Graduate Assistants," 35–36. On the "modes" and "methods" of current-traditional rhetoric, see Connors, *Composition-Rhetoric;* Crowley, *Methodical Memory.*

9. UW Department of English, "Syllabus for English 1b," spring 1953.

10. Ibid.

11. This was still evident fifteen years later in what Susan McLeod remembered as an hour-long lesson on commas from Ednah Thomas (Susan McLeod, interview with David Fleming, June 30, 2005).

12. Thomas, *Evaluating Student Themes.*

13. Note the letter from student Anthony Elkan to chair Simeon Heninger in Nov. 1968, complaining about departmental ownership of his themes, and Heninger's reply in Dec. 1968, suggesting that the student make carbon copies (see chap. 5).

14. Students had fifty minutes to write a theme giving advice, based on a semester's experience at the university, to prospective college students currently in high school. The fourteen themes selected for the book included three judged "unsatisfactory," eight deemed of "middle" quality, and three "superior," though it should be said that the booklet is not about grading per se; that marginal comments concerning spelling, mechanical, and grammatical errors are omitted; and that the point of the long, detailed, and thoughtful terminal comments is not to criticize, rank, or justify negative or positive evaluations, but to give each student a sense of his or her work as a whole, to recognize his or her strengths and weaknesses as a writer, and to point the way toward improvement. As Thomas herself put it in the "Foreword," the teacher's primary concern in the terminal comment on any student's theme "is not this particular paper as an end in itself but the development of writing skill for the student's use all his life" (*Evaluating Student Themes,* iv).

Although the book was mainly the work of Ednah Thomas, and became indelibly associated with her, the copyright page includes the following note: "This pamphlet has grown out of a project undertaken by the Committee on the Training of Teachers, Department of English, University of Wisconsin: Robert C. Pooley, Chairman, Edgar W. Lacy, George B. Rodman, John R. Searles, Ednah S. Thomas, and Helen C. White" (ii).

15. Here's what Thomas has to say about the writing process: "Ideally, let us conceive of the writing process as consisting of three parts: preparation, realization, and follow-through. In all three, both teacher and student are actively concerned, united in a common interest in and respect for the student's work. . . . The assignment should be given well in advance and the purpose clearly stated. . . . [The student] should have a chance to ask questions, and he should understand thoroughly what he is about to do. He should realize he is expected to think before he writes, to write a first draft, to revise, and to make a final fair copy" (*Evaluating Student Themes,* iii–iv). But even this somewhat early nod to process betrays its setting in a thoroughly current-traditional writing pedagogy: the collected themes in the pamphlet are all examples of impromptu writing, the students given fifty minutes to get their essays "right" without much chance for "preparation, realization, and follow-through." And Thomas goes on to admit that the point of the marginal comments on student papers (examples of which are not included in the pamphlet) is to prompt "corrections" by the student of mechanical and grammatical errors, while the extensive terminal comments that Thomas models (quite brilliantly), and that the pamphlet became surprisingly well known for, are not meant to guide actual revision, but merely to help the student develop more generally as a writer—an admirable goal, but far removed from the much

more extensive process-based pedagogy that would usher in the new composition paradigm of the 1970s.

16. Ibid., v.

17. Brereton, *Origins of Composition Studies,* 438. See also the post by Arizona State University Polytechnic English professor Barry Maid to the WPA-L discussion list, dated Jan. 14, 2005, regarding his experiences as an undergraduate student in freshman English at UW in the mid-1960s, in a section whose TA seemed to think that the purpose of the course was error hunting.

18. UW-Madison, Office of the Registrar, "Enrollments 1888 to Present." As these data reveal, the number of graduate students at UW increased from 911 in 1945 to 9,063 in 1967. The numbers of graduate student teaching assistants (TAs) similarly rose. According to the "Report of Committee on Teaching Assistant System" (the "Mulvihill Report"), between 1955 and 1965, the number of TAs at UW grew 155 percent, from 624 to 1,170 (21, n. 1) (University of Wisconsin, Madison campus, Faculty Document 183, Feb. 5, 1968).

19. UW-Madison, Office of the Registrar, "Enrollments 1888 to Present."

20. Lacy, "Safeguards for Satisfactory Functioning," 36.

21. Garlington, "Advantages and Disadvantages of the System," 35. By the late 1960s, however, all sections of all versions of Freshman English at UW—English 101, 102, and 181—were TA taught (see, e.g., attachment 2 on English 181, in William Lenehan [director, Freshman English] to Simeon Heninger [chair, English Department], memo, Aug. 21, 1969).

22. Thomas, "Devices for Training Graduate Assistants," 35–36.

23. Merritt Hughes to high school teacher, May 14, 1953 (emphasis in original).

24. See UW English Department committee assignment sheets, beginning in the early 1930s.

25. Michael Bernard-Donals to author, email, Oct. 11, 2004, with link to *Wisconsin State Journal* obituary, Oct. 10, 2004.

26. UW English Department, list of TAs, 1969–70.

27. UW English Department, "1969–1970 TAships in English."

28. Lacy, Lenehan, and Thomas, "Master Assistants at the University of Wisconsin." See also UW English Department, Minutes of the Departmental Committee, Mar. 15, 1966.

29. Lacy, Lenehan, and Thomas, "Master Assistants at the University of Wisconsin," 637.

30. Ibid.

31. Ibid. Freshman enrollment went from 5,358 in fall 1964 to 6,342 in fall 1965 (UW-Madison, Office of the Registrar, "Enrollments 1888 to Present").

32. UW-Madison, Office of the Registrar, "Enrollments 1888 to Present." See also "Information for TAs," 1966–68.

33. McLeod, interview, June 30, 2005.

34. Virginia (Joyce) Davidson, interview with David Fleming, Aug. 24, 2005.

35. Burr Angle, interview with David Fleming, Oct. 11, 2005, Nov. 22, 2005.

36. Freshman English Policy Committee (chair, William Lenehan) to prospective 1969–70 TAs, memo, May 14, 1969; Lenehan to Heninger, memo, Aug. 21, 1969. The inclusion of literary materials in UW's Freshman English course was not new: a collection of short stories was used in English 1a as early as 1917; novels and plays were the central texts of 1b in the mid-1920s, when the course featured Hardy's *Return of the Native;* in the 1930s "better" students in the program were getting "Masterpieces of Literature" from day one; and in 1953 students in 1b were writing about Thackeray's *Henry Esmond.*

37. Freshman English Policy Committee to prospective 1969–70 TAs, memo, May 14, 1969.

38. Ibid. We know from interviews with TAs that during the previous fall (1968), students in 102 were using Porter Perrins's *Writer's Guide and Index to English* and the *Norton Reader*.

39. Ibid. They also took two tests: a six-week exam and a final, both of which included writing an impromptu theme.

40. Thomas, "Devices for Training Graduate Assistants," 35–36; Freshman English Policy Committee to prospective 1969–70 TAs, memo, May 14, 1969.

41. For these current-traditional techniques, see Connors, *Composition-Rhetoric*.

42. Freshman English Policy Committee to prospective 1969–70 TAs, memo, May 14, 1969.

43. Davidson, interview, Aug. 24, 2005.

44. The essay, by Allan Seager, originally appeared in *Sports Illustrated*, Oct. 29, 1962. It's also mentioned in TA Pauline Lipman's letter to the editor of the *Daily Cardinal*, Nov. 25, 1969 (quoted extensively in chap. 6).

45. McLeod, interview, June 30, 2005.

46. Jean Turner, interview with David Fleming, Nov. 9, 2005.

47. See Brown and Silber, *War at Home;* Maraniss, *They Marched into Sunlight*.

48. Turner, interview, Nov. 9, 2005.

49. "Department of English: Training of Teaching Assistants," 1966–67.

50. McLeod, interview, June 30, 2005.

51. Davidson, interview, Aug. 24, 2005.

52. McLeod, interview, June 30, 2005.

53. Ira Shor, interview with Mira Shimabukuro, July 13, 2005; Turner, interview, Nov. 9, 2005.

54. Davidson, interview, Aug. 24, 2005.

55. Gender issues surface occasionally in the materials we uncovered, sometimes in surprising places. Former TA and graduate student Virginia (Joyce) Davidson came to UW in the 1960s specifically because the English Department there was thought to be a good place for female scholars, with Madeleine Doran, Ruth Wallerstein, Rosamund Tuve, and Helen White all prominent members of the faculty. "I wanted to work with women," she said (interview, Aug. 24, 2005). The department was far from a feminist utopia, however. Lynne Cheney, writing a dissertation at UW on Matthew Arnold, "found it impossible to land a mentor on the English faculty, which she considered sexist; even the noted scholar Madeline Doran seemed interested only in helping male grad students, she thought" (Maraniss, *They Marched into Sunlight*, 113). Davidson also fell afoul of Doran's alleged preference that her female students be married to their work (interview, Aug. 24, 2005). Jean Turner, meanwhile, used feminist analysis in her teaching and considered it a badge of honor to finish her PhD when so many of her colleagues did not (of the nine who left with her in 1970 to begin a commune in Baltimore, she was the only one who completed her dissertation: "finishing things" was a feminist principle for her (interview, Nov. 9, 2005).

56. Davidson, interview, Aug. 24, 2005.

57. Turner, interview, Nov. 9, 2005. After reading an earlier draft of this chapter in which I seemed to sympathize too much with Ednah Thomas and Joyce Steward, Ira Shor wrote that he wasn't willing to let them off the hook that easily: "Should Ednah and Joyce also be blamed for the predicament or only Lacy, the easy target? They were the 'comp

women,' bullied and disrespected by the male PhD lit authorities. They represented the oppressed margins to which 'comp' had been relegated. Perhaps they could do no more? Perhaps they could not have known how to do anything differently? I wonder. They certainly decided to take no risks and certainly did the best they could for themselves—getting university-level work, offices, and wages—without PhDs in hand. Loyal, gifted, smart, and dedicated, grunt workers like Ednah and Joyce facilitated the subordination of 'comp' to 'lit.' . . . They were the local agents for keeping 'comp' large, unworkable, underfunded, and inferior—whom Lacy and others could not have done without. . . . Not only did Thomas and the others enforce this subordinate status of 'comp' in the 'lit' departments, but they also never let us know that there was a real comp/rhet professional community. . . . Surely Thomas and the others must have known about . . . the CCCC—but they never introduced us to these resources, accepting the subordination of themselves and of 'comp' teaching" (Ira Shor to David Fleming, email, Aug. 21, 2006).

58. McLeod, interview, June 30, 2005.

59. Davidson, interview, Aug. 24, 2005.

60. Turner, interview, Nov. 9, 2005.

61. Shor, interview, July 13, 2005.

62. See post to WPA-L, Jan. 13, 2005.

63. McLeod, interview, June 30, 2005. Something of Thomas's "essential humanity," as well as her strictness, shows through at the end of her "Foreword to Teachers" in *Evaluating Student Themes,* where she writes, "Virginia Woolf points out the responsibility and importance of the reader who judges books 'with great sympathy and yet with great severity.' Does not this apply also to us? Our severity, sympathetically expressed, takes the form of assuming that the student will do the best work of which he is capable. Our sympathy, severely accompanied by recognition of the truth that any discipline requires care and pains, takes the form of realizing that the student is an individual, different from his teacher, with problems, weaknesses, and strengths of his own. We express both severity and sympathy by our interest in and respect for his work" (vi). Joyce Steward, in her interview with Brad Hughes in 2002, said that Ednah Thomas always urged teachers to "find the good in the paper first" (Oral History Program, UW-Madison, Archives, #592, 2002). See also Rich Haswell's "1955 and Ednah Thomas Takes on the Grammar Police," in which Haswell calls Thomas's four-page foreword to *Evaluating Student Themes* "remarkably contemporary." Thomas herself wrote in the booklet that the teacher's aim in commenting is not to do the work for the student, but "to stimulate and guide the student to assume responsibility for doing it." The teacher should require corrections only for specific errors, with "general comments to be applied to the next assignment." The teacher ought to "recognize strength as well as weakness." And she noted that in the first-year writing program at Wisconsin, teachers provided "a grade report at stated intervals but no grade on individual themes" (*Evaluating Student Themes*).

64. McLeod, interview, June 30, 2005; Turner, interview, Nov. 9, 2005; Angle, interview, Oct. 11, 2005, Nov. 22, 2005; Davidson, interview, Aug. 24, 2005.

65. S. Rosenberg, *American Economic Development,* 103–4.

66. Shiller, *Irrational Exuberance,* 7–8. The late 1960s and early 1970s were a period of stock-market decline, however. By Dec. 1974, real stock prices were down 56 percent and would not return to their Jan. 1966 levels until 1992.

67. Marwick, *Sixties,* 36.

68. Ibid., 16–20.

69. See U.S. Census Mini Historical Statistics, from *2003 Statistical Abstract of the United States*, HS-21.

70. Nathan, *My Freshman Year*, 148–49.

71. Cronon and Jenkins, *University of Wisconsin*, 4: 228; UW-Madison, Office of the Registrar's "Enrollments 1888 to Present."

72. UW-Madison, Office of the Registrar, "Enrollments 1888 to Present."

73. Ibid. The staggering increases in college freshmen nationwide between 1963 and 1965 are a direct reflection of the "birth" of the "baby boom" eighteen to twenty years before. The College Entrance Examination Board's *On Further Examination*, discussing SAT scores between 1963 and 1977, described the number of eighteen-year-olds in 1964–65 as appearing "so high as to suggest error," but then confirmed the dramatic increase by looking at birth statistics for 1945–46 and 1946–47 (4).

74. "Federal and state governments have profoundly affected the possibilities (and aspirations) for higher education by providing student financial aid and subsidized public higher education. Apart from the G.I. Bill, federal efforts began in 1958 with the National Defense Education Act (which authorized low-interest loans to students) and have consistently expanded since then. College Work-Study was added in 1964, and Educational Opportunity Grants and Guaranteed Student Loans in 1965" (Carroll and Morrison, "Demographic and Economic Influences," 105–6).

75. UW-Madison, Office of the Registrar, "Enrollments 1888 to Present."

76. Cronon and Jenkins, *University of Wisconsin*, 4: 5.

77. Robert Rosenzweig, *The Political University: Policy, Politics, and Presidential Leadership in the American Research University* (Baltimore: Johns Hopkins University Press, 1998), 2 (quoted in Maurrasse, *Beyond the Campus*, 15).

78. Cronon and Jenkins, *University of Wisconsin*, 4: 261.

79. Geiger, "Sputnik and the Academic Revolution," 1.

80. Kerr, *Uses of the University*, 35.

81. Modern Language Association, *Final Report*.

82. Sperber, "How Undergraduate Education Became College Lite."

83. See, e.g., Copperman, "Literacy and the Future of Print," 115; College Entrance Examination Board, *On Further Examination*, 5; Cronon and Jenkins, *University of Wisconsin*, 4: 431 (on 1958's National Defense Education Act); Geiger, "What Happened after Sputnik?" and "Sputnik and the Academic Revolution." It's also possible that economic expansion, increasing affluence, continuing urbanization, improved nutrition, and internationalization contributed to this trend as well.

84. See, e.g., Buhle, *History and the New Left*.

85. Cronon and Jenkins, *University of Wisconsin*, 4: 210, 432.

86. UW-Madison, Office of the Registrar, "Enrollments 1888 to Present."

87. College Entrance Examination Board, *On Further Examination*; Scheuneman, "Differences between SAT Math and Verbal Scores." See chap. 7 for the post-1965 decline in test scores in this country.

88. Cronon and Jenkins, *University of Wisconsin*, 4: 226–27. But we should be careful about "decline" narratives regarding the late 1960s. See N. Rosenberg, "Sixties," for other ways to view the period—for many groups, women, e.g., the 1960s got arguably *better* as the decade went on. The main point here, however, is not that conditions at the university

in any way *declined* in the 1960s, but that they changed, and that projects like Freshman English, at least from the point of view of its faculty administrators, did not adapt.

89. Charles Scott, interview with Laura Smail, Oral History Program, UW-Madison, Archives, #195, 1980.

90. Madeleine Doran, interview with Laura Smail, Oral History Program, UW-Madison, Archives, #31, 1977. For a less rosy view of this period, see Joyce Carol Oates's memoir of her year (1960–61) as an English MA student at UW ("Nighthawk").

91. For the number of graduate students campuswide, see UW-Madison, Office of the Registrar, "Enrollments 1888 to Present." As we've seen, the increases started before this, essentially in the late 1950s. As for English Department faculty, in 1963, eleven new faculty members were hired (Scott, interview, 1980), but it was in 1965–67 that the numbers probably reached a crisis point: in terms of freshmen, majors, and graduate students alike.

92. Ricardo Quintana, memo re: English Department FTE's, 1960.

93. Simeon (Tim) Heninger to Dean Leon Epstein, memo, Apr. 22, 1969. Heninger predicts in the memo that few of the twenty-five assistant professors would be tenured.

94. Ednah Thomas, remarks to the Departmental Committee, quoted in UW English Department, Minutes of the Departmental Committee, Mar. 15, 1966. See also Mark Eccles, interview with Barry Teicher, Oral History Program, University of Wisconsin-Madison, Archives, #508, 1997.

95. Lacy, Lenehan, and Thomas. "Master Assistants at the University of Wisconsin"; "Department of English: Training of Teaching Assistants," 1966–67, 1.

96. Scott, interview, 1980; Walter Rideout, interview with Laura Smail, Oral History Program, UW-Madison, Archives, #88, 1976.

97. UW English Department, Minutes of the Departmental Committee, Apr. 2, 1968; Scott, interview, 1980.

98. See, e.g., Buhle, *History and the New Left.*

99. McLeod, interview, June 30, 2005.

100. Cronon and Jenkins, *University of Wisconsin,* 4: 450ff. Ira Shor confirmed this development in an email communication to David Fleming, Aug. 21, 2006.

101. Maraniss, *They Marched into Sunlight;* Van Ells, "More Than a Union."

102. Maraniss, *They Marched into Sunlight;* Cronon and Jenkins, *University of Wisconsin,* 4: 469.

103. Cronon and Jenkins, *University of Wisconsin,* 4: 478ff.

104. Heninger to Epstein, memo, Apr. 22, 1969. There were around 800 undergraduate majors and 70 faculty members in the department at the time. By comparison, in 1960, there were around 300 undergraduate majors, 274 graduate students (110 MA students and 164 at the PhD level), and 25 faculty members in the department (UW English Department, Minutes of the Departmental Committee, Sept. 20, 1960). In the mid-2000s, the respective numbers were, roughly speaking, 800 majors, 200 graduate students, and 55 faculty members.

105. Rideout, interview, 1976.

106. UW English Department, Minutes of the Departmental Committee, Sept. 25, 1967.

107. UW English Department, Minutes of the Departmental Committee, Mar. 19, 1968, 3–4, and May 7, 1968, 2–10—this latter meeting went from 4:35 to 8:15 P.M. and was almost entirely concerned with the Marten case; see assorted other documents from both chair and TAA, Mar.–May 1968, as well as Rideout, interview, 1976.

108. Simeon K. Heninger to English Departmental Committee, memo, Sept. 12, 1968.

109. UW English Department, Minutes of the Departmental Committee, Sept. 23, 1968, 3.

110. UW English Department, Minutes of the Departmental Committee, Oct. 8, 1968. Heninger provided his own estimate of TA attendance at various meetings, 1968–69, in a memo to the English Departmental Committee, Oct. 20, 1969.

111. UW English Department, Minutes of the Departmental Committee, Sept. 23, 1968, 3. A letter from an anonymous TA after the Sept. 17, 1968, meeting, kept in the department files, expresses sympathy with Heninger and describes the TAs as divided among those with "sincere and heartfelt . . . distresses and complaints"; another group of "apparently sincere, but disturbed and hostile, romantics"; and a "small band of hard-core, very shrewd, possibly Marxist-oriented anarchists."

112. My knowledge of this event comes from an Oct. 1968 petition with thirty-six TA signatures, as well as various English Students Association documents and local news accounts.

113. Lenehan to Heninger, memo, Aug. 21, 1969; Simeon Heninger to English 102/181 TAs, memo, Oct. 22, 1968. Lenehan urges TAs not to withhold six-week grades to freshmen "as a means of protesting the present grading system."

114. UW English Department, Minutes of the Departmental Committee (including appendices), Apr. 29, 1969; Edwin Young, chancellor, UW-Madison, and Robert L. Muehlenkamp, president, TAA, "Young's 'Position'—Our Response," Mar. 31, 1969.

115. Shor, interview, July 13, 2005; cf. Turner, interview, Nov. 9, 2005.

116. See also Van Ells, "More Than a Union," on TAA demands; see Cronon and Jenkins on the TAA strike and demands for TAs' role in educational planning (*University of Wisconsin*, 4: 494ff, 498, 503). "The goals of the TAA are: to better the Conditions of Employment of TA's and to improve the quality of Education at the U.W." (TAA, "General Policy Statement," quoted in Craig, "Graduate Student Unionism," 83).

117. See, e.g., Mosse, "New Left Intellectuals."

118. Karnow, *Vietnam*.

119. Cronon and Jenkins, *University of Wisconsin*, 4: 449–50.

120. Ibid., 4: 453, 508.

121. UW president Fred Harrington resigned after the bombing of Cambodia, and English chair Tim Heninger apparently became strongly antiwar during his time at UW (Scott, interview, 1980).

122. Maurrasse, *Beyond the Campus*, 15.

123. This was a more specific problem than whether an institution of higher education could be a liberal arts college, a graduate school, and a professional school at the same time. That had already been answered in the affirmative by Van Hise's "combination university" of the late nineteenth century (Curti and Carstensen, *University of Wisconsin*, 2: 30; Cronon and Jenkins, *University of Wisconsin*, 4: 1–2). What I'm talking about here is whether the university could handle the often conflicting demands of the Cold War: both rapidly increased undergraduate enrollment in a cultural and economic situation calling for high general skills *and* rapidly increased demands on faculty for world-class original research.

124. Maurrasse, *Beyond the Campus*, 15; Sampson, "What Is a University?"

125. This interpretation of the contradiction built into U.S. higher education in the 1960s—the competing demands (both federally supported) for access, on the one hand, and specialized research, on the other—and how this played out in the fraught staffing of

and attitudes toward general education classes like first-year composition is taken in part from remarks by David Laurence and John Guillory, as summarized in "The History of the Job Crisis in the Modern Languages," in the Modern Language Association's *Final Report*.

126. Geiger, "What Happened after Sputnik?" 356.

127. Ibid., 354–55.

128. Ibid., 355.

129. Ibid., 360.

130. Ibid., 361.

131. Geiger, "Sputnik and the Academic Revolution," 1.

132. Ibid., 2.

133. Ibid., 4.

134. Ibid., 5.

135. Ibid.

136. Ibid.

137. David Lawrence and John Guillory, in "The History of the Job Crisis in the Modern Languages," in the Modern Language Association's *Final Report*.

138. Dubin and Beisse, "Assistant."

139. "To a considerable extent, the higher education system fed on itself. Its rapid expansion demanded more college faculty, thereby stimulating expansion of postgraduate education. During the 1960s, many college graduates were channeled into postgraduate schools rather than directly into the labor force; that trend was so marked that the proportion of college graduates among all new labor-force entrants actually declined. In effect, large numbers of college graduates were in a postgraduate holding pattern" (Carroll and Morrison, "Demographic and Economic Influences," 105).

140. Dubin and Beisse, "Assistant," 525.

141. Ibid. Note that Dubin and Beisse's data do not even include academic years 1964–65 and 1965–66, which recorded some of the largest increases in U.S. undergraduate and graduate enrollment in history and which put even further strain on the demographic situation just described.

142. See above, n. 139. It's also clear, of course, that graduate enrollments were rising in response to the military draft.

143. Orr, "Job Market in English." Of our interviewees, three of six former TAs never got their PhD's; in Jean Turner's Baltimore group, only one of nine did (Turner, interview, Nov. 9, 2005). The economy couldn't keep up with these numbers either: by the end of the 1960s, unemployment was rising and productivity was in decline, problems that could be traced not only to the huge expansion of the previous years and the mounting costs of war but also to structural developments like worldwide deindustrialization. The bloom was off the U.S. economic rose, and there were hints of insecurity to come.

4. Faculty Withdrawal, 1966–1969

1. UW English Department, Minutes of the Departmental Committee, Mar. 6, 1968.

2. UW English Department, "Interim Report of the Ad Hoc Committee to Study Undergrad Course Offerings," Feb. 26, 1968 (approved by the UW English Department Curriculum Committee, Feb. 27, 1968) (emphasis in original).

3. "Report from Department of English on Change in Placement Procedures," Letters and Science Faculty Document 141, May 15, 1968, p. 2 (emphasis in original).

4. Appendix to UW English Department, "Interim Report of the Ad Hoc Committee to Study Undergrad Course Offerings," Feb. 26, 1968. For comparison's sake, 57 percent of the 2006 freshman class at UW ranked in the top 10 percent of their high school class (see http://www.news.wisc.edu/13013.html).

5. See also table 7.1 for figures from the Task Group on Student Writing and Speaking (Lee Hansen, chair) of the UW-Madison Committee on Undergraduate Education (Bassam Z. Shakhashiri, chair), "Improving the Writing Skills of Undergraduate Students," Apr. 1976, which show higher freshman scores on a variety of measures in 1968 compared to 1963.

6. Frank Battaglia, interview with Mira Shimabukuro, Oct. 18, 2005.

7. Davidson, interview, Aug. 24, 2005.

8. McLeod, interview, June 30, 2005.

9. Robert Muehlenkamp, interview with Rasha Diab, Dec. 7, 2005.

10. College Entrance Examination Board, *On Further Examination;* Scheuneman, "Differences between SAT Math and Verbal Scores." But as indicated in n. 5 above, figures from the 1976 Shakhashiri report suggest that 1968 was indeed the high point for student scores at UW. For conflicting accounts of the "great decline" in SAT scores from 1963 to 1980, see Stedman and Kaestle, "Literacy and Reading Performances"; Herrnstein and Murray, *Bell Curve.*

11. Emig, *Composing Processes of Twelfth Graders.*

12. Crowley, "Around 1971"; Fleming, "Rhetoric Revival"; Nystrand, "Janet Emig, Frank Smith." Emig studied the writing of five girls and three boys, six of whom were white, one black, and one Chinese American (*Composing Processes of Twelfth Graders,* 29), from a variety of economic backgrounds and a diverse range of high schools in metropolitan Chicago, from an all-white upper-middle-class suburban school, to a racially and economically mixed high school in a small city north of Chicago, to a racially mixed and lower-middle-class suburban high school in an industrial area west of the city, to an almost all-black ghetto school in Chicago, to a university-affiliated lab school. Six of the students were "above average" in ability and two "average," the former identified by their schools as "good" writers. For more on Emig's career, see Nystrand, "Janet Emig, Frank Smith."

13. Emig, *Composing Processes of Twelfth Graders,* 99.

14. Ibid., 50.

15. Ibid., 97.

16. Ibid., 70.

17. Ibid., 98.

18. Ibid., 4.

19. Ibid., 97.

20. Ibid., 93.

21. Ibid., 93, 72.

22. See chap. 7.

23. Kerr, *Uses of the University,* 116–17.

24. In a letter to Ednah Thomas dated May 22, 1969, UW English Department chair Simeon (Tim) Heninger talks about "our responsibilities to culturally disadvantaged students whom the university recruits, and especially about the need for special instruction in English to help them through the first year here."

25. On federally fueled, post-*Sputnik* gains in the educational achievement of U.S. students, see Copperman, "Literacy and the Future of Print," 115; College Entrance Examination

Board, *On Further Examination,* 5: "It is generally assumed that the increase in SAT scores in the early 1960s, especially the spurt that made 1963 a high year, may have reflected the results of the post-Sputnik acceleration of educational effort in this country." Thanks to the National Defense Education Act (NDEA), one billion dollars was spent on student loans, scientific equipment for schools and colleges, and scholarships between 1958 and 1964, federal support for research and education essentially tripling, with most of it benefiting the study of math, science, engineering, and foreign languages. But even outside those areas, the NDEA ushered in a more activist federal government in educational matters (see Geiger, "Sputnik and the Academic Revolution").

26. In a so-called strong composition course, first-year general education writing instruction is affirmed even as it is disattached from the project of remedialism (see Sullivan et al., "Student Needs and Strong Composition").

27. UW English Department, Minutes of the Departmental Committee, Sept. 25, 1967, 2.

28. See Curriculum Review Committee (David E. Cronon, chair) of the UW College of Letters and Science, "English Composition Survey," Apr. 1970. That survey's findings were later summarized as follows: "A clear majority of respondents said they were dissatisfied or very dissatisfied with the effectiveness of the freshman composition courses. Yet over two-thirds of the freshmen and half the seniors expressed support for some course, either required or voluntary, on writing improvement. . . . A sizeable majority (72 percent of freshmen and 62 percent of seniors) thought an ideal composition course should 'develop writing skills,' as contrasted with approximately 10 percent favoring 'critical thinking,' the current buzzword of radical activists" (Cronon and Jenkins, *University of Wisconsin,* 4: 290–91).

29. "Survey English TAs Elsewhere," *TAA Newsletter* 1, no. 2 (1968): 1–2.

30. William T. Lenehan's memo to Simeon K. Heninger, dated Aug. 21, 1969, written when Lenehan was not yet forty years old, betrays a curious world-weariness about pedagogical theory—there's nothing new under the sun, this is a difficult and frustrating course, etc. At one point, Lenehan writes that few new ideas in teaching composition ever crop up.

31. UW English Department, Minutes of the Departmental Committee, May 9, 16, 1967.

32. Scott, interview, 1980.

33. UW English Department, Minutes of the Departmental Committee, May 9, 1967, 2.

34. Ibid.

35. Ibid.

36. UW English Department, Minutes of the Departmental Committee, May 16, 1967.

37. UW English Department, Minutes of the Departmental Committee, Mar. 6, Apr. 30, 1968.

38. David Middleton, "The Ad Hoc Committee Meetings: An Interpretation," spring 1968, 1–2.

39. Ibid., 1.

40. Middleton also provides some evidence for the predetermined nature of the decision about English 101: "We have since learned . . . that the freshman/sophomore English program is in fact changed for next year, to include one semester of comp and a two semester sequence of literature-oriented work. This decision appears to me to have been made before we ever met with the committee" (ibid., 1).

41. See Cronon and Jenkins, *University of Wisconsin,* 4:289ff. Still, this doesn't explain why faculty and students were enthusiastic supporters of other required courses.

42. UW English Department, Minutes of the Departmental Committee, Mar. 6, 1968, Nov. 18, 1969.

43. Heninger to Epstein, memo, Apr. 22, 1969.

44. Mulvihill Report, Faculty Document 183, Feb. 5, 1968.

45. Ibid., 21, n. 1.

46. "TAA Speaks on 10D," n.d., TAA archives, Madison, 2.

47. Dubin and Beisse, "Assistant."

48. Ibid., 531. Thus, English TA Gary Kline would argue in a fall 1969 Departmental Committee meeting that the TAs' motion for control of the Freshman English Policy Committee "should not be interpreted as a bid for autonomy, but rather as a desire to work within the structure" (UW English Department, Minutes of the Departmental Committee, Oct. 28, 1969, 2).

49. Dubin and Beisse, "Assistant," 530. Compare the untitled essay on the contradictions of being both an instructor and a graduate student by James Naremore in Middleton, "Ad Hoc Committee Meetings," and the discussion of the "nebulous" position of TAs in Craig, "Graduate Student Unionism."

50. Dubin and Beisse, "Assistant," 530.

51. Ibid., 531. Compare the remarks of Professor Howard Weinbrot in UW English Department, Minutes of the Departmental Committee, Oct. 28, 1969 (see chap. 6).

52. During the 1970 TAA strike at UW, associate professor of math Patrick Ahern admitted, "I and some of my colleagues have not paid enough attention to undergraduate education and have been apathetic toward education reform" (Van Ells, "More Than a Union," 120).

53. Report of the Committee on the Teaching Assistant System, 4. In 1967–68, the English Department appointed all TAs on a year-by-year (and sometimes semester-by-semester) basis for a maximum of five years. Note that whereas 77 percent of faculty in the humanities claimed that their TAs were among their best graduate students, this was true for only 11 percent of faculty in the biological sciences (ibid., 3).

54. Ibid., 6.

55. Ibid., 10.

56. Ibid., 11.

57. Ibid., 14 (emphasis in original).

58. Ibid., 16.

59. UW English Department, Minutes of the Departmental Committee, May 21, 1968.

60. UW English Department, "Recommendation Concerning English 200," approved in Departmental Committee, Apr. 30, 1968.

61. See chap. 3, nn. 110–11.

62. UW English Department, Minutes of the Departmental Committee, Oct. 8, 1968, 4.

63. Ibid.

64. Ibid, 4, 2 (see also the appendix to the minutes from the Curriculum Committee: "Recommendation Concerning the Participation of Teaching Assistants in Certain Policy Committees of the English Department," Oct. 8, 1968).

65. UW English Department, Minutes of the Departmental Committee, Oct. 8, 1968.

66. Ibid., 4, 8.

67. UW English Department Curriculum Committee, "Recommendation Concerning the Participation of Teaching Assistants," Oct. 8, 1968. In Sept., Lenehan had requested the addition of TAs to the committee, though he had proposed three TA members rather than four (William Lenehan to Simeon Heninger, memo, Sept. 19, 1968).

68. Lenehan to Heninger, memo, Aug. 21, 1969.

69. There are indications, however, that the main period of meetings was late spring, from about Mar. 10 to May 26, 1969, when the group met weekly to revise the English 102 syllabus.

70. Lenehan to Heninger, memo, Aug. 21, 1969, 1–2.

71. Ibid., 2–3.

72. Ibid. (emphasis in original).

73. UW English Department, Report on English 101 by Ednah Thomas, Director of the Course, with appendices from TAs Jeanie Peterson, John Pirri, Mary Richards, Michael Stroud, and Sharon Wilson, Feb. 5, 1969.

74. Morale among the English 101 staff, unlike in English 102, seems to have been consistently high during this period. Jean Turner, who taught English 101 in 1969–70, loved the course. It was a real experiment, collective, collaborative, invigorating: "We were very earnest," she said (interview, Nov. 9, 2005).

75. Memos from May 1969 about English 101 (S. K. Heninger, William Lenehan, Dean Leon Epstein, Ednah Thomas).

76. UW English Department, Report on English 101, 7.

77. On the theory that some students' struggles with standard English were caused by dialect interference, TA Burr Angle taught an experimental section of English 101 in fall 1969, subtitled "Special Section for Black Americans," that was meant to give students focused phonological and syntactic help with Standard English (Burr Angle, "Syllabus for English 101"). But in a spring 1970 follow-up, he argued that his hypothesis about dialect interference had been wrong (Burr Angle, report dated Apr. 20, 1970). He wrote that, although the students came from "very segregated and very Black cultures," they knew Standard English well and were able to use it when required. The study of Black English did seem to help the students' "linguistic self-confidence," however, and this was important since, according to Angle, the students' difficulties (according to him, they were among the lowest scorers on the university's multiple-choice entrance examination) stemmed not from dialect interference, "but from a lack of confidence in their abilities to write academic Standard English and from an *ignorance* of the rhetorical frames and models used in college writing" (emphasis in original). A year later, in the spring of 1970, the staff of English 101, now without Ednah Thomas signing off, wrote a somewhat more strident report on teaching the course than they had a year earlier ("Teaching Staff Report on English 101, 1969–1970," Apr. 28, 1970). They remained, however, convinced that the typical English 101 student's biggest problem was psychological, namely, lack of confidence in his or her writing ability, and that the solution required giving English 101 TAs "a free hand in terms of classroom methodology, course content, and grading." Throughout, the group called for flexibility, patience, sympathy, variety, and personal contact: "It is extremely important to take the content of the papers seriously, for that is an essential first step in building the student's self-esteem, confidence, and ability to say what he wants to say." The stated aim of the course should be "to encourage and develop the student's own abilities to think and to read critically, which are prior to and necessary for development of acceptable writing

skills." Still recommending that all sections of the course be scheduled at 12:05 P.M., that class size be limited to twelve students, and that seating be circular, the group proposed that students themselves decide how to divide up class meetings and what should be done in them.

78. "english," *TAA Newsletter* 1, no. 4 (1968): 6–7.

5. TA Experimentation, 1966–1969

1. Another 283 students were enrolled in English 102 in the spring of 1970, the last semester it was officially offered—a few of them may have failed the course the previous fall, but most, we speculate, either took English 101 in the fall and then English 102 in the spring or waited until spring 1970 to fulfill their Freshman English requirement, going straight into English 102. An additional 21 students in two sections were still in English 101 in the spring of 1970, accounting for the odd fact that English 102 was still being offered in a dozen or so sections in 1970–71, i.e., after it had already been abolished.

2. On the total number of TAs, see Heninger to English Departmental Committee, memo, Oct. 20, 1969, 2; see also the English Department's June 1969 TAA list for 1969–70, which puts the number at 155. On 101 TAs in English 102 that fall, see William T. Lenehan to Simeon K. Heninger, memo, Sept. 25, 1969.

3. I'll have more to say about this document in chap. 6.

4. Lenehan to Heninger, memo, Aug. 21, 1969, 3. The one exception to all this was the short-lived and rather freewheeling experiment in remedializing English 101.

5. Davidson, interview, Aug. 24, 2005.

6. Turner, interview, Nov. 9, 2005.

7. McLeod, interview, June 30, 2005. In a Jan. 14, 2005, post to the WPA-L online discussion list, Susan McLeod wrote, "I sometimes feel that I should try to locate some of my students from that time and offer them a refund."

8. Shor, interview, July 13, 2005.

9. Ibid.

10. Lenehan to Heninger, memo, Aug. 21, 1969 ("Agenda," 4).

11. "Contract Proposal for English 102 and 200," English Department TAA, 1969. TAs participating in the seminars would be paid at a one-twelfth rate per semester for on-the-job training. Money would also be made available "for use by TAs in sponsoring films, forums, plays, and speakers relevant to the interests and concerns (academic and political) of 102 and 200 teachers and students."

12. David Foster, "Reflections in a Jaundiced Eye," *Critical Teaching* 1 (September 1968): 51 (TAA archives). (The short-lived TAA journal *Critical Teaching* is only available in the TAA archives in Madison; *Critical Teaching* articles are thus cited in the notes rather than being listed in the bibliography.)

13. "Education Report," *TAA Newsletter* 3, no. 1 (1969): 2.

14. Neill, *Summerhill*. The Summerhill School, in Suffolk, England, was founded in 1921 by A. S. Neill, a progressive Scottish educator, and his first wife, for primary- and secondary-school-aged children. It is still in operation today, and still controversial, under the leadership of Neill's daughter. In A. S. Neill's words, Summerhill was designed to "allow children freedom to be themselves"; in order to accomplish this, the school renounced "all discipline, all direction, all suggestion, all moral training, all religious instruction." It was

based on the idea "that a child is innately wise and realistic. If left to himself without adult suggestion of any kind, he will develop as far as he is capable of developing" (4). Children have lessons at the school, but they're optional, and thus the focus is not on *teaching* but on the child's self-initiated *learning*: "Whether a school has or has not a special method for teaching long division is of no significance, for long division is of no importance except to those who *want* to learn it. And the child who *wants* to learn long division *will* learn it no matter how it is taught" (5). According to Neill, "there is a lot of learning in Summerhill. Perhaps a group of our twelve-year-olds could not compete with a class of equal age in handwriting or spelling or fractions. But in an examination requiring originality, our lot would beat the others hollow" (6). Summerhill is referenced in the following *Critical Teaching* articles: Margaret Blanchard, "Preface: 'There's no success like failure, and failure's no success at all,'" and Anne Mulkeen, "Workshop in Communication" (both in vol. 1); Karl Tunberg, "Radical Speech" (vol. 2).

15. "Education Report," 2.

16. Shor, interview, July 13, 2005.

17. McLeod, interview, June 30, 2005.

18. "Survey English TAs Elsewhere," 2.

19. *Critical Teaching* 1 (Sept. 1968) (TAA archives).

20. TAA *Newsletter* 1, no. 4 (1968), 5.

21. Ibid.

22. See, e.g., UW English Department, Report on English 101; William T. Lenehan to Simeon K. Heninger, re: English 101, May 1969; Turner, interview, Nov. 9, 2005; UW English Department, Minutes of the Departmental Committee, Oct. 28, 1969; various *Critical Teaching* articles.

23. Muehlenkamp, interview, Dec. 7, 2005.

24. Ibid.

25. English TAA stewards, Minutes of TA Staff Meeting, Oct. 13, 1969.

26. UW English Department, Minutes of the Departmental Committee, Oct. 28, 1969.

27. Pauline Lipman, letter to the editor, *Daily Cardinal,* Nov. 25, 1969; McLeod, interview, June 30, 2005.

28. Susan McLeod, personal communication with David Fleming.

29. UW English Department, Report on English 101.

30. Lenehan to Heninger, memo, Aug. 21, 1969.

31. Ibid. (attachment 2). See also "Survey English TAs Elsewhere," 2.

32. Lenehan to Heninger, memo, Aug. 21, 1969, 2–3.

33. Ironically, the TAs' preference for increasing the literary content of English 102 is also an effective rejoinder to the charge that, in the words of former chair Walter Rideout, they were simply using the course "to argue against the war" (Rideout, interview, 1976). In fact, the fullest narrative of a radical English 102 class that we possess, Bob Muehlenkamp's 1968 article in *Critical Teaching,* is essentially the story of his students' reading of Joyce's *Dubliners* ("Growing Free," *Critical Teaching* 1 [September 1968]: 44–50 [TAA archives]).

34. Heninger to English Departmental Committee, memo, Sept. 12, 1968 (emphasis added).

35. Quinn and Dolan, *Sense of the Sixties,* vii–viii.

36. Sea Unido, "Becoming a Radical Teacher," *Critical Teaching* 2 (September 1969): 56 (TAA archives).

37. Shor, interview, July 13, 2005.

38. Ibid.

39. Debbie Soglin, "Panel Terms Literature Relevant," *Daily Cardinal*, Mar. 22, 1969, 5.

40. Ibid.

41. Shor, interview, July 13, 2005.

42. Davidson, interview, Aug. 24, 2005.

43. McLeod, interview, June 30, 2005.

44. Angle, interview, Oct. 11, 2005, Nov. 22, 2005.

45. UW Department of English, Minutes of the Departmental Committee, Feb. 15, 1969, 3.

46. Richard Damashek, letter to the editor, *Daily Cardinal*, Nov. 25, 1969.

47. Emig, *Composing Processes of Twelfth Graders*, 100.

48. Shor, interview, July 13, 2005.

49. Muehlenkamp, interview, Dec. 7, 2005.

50. Neill, *Summerhill*, 12.

51. Duberman, "Experiment in Education."

52. Ibid., 322, 321.

53. Ed Zeidman and Linda Zeidman, "Bringing It All Back Home," *Critical Teaching* 2 (September 1969): 15–19 (TAA archives).

54. Anonymous, "Reviving Freshman English," *Critical Teaching* 1 (September 1968): 35 (TAA archives).

55. Ibid., 36–37 (emphases in original).

56. Ibid., 38.

57. Muehlenkamp, "Growing Free."

58. Ibid., 45.

59. Ibid., 47.

60. Ibid.

61. UW English Department, Minutes of the Departmental Committee, Oct. 28, 1969.

62. English Students Association, statement about suspending normal class hours to discuss upcoming presidential election, Nov. 4, 1968.

63. Unido, "Becoming a Radical Teacher," 51–58.

64. Ibid., 51–52.

65. UW English Department, Report on English 101.

66. Duberman, "Experiment in Education."

67. TAA, "The Evils of the Grading System," n.d., TAA archives.

68. TAA, "History," n.d., p. 2, TAA archives. See also Van Ells, "More Than a Union"; Maraniss, *They Marched into Sunlight*. In May 1966, TAs at UW objected to the connection between the grades they gave male students and the military draft. This is why "thirty five TAs calling themselves the Teaching Assistants for Re-evaluation and Renewal of Education (TARRE) passed a resolution reiterating the demand for a student-faculty committee and threatened to withhold grades 'until they were no longer a life and death issue'" (Van Ells, "More than a Union," 104). When it took the TARRE TAs two days to find a faculty member willing to read their resolution at the Faculty Senate (May 25, 1966), they realized that they needed representation as teaching assistants. To them, this situation "exposed the ambiguous role of the teaching assistant in the university community," since they were in the "nether world between student and faculty" (ibid., 105). Judy Craig later wrote in her study

of the union, "Twenty-five teaching assistants, part of the nebulous group who are fully accepted and enjoy the rights of neither the faculty world nor the student world, voted to incorporate as the University Teaching Assistants' Association" (*Graduate Student Unionism*, 54).

69. Heninger to English 102/181 TAs, memo, Oct. 22, 1968.

70. Lenehan to Heninger, memo, Aug. 21, 1969.

71. Cronon and Jenkins, *University of Wisconsin*: 4: 287–88, 476.

72. Lenehan to Heninger, memo, Aug. 21, 1969.

73. UW English Department, Minutes of the Departmental Committee, Nov. 4, 1969 (see chap. 6 for the details of Lenehan's remarks at this meeting).

74. TAA, "Evils of the Grading System."

75. Inez Martinez, "The Degrading System," *Critical Teaching* 1 (September 1968): 4–6 (TAA archives).

76. Turner, interview, Nov. 9, 2005.

77. Muehlenkamp, interview, Dec. 7, 2005.

78. McLeod, interview, June 30, 2005; see also her Jan. 2005 email post to WPA-L about a 1968–69 experiment in giving all As.

79. Anonymous, "Reviving Freshman English," 35–36.

80. Muehlenkamp, "Growing Free."

81. Ibid.

82. Ibid.

83. Blanchard, "Preface," 1.

84. Muehlenkamp, "Growing Free."

85. Ibid., 49–50.

86. Tassoni and Thelin, *Blundering for a Change*, 2–3.

87. Ibid., 5.

88. Ibid. Tassoni and Thelim are quoting here from Robert P. Yagelski.

89. UW English Department, Minutes of the Departmental Committee, Oct. 28, 1969.

90. Emig, Composing *Processes of Twelfth Graders*, 89.

91. Anthony Elkan to Simeon K. Heninger, Nov. 1968.

92. Simeon K. Heninger to Anthony Elkan, Nov. 1968.

93. DeKoven, *Utopia Limited*.

94. Ibid., 124.

95. Ibid., 4.

96. Ibid., 200.

97. Duberman, "Experiment in Education," 339.

98. Sampson, "What Is a University?" 561.

99. Sampson, "What Is a University?" 563. For a defense of "value-free" inquiry by the UW faculty at this time, see the "Majority Statement" of the Ad Hoc Committee on Mode of Response to Obstruction, Interview Policy, and Related Matters, University of Wisconsin, Madison campus, Mar. 13, 1968, excerpted as "The Logic of Neutrality" in vol. 1 of *The University Crisis Reader*.

100. Ibid.

101. Ibid., 564.

102. Muehlenkamp, "Growing Free."

103. Ibid., 44–45.

104. Unido, "Becoming a Radical Teacher," 51–58.

105. Nystrand, Greene, and Wiemelt, "Where Did Composition Studies Come From?" I am not the first to note that the 1960s critique of current-traditionalism was based largely on this preference for meaning over form. Nystrand, Greene, and Wiemelt illuminate the historical shift from formalist accounts of language and symbolic activity (e.g., New Criticism, current-traditional rhetoric, behavioral psychology), which locate meaning in the text, to those that locate it in the reader or writer, including theories influenced by the Cambridge revolution in cognitive psychology, and oppose all forms of formalism, structuralism, and behaviorism. But they trace that turn among researchers and in fact see the rise of composition almost exclusively as a disciplinary or scientific phenomenon rather than a pedagogical one. The two historical developments are obviously connected, but it's important, I believe, to bring teachers back into the timeline, especially forgotten teachers like English graduate student TAs at UW in the late 1960s.

106. Shor, interview, July 13, 2005.

107. Ibid. For other examples of 1960s humanism, see Sampson, "What Is a University?"; Dixon, *Growth through English;* Emig, *Composing Processes of Twelfth Graders.*

108. See Brodkey, *Writing Permitted in Designated Areas Only;* Hairston, "Diversity, Ideology, and Teaching Writing."

109. Turner, interview, Nov. 9, 2005.

110. Shor, interview, July 13, 2005.

111. Muehlenkamp, interview, Dec. 7, 2005.

112. Pauline Lipman, letter to the editor, *Daily Cardinal,* Nov. 25, 1969

113. Simeon K. Heninger to Dean Leon Epstein, May 23, 1969.

114. UW English Department, Minutes of the Departmental Committee, Oct. 28, 1969.

115. At a Departmental Committee meeting in late 1968, one professor complained that some graduate students "seemed to think that effective teaching was a far better criterion for reappointment than was excellence in graduate course-work" (UW English Department, Minutes of the Departmental Committee, Dec. 17, 1968, 1); see also TA David Middleton's spring 1968 remarks in "The Ad Hoc Committee Meetings: An Interpretation" apropos the Mulvihill Report: "The sad thing is that altho' we are getting some cover as teachers, we stand stark naked as graduate students. We are required by the department to be 'good' on two counts (as TAs and as students) but are protected by the department on only one of them. . . . In order to get rid of a TA all the University has to do is suspend or expel him as a student" (1–2).

116. Heninger to Epstein, memo, Apr. 22, 1969.

117. UW English Department, Minutes of the Departmental Committee, Apr. 29, 1969, 3.

118. For more on this crucial statute, see chap. 6.

6. 1969 Breakdown

1. Lenehan to Heninger, Sept. 25, 1969.
2. Joseph Carr to English Department TAs, Oct. 13, 1969.
3. Ibid.
4. Lenehan to Heninger, Sept. 25, 1969.
5. Ibid.

6. Carr to English Department TAs, Oct. 13, 1969.

7. Ibid.

8. Ibid. (emphasis in original).

9. Ibid. (emphasis in original).

10. English TAA stewards, minutes of TA staff meeting, Oct. 13, 1969.

11. Simeon K. Heninger to TAs, memo, Oct. 7, 1969.

12. English TAA stewards, minutes of TA staff meeting, Oct. 13, 1969.

13. Ibid.

14. Ibid., 2.

15. Later, the TAs proposed six TAs, two undergraduates, and one faculty adviser for the Freshman English Policy Committee—this is apparently the "collaborative" group that Lipman refers to in her letter to the *Daily Cardinal* on Nov. 25, 1969.

16. Attendance at this meeting—which was reported as 85 by the TAA stewards but only 68 by Heninger himself and included only 58 (of a total of 158 TAs) in the final vote on the motion to reconstitute the Freshman English Policy Committee—became an issue both for Heninger in his Oct. 20, 1969, memo to the Departmental Committee (claiming that poor attendance at this and other meetings made any such decision illegitimate) and for the "Third View" memo, which refused to interpret lack of attendance as apathy and which referred to an Oct. 27 anonymous memo from a TA accusing inactive TAs of apathy.

17. The minutes appear to be an accurate record of the meeting. Nothing is disputed by any later documents; Heninger, as seen in n. 16 above, offered in his Oct. 20 memo to the faculty a different estimate of TA attendance at the meeting, but there's no dispute about the final vote, and Heninger himself summarizes one moment, when he asked the TAs if they felt their academic freedom had been violated by the policies of the Freshman English program, in words almost identical to the TAA stewards' minutes: "When I asked rhetorically, 'Do you really feel that your academic freedom is appreciably curtailed,' there was a loud chorus of 'yes.'" Compare the TAA minutes: "Mr. Heninger then asked the body if they felt their academic freedom was being violated." Almost everyone responded 'yes.'"

18. Robert Doremus, interview with Laura Smail Oral History Program, UW-Madison, Archives, #32, 1976.

19. Simeon K. Heninger, notes to self, written around Oct. 13, 1969.

20. Heninger to English Departmental Committee, memo, Oct. 20, 1969.

21. Ibid., 1.

22. Ibid., 4.

23. Ibid.

24. At the previous week's meeting, Heninger read the TAs' Oct. 13 motion "that the faculty be instructed to establish a committee to administer English 102 composed of seven TA's and one faculty advisor; that no further action be taken on the existing English 102 committee until action is taken on the first part of this motion" (UW English Department, Minutes of the Departmental Committee, Oct. 21, 1969). He pointed out that discussion on the motion in the Departmental Committee must involve teaching assistants, and he asked the department for permission to invite TAs to attend the next faculty meeting on Oct. 28 and asked that they be allowed to speak there. According to the minutes of that meeting, "He asked also that the departmental members sit in a group to conduct the discussion in solidarity." He noted that the issue would be the only thing discussed at the meeting, but that the normal time limit would apply and that it was not necessary to resolve the problem at this meeting: "It was noted, however, that the present impasse was very

serious." The motion to invite teaching assistants to and allow them to speak at the Oct. 28 Departmental Committee meeting passed unanimously.

25. UW English Department, Minutes of the Departmental Committee, Oct. 28, 1969, 1 (emphasis in original).

26. Ibid., 2.

27. Ibid.

28. Ibid.

29. Ibid., 2–3.

30. Ibid., 3.

31. Ibid.

32. Ibid., 4.

33. Ibid.

34. Ibid.

35. Ibid., 5.

36. Ibid.

37. Ibid.

38. Ibid., 6.

39. Ibid.

40. Ibid.

41. Ibid.

42. Ibid., 7 (emphasis added).

43. The line here between "taking responsibility" for English 102 and "seeking autonomy" in that assignment is probably a thin one, but the evidence suggests that even the more radical TAs at UW did *not* see a new TA-led policy committee as simply a way to license whatever any individual TA wanted to do pedagogically. For one thing, the TAs at this time were intensely collaborative in their political and professional tactics—they were inveterate meeting goers and committee formers, nearly soviet in their organizational tendencies. In the fullest statement we've found of what new institutional structures would have looked like under the TAs' vision, the development of "model syllabi, reading lists and course guidelines" and the publication of "successful experiments in course form and content" in those courses would be the responsibility of neither faculty administrators nor individual unsupervised TAs, but of TA-led policy committees (comprised of six TAs, two undergraduate students, and one faculty member) that would submit proposed syllabi and guidelines to a plenary meeting of all TAs for approval ("English Department TAA, Contract Proposal for English 102 and 200," fall 1969). The point of the TAs' Oct. 13, 1969, motion, in other words, was not individual academic freedom for themselves, though they clearly supported reasonable protection of such freedom, but rather the overall improvement of the course. As good Summerhillians would have put it, the freedom needed for growth is not license to do as one pleases (see Erich Fromm's introduction to Neill, *Summerhill*).

44. "A Third View" does not contain a date, but I believe it was written and distributed sometime on or around Oct. 30, 1969.

45. "A Third View."

46. Edgar W. Lacy, draft proposal regarding elimination of English 102, Nov. 1, 1969. The proposal bears language Lacy had been using about Freshman English for at least a year and a half, and he's the one who introduced a slightly revised version of it as a formal motion in the Departmental Committee meeting of Nov. 11.

47. UW English Department, Minutes of the Departmental Committee, Nov. 4, 1969.

48. Ibid., 1.

49. Ibid.

50. Ibid., 2. The page number here actually reads "page 4," but I believe that this is an error and that it is page 2 of the minutes. Because of this and what appears to be a syntactic gap between the two pages, I thought for a long time that two pages of these minutes were missing. I no longer think so—though if they are in fact two pages long, the minutes of the Nov. 4, 1969, meeting of the English Departmental Committee (which went from 3:30 to 5:45 P.M.) are uncharacteristically short for this period.

51. Lacy is apparently referring here to Greenbaum, "Tradition of Complaint."

52. UW English Department, Minutes of the Departmental Committee, Nov. 4, 1969, 2.

53. Lenehan to Heninger, memo, Aug. 21, 1969.

54. Susan Moseley, "Frosh English Cancelled for 'Political Reasons': TA's Charge," *Daily Cardinal,* Nov. 21, 1969, 3.

55. UW English Department, Minutes of the Departmental Committee, Nov. 11, 1969.

56. Ibid., 2, 3.

57. Ibid.

58. UW English Department, Minutes of the Departmental Committee, Nov. 18, 1969.

59. Moseley, "Frosh English Cancelled"; Susan Moseley, "TA's Locked Out by Heninger: Has Freshman English Been Abolished?" *Daily Cardinal,* Nov. 19, 1969.

60. UW English Department, Minutes of the Departmental Committee, Nov. 18, 1969, 1.

61. Battaglia, interview, Oct. 18, 2005.

62. UW English Department, Minutes of the Departmental Committee, Nov. 18, 1969, 2.

63. Ibid.

64. UW English Department, Minutes of the Departmental Committee, Nov. 18, 1969, 2. The final proposal, titled "Proposal to Cease Offering English 102 and English 181" and dated Nov. 18, 1969, is almost identical to the Nov. 1 draft printed above. I include it here, noting in italics the somewhat emended ending:

> On April 1, 1968, the Department of English reported to the University Faculty that, because "the great bulk of entering freshmen have profited from stepped-up high school training and are not receptive to more than one semester of college composition," these students should be assigned, on the basis of placement tests, to English 102 rather than to English 101 (followed by English 102).
>
> The Department now feels that the needs of most students would be best served by shifting to each undergraduate department the responsibility for offering whatever training in composition, if any, a department may decide is needed by its undergraduate majors. In order to ensure that those students who need and may profit from additional instruction in composition will be selected to receive this instruction, the Department of English will be glad to *suggest to departments ways of developing procedures for handling their majors, and to suggest to referred students opportunities for supplementary aid. Although the Department of English will continue to test entering freshmen in order to assign to English 101 the small number who need that remedial course, the Department, at the end of the current academic year, will cease to offer English 102 and English 181* (emphasis added).

65. UW English Department, Minutes of the Departmental Committee, Nov. 18, 1969, 2.

66. William T. Lenehan to English Department Teaching Assistants, memo, Nov. 19, 1969.

67. Cf. Simeon K. Heninger to English Department Teaching Assistants, memo on reappointment for 1970–71, Dec. 8, 1969.

68. Lenehan to English Department Teaching Assistants, memo, Nov. 19, 1969.

69. Ibid. See also William T. Lenehan, "Report from the Department of English," Nov. 1969. English TA Richard Damashek specifically objected to this sentence in his Nov. 25, 1969, letter to the *Daily Cardinal.*

70. Minutes of the UW College of Letters and Science Faculty Meeting, Nov. 24, 1969, 1 (emphasis in original).

71. See chap. 1, n. 83.

72. Smith, "Composition Requirement."

73. It is true, as well, that the late 1960s saw a general trend on American campuses away from required courses in general. On this, see Cronon and Jenkins, *University of Wisconsin,* 4: 289; UW Faculty Document 148, Apr. 21, 1970. As noted above, however, I don't believe this explains the speed or totality of what happened to Freshman English at UW in 1968 and '69. It's also significant, as shown in the previous chapter, how seemingly unanimous the negative response to the department's move in 1969 was and how persistently a reinstated writing requirement was proposed in the quarter century after the abolition of 102. If students and TAs seemed ideologically opposed to requirements of this kind, they didn't seem to apply that opposition to Freshman English after it was abolished.

74. William T. Lenehan, Director of Freshman English, "Means for Attaining Student Writing Effectiveness without Required Freshman English, A Preliminary Report," Feb. 1970.

75. Pooley, interview, 1972.

76. Ibid.

77. Doran, interview, 1977.

78. Rideout, interview, 1976.

79. Scott, interview, 1980.

80. Muehlenkamp, interview, Dec. 7, 2005.

81. Steward, interview, 2002.

82. Edwin Young, interview with Laura Smail, Oral History Program, UW-Madison, Archives, #117, 1977.

83. The TAs too seem to have interpreted the abolition of English 102 as having to do mainly with them: both Pauline Lipman and Richard Dameshek, writing in the *Daily Cardinal* a week after the vote, claimed it was meant to eliminate the TAs' power base, to exact revenge against unruly insubordinates, and to punish TAs for their classroom experiments (Pauline Lipman and Richard Damashek, letters to the editor, *Daily Cardinal,* Nov. 25, 1969).

84. Cronon and Jenkins, *University of Wisconsin,* 4: 290.

85. Ibid., 4: 290–91.

86. As for the whole question of interpersonal tensions in UW's English Department during the fall 1969 semester, there were signs of faculty-TA discord in the department well before Oct. 1969. Recall, e.g., Heninger's fall 1968 semester-opening memo ("we must protect ourselves from . . . chaos and old night"), which the TAs read as a personal attack on them (Heninger to English Departmental Committee, memo, Sept. 12, 1968). And during that semester in particular, a variety of problems emerged between the faculty and TAs,

involving such issues as grades, the alleged presence of undercover police officers in English 102 classrooms, and the question of whether TAs should be more involved in course planning and policy. It should also be said, however, that the overall faculty attitude in the department toward graduate student TAs during this period appears to have been quite positive. As we saw in chap. 4, in the fall of 1968, Tim Heninger described as "legitimate" the TAs' "desire to know where they belong in the department," claiming that "they should in reality be at least partially responsible for the courses which they teach" (UW English Department, Minutes of the Departmental Committee, Oct. 8, 1968). And just a month before his fateful Sept. 1969 meeting with Joe Carr, Bill Lenehan praised the TAs who had worked on the English 102 Policy Committee the previous year, writing in his Aug. 21, 1969, memo to Heninger that, despite frustrations arising from the TAs' lack of experience and despite the polarized climate of the campus that semester (spring 1969), the committee's discussions had been "consistently relevant and civilized" (2), all the members, faculty and teaching assistants alike, "consistently open-minded" (2), the TAs in particular adding a "concrete awareness of what is happening in the classroom" (3), their overall presence "making a sufficiently significant contribution that I strongly recommend its continuance." And although he was thinking mainly of the English 101 teachers whose spring 1969 report on developments in that course he had read, Leon D. Epstein, dean of the College of Letters and Science, had this to say about the English Department TAs in May 1969: "My own impression . . . is that we . . . have a remarkably devoted and intelligent staff" (Epstein to Simeon K. Heninger, May 20, 1969). The TAs themselves, as a campus-wide group, put it this way in the spring of 1969: "Most administrators concerned with teaching admit that TAs are excellent teachers: many TAs have previous college teaching experience (see Mulvihill, p. 8); most TAs have MA degrees; TAs of necessity fit the scholar (learner)-teacher role held as ideal in American Universities; TAs are closer to and therefore more understanding of students' needs and in fact have the only personal contact with students in lecture-discussion courses; TAs (by their own and faculty consensus: see Mulvihill, p. 7) are vital and interested in teaching" ("TAA Speaks on 10D," 2). And even during the Oct. and Nov. 1969 Departmental Committee meetings cited above, when aspersions were being cast on the TAs, the criticism was sometimes tempered with praise. At the Oct. 28 Departmental Committee meeting, e.g., when a TA asked how many faculty members taught English 102 and how qualified the TAs were who taught it, Walter Rideout answered that "few faculty members teach English 102, and that most TAs do it very well" (5). And we've already seen that, at the Nov. 4 meeting, Eric Rothstein wondered aloud whether "deviation from the course by TAs was so great as Professor Lenehan had implied," suggesting that at least one senior faculty member thought the picture of misconduct may have been overdrawn. The attitude toward the course itself was also quite strong in the months leading up to the fall 1969 semester. In May of that year, Heninger praised Lenehan and the Freshman English Policy Committee "for a splendid job of keeping English 102 a vital course" (Simeon K. Heninger to William T. Lenehan, May 13, 1969), and as we've seen, course director Lenehan's late Aug. 1969 memo summarizing the work of the policy committee over the previous year, and sent to Heninger just a month before Joe Carr first approached him, gives no hint whatsoever that anybody—faculty, TA, or student—thought the course unneeded, poorly taught, or in administrative dire straits (Lenehan to Heninger, memo, Aug. 21, 1969).

87. Heninger to English 102/181 TAs, memo, Oct. 22, 1968; Lenehan to Heninger, memo, Aug. 21, 1969.

Note to Page 154

88. See, e.g., n. 86 above.

89. Lenehan to Heninger, memo, Aug. 21, 1969.

90. "Third View," Oct. 30, 1969.

91. McLeod, interview, June 30, 2005; Davidson, interview, Aug. 24, 2005; Turner, interview, Nov. 9, 2005.

92. Heninger to English Departmental Committee, memo, Oct. 20, 1969. Most of those 186 TAs were teaching either English 101 (104 students in 6 sections), English 102 (3,938 in 187 sections), or English 181 (probably about 300 if we go by the proportion in fall 1969). (Heninger had estimated in Apr. 1969 that there were 4,500 students in those three courses the previous fall, which would be about 79 percent of the 5,716 total freshmen enrolled [Heninger to Epstein, memo, Apr. 22, 1969].)

93. See, e.g., TA efforts at moderation during the Oct. 28, 1969, Departmental Committee meeting; the compromise efforts of professors Lenehan, Henning, and Kimbrough during the Nov. 18, 1969, Departmental Committee meeting; and Professor Kimbrough's renewed motion for moderation during the Feb. 10, 1970, Departmental Committee meeting. For Turner's quote, see Turner, interview by David Fleming, Nov. 9, 2005.

94. "english," 6–7.

95. English TAA stewards, Minutes of TA Staff Meeting, Oct. 13, 1969.

96. Petition with thirty-six TA signatures concerning the presence of police in English 102 classroom, Oct. 1968.

97. Heninger to English Departmental Committee, memo, Oct. 20, 1969.

98. As reported by Heninger in the English Departmental Committee meeting of Oct. 8, 1968.

99. A chart listing sixty named English TAs from this period, according to their mention in twenty-seven separate documents from the time, is available from the author.

100. See the chart mentioned in the preceding note. Those eleven are Tim Drescher, Steve Groark, Bill Huttanus, Gary Kline, Michael Krasny, Elliot Lieberman, Pauline Lipman, Bob Muehlenkamp, Jeff Sadler, Ira Shor, and Jean Turner. Thus, of 158 TAs on staff that semester, 113 (72 percent) were members of the TAA; 61 (39 percent) show up in at least one other document from the time: a petition, minutes of a meeting, etc.; 24 (15 percent) show up at least twice; and 11 (7 percent) show up three or more times—though these last three figures include TAs from two different academic years when the Freshman English staffs didn't overlap perfectly.

101. UW English Department, Minutes of the Departmental Committee, Oct. 28, 1969.

102. Anonymous TA to Heninger, written after Sept. 17, 1968, TA staff meeting.

103. UW English Department, Minutes of the Departmental Committee, Oct. 28, 1969, 6.

104. The Sept. 30, 1968, TA vote advocating increased participation in course policy committees was 60–14–1, as reported by Heninger at the Oct. 8, 1968, English Departmental Committee meeting; the Oct. 13, 1969, TA vote for essentially taking over the Freshman English Policy Committee was 41–17, as reported by the TAA stewards in their minutes of that meeting.

105. "english," 6–7.

106. Quoted in Maraniss, *They Marched into Sunlight*, 370. But we should be cautious about ideologically pigeonholing anyone from this period: in a later interview, Cheney

complained that, while writing her dissertation at UW on Matthew Arnold, she "found it impossible to land a mentor on the English faculty, which she considered sexist; even the noted scholar Madeline Doran seemed interested only in helping male grad students, she thought" (ibid., 113). Maraniss has something similar to say about TA Michael Krasny, who was teaching freshman composition in the Commerce Building on the day of the Dow Strike. According to Maraniss, Krasny adopted the prevailing TA attitude of the day, making his classroom less structured, more student centered, more relevant; and he was an active member of the protest movement. But having grown up in a working-class neighborhood, Krasny was repelled by the hostility toward police and soldiers shown by some of the protestors (ibid., 365). We heard similar accounts of moderate or liberal TAs breaking from their more radical colleagues at times.

107. Heninger to Epstein, memo, Apr. 22, 1969; Rideout, interview, 1976.

108. McLeod, interview, June 30, 2005.

109. Ibid.

110. Davidson, interview, Aug. 24, 2005.

111. McLeod, interview, June 30, 2005.

112. Angle, interview, Oct. 11, 2005, Nov. 22, 2005.

113. Cronon and Jenkins, *University of Wisconsin,* 4: 453, 508. Surprisingly, in the fall of 1968, a plurality of college students supported Richard Nixon in the presidential election— see the "Introduction" to the special Winter 1968 issue of *Daedalus,* devoted to "The Student Left in Higher Education."

114. See TAA penetration numbers, from 1966 to spring 1969, in Van Ells, "More Than a Union." See also TAA "History," which says that "participation in a 1967 student strike to protest police brutality against antiwar demonstrators led to a fourfold increase in the organization's membership" (2), but that the TAA did not become "broadly representative" until the Jan. 1969 attempt by the Wisconsin state legislature to increase TA tuition—by then a majority (about 900?) of 1,900 TAs designated the TAA as their bargaining agent, which was confirmed in a May 1969 campus-wide election.

115. In her interview, Jean Turner remembered a different set of proportions. She claims that the activist TAs made up the largest group on the staff and that the remainder could be divided among the mostly older, married, "solid citizens," on the one hand, and the academically ambitious and apolitical, on the other. Turner argued that the radical TAs eventually won over the first of these groups, but not the second. She also claimed at one point, when asked about Joseph Carr, that " *none of us* was following the standard syllabus" (emphasis added) (Turner, interview, Nov. 9, 2005). I follow Turner in her tripartite grouping of the TAs, with the middle bloc being the key "swing" component, but I believe that the radical group was probably smaller than she remembers and that her claim of universal abandonment of the standard syllabus is overstated—interviews with Susan McLeod and Virginia Davidson suggest that many TAs, including even "moderate" ones, were doing their best to teach the course as Ednah Thomas and Joyce Steward intended (McLeod, interview, June 30, 2005; Davidson, interview, Aug. 24, 2005).

116. UW English Department, Minutes of the Departmental Committee, Oct. 28, 1969, 5. In his 1976 interview, Rideout estimated that, in the late 1960s, 30–40 percent of TAs were not teaching English 102 as intended (Rideout, interview, 1976).

117. UW English Department, Minutes of the Departmental Committee, Nov. 11, 1969.

118. Mulvihill Report, Feb. 5, 1968.

119. See, e.g., Bates, *Rads.*

120. See Marianne DeKoven's annotation for Isserman and Kazin's book (*Utopia Limited,* 339–40).

121. Moseley, "TA's Locked Out by Heninger." Hanson is well known to readers of Maraniss, *They Marched into Sunlight.*

122. "UW 'Flunks Out' of Basic English," *Wisconsin State Journal,* Nov. 19, 1969; "TAs Hit U. Secrecy after Ban from English Meeting: Were Freshman Courses Dropped?" *Capital Times,* Nov. 19, 1969.

123. "Freshman English Abolished: Over Protests of TAs," *Daily Cardinal,* Nov. 20, 1969; "U.W. Drops Freshman Composition Courses: Change Will Take Effect Next Fall," *Capital Times,* Nov. 20, 1969.

124. Moseley, "Frosh English Cancelled."

125. Pauline Lipman, letter to the editor, *Daily Cardinal,* Nov. 25, 1969; Richard Damashek, letter to the editor, *Daily Cardinal,* Nov. 25, 1969.

126. Pauline Lipman, letter to the editor, *Daily Cardinal,* Nov. 25, 1969

127. Petition from Non-TA English Graduate Students objecting to abolition of 102 and 181, Nov. 1969.

128. Professor Millard Susman, Department of Genetics (UW-Madison), to Simeon K. Heninger, Chair, Department of English, Nov. 19, 1969, 1–2 (emphasis in original).

129. S. K. Heninger to Professor Millard Susman, Department of Genetics, Dec. 10, 1969.

130. Dean George W. Sledge, College of Agriculture and Life Sciences, to S. K. Heninger, Chair of the English Department, Dec. 3, 1969.

131. William T. Lenehan, Director of Freshman English, to Dean George W. Sledge, College of Agriculture and Life Sciences, Dec. 9, 1969.

132. Ibid., 1.

133. Ibid., 2.

134. Professor Roy E. Tuttle, Professor of Business and Chair of the Undergraduate Studies Committee of the UW School of Business, to his Dean, E. A. Gaumnitz, Dec. 24, 1969. Gaumnitz then copied the letter to Dean of Letters and Science Stephen Kleene and English Department Chair Simeon K. Heninger.

135. Ibid., 1–2 (emphasis in original).

136. Professor G. R. Stairs, Chair of the Department of Forestry to William T. Lenehan, Jan. 15, 1970.

137. William T. Lenehan to Professor G. R. Stairs, Jan. 26, 1970.

138. Lenehan, "Means for Attaining Student Writing Effectiveness."

139. It's possible that Lenehan learned this distinction from Lacy, who had described, as early as 1952, the aim of English 1a as the achievement of "*clear* and direct expression" and the aim of English 1b as "*effective* and interesting expression" (emphases added) (see chap. 3).

140. Fred R. Rickson, Assistant Prof. of Botany, to Chancellor Edwin Young, Mar. 11, 1971.

141. Ibid., 2.

142. Ibid. Chancellor Young forwarded Rickson's letter to English Department chair Charles Scott, who replied on Mar. 19, 1971. In his letter, Scott countered Rickson's claims about the universal need for a basic first-year writing course by arguing that only some

students need such instruction, ably provided, he wrote, by English 100 for foreign students, English 101 for disadvantaged ones, and the Writing Laboratory for any students looking for assistance of any kind with their writing. He argued against Rickson's assertion that UW students could take courses from algebra to zoology, but not writing, by pointing to the various intermediate composition and creative writing classes offered by the department. And he took issue with the implication that the department "had abdicated its responsibility" for teaching introductory-level courses by noting the four thousand or so students enrolled that year in English 200, 205, 209, and 211—though he failed to include here the information that those courses were literary in focus and intended for sophomores.

143. Richard Damashek, letter to the editor, *Daily Cardinal,* Nov. 25, 1969, 6.

144. Franklin Wiener to Tim Heninger, Nov. 24, 1969, 1–2. Wiener ended his letter wondering "if it really matters" that UW students would graduate without sufficient training in composition. Heninger replied about two weeks later with a two-sentence letter: "Yes, it does matter. Thank you for your letter."

145. Simeon K. Heninger to Chancellor Edwin Young, Feb. 4, 1970.

146. Bob Kimbrough, handwritten note in English Department files, early Feb. 1970.

147. UW English Department, Minutes of the Departmental Committee, Feb. 10, 1970.

148. Ibid.

149. Minutes of the UW-Madison College of Letters and Science Faculty Meeting, May 18, 1970, 3 (emphasis in original).

150. Scott, interview, 1980.

151. According to Stephen Carroll and Peter Morrison, by the early 1970s, the "euphoria of the 1960s" had given way to "widespread concern for the survival of higher education." Between 1964 and 1969, e.g., degree-credit enrollments in U.S. institutions of higher education had risen by 60 percent; between 1969 and 1974, the growth rate was only 19 percent. And "as the enrollment curve flattened, so did the growth of financial support, which had more than tripled during the 1960s" ("Demographic and Economic Influences," 101–2).

7. Aftermath, 1970–1996

1. UW College of Letters and Science, Report of the Curriculum Review Committee, Apr. 19, 1971. The committee had been appointed by new Letters and Science dean Stephen Kleene in Nov. 1969 to respond to increasing complaints about undergraduate requirements. It was chaired by history professor David Cronon and had eight faculty and five student members (Cronon and Jenkins, *University of Wisconsin,* 4: 289–94).

2. UW College of Letters and Science, Report of the Curriculum Review Committee, Apr. 19, 1971, 2.

3. Ibid.

4. The other three were "competency in utilizing the modes of thought characteristic of the major areas of knowledge; a knowledge of man's basic cultural heritage; and a thorough understanding of at least one subject area" (3).

5. Ibid., 5.

6. Ibid., 10.

7. See, e.g., Stone, "Bonehead English," 106; Scully, "Crisis in English Writing." See also Bazerman et al., *Reference Guide to Writing across the Curriculum,* chap. 3.

8. Sheils, "Why Johnny Can't Write," 58.

9. College Entrance Examination Board, *On Further Examination.* The charge to the group from College Board president S. P. Marland Jr. included the following: "No topic related to the programs of the College Board has received more public attention in recent years than the unexplained decline in scores earned by students on the Scholastic Aptitude Test" (iii).

10. Ibid., 1, 5. In *The Bell Curve,* Herrnstein and Murray call the "great decline" of mean math and verbal SAT scores from 1963 to 1980 "the most frequently published trendlines in American education circles" (425).

11. College Entrance Examination Board, *On Further Examination,* 1.

12. Ibid., 8–12.

13. Ibid., 13.

14. Ibid., 15.

15. Ibid., 18.

16. Ibid., 18, 24.

17. Ibid., 19–20.

18. Ibid., 46.

19. Ibid., 25. "Our strong conviction is that concern about declining SAT-Verbal scores can profitably be concentrated on seeing to it that young people do more reading that enhances vocabulary and enlarges knowledge and experience, and more writing that makes fledgling ideas test and strengthen their wings" (ibid., 27).

20. Ibid., 28–31.

21. Ibid., 37. What almost none of these researchers mentions is the massive economic transformation of the early 1970s, including wide-scale deindustrialization and globalization, generally regarded now as ushering in the "new economy" of our own time.

22. Ibid., 48.

23. On CCCC's "Students' Right to their Own Language," see http://www.ncte.org/ library/NCTEFiles/Groups/CCCC/NewSRTOL.pdf: "We affirm the students' right to their own patterns and varieties of language—the dialects of their nurture or whatever dialects in which they find their own identity and style. Language scholars long ago denied that the myth of a standard American dialect has any validity. The claim that any one dialect is unacceptable amounts to an attempt of one social group to exert its dominance over another. Such a claim leads to false advice for speakers and writers, and immoral advice for humans. A nation proud of its diverse heritage and its cultural and racial variety will preserve its heritage of dialects. We affirm strongly that teachers must have the experiences and training that will enable them to respect diversity and uphold the right of students to their own language."

24. Herrnstein and Murray, *Bell Curve.*

25. Ibid., 426.

26. Ibid., 430.

27. Ibid., 433, 432.

28. Stedman and Kaestle, "Literacy and Reading Performance."

29. Ibid., 20.

30. Ibid., 21.

31. Ibid.

32. Ibid., 22.

33. Though some departments required their students to complete specially designed writing courses, some considered completion of coursework in the major "indicative of having achieved writing competence" (Task Group on Student Writing and Speaking [Lee Hansen, chair] of the UW Committee on Undergraduate Education [Bassam Z. Shakhashiri, chair], "Improving the Writing Skills of Undergraduate Students," Apr. 1976, 5).

34. Ibid., 3.

35. Ibid., 2–3.

36. Ibid., 6.

37. UW-Madison, Report of the Special Committee on Improving the Quality of Student Writing Skills, Feb. 1977.

38. UW-Madison Teaching Assistants Association, "The First Thirty-Five Years and Beyond," http://www.taa-madison.org/history.html.

39. Other committee members were Jean Brenkman, Nathan Blount, Standish Henning, Edgar Lacy, Douglas Leonard, Dan Lochman, Abigail McCann, and George Rodman (committee member Joyce Steward was on leave that semester).

40. UW-Madison English Department, Report of the Committee on Composition Programs (Charles Scott, chair), Dec. 1980, 1–2.

41. Ibid., 3.

42. Ibid.

43. Ibid., 4.

44. Ibid, 5.

45. Ibid., 6.

46. Ibid.

47. Ibid.

48. Ibid., 7.

49. Ibid., 6.

50. See Westphal-Johnson and Fitzpatrick, "Role of Communication and Writing Intensive Courses"; "Mission and Purpose of the UW-Madison General Education Requirements," available at http://www.ls.wisc.edu/gened/.

51. UW-Madison, Report of the Committee on Undergraduate Education (Lloyd Bitzer, chair). Faculty Document 1065a, Aug. 20, 1993; supplemented with recommendations Mar. 15, 1994; amended Oct. 7, 1996.

52. Ibid.

53. See http://www.ls.wisc.edu/gened/documents/CommACriteria.pdf.

8. Conclusion: Freshman Composition at the Turn of the New Century

1. The phrase "surprise action" is from Cronon and Jenkins, *University of Wisconsin,* 4: 291.

2. See Fleming, "Rhetoric Revival."

3. Ibid.

4. Roemer, Schultz, and Durst, "Reframing the Great Debate on First-Year Writing."

5. Ibid., 7.

6. See chap. 1, n. 59.

7. Heninger to Epstein, memo, Apr. 22, 1969, 4.

8. Heninger to Epstein, May 23, 1969.

9. Ibid.

10. Lenehan to Heninger, memo, Aug. 21, 1969, 3.

11. James Naremore, "The Ad Hoc Committee Meetings: An Interpretation," spring 1968, p. 2, TAA archives.

12. As quoted in Masters, *Practicing Writing*, 216.

13. Composition, writes David Bartholomae, is "a good field to work in, but you have to be willing to pay attention to common things" ("What Is Composition," 28).

14. Scott, interview, 1980; Heninger to Epstein, memo, Apr. 22, 1969.

15. Smit, *End of Composition Studies*.

16. Pauline Lipman, letter to the editor, *Daily Cardinal*, Nov. 25, 1969.

17. Curti and Carstensen, *University of Wisconsin*, 1: 3–34.

18. Cronon and Jenkins, *University of Wisconsin*, 4: 1–2.

19. Angle, interview, Oct. 11, 2005, Nov. 22, 2005.

20. I'm influenced here by Rebekah Nathan's summary of Turner in *My Freshman Year*.

21. As quoted in Readings, *University in Ruins*, 147.

22. Ibid., 147–48.

23. See Warner Taylor's survey, reprinted in Brereton, *Origins of Composition Studies*, 555: "Almost everyone is in theory committed to the principle that Freshmen deserve the best, but the principle is more often violated than not. . . . When I came to Wisconsin 18 years ago [i.e., in 1911], every member of the department save one, who had never taught in the course, had at least one section of Freshman English. It was a policy of the department. Today I am the only [faculty member] instructing in the regular course." Taylor reported that, at Wisconsin, Minnesota, Ohio State, and Iowa, only 6.7 percent of teachers of professional rank in English taught Freshman English. Women, meanwhile, were teaching 44 percent of Freshman English sections at large (more than three hundred freshmen) midwestern institutions (ibid., 558). Nationwide, 47 percent of large institutions used TAs: 48 percent in the Midwest, 59 percent in the West, 37 percent in the East, and 43 percent in the South. At small institutions, it was 18 percent (ibid., 562). "The graduate-student teacher has apparently come to stay. Universities find him useful. Not only does he bring youthful eagerness and a spirit of ready cooperation to his new profession, but he adds to the numbers in the graduate schools—a condition wholly acceptable to those responsible for the creation of Masters of Arts and Doctors. There is, of course, potential danger in the situation: it's a question of sane balance in the composition of a staff. Chairmen of departments who put the needs of Freshmen English first will see to it that there is a ponderable nucleus of experienced instructors on the first-year corps. Any large university can gracefully absorb a certain percentage of novitiate teachers; but the determination of the danger point is a matter for informed deliberation" (ibid., 562).

24. Greenbaum, "Tradition of Complaint."

Bibliography

Abbott, Don Paul. "Rhetoric and Writing in Renaissance Europe and England." In *A Short History of Writing Instruction from Ancient Greece to Twentieth Century America*, ed. James J. Murphy, 95–120. Davis, CA: Hermagoras Press, 1990.

Adams, Charles Francis, Edwin Lawrence Godkin, and George R. Nutter. "Report of the Committee on Composition and Rhetoric." 1897. In Brereton, *Origins of Composition Studies*, 101–27.

Adams, Charles Francis, Edwin Lawrence Godkin, and Josiah Quincy. "Report of the Committee on Composition and Rhetoric." 1892. In Brereton, *Origins of Composition Studies*, 73–100.

Adams, Katherine H. "At Wisconsin: A Progressive Writing Curriculum for Advanced Students." In *Progressive Politics and the Training of America's Persuaders*, 39–69. Mahwah, NJ: Lawrence Erlbaum, 1999.

Adelman, Clifford. *The New College Course Map and Transcript Files: Changes in Course-Taking and Achievement 1972–1993*. Washington, DC: U.S. Department of Education, Office of Educational Research and Improvement, National Institute on Postsecondary Education, Libraries, and Lifelong Learning, 1995.

Aristotle. *On Rhetoric: A Theory of Civic Discourse*. Ed. George Kennedy. 2nd ed. New York: Oxford University Press, 2006.

Baron, Denis. "No Students Left Behind: Why Reports on the Literacy Crisis from the Spellings Commission, the ACT, and the ETS Just Don't Read America's Literacy Right." *CCC* 61, no. 1 (2009): W424–35.

Bartholomae, David. "What Is Composition and (if You Know What That Is) Why Do We Teach It?" In *Composition in the Twenty-First Century: Crisis and Change*, ed. Lynn Z. Bloom, Donald A. Daiker, and Edward M. White, 11–28. Carbondale: Southern Illinois University Press, 1996.

Bates, Tom. *Rads: The 1970 Bombing of the Army Math Research Center at the University of Wisconsin and Its Aftermath*. New York: Harper Collins, 1992.

Bazerman, Charles, Joseph Little, Lisa Bethel, Teri Chavkin, Danielle Fouquette, and Janet Garufis. *Reference Guide to Writing across the Curriculum*. Anderson, SC: Parlor Press and the WAC Clearinghouse, 2005. Available at http://wac.colostate.edu/books/bazerman_wac/.

Bell, Daniel. *The Reforming of General Education: The Columbia College Experience in Its National Setting*. New York: Columbia University Press, 1966.

Bledstein, Burton J. *The Culture of Professionalism: The Middle Class and the Development of Higher Education in America*. New York: Norton, 1976.

Bok, Derek. *Our Underachieving Colleges: A Candid Look at How Much Students Learn and Why They Should Be Learning More*. Princeton: Princeton University Press, 2006.

Braddock, Richard, Richard Lloyd-Jones, and Lowell Schoer. *Research in Written Composition*. Urbana: National Council of Teachers of English, 1963.

Brandt, Deborah. *Literacy in American Lives.* Cambridge: Cambridge University Press, 2001.

Brannon, Lil. "(Dis)Missing Compulsory First-Year Composition." In Petraglia, *Reconceiving Writing,* 239–48.

Brenner, Robert. *The Economics of Global Turbulence.* London: Verso, 2006. Originally published in *New Left Review* 229 (May–June 1998).

Brereton, John C., ed. *The Origins of Composition Studies in the American College, 1875–1925: A Documentary History.* Pittsburgh: University of Pittsburgh Press, 1995.

Brint, Steven, Kristopher Proctor, Scott Patrick Murphy, Lori Turk-Bicakci, and Robert A. Hanneman. "General Education Models: Continuity and Change in the U.S. Undergraduate Curriculum, 1975–2000." *Journal of Higher Education* 80, no. 6 (2009): 605–42.

Brodkey, Linda. *Writing Permitted in Designated Areas Only.* Minneapolis: University of Minnesota Press, 1996.

Brown, Barry Alexander, and Glenn Silber. *The War at Home.* Documentary film. Catalyst Media and Wisconsin Educational Television Network, 1979.

Brown, Stuart C., Paul R. Meyer, and Theresa Enos. "Doctoral Programs in Rhetoric and Composition." *Rhetoric Review* 12, no. 2 (1994): 237–412.

Buhle, Paul, ed. *History and the New Left: Madison 1950–1970.* Philadelphia: Temple University Press, 1989.

Carroll, Stephen J., and Peter A. Morrison. "Demographic and Economic Influences on the Growth and Decline of Higher Education." In *Easing the Transition from Schooling to Work,* ed. Harry F. Silberman and Mark B. Ginsburg, 101–8. Vol. 16 of *New Directions for Community Colleges,* ed. Arthur M. Cohen and Florence B. Brawer. San Francisco: Jossey-Bass, 1976.

Clark, Gregory, and S. Michael Halloran. *Oratorical Culture in America: Essays on the Transformation of Nineteenth-Century Rhetoric.* Carbondale: Southern Illinois University Press, 1993.

College Entrance Examination Board. *On Further Examination: Report of the Advisory Panel on the Scholastic Aptitude Test Score Decline.* New York: College Entrance Examination Board, 1977.

Connors, Robert J. "Composition History and Disciplinarity." In *Selected Essays of Robert J. Connors,* ed. Lisa Ede and Andrea Lunsford, 405–22. Boston: Bedford/St. Martin, 2003.

———. *Composition-Rhetoric: Backgrounds, Theory, and Pedagogy.* Pittsburgh: University of Pittsburgh, Press, 1997.

———. "The New Abolitionism: Toward a Historical Background." In Petraglia, *Reconceiving Writing,* 3–26.

Copperman, Paul. "Literacy and the Future of Print: The Decline of Literacy." *Journal of Communication* 30, no. 1 (1980): 113–22.

Corbett, Edward P. J. "A History of Writing Program Administration." In *Learning from the Histories of Rhetoric: Essays in Honor of Winifred Bryan Horner,* ed. Theresa Enos, 60–71. Carbondale: Southern Illinois University Press, 1993.

Craig, Judy. "Graduate Student Unionism." PhD dissertation, University of Wisconsin-Madison, 1986.

Cronon, E. David, and John W. Jenkins. *The University of Wisconsin: A History.* 2 vols. (3 and 4). Vol. 3, *1925–1945: Politics, Depression, and War.* Vol. 4, *1945–1971: Renewal to*

Revolution. Madison: University of Wisconsin Press, 1994. Available at http://digicoll. library.wisc.edu/UW/subcollections/CurtiUWHistAbout.html.

Crosby, Harry H., and George F. Estey. *College Writing: The Rhetorical Imperative.* New York: Harper and Row, 1968.

Crowley, Sharon. "Around 1971: The Emergence of Process Pedagogy." In *Composition in the University,* 187–214.

————. *Composition in the University: Historical and Polemical Essays.* Pittsburgh: University of Pittsburgh Press, 1998.

————. *The Methodical Memory: Invention in Current-Traditional Rhetoric.* Carbondale: Southern Illinois University Press, 1990.

————. "A Personal Essay on Freshman English." In *Composition in the University,* 228–49. Originally published in *Pre/Text* 12 (1991).

Curti, Merle Eugene, and Vernon Rosco Carstensen. *The University of Wisconsin: A History, 1848–1925.* 2 vols. (1 and 2). Vol. 1, *1925–1945.* Vol. 2, *1945–1971.* Madison: University of Wisconsin Press, 1949. Available at http://digicoll.library.wisc.edu/UW/subcollections/ CurtiUWHistAbout.html.

DeKoven, Marianne. *Utopia Limited: The Sixties and the Emergence of the Postmodern.* Durham: Duke University Press, 2004.

Dixon, John. *Growth through English.* Reading, UK: National Association for the Teaching of English, 1967.

Donahue, Patricia, and Gretchen Flesher Moon, eds. *Local Histories: Reading the Archives of Composition.* Pittsburgh: University of Pittsburgh Press, 2007.

Doremus, Robert, Edgar W. Lacy, and George B. Rodman. *Patterns in Writing.* New York: William Sloane Associates, 1950.

Douglas, Wallace. "Rhetoric for the Meritocracy." Chapter in *English in America: A Radical View of the Profession,* by Richard Ohmann, 97–132. New York: Oxford University Press, 1976.

Duberman, Martin. "An Experiment in Education." *Daedalus* 97, no. 1 (1968): 318–41.

Dubin, Robert, and Beisse, Fredric. "The Assistant: Academic Subaltern." *Administrative Science Quarterly* 11, no. 4 (1967): 521–47.

Ehrenreich, Barbara. *Fear of Falling: The Inner Life of the Middle Class.* New York: Harper Collins, 1989.

Ehrenreich, Barbara, and John Ehrenreich. "The Professional-Managerial Class." *Radical America* 11, no. 2 (1977): 7–31. (Continued in "The New Left and the Professional-Managerial Class." *Radical America* 11, no. 3 [1977]: 7–22.)

Emig, Janet. *The Composing Processes of Twelfth Graders.* Urbana: National Council of Teachers of English, 1971.

Fleming, David. "Becoming Rhetorical: An Education in the Topics." In *The Realms of Rhetoric: Inquiries into the Prospects for Rhetoric Education,* ed. Deepika Bahri and Joseph Petraglia, 93–116. Albany: State University of New York Press, 2003.

————. "Rhetoric Revival or Process Revolution? Revisiting the Emergence of Composition-Rhetoric as a Discipline." In *Renewing Rhetoric's Relation to Composition: Essays in Honor of Theresa Jarnagin Enos,* ed. Shane Borrowman, Stuart Brown, and Thomas Miller, 25–52. New York: Routledge, 2009.

Gaonkar, Dilip. "Rhetoric and Its Double: Reflections on the Rhetorical Turn in the Human Sciences." In *The Rhetorical Turn: Invention and Persuasion in the Conduct of Inquiry,* ed. H. W. Simons, 341–66. Chicago: University of Chicago Press, 1990.

Garlington, Jack O. "Advantages and Disadvantages of the System." In "The Graduate Assistant and the Freshman English Student: A Panel Discussion," rec. T. J. Kallsen. *CCC* 5, no. 1 (1954): 35.

Gee, James Paul. *Situated Language and Learning: A Critique of Traditional Schooling.* New York: Routledge, 2004.

———. *Social Linguistics and Literacies: Ideology in Discourses.* 3rd ed. London: Routledge, 2008.

Geiger, Roger L. "Sputnik and the Academic Revolution." Paper presented at Federal Support for University Research: Forty Years after the National Defense Education Act, October 1, 1998. Available at http://cshe.berkeley.edu/events/ndeaconference1998/geiger.htm.

———. "What Happened after Sputnik? Shaping University Research in the United States." *Minerva* 35, no. 4 (1997): 349–67.

Godkin, E. L. "The Illiteracy of American Boys." *Educational Review* 8 (1897): 1–9.

Goggin, Maureen Daly. *Authoring a Discipline: Scholarly Journals and the Post–World War II Emergence of Rhetoric and Composition.* Mahwah, NJ: Lawrence Erlbaum Associates, 2000.

Goggin, Maureen Daly, and Susan Kay Miller. "What Is New about the 'New Abolitionists': Continuities and Discontinuities in the Great Debate." *Composition Studies* 28, no. 2 (2000): 85–112.

Graff, Gerald. *Professing Literature: An Institutional History.* Chicago: University of Chicago Press, 1987.

Greenbaum, Leonard. "The Tradition of Complaint." *College English* 31, no. 2 (1969): 174–87.

Hairston, Maxine. "Diversity, Ideology, and Teaching Writing." *CCC* 43, no. 2 (1992): 179–95.

Halloran, S. Michael. "Rhetoric in the American College Curriculum: The Decline of Public Discourse." *Pre/Text* 3, no. 3 (1982): 245–69.

Hamalian, Leo, and Frederick R. Karl, eds. *The Shape of Fiction: British and American Short Stories.* New York: McGraw-Hill, 1967.

Harris, Joseph. "After Dartmouth: Growth and Conflict in English." *College English* 53, no. 6 (1991): 631–46.

———. *A Teaching Subject: Composition since 1966.* Upper Saddle River, NJ: Prentice Hall, 1997.

Hartzog, Carol P. *Composition and the Academy: A Study of Writing Program Administration.* New York: MLA, 1986.

Haswell, Rich. "1955 and Ednah Thomas Takes on the Grammar Police." *CompPanels: Images from the Annals of Composition* 12 (November 2003). Available at http://comppile.org/comppanels/comppanel_12.htm.

Herrnstein, Richard J., and Charles Murray. *The Bell Curve: Intelligence and Class Structure in American Life.* New York: Simon and Schuster, 1994.

Hill, Adams Sherman. "An Answer to the Cry for More English." 1879. In Brereton, *Origins of Composition Studies,* 45–57.

Horner, Bruce, and John Trimbur. "English Only and U.S. College Composition." *CCC* 53, no. 4 (2002): 594–630.

Hourigan, Maureen M. *Literacy as Social Exchange: Intersections of Class, Gender, and Culture.* Albany: State University of New York Press, 1994.

Karnow, Stanley. *Vietnam: A History.* Rev. ed. New York: Penguin, 1991.

Kaufer, David S., and Kathleen M. Carley. *Communication at a Distance: The Influence of Print on Sociocultural Organization and Change.* Hillsdale, NJ: Lawrence Erlbaum Associates, 1993.

Kernan, Alvin. "Literacy Crises, Old and New Information Technologies and Cultural Change." *Language and Communication* 9, nos. 2–3 (1989): 159–73.

Kerr, Clark. *The Uses of the University.* 1963. 5th ed. Cambridge: Harvard University Press, 2001.

Kitzhaber, Albert R. "Death—or Transfiguration?" *College English* 21, no. 7 (1960): 367–73.

———. *Rhetoric in American Colleges, 1850–1900.* 1953. Dallas: Southern Methodist University Press, 1990.

Lacy, Edgar W. "Safeguards for Satisfactory Functioning of the System." "The Graduate Assistant and the Freshman English Student: A Panel Discussion," rec. T. J. Kallsen. *CCC* 5, no. 1 (1954): 36.

Lacy, Edgar W., William Lenehan, and Ednah S. Thomas. "Master Assistants at the University of Wisconsin," *College English* 27, no. 8 (1966): 637–38.

Lacy, Edgar W., and Ednah S. Thomas. *Guide for Good Writing: A Composition Text for College Students.* Harrisburg, PA: Stackpole and Heck, 1951.

Lamos, Steve. "Literacy Crisis and Color-Blindness: The Problematic Racial Dynamics of Mid-1970s Language and Literacy Instruction for 'High-Risk' Minority Students." *CCC* 61, no. 2 (2009): W125–28.

Laurence, David, Natalia Lusin, and Stephen Olsen. "Report on Trends in the MLA *Job Information List,* September 2007." New York: Modern Language Association, 2007. Available at http://www.mla.org/pdf/report_on_trends_in_jil_se.pdf (text of report) and http://www.mla.org/pdf/tables_and_figures_for_jil.pdf (tables and figures).

Light, Richard J. *Making the Most of College: Students Speak Their Minds.* Cambridge: Harvard University Press, 2001.

"The Logic of Neutrality." In *The University Crisis Reader,* vol. 1, *The Liberal University under Attack,* ed. Immanuel Wallerstein and Paul Starr, 61–62. New York: Vintage Books, 1971.

Maraniss, David. *They Marched into Sunlight: War and Peace, Vietnam and America, October, 1967.* New York: Simon and Schuster, 2003.

Marwick, Arthur. *The Sixties: Cultural Revolution in Britain, France, Italy, and the United States, c. 1958–c. 1974.* Oxford: Oxford University Press, 2001.

Masters, Thomas. *Practicing Writing: The Postwar Discourse of Freshman English.* Pittsburgh: University of Pittsburgh Press, 2004.

Mastrangelo, Lisa S. "Learning from the Past: Rhetoric, Composition, and Debate at Mount Holyoke College." *Rhetoric Review* 18, no. 1 (1999): 46–64.

Maurrasse, David J. *Beyond the Campus: How Colleges and Universities Form Partnerships with Their Communities.* New York: Routledge, 2001.

McHale, Brian. "1966 Nervous Breakdown; or, When Did Postmodernism Begin?" *MLQ* 69, no. 3 (2008): 391–413.

Menand, Louis. "The Ph.D. Problem." *Harvard Magazine,* November–December 2009: 27–31, 91. Reprinted from Louis Menand, *The Marketplace of Ideas.* New York: Norton, 2009.

Merritt, Travis, R., ed. *Style and Substance: Reading and Writing Prose.* New York: Harcourt, Brace and World, 1969.

Miller, Gary E. *The Meaning of General Education: The Emergence of a Curriculum Paradigm.* New York: Teachers College Press, 1988.

Miller, Thomas P. *The Formation of College English: Rhetoric and Belles Lettres in the British Cultural Provinces.* Pittsburgh: University of Pittsburgh Press, 1997.

Modern Language Association. *Final Report of the Committee on Professional Employment.* Sandra Gilbert, chair. New York: MLA, 1997. *PMLA* 113 (1998): 1154–87 and *ADE Bulletin* 119 (Spring 1998): 27–45. Available at http://www.mla.org/prof_employment.

Moghtader, Michael, Alanna Cotch, and Kristen Hague. "The First-Year Composition Requirement Revisited: A Survey." *CCC* 52, no. 3 (2001): 455–67.

Moran, Charles. "How the Writing Process Came to UMass/Amherst: Roger Garrison, Donald Murray, and Institutional Change." In *Taking Stock: The Writing Process Movement in the 90s,* ed. Lad Tobin and Thomas Newkirk, 133–52. Portsmouth, NH: Boynton/Cook, 1994.

Mosse, George. "New Left Intellectuals/New Left Politics." In *History and the New Left,* ed. Paul Buhle, 233–38. Philadelphia: Temple University Press, 1989.

Murphy, James J., ed. *A Short History of Writing Instruction from Ancient Greece to Twentieth Century America.* Davis, CA: Hermagoras Press, 1990.

Nathan, Rebekah (pseud.). *My Freshman Year: What a Professor Learned by Becoming a Student.* Ithaca: Cornell University Press, 2005.

National Commission on Excellence in Education. *A Nation at Risk: The Imperative for Educational Reform.* Washington, DC: U.S. Department of Education, 1983.

National Commission on Writing in America's Schools and Colleges. *The Neglected "R": The Need for a Writing Revolution.* New York: College Board, 2003.

Neill, A. S. *Summerhill: A Radical Approach to Child Rearing.* New York: Hart, 1960.

Nystrand, Martin. "Janet Emig, Frank Smith, and the New Discourse about Writing and Reading; or, How Writing and Reading Came to Be Cognitive Processes in 1971." In *Towards a Rhetoric of Everyday Life: New Directions in Research on Writing, Text, and Discourse,* ed. Martin Nystrand and John Duffy, 121–44. Madison: University of Wisconsin Press, 2003.

Nystrand, Martin, Stuart Greene, and Joseph Wiemelt. "Where Did Composition Studies Come From? An Intellectual History." *Written Communication* 10, no. 3 (1993): 267–333.

Oates, Joyce Carol. "Nighthawk: A Memoir of a Lost Time." *Yale Review* 89, no. 2 (2001): 56–72.

Ohmann, Richard. "The Strange Case of Our Vanishing Literacy." In *Politics of Letters,* 230–35. Middletown, CT: Wesleyan University Press, 1987.

Orr, David. "The Job Market in English and Foreign Languages." *PMLA* 85, no. 6 (1970): 1185–98.

Petraglia, Joseph. "Introduction: General Writing Skills Instruction and Its Discontents." In Petraglia, *Reconceiving Writing,* xi–xvii.

———, ed. *Reconceiving Writing, Rethinking Writing Instruction.* Mahwah, NJ: Lawrence Erlbaum, 1995.

Postman, Neil, and Charles Weingartner. *Teaching as a Subversive Activity.* New York: Delta, 1969.

Quinn, Edward, and Paul J. Dolan, eds. *The Sense of the Sixties.* New York: Free Press, 1968.

Readings, Bill. *University in Ruins.* Cambridge: Harvard University Press, 1996.

Reid, Ronald F. "The Boylston Professorship of Rhetoric and Oratory, 1806–1904: A Case Study in Changing Concepts of Rhetoric and Pedagogy." *Quarterly Journal of Speech* 45, no. 3 (1959): 239–57.

Rice, Warner G. "A Proposal for the Abolition of Freshman English, as It Is Now Commonly Taught, from the College Curriculum." *College English* 21, no. 7 (1960): 361–67.

Roemer, Marjorie, Lucille M. Schultz, and Russel K. Durst. "Reframing the Great Debate on First-Year Writing." *CCC* 50, no. 3 (1999): 377–92.

Rose, Mike. "The Language of Exclusion: Writing Instruction at the University." *College English* 47, no. 4 (1985): 341–59.

Rosenberg, Norman L. "The Sixties." In *The Oxford Companion to United States History,* ed. Paul S. Boyer, 710–13. New York: Oxford University Press, 2001.

Rosenberg, Samuel. *American Economic Development since 1945: Growth, Decline and Rejuvenation.* New York: Palgrave Macmillan, 2003.

Russell, David R. "American Origins of the Writing-across-the-Curriculum Movement." In *Writing, Teaching, and Learning in the Disciplines,* ed. Anne Herrington and Charles Moran, 22–42. New York: Modern Language Association, 1992.

———. "Romantics on Writing: Liberal Culture and the Abolition of Composition Courses." *Rhetoric Review* 6, no. 2 (1988): 132–48.

———. *Writing in the Academic Disciplines, 1870–1990.* Carbondale: Southern Illinois University Press, 1991.

Sampson, Ronald. "What Is a University?" *Nation,* May 5, 1969, 560–65.

Scheuneman, Janice Dowd. "Differences between SAT Math and Verbal Scores: A 50-Year History." *College Board Review,* no. 188 (August 1999): 26–27.

Scully, M. G. "Crisis in English Writing." *Chronicle of Higher Education,* September 23, 1974: 1, 6.

Shaughnessy, Mina. *Errors and Expectations: A Guide for the Teacher of Basic Writing.* New York: Oxford University Press, 1977.

Sheils, Merrill. "Why Johnny Can't Write." *Newsweek,* December 8, 1975, 58–65.

Shiller, Robert. *Irrational Exuberance.* 2nd ed. Princeton: Princeton University Press, 2005.

Shor, Ira. *Culture Wars: School and Society in the Conservative Restoration.* 1986. Chicago: University of Chicago Press, 1992.

Siff, David. "The Sense of Nonsense: An Approach to Freshman Composition." *CCC* 27, no. 3 (1976): 271–77.

Sirc, Geoffrey. *Composition as a Happening.* Logan: Utah State University Press, 2002.

Smit, David W. *The End of Composition Studies.* Carbondale: Southern Illinois University Press, 2004.

Smith, Ron. "The Composition Requirement Today: A Report on a Nationwide Survey of Four-Year Colleges and Universities." *CCC* 25, no. 2 (1974): 138–48.

Sperber, Murray. "How Undergraduate Education Became College Lite—and a Personal Apology." In *Declining by Degrees: Higher Education at Risk,* ed. Richard H. Hersh and John Merrow, 131–43. New York: Palgrave Macmillan, 2005.

Stedman, Lawrence C., and Carl F. Kaestle. "Literacy and Reading Performance in the United States, from 1880 to the Present," *Reading Research Quarterly* 22, no. 1 (1987): 8–46.

Stevens, Anne H. "The Philosophy of General Education and Its Contradictions: The Influence of Hutchins." *Journal of General Education* 50, no. 3 (2001): 165–91.

Stewart, Donald C. "Harvard's Influence on English Studies: Perceptions from Three Universities in the Early Twentieth Century." *CCC* 43, no. 4 (1992): 455–71.
———. "Two Model Teachers and the Harvardization of English Departments." In *The Rhetorical Tradition and Modern Writing,* ed. James J. Murphy, 118–29. New York: MLA, 1982.
Stone, Marvin. "Bonehead English," *Time,* November 11, 1974, 106.
Stygall, Gail. "At the Century's End: The Job Market in Rhetoric and Composition." *Rhetoric Review* 18, no. 2 (2000): 375–89.
Sullivan, Frank J., Arabella Lyon, Dennis Lebofsky, Susan Wells, and Eli Goldblatt. "Student Needs and Strong Composition: The Dialectics of Writing Program Reform." *CCC* 48, no. 3 (1997): 392–409.
Tassoni, John Paul, and William H. Thelin. *Blundering for a Change: Errors and Expectations in Critical Pedagogy.* Portsmouth, NH: Boynton/Cook, 2000.
Taylor, Warner. *National Survey of Conditions in Freshman English.* Madison: University of Wisconsin Bureau of Educational Research, Bulletin no. 11 (1929). In Brereton, *Origins of Composition Studies,* 545–62.
Thomas, Ednah S. "Devices for Training Graduate Assistants." In "The Graduate Assistant and the Freshman English Student: A Panel Discussion," rec. T. J. Kallsen. *CCC* 5, no. 1 (1954): 35–36.
———. *Evaluating Student Themes.* Madison: University of Wisconsin Press, 1955.
Trimbur, John. "Changing the Question: Should Writing Be Studied?" *Composition Studies* 31 (Spring 2003): 15–24.
U.S. Department of Education, National Center of Education Statistics. *The Condition of Education 2004.* Available at http://nces.ed.gov/pubs2004/2004077.pdf.
Van Ells, Mark K. "More Than a Union: The Teaching Assistants Association and Its 1970 Strike against the University of Wisconsin." *Michigan Historical Review* 25, no. 1 (1999): 103–124.
Varnum, Robin. "From Crisis to Crisis: The Evolution towards Higher Standards of Literacy in the United States." *Rhetoric Society Quarterly* 16, no. 3 (1986): 145–65.
Vogt, W. Paul. *Dictionary of Statistics and Methodology.* Newbury Park, CA: Sage, 1993.
Weidner, Heidemarie Z. "A Chair 'Perpetually Filled by a Female Professor': Rhetoric and Composition Instruction at Nineteenth-Century Butler University." In *Local Histories: Reading the Archives of Composition,* ed. Patricia Donahue and Gretchen Flesher Moon, 58–76. Pittsburgh: University of Pittsburgh Press, 2007.
Westphal-Johnson, Nancy, and Mary Anne Fitzpatrick. "The Role of Communication and Writing Intensive Courses in General Education: A Five Year Case-Study of the University of Wisconsin-Madison. *JGE: The Journal of General Education* 51, no. 2 (2002): 73–102.
Williams, Bronwyn T. "Why Johnny Can Never, Ever Read: The Perpetual Literacy Crisis and Student Identity." *Journal of Adolescent and Adult Literacy* 51, no. 2 (2007): 178–82.
Wooley, Edwin. *Handbook of Composition.* Boston: D. C. Heath, 1907.
Young, Richard, and Maureen Daly Goggin. "Some Issues in Dating the Birth of the New Rhetoric in Departments of English: A Contribution to a Developing Historiography." In *Defining the New Rhetorics,* ed. Theresa Enos and Stuart C. Brown, 22–43. Newbury Park, CA: Sage, 1993.

Index

Cronon, E. David *(cont.)*,
as co-author of *University of Wisconsin: A History* (Vols. 3–4), 19, 40, 61–68, 154, 205, 213n60, 214n65, 219n68, 225n71, 225n83, 225–26n88, 226nn102–3, 227n116, 227nn119–20, 227n123, 230n28, 231n41, 236n71, 241n73, 248n1
Crowley, Sharon, 26, 214n77, 215n85, 221n8, 229n12
current-traditionalism in freshman composition, 23, 26, 47–50, 55 table 3.1, 57, 94, 128, 197, 214n77, 221n8, 221n11, 221–22n15, 222n17, 223n41, 237n105. *See also* belletristic approach to freshman composition; clarity, correctness, and effectiveness as goals of student writing at UW; Emig, Janet; "idea course" (Freshman English at UW, 1916–1946); meaning and form in freshman composition; modes of discourse in current-traditional freshman composition; pedagogical experiments of UW English TAs in late 1960s
Curriculum Committee (UW English Dept.), 74, 87, 134, 136, 139, 228n2, 231n64, 232n67
Curriculum Review Committee (UW College of Letters and Science, 1971), 80, 149, 171, 173–75, 181, 230n28, 246n1
Curti, Merle Eugene (*University of Wisconsin: A History*, Vols. 1–2), 30, 36, 205, 210n6, 216n1, 216nn3–5, 216n9, 216n11, 216–17nn13–20, 217n22, 217nn25–28, 217n37, 217n39, 218n44, 218n46, 227n123

Daily Cardinal, 66, 102, 107–8, 129, 145–46, 157, 162–63, 170, 203, 223n44, 235n39, 238n15, 241n69, 241n83
Damashek, Richard (English TA, UW), 108, 162, 170, 241n69, 241n83
Dartmouth Conference (Anglo-American Seminar on the Teaching and Learning of English) (1966), 23, 94
Davidson, Virginia (Joyce) (English TA, UW), 53, 55–58, 77, 94, 106, 155, 160, 172, 223n55, 244n115
decentering classroom authority, 24, 108–13. *See also* critical humanism in 1960s higher education; democratic education; pedagogical experiments of UW English TAs in late 1960s

"de-grading" teacher-student communication, 24, 49, 67, 83–84, 101, 110, 115, 116–21, 124, 144–45, 154, 156, 224n63, 227n113, 235n68. *See also* Committee on Grading (UW); critical humanism in 1960s higher education; democratic education; pedagogical experiments of UW English TAs in late 1960s; Peterson Building sit-in (UW, 1966); military draft
DeKoven, Marianne, 124–25, 127, 214n78, 215n80, 245n120
democratic education, 69, 108–13, 162–63. *See also* critical humanism in 1960s higher education; decentering classroom authority; "de-grading" teacher-student communication; employing relevant materials and topics; opening syllabi to emergent needs and desires; pedagogical experiments of UW English TAs in late 1960s; Students for a Democratic Society (SDS)
demographic, economic, and sociocultural factors in the history of U.S. higher education: 7–8, 15, 23–25, 30–31, 37, 39, 40, 44–45, 47, 50, 53, 58–73, 60 fig. 3.1, 72 table 3.2, 73 table 3.3, 79–80, 83, 104, 175–81, 196, 215n84, 217n20, 220n87, 222n18, 222n31, 224n66, 225nn73–74, 225n83, 225–26n88, 226n91, 226n104, 228n139, 228n141, 228n143, 246n151, 247n21. *See also* "the long sixties" in U.S. higher education; SAT
Departmental Committee (UW English Dept.), 63, 66, 67, 75, 77, 80, 82, 86–87, 131, 136, 161, 163, 190, 220n4, 222n28, 226n104, 226n107, 231n48, 237n115, 241–42n86; fall 1969 meetings of: Oct. 21, 1969 (238–39n24); Oct. 28, 1969 (113, 130, 138–42, 157–58, 161, 238–39n24, 243n93); Nov. 4, 1969 (143–45, 150, 155, 240n50); Nov. 11, 1969 (145–46, 239n46); Nov. 18, 1969 (83, 146–48, 162, 170–71, 240n64, 243n93); Heninger's Oct. 20, 1969, memo to: 137–38, 155, 156 table 6.1, 157, 233n2, 238n16, 243n92; spring 1970 meetings of: 171, 243n93
Dewey, John, 212n52
Dewoskin, Ron (English TA, UW), 141
"disadvantaged" students at UW in 1960s, 80, 115, 144, 229n24, 232–33n77,

English 181 (UW) Honors Freshman English (1963–1970), 75, 93, 102–3, 147–49, 154, 163, 165, 171, 174, 222n21, 240n64, 243n92. *See also* English 11 (UW); Honors Freshman English at UW; stratification of student writers at UW by skill level

English 200 (UW) Introduction to Literature, 58, 75, 82, 86–87, 93, 95, 135, 137, 141, 143, 149, 156, 230n40, 231n60, 233n11, 239n43, 245–46n142

English 201 (UW) Intermediate Composition, 135, 183 table 7.1, 185, 187–88, 189, 213n64

English 309 (UW) Composition for English Teachers, 52

English 315 (UW) Advanced Composition, 213n64

English 700 (UW) Introduction to Composition Studies, 187–88, 190

English 723 (UW) Critical Methods, 188

English 900 (UW), Language and Cognition in the Composing Process, 190

English 901 (UW), Structure of Written Communication, 190

English A (Harvard), 5, 32, 36, 209n1 (chap. 1), 210n6

English as a Second Language at UW, 189, 213–14n64, 245–46n142. *See also* English monolingualism in U.S. higher education

English Journal (NCTE), 36

English monolingualism in U.S. higher education, 1, 29, 31. *See also* English as a Second Language at UW

English Students Association (UW), 98, 114, 129, 201, 214n68, 227n112

Enos, Theresa, 212n42

enrollment at UW. *See* demographic, economic, and sociocultural factors in the history of U.S. higher education

entrance (or placement) exam. *See* admissions exam (higher education); College Qualification Examination (CQE); SAT

Epstein, Leon (dean, College of Letters and Science, UW), 65, 74, 83, 87, 90, 129, 131, 200, 203, 226n93, 232n75, 241–42n86, 243n92

ethnic studies programs and requirements, 24, 191–92. *See also* Black Strike (UW, 1969); civil rights struggles of 1960s

Evaluating Student Themes (UW) (1955), 49–50, 56, 57–58, 94, 221–22nn14–16, 224n63. *See also* Thomas, Ednah

Executive Committee (UW English Dept.), 64

exemption from Freshman English (UW), 39, 41–42, 45, 75, 144, 165, 171, 174, 184, 185, 191–93, 219n78. *See also* Honors Freshman English at UW; stratification of student writers at UW by skill level

Faculty Senate (UW), 76, 86, 149, 171, 173, 185, 191, 235–36n68

faculty withdrawal from general education teaching in 1960s. *See* research profile of faculty vis-à-vis general education duties

Feltskog, Elmer (English prof., UW), 87, 118

Fleming, David, 213n59, 213n64, 214n74, 215n83, 229n12, 248n2

Foerster, Norman (English prof., UW) 43, 218n46

formal considerations in writing. *See* belletristic approach to freshman composition; current-traditionalism in freshman composition; meaning and form in freshman composition; modes of discourse in current-traditional freshman composition

Foster, David (English TA, UW), 95, 99, 100 fig. 5.1

Frankenburger, David (rhetoric prof. UW), 29, 31, 33

Freeman, John Charles (English prof., UW), 29, 31

freshman composition in the U.S., 1–14, 22–27, 37, 39, 80, 114, 195–207, 209–10nn1–7, 213n62, 215n83, 217n30. *See also* abolition (or relaxation) of freshman composition requirement; Freshman English at UW; English A (Harvard); commonness of freshman composition; generality as feature of freshman composition; liminality as feature of freshman composition; literacy crises in U.S. history; the midwest as geographic heart of freshman composition; "myth of transience" in history of freshman composition; universality as feature of freshman composition

Marwick, Arthur, 215n81, 224n67
master teaching assistants (UW), 52–53, 56, 64, 83
Mastrangelo, Lisa S., 220n2
Maurrasse, David J., 225n77, 227n122, 227n124
McGlinchy, Tom (English TA, UW), 139, 140
McHale, Brian, 215n81
McLeod, Susan (English TA, UW), 53, 56, 57–58, 65, 66, 77, 94, 98, 102, 106, 119, 155, 159, 160, 221n11, 233n7, 236n78, 244n115
meaning and form in freshman composition, 8, 49, 55–56, 57, 78–79, 89, 102–3, 109, 111–12, 113–15, 121, 123–28, 140, 237n105. *See also* belletristic approach to freshman composition; clarity, correctness, and effectiveness as goals of student writing at UW; current-traditionalism in freshman composition; "idea course" (Freshman English at UW, 1916–1946); pedagogical experiments of UW English TAs in late 1960s; Emig, Janet; process paradigm in writing instruction
"Means for Attaining Student Writing Effectiveness" at UW (Lenehan), 94, 166–69. *See also* writing across the curriculum at UW
Melville, Joyce, 190
Menand, Louis, 209n2
Mennis, Bernice (English TA, UW), 99, 100 fig. 5.1
Meyer, Paul R., 212n42
middle class, 6–8, 179. *See also* professional-managerial class (PMC)
Middleton, David (English TA, UW), 82, 230n40, 237n115. *See also* Ad Hoc Committee to Study Undergraduate Course Offerings (UW English Dept., 1968)
midwest as geographic heart of freshman composition in the U.S., 3, 18, 210n6
Mifflin Street Riot (UW, 1969) 66, 107, 199
Miko, Richard (English TA, UW), 105
military draft, 68, 83–84, 102, 117–19, 228n142, 235–36n68. *See also* "de-grading" teacher-student communication; Peterson sit-in; TAA; Vietnam War
Miller, Gary E., 212n52
Miller, Susan Kay, 215n85

Miller, Thomas P., 210n6
MLA. *See* Modern Language Association
Modern Language Association (MLA), 10, 95 (*PMLA*), 225n81, 227–28n125
modes of discourse in current-traditional freshman composition, 47–48, 55–57, 55 table 3.1, 93, 221n8. *See also* belletristic approach to freshman composition; current-traditionalism in freshman composition; literature, use in freshman composition of
Moghtader, Michael, 215n83
Moon, Gretchen Flesher, 209n1 (chap. 1)
Moran, Charles (English prof., UW), ix
Morrison, Peter A., 220n87, 225n74, 228n139, 246n151
Mosse, George (history prof., UW), 227n117
Mount Holyoke College, 46, 220n2
Muehlenkamp, Bob (English TA, UW), 77, 94, 99, 100 fig. 5.1, 101, 109, 111–13, 114–15, 119–22, 126, 129, 131, 139–40, 145, 153, 157, 195, 227n114, 234n33, 243nn99–100. *See also* pedagogical experiments of UW English TAs in late 1960s; Teaching Assistant Association of UW (TAA)
Mulkeen, Anne (English TA, UW), 99, 100 fig. 5.1, 233–34n14
Mulvihill, Edward R. (Spanish prof., UW). *See* Mulvihill Report
Mulvihill Report (Committee on the Teaching Assistant System, UW, 1966–1968), 82, 83–88, 130–32, 161, 222n18, 237n115, 241–42n86
Murphy, James J., 216n8
Murray, Charles (*The Bell Curve*), 179–80, 229n10, 247n10
Murray, Donald, 23, 95
"myth of transience" in history of freshman composition, 8–9, 13, 32, 51, 211n34, 212n37, 217n30, 217n36. *See also* freshman composition in the U.S.; high school, writing in; liminality as feature of freshman composition; literacy crises in U.S. history; Rose, Mike

Naremore, James (English TA, UW), 201–2, 231n49
Nathan, Rebekah, 225n70
National Council of Teachers of English (NCTE), 3, 36 (*English Journal*), 78

National Defense Education Act (NDEA), 159, 225n74, 225n83, 229–30n25
National Survey of Conditions in Freshman English (1929). *See* Taylor, Warner
Nation At Risk, A (1983), 4–5
Neill, A. S. See *Summerhill*
new rhetorics, the, 22–24, 94, 197, 214n75. *See also* rhetorical education at UW
New University Conference, 96
Nixon, Richard, 107, 160, 244n113. *See also* Vietnam War; Watergate
Normal Department (UW), 28, 34
Norton Reader, 54, 56, 223n38. *See also* "Joys of Sport at Oxford"
Nutter, George R. *See* Committee on Composition and Rhetoric (Harvard)
Nystrand, Martin (English prof, UW), 126–27, 190, 213n64, 229n12, 237n105

Oates, Joyce Carol (English MA student, UW), 226n90
Ohmann, Richard, 5, 7, 202, 211n19
Olsen, Stephen, 212n43
On Further Examination (College Board), 177–80, 225n73, 225n83, 225n87, 229n10, 229–30n25, 247n9. *See also* Scholastic Aptitude Test (SAT)
opening syllabi to emergent needs and desires, 24, 90, 113–16, 140. *See also* critical humanism in 1960s higher education; democratic education; English 101, remedialization of; pedagogical experiments of UW English TAs in late 1960s
Oral History Program, University of Wisconsin-Madison Archives, 17, 19–20, 152–53
oratory, public speaking, and debate at UW, 3, 29–31, 33, 34, 175, 191–94, 216n13, 216–17n17. *See also* Communication Arts Dept. (UW)

participatory democracy, 96, 109, 123, 125. *See also* critical humanism in 1960s higher education; de-centering classroom authority; democratic education; pedagogical experiments of UW English TAs in late 1960s; Students for a Democratic Society (SDS)
Patterns in Writing (Doremus, Lacy, and Rodman), 48

pedagogical experiments of UW English TAs in late 1960s, 93–132, 123 fig. 5.2. *See also* decentering classroom authority; "de-grading" teacher-student communication; employing relevant materials and topics; opening syllabi to emergent needs and desires
personal growth as goal of 1960s radical pedagogy, 117, 124–25, 127–28, 214n78. *See also* critical humanism in 1960s higher education; DeKoven, Marianne; Duberman, Martin; meaning and form in freshman composition; pedagogical experiments of UW English TAs in late 1960s
Peterson Building sit-in (UW, 1966), 65, 68, 84. *See also* Mulvihill Report; Teaching Assistants Association of UW (TAA)
Peterson, Jeanie (English TA, UW), 232n73
Petraglia, Joseph, 212n46
Pirri, John (English TA, UW), 232n73
placement (higher education). *See* admissions exam
PMC. *See* professional-managerial class
Pochmann, Henry (English prof., UW), 42, 139, 146
Pohl, Connie (English TA, UW), 101, 136
Pondrom, Cyrena (English prof., UW), 105–6
Pooley, Robert (English prof., UW), 45, 46, 51, 152, 220n1, 221n14
process paradigm in writing instruction, 22–24, 26, 50, 78, 113, 188, 190, 193, 197, 202, 213n64, 221–22n15. *See also* clarity, correctness, and effectiveness as goals of student writing at UW; current-traditionalism in freshman composition; Emig, Janet; meaning and form in freshman composition; pedagogical experiments of UW English TAs in late 1960s; personal growth as goal of 1960s writing pedagogy
professional-managerial class (PMC), 6–8, 31–32, 44, 220n87. *See also* Ehrenreich, Barbara; Ehrenreich, John; middle class, the
public speaking at UW. *See* oratory, public speaking, and debate at UW
Purdue University, 3, 62

Index

tural factors in the history of U.S. higher education
Schoer, Lowell (*Research in Written Composition*), 22
Scholastic Aptitude Test. *See* SAT
Schultz, Lucille M., 215n85, 248n4
Scott, Charles (English prof., UW), 63–64, 81, 153, 172, 173, 187, 203, 226n91, 227n121, 245–46n142
Scott, Fred Newton, 212n41
SDS. *See* Students for a Democratic Society
Sense of the Sixties (Quinn and Dolan), 96, 104, 133–34. *See also* Carr, Joseph; employing relevant materials and topics; textbooks in Freshman English at UW
Shagass, Carla (English TA, UW), 99, 100 fig. 5.1
Shakhashiri, Bassam (chemistry prof., UW), 181. *See also* Shakhashiri Report
Shakhashiri Report ("Improving the Writing Skills of Undergraduate Students," Task Group on Student Writing and Speaking, Committee on Undergraduate Education, UW, 1976), 181–85, 183 table 7.1, 229n5, 229n10, 248n33. *See also* literacy crises in U.S. history
Shape of Fiction (Hamalian and Karl), 54, 133
Shaughnessy, Mina, 211n27. *See also* "basic writing" at UW
Shiller, Robert, 59, 224n66
Shor, Ira (English TA, UW), 17, 57, 58, 67–68, 94–95, 97–98, 104–6, 109, 127, 129, 140–41, 214–15nn78–79, 223–24n57, 226n100, 243nn99–100
Silber, Glenn (*The War at Home*), 19, 214n66, 223n47
Siff, David (English prof., UW), 100 fig. 5.1, 107, 141, 146
Sledge, George (dean, College of Agriculture and Life Sciences, UW), 164
Sloan, Tim (English TA, UW), 136
Smit, David W., 26, 212n46, 215n85, 249n15
Smith, Ron, 150, 215n83
Special Committee on Improving the Quality of Student Writing Skills (UW, 1977), 185
Sperber, Murray, 62
Sputnik I, 5, 25, 61–62, 69–71, 79–80, 83, 203, 229–30n25. *See also* "academic revolution" of the late 1950s and early 1960s; Geiger, Roger; research profile

of faculty vis-à-vis general education duties; SAT, scores rising from late 1950s through early 1960s
Stairs, G. R. (forestry prof., UW), 165–66
Stedman, Lawrence C., 180–81, 229n10. *See also* SAT
Sterling Hall. *See* Army Math Research Center (UW)
Stevens, Anne H., 212–13n52
Steward, Joyce (English prof., UW), 52, 53, 57, 87, 118, 140, 143, 153, 191, 213n64, 222n25, 223–24n57, 224n63, 244n115, 248n39
Stewart, Donald C., 210n6
stratification of student writers at UW by skill level, 38, 39, 41–43, 47, 75, 79, 218–19nn62–63, 220n4. *See also* "awkward squad" at UW; "basic writing" at UW; demographic, economic, and sociocultural factors in the history of U.S. higher education; English 0 (UW); English 11 (UW); English 101 (UW), remedialization of; English 181 (UW); high school, writing in; honors Freshman English at UW; *Evaluating Student Themes*; exemption from Freshman English at UW; Sub-Freshman English at UW
Stroud, Michael (English TA, UW), 87–88, 118, 232n73
Students for a Democratic Society (SDS), 66, 107, 109, 125, 129, 201
"Students' Right to their Own Language" (CCCC, 1974), 179, 247n23
Stygall, Gail, 212n44
Style and Substance (Merritt), 54
Sub-Freshman English at UW, 38–39, 41–42, 219n78. *See also* "awkward squad" at UW; "basic writing" at UW; English 0 at UW; English 101, remedialization of
Sullivan, Frank J., et al., 215–16nn85–86, 230n26
Summerhill (Neill), 96, 109–10, 122, 233–34n14, 239n43
SUNY Albany, 215–16n86
Susman, Millard (genetics prof., UW), 163–64
syllabus reform in Freshman English (UW). *See* opening syllabi to emergent needs and desires